T0219962

Cyber-Humans

Woodrow Barfield

Cyber-Humans

Our Future with Machines

 Springer

Copernicus Books is a brand of Springer

Woodrow Barfield
Chapel Hill, NC
USA

ISBN 978-3-319-25048-9   ISBN 978-3-319-25050-2   (eBook)
DOI 10.1007/978-3-319-25050-2

Library of Congress Control Number: 2015952027

Springer Cham Heidelberg New York Dordrecht London

Copernicus Books is a brand of Springer
Springer International Publishing AG Switzerland is part of Springer Science+Business Media
(www.springer.com)

This book is dedicated to my daughter, Jessica, both athlete and scholar; to the memory of my wonderful and supportive parents, my sister Linda, to my nieces Melissa and Sky, Cousin Paula, and all the relatives in South Florida, Oregon, Virginia, and California. Dr. Conrad Kraft is also remembered for his friendship, scholarship, and mentorship. I also dedicate this book to Watson, and all other artificial intelligences that will follow, and I look forward to their book review and to the books they will write and to the science they will discover.

Preface

In the mid-1980s I was a graduate student of Industrial and Systems Engineering at Purdue University in Indiana. My research revolved around the topic of how to make computers easier for people to use. At that time the fields of artificial intelligence and robotics were still in their infancy; and a human was a component of every system, either providing manual input or performing supervisory control. With a human brain containing about 85–100 billion neurons and approximately 100 trillion synapses, and with sensors containing remarkable capabilities, determining how technology could best serve humans was a challenging research topic. The theme that the purpose of technology was to serve as a tool for humans, was the dominant view when I was a graduate student in engineering and still is. But later my thinking about technology with regard to its role in serving humanity was to change, and eventually led to the writing of this book. While at Purdue, with limited space for graduate students, I shared an office with other students who were studying aeronautical engineering, manufacturing, and robotics. As I engaged my fellow graduate students in conversation about the topic of their research, I realized that while I was trying to design systems that were easier for humans to use, the other graduate students were trying to design systems that were completely automated; that is, had no human in the system at all. These fascinating and wide ranging discussions were my first introduction to robotics, artificial intelligence, and automation.

After graduation, I took a faculty position and did work primarily in the area of virtual reality, augmented reality, and wearable computers and taught a course on the supervisory control of robots. As my career developed, I became interested in more of the big picture of how technology, science, and policy interrelated. This new line of thinking led me to papers in the area of human rights (for artificial intelligence) and intellectual property, which then led me to law school and later to the LLM program in intellectual property law and policy at the University of Washington. This book details much of my engineering knowledge regarding the design of systems for human use, my formal training in law, and from years of research and scholarship on the design of virtual and augmented reality systems and wearable computers.

While in graduate school I became aware of another accelerating trend occurring in technology—the enhancement of humans using techniques that were just being discovered in genetics, and the practice of equipping humans with biotechnology to treat a range of disabilities. For frame of reference, in the early 1980s, William DeVries implanted an artificial heart, the Jarvik-7, in a patient with the intention that the implant be long-lasting (it worked for a few months). More recently, French heart transplant specialists developed a prototype of the world's first fully implantable artificial heart, designed to beat for at least five years. Since the first attempts at using technology to enhance humans, advances in technology have led to the ability to replace or enhance a surprising amount of human physiology and anatomy. In fact, over the coming decades, humankind will, for the first time in the history of our species, be able to actively supersede our own physiology and anatomy. And as the nascent technology of prosthetics and neuromorphic chips develops, sometimes this century we may be able to bolster our memory and recall with brain implants; and to think faster, focus our attention better, react faster, run more swiftly, and possibly have superhuman strength. When I consider the enhancement of the human body with technology, my conclusion is that we are in the process of becoming the technology, and not just the passive recipient of its benefits.

For a host of reasons, technology is being developed and used for many purposes thought not possible even a few years ago: for example, assisting the handicapped and disabled (restoring sight for the blind, sound where there is a hearing deficit, or equipping people with exoskeletons to enable movement for those lacking mobility); for those who want to hack their body (a term used for people who seek to self-modify their body to extend the range of their senses, the topic of a chapter in this book); and ominously, for the cyborg-soldier of the future. However, while humans are being equipped with more-and-more technology, our cognitive abilities, which derive from our genetic blueprint, have remained relatively the same for thousands of years. In contrast, operating under the law of accelerating returns, which states that the rate of technological change is exponential, machines are quickly gaining in intelligence, sensory, and motor capabilities.

While technology is being used to enhance human capabilities, fight disease, and to allow new forms of expression, technology itself is becoming smarter, more human-like (i.e., an android, which is a robot designed to have a human appearance), and before midcentury could exceed humans in intelligence (referred to as the Singularity, the topic of Chap. 2). If so, a number of policy and legal issues will ensue regarding the relations between humans and our intelligent machines. Often when challenged by advances across many areas of human endeavor, our relevant laws and governmental policies have lagged behind technological breakthroughs. Consider the ethical, policy, and legal issues raised by the use of drones, or with autonomous robotic soldiers should they enter the battlefield. How about tort law and specifically negligence and strict liability when robots harm humans, or from a social justice perspective, the deep digital divide which may result when some humans are physically and cognitively enhanced by technology and others are left behind? Further, consider how humanity should respond if artificially intelligent machines attain or surpass human levels of intelligence and argue for rights. For example, should we extend the rights that humans receive in most industrialized nations—such as political rights and liberties, to artificially intelligent machines; or would it be prudent to deny such rights to nonhuman beings? And finally, consider the main theme of this book—should we merge with artificially intelligent machines, or risk being surpassed and becoming inconsequential or even extinct?

One significant impact that will be made by developments in enhancement technology and the emergence of machines with artificial intelligence will be on the law—specifically creating motivations for the passage of new laws and also discovering novel ways to use existing laws to apply in a human society intertwined with smart machines. The law can be found in Constitutions, statutes, government and industry regulations, and the judge-made decisions resulting from cases argued in court. When writing a law review article, the author is comforted when cases have been decided on the issue of interest. This is because the court will have heard the facts, examined the issues, listened to witnesses, and decided how the law applies. However, when dealing with the topic of cyborgs and artificially intelligent machines, we are just now at the stage where disputes are beginning to occur. For example, in 2012 Professor Steve Mann one of the first human–machine "cyborgs" living amongst us, was assaulted at a restaurant in Paris based on his appearance and technical capabilities as a cyborg. Since Steve has natural personhood status (a legal status granting him a range of rights), he could initiate a civil lawsuit on his own behalf (possibly for assault and battery). However, artificially intelligent machines have not yet reached a level of cognitive development to argue for personhood status, thus, they currently lack individual rights and the ability to defend their interests. But if in the future an artificially intelligent machine claimed to be sentient and subsequently argued for rights (at the time of this writing, it has been argued that an AI software bot posing as a teenage boy has passed the Turing test), the public should stay tuned, a tipping point would have been reached and it will get interesting.

To indicate the widespread interest in the topic of this book, let me briefly introduce some of the comments of renowned Cosmologist Sir Martin Rees, by conveying some of his highly interesting observations about our future—what some have termed the Post-Human era. Professor Rees rightly notes that there are chemical and metabolic limits to the size and processing power of organic brains which results in issues of bandwidth limitations and speed of information processing for humans. Furthermore, he notes that such limitations are not competitive with the raw processing power of computers and their march toward artificial general intelligence. But while some think that artificial intelligence is becoming our competition, prominent scientists such as Hans Moravec think of artificial intelligence as humanity's natural future evolutionary path. Agreeing with Rees, I conclude that the potential for further development of artificial intelligence could be as dramatic as the evolution from single-celled organisms to the humans that exist today. So, looking beyond the horizon, Rees eloquently states that "in the far future, it won't be the minds of humans, but those of machines, that will most fully understand the cosmos—and it will be the actions of autonomous machines that will most drastically change our world, and perhaps what lies beyond."

This book is about the technical, legal, and policy issues which are raised when humans and artificially intelligent machines are enhanced by technology. I discuss cyborgs, bionic humans, and machines with increasing levels of intelligence by linking a chain of fascinating subjects together—the technology of cognitive, motor, and sensory prosthetics; biological and technological enhancements to humans; and body hacking and brain–computer interfaces. Each of these technologies combines to tell the story of where we are going as a species, what policies to consider, and how the law and policy must adapt to accommodate the future of human-technology combinations. My goal in writing this book is to inform the public of what may be coming this century in terms of human cybernetic enhancements, artificially intelligent machines, and the development of cyborgs. I also aim to initiate debate among academicians on a range of scholarly topics, which often receive inadequate coverage in law and technology courses. In the coming decades, the decisions we make as a society, or more generally, as a species regarding how we enhance ourselves and create machines that may replace us, will affect the very essence of what it means to be human, nothing could be more compelling and important for humanity.

Chapel Hill, USA   Woodrow Barfield

Acknowledgments

Beverley Ford, Editorial Director at Springer, has been a great resource and contact person with the press, a reader of chapters, and a gentile prodder of deadlines. Without her support and encouragement, this book would not have been written. And also from Springer, James Robinson is thanked for his editorial assistance as is Helen Desmond. In addition, Gowtham Chakravarthy is thanked for his production work. Further, I thank Laura N. Gasaway, Paul B. Eaton Distinguished Professor of Law Emeritus, at the University of North Carolina, School of Law for her insightful comments on intellectual property law. Also, Makiko Kashioka from Osaka University is gratefully acknowledged for her help in providing images of androids. Most importantly, I thank Ed Cockrell, poet and science fiction short-story writer, for not only reading the chapters and providing edits, but for his numerous meetings with me in which we discussed the material in this book and his thoughts on the future. Finally, my students have always been a source of ideas, as have the colleagues I have worked with throughout my career, including the faculty in intellectual property law at the University of Washington and particularly Jonathan Franklin.

Contents

About the Author

Woodrow Barfield headed the Sensory Engineering Laboratory at the University of Washington where he was a Professor of Industrial and Systems Engineering. His research revolved around the design and use of wearable computers and augmented reality systems. He received the Presidential Young Investigator Award from the National Science Foundation, and served as a senior editor of Presence: Teleoperators and Virtual Environments. Dr. Barfield is currently an associate editor of the Virtual Reality Journal and is the senior editor of the first and second editions of *"Fundamentals of Wearable Computers and Augmented Reality."* Dr. Barfield earned a Ph.D. in Engineering from Purdue University and the JD degree and an LLM in intellectual property law and policy, serving as an editor of the *Journal of Law, Technology & Arts*. He has over 350 publications and major presentations, including keynote addresses and articles in engineering and law review journals. He currently lives in Chapel Hill, North Carolina.

Other Books by the Author

Barfield, W., and Caudell, T., 2001, eds., *Fundamentals of Wearable Computers and Augmented Reality, 1st edition,* Lawrence Erlbaum Press, Malwah, New Jersey.

Barfield, W., 2015, ed., *Fundamentals of Wearable Computers and Augmented Reality, 2nd edition,* CRC Press, New York.

Barfield, W., and Dingus, T., 1997, eds., *Human Factors in Intelligent Transportation Systems,* Psychology Press, New York.

Barfield W., and Furness, T., 1995, eds., *Virtual Environments and Advanced Interface Design,* Oxford University Press, 1995.

Majchrzak, A., Chang, T-C., Barfield, W., Eberts, R. E., & Salvendy, G., 1987, *Human Aspects of Computer-Aided Design,* London: Taylor and Francis, Ltd.

A Brief Comment About Predictions and Examples Used in the Book

The most important question posed by books on the Singularity, and discussed by futurists and authors such as Ray Kurzweil, Rodney Brooks, Kevin Warwick, Hans Moravec, Nick Bostrom, James Barrat, and Martine Rothblatt, is whether artificial intelligence will eventually pass humans in general intelligence, and gain consciousness. I don't profess to know the answer with any certainty, but I do have the opinion that it will happen. I find it interesting that many of the debates on whether humans may be surpassed in intelligence by an artificial intelligence focuses on *when* it could happen (not *if*)—with predictions that this transformative event will occur by midcentury, the latter half of this century, or sometime next century. However, if one considers the age of this planet (over 45 million centuries), or the amount of time that has passed since humans evolved to live on this planet, or even since humans started recording history, being off by a century or two is insignificant, some would even say a rounding error. But in my view Ray Kurzweil's argument that the Singularity is near, is convincing, so I wrote this book to add to the conversation on how humanity should respond to the emergence of cyborgs and artificial intelligence. Further, to make a specific point about technology, law, and policy in an "age of cyborgs," in several chapters I often used existing "cyborgs" Steve Mann, Neil Harbisson, and Kevin Warwick as examples. They certainly aren't the only cyborgs living amongst us, you, or your neighbor may be equipped with cyborg technology in the form of a heart pacer or artificial limb. In fact, cumulatively, millions of people worldwide are equipped with cochlear implants, retinal prosthesis, and artificial limbs. However, I consistently used Steve, Neil, and Kevin as examples because they are not only pioneers in "wearable and implantable computing technology," they have also been the subject of the popular media and in Steve's case a documentary (Cyberman, 2002). In several chapters I also discuss the work of Dr. Theodore Berger of the University of Southern California on the design of an artificial hippocampus; this is because his work cuts across several topics discussed in this book and I view his work as essential for our cyborg future. In terms of examples of cutting-edge cyborg technology, and start-up companies developing amazing technologies in artificial intelligence, robotics, and neuroprosthesis, I expect some of the companies discussed in this book will have failed by the time this book is in the hands of the reader, or that some of the projects discussed in this book will have not met the initial promise and are no longer being developed. But if that is the case, there is no doubt that other companies and projects will have started, which the reader will surely read about in the news and that will lead to the amazing future described in this book.

Further Reading

Cyberman (2001) Based on the "Cyborg Experiences" of Steve Mann, Directed by Michael Allder, Written by David Wearer and Bridgot Newsom, distrubted by Canadian Broadcasting Corperation (CBC)

Chapter 1
The Technological Future

Introduction

Let me start the book with a controversial and bold statement—our future is to merge with artificially intelligent machines! How I reached that conclusion is the subject of this book. I don't mean to imply that in the coming decades we humans will look and act like robots on an assembly line, rather, that we will be equipped with so much technology, including computing devices implanted within the brain itself, that we will have been transformed from a biological being into a technology-based being, evolving under laws of technology, more so than under the laws of biological evolution. At the same time that we are becoming more "machine like" (or "cyborg like"), advances in robotics, artificial intelligence, neuroscience, and materials engineering are allowing scientists to create intelligent machines that have sophisticated human—like functionality and are rapidly gaining in intelligence—"they" are becoming like us. I see the logical outcome of technological advancements in robotics, artificial intelligence, prosthesis, and brain implants, as a future merger between humans and machines.[1] This will not be a conscious decision made by humanity, but will be a gradual process, and inevitable. But not so gradual as to take centuries, but in all likelihood something that will happen this century or early next.

As a confession, I may have played a small role in this outcome (our future merger with machines), because as a faculty in engineering, I headed a research laboratory whose goal was to design wearable computing and sensor technology that was fully integrated with the human body. In the early 1990s, I began to formalize my thinking about the future direction of technology, and wrote about it in

---

[1]Of course, while seminal robot experts and artificial intelligence pioneers such as Hans Moravec hold the view that our future is to merge with machines, many experts disagree, and others argue that humanity should stop this outcome from occurring.

© Springer International Publishing Switzerland 2015
W. Barfield, *Cyber-Humans*, DOI 10.1007/978-3-319-25050-2_1

2001, in a chapter 1 co-authored, *Computing Under the Skin*, in which my colleagues and I argued for the use of sensors and cyborg implants to fix, repair, replace, and enhance damaged human anatomical and physiological systems.[2] At the time, my colleagues and I also mused about the future directions of "wearable" devices, making predictions about technology that are being implemented today. But in hindsight, it seems that we didn't go far enough predicting the future that has unfolded and we were too conservative in stating how close we are to the Singularity and afterwards Posthuman age.

Much of my work on the design and use of "wearable" technology was published in two books I co-edited, *Virtual Environments and Advanced Interface Design,* and *Fundamentals of Wearable Computers and Augmented Reality.*[3] Since the publication of the first edition of these books over a decade ago, the landscape in human enhancement technology and artificial intelligence has changed dramatically. To address these changes, I wrote this book to present an up-to-date summary of recent advances in genetics, prosthesis, and brain-computer interfaces; and to discuss current efforts to create artificially intelligent machines that learn and solve problems in ways not predicted by humans. Another goal in writing this book was to generate discussion among the public on the law and policies which should be enacted as humans are enhanced by technology, and as artificially intelligent machines gain human, or beyond human, levels of intelligence. Given the nature of the topics presented in this book, the discussion will be wide ranging cutting across diverse fields such as biology, engineering, ethics, and law.

As often stated by Google's Ray Kurzweil, the rate of technological change in engineering, medicine, and computer science is accelerating.[4] In some areas, what was science fiction just 10–20 years ago is now mainstream science. If advances in several key technologies continue to accelerate, the twenty-first century will indeed be a time of great change, amazing developments, and unique challenges for humanity. As predicted by computer scientists, engineers, and philosophers, by the end of the twenty-first century, advances in science and engineering will have led to such significant changes in the structure of our bodies that the very nature of what it means to be human will be questioned. On this point, the science fiction writer William Gibson, who coined the term "cyberspace" in the short story *"Burning Chrome,"*[5] sees a "cyborg" future for humanity which includes implantations of silicon chips into the human brain modified with DNA. Fast forward to Professor Theodore Berger's

---

[2]Dwight Holland, Dawn J. Roberson, and Woodrow Barfield, 2001, Computing Under the Skin, in Woodrow Barfield and Thomas Caudell (eds), *Fundamentals of Wearable Computers and Augmented Reality*, CRC Press.

[3]Woodrow Barfield and Thomas Caudell, *id.*; Woodrow Barfield and Thomas Furness (eds.), 1995, *Virtual Environments and Advanced Interface Design*, Oxford University Press.

[4]Perhaps Ray Kurzweil is most recognized for his ideas about the Law of Accelerating Returns discussed in his seminal book, Ray Kurzweil, 2006, The Singularity is Near, When Humans Transcend Biology, Penguin Books.

[5]William Gibson, 2003, Burning Chrome, Harper Voyager Press. Gibson coined the term "cyberspace" in the 1980s.

laboratory at the University of Southern California, where our cyborg future is being designed now in the form of remarkable neuroprosthetic devices.

Enhancing Humans

According to Sidney Perkowitz writing in *"Digital People: From Bionic Humans to Androids,"*[6] there are two main ways to categorize artificial enhancements of humans: firstly, as functional prosthetic devices and implants, such as artificial limbs, replacement knees and hips, and vascular stents (which aid in the flow of blood in blocked arteries); and secondly, as cosmetic or vanity implants, like hair plugs, false teeth, artificial eyes, and breast implants. This book concerns both categories of enhancements, and it is interesting to note that the efforts of some researchers to develop human-like robots, could be thought of as cosmetic or vanity enhancements to the machine, as such enhancements may be nonfunctional. Enhancement technologies may also occur in a multitude of ways, supported by a variety of technologies, in which human beings enhance their looks, abilities, features, or functions. In fact, enhancements to the human body range from performance enhancing drugs, plastic surgery and silicone implants for (perceived) beauty purposes, to bionic limbs and chip-enhanced cognition in humans. While the distinguishing feature of "cyborg" enhancement technology is to improve human functioning above 'normal' or 'average', many technologies for enhancement are being used for medical or regenerative purposes; for example, plastic surgery for burn victims or prostheses for lost limbs; the purpose in these cases being to bring the people 'back to normal'.

In addition to efforts to enhance the human body with a range of technologies, other important progress is being made in robotics and artificial intelligence that is also setting the stage for a human-machine merger. Due to major improvements in algorithms and sensors, machines are becoming more autonomous, software is becoming 'smarter', and robots are being developed that are beginning to look and act more like humans than machines (see Chaps. 3, *The Law of Artificially Intelligent Brains*, and 7, *The Law of Looks and Artificial Bodies*). In fact, one area of research in robotics is towards developing realistic looking robots that mirror human appearance (i.e., androids); another strand is towards developing facial features that cause a robot to appear as if expressing emotions; in particular, facial expressions like smiling or raising eyebrows. Once 'humanoid' robots are equipped with artificial intelligence—and thus acquire more autonomy from their human masters—the vision of an android in the spirit of Star Trek's "Data" might become a reality. At this point one can imagine two interesting scenarios: firstly, that the world may become populated by different types of species than those we see around us today: non-enhanced and enhanced humans, cyborgs, robots, and

---

[6]Sidney Perkowitz, 2004, Digital People: From Bionic Humans to Androids, Joseph Henry Press.

androids among them, all of which will function, in different but perhaps also in similar ways, in day-to-day social life.[7] And secondly, from advances in technology there could emerge one intelligent species, based on the merger of human and machine. In my view, before humanity could eventually merges with machines, there will be several intermediate forms of human-machine combinations, some of which we will term cyborgs. Again, when I speak of "merging with machines," I mean equipping humans with the technology (typically information technologies) to enhance the human body and mind, to go beyond current capabilities, essentially, to become more "cyborg-like." Throughout this book, I refer to the technology to enhance the human body and mind as "cyborg technologies." And I refer to the "cyborg future," "cyborg age," or coming "age of cyborgs," to refer to the future in which we will become equipped with technology to repair, replace, and extend our senses, and cognitive functions. An "emerging cyborg law," then is the legal issues which will be important to consider for our technological future. Further, whether a complete machine body containing a human consciousness uploaded to a machine architecture is a human or machine, is an interesting philosophical question, and the subject of discussions by various authors (see Chap. 7: *The Law of Looks and Artificial Bodies*).[8]

The vision of a future world populated by humans, cyborgs, intelligent robots, and androids raises many interesting questions. One such question is what this development means for fundamental or constitutional rights for the range of intelligent beings that may exist in the near future. Will cyborgs be considered human enough to still be bearers of 'human' rights? Can androids claim 'human' rights if they look and function in the same way in society as humans or cyborgs? And can human beings keep robots under control as they become increasingly autonomous; in other words, will robots comply with Asimov's three laws of robotics, or will they, like HAL in *2001—A Space Odyssey*, revolt and try and control humans? Society has been warned of this very outcome by physicist Stephen Hawking and entrepreneur and CEO of Telsa Motors Elon Musk.[9] Some argue that since cyborgs will evolve in gradual steps from the human species, they will most likely be considered humans by future generations. The scenario may work out as follows—as soon as different enhancement technologies are adopted by a critical mass, after the initial pioneers, enhanced humans will simply be the new appearance of the human species. As a result, it is argued that cyborgs will be the

[7]See Human enhancement, at: http://www.fidis.net/resources/identity-use-cases-scenarios/human-enhancement-robots-and-the-fight-for-human-rights/.

[8]Patrick Lin and Keith Adney, 2014, Robot Ethics: The Ethical and Social Implications of Robotics, MIT Press.

[9]Rory Cellan, Stephen Hawking Warns Artificial Intelligence Could End Mankind, BBC News, at http://www.bbc.com/news/technology-30290540; Ellie Zolfaghariford and Victoria Woollastan, 2–15, Could robots turn people into PETS? Elon Musk claims artificial intelligence will treat humans like 'labradors', at: http://www.dailymail.co.uk/sciencetech/article-3011302/Could-robots-turn-people-PETS-Elon-Musk-claims-artificial-intelligence-treat-humans-like-Labradors.html.

inheritors of human rights that exist today.[10] Now suppose that robots and artifi-
cially-intelligent machines perform similar functions as cyborgs do, and perhaps
even become androids who are in looks and functions equivalent to cyborgs, then
should they not have the same catalogue of rights? This issue will require substantial debate in society and legal academia.

Another issue that technologically enhanced people may raise is whether a
social, or digital divide will develop between enhanced and non-enhanced humans.
Human rights can play an important part in this debate: because they lay down
the basic rules for treating people. At first sight, the right to non-discrimination
will provide substantial guidance: non-enhanced people should not be treated une-
qually. However, what is 'unequal', if in the future enhanced humans are different
in important ways from non-enhanced humans? For example, if an employer can
choose between an unenhanced person with an IQ of 120 and a cyborg with an
IQ of 260 or beyond, does he discriminate if he chooses the cyborg? This is just
one example of questions concerning specific human rights in relation to human
enhancement that merit public debate.

Humans, Bionics, and Cyborgs

As we become equipped with prosthesis and brain implants, we are moving
beyond the human capabilities provided by our evolutionary history and coded in
our genes. Since I believe technological advances are leading humanity towards a
"cyborg" future and an eventual merger with machines; I should define some basic
terms. Let's start with one of the main characters in this book—a "cyborg".
Generally, a cyborg is a human-machine combination that has certain physiological and intellectual processes aided or controlled by mechanical, electronic, or
computational devices. "Cyborg," is actually a compound word derived from
cybernetics and organism, and was coined by Manfred Clynes[11] in 1960 to
describe the need for mankind to artificially enhance biological functions in order
to survive in the hostile environment of Space.

To introduce some other basic terms, "transhuman" is a term that refers to an
evolutionary transition from the human to the Posthuman. To transhumanist thinkers, a Posthuman is a hypothetical future being "whose basic capacities so radically exceed those of present humans as to be no longer unambiguously human by
our current standards."[12] The difference between the Posthuman and other hypothetical sophisticated non-humans is that a Posthuman was once a human, either in

---

[10]Human enhancement, robots, and the fight for human rights, at: http://www.fidis.net/resources/
identity-use-cases-scenarios/human-enhancement-robots-and-the-fight-for-human-rights/.

[11]M. E. Clynes and N. S. Kline, 1960, Cyborgs and Space, *Astronautics*, 26–27, 74–75.

[12]Posthuman, Wikipedia, https://en.wikipedia.org/wiki/Posthuman.

its lifetime or in the lifetimes of some or all of its direct ancestors.[13] As such, a prerequisite for a Posthuman is a transhuman, the point at which the human being begins surpassing his or her own limitations, but is still recognizable as a human person. In this sense, the transition between human and Posthuman may be viewed as a continuum rather than an all-or-nothing event.

The field of cybernetics is concerned with communication and control systems involving living organisms and machines. The artificial parts used to create cyborgs do more than replace the main functionality of an organ or limb, they add to, enhance, or replace the computational abilities of biological systems. In a typical example of a cyborg, a human fitted with a heart pacemaker might be considered a cyborg, since s/he is incapable of surviving without the mechanical part whose computational capabilities are essential. As a more extreme example of a cyborg, some would view clothing as a cybernetic modification of skin; because it enables us to survive in drastically different environments by the use of materials that aren't naturally existing in those environments. In my conceptualization of a cyborg, if the clothing had computational capabilities that aided the wearer,[14] then I would conclude that the "clothing enhanced human" was a cyborg. However, in almost every case, throughout this book the "cyborgs" I discuss are the result of being enhanced with technology worn on or integrated into the body.

In the popular culture the terms "bionic human" and "cyborg" are often used interchangeably to refer to any human enhanced with technology. However, I draw the distinction that while a bionic human is a person that has been enhanced by mechanical or biological means; going a step further, a cyborg has computational processes enhanced or aided by technology, the goal being to go beyond current human sensory and cognitive abilities. Interestingly, while there are clearly many bionically enhanced people, there are also cyborgs living amongst us now. If we want to determine how many cyborgs or bionic humans there are, the number will depend on the definition used. For example, if by using the term "bionic human," one means to signify a person who is artificially enhanced in some way, then the digestion of medicine would create a bionic human and there would be literally hundreds of millions of such beings alive today. If, however, one meant that to be a "bionic human" a certain number of human parts were replaced by mechanical implants and prosthesis, then the number of such humans would not number in the hundreds of millions, but in the millions. According to one commentator, many current people could be defined as "bionic," in that eight to ten percent of the U.S. population, that is, approximately 25 million people, currently have some sort of artificial part- a number expected to grow as the population ages. In fact, just considering the sense of audition, thousands of cochlear implants are currently in use, including some placed in deaf children.

Finally, if one meant that to be a "cyborg" that a brain function was artificially enhanced or replaced, then the number of such people would likely be in the

---

[13]Id.

[14]Kate Hartman, 2014, Make: Wearable Electronics: Design, Prototype, and Wear Your Own Interactive Garments, Maker Medic Inc. Publisher.

thousands, a number expected to increase dramatically in the next 10 years. As an example of brain implant technology currently being used, starting in the late 1990s physicians have implanted electrodes into the brains of patients in the hope of developing a computer-brain interface which would allow those "locked-in " their bodies to operate a robotic arm or move a cursor on a screen. Further, technology that may allow memories to be digitally stored in the brain is under development. The neuroprosthesis (artificial hippocampus) referred to earlier and that is being designed and tested by Theodore Berger and his team at the University of Southern California[15] and by Dr. Sam A. Deadwyler and Dr. Robert Hampson of Wake Forest Baptist Medical Center could serve this purpose.[16]

In many discussions of enhanced humans, whether a person equipped with technology is termed bionic or cyborg, is not an important distinction—most people use the terms interchangeably to refer to any person equipped with technology. But under the law, the degree to which a person is enhanced by technology could matter. For example, under disability law a person with a given handicap may need to be accommodated by an employer; but the type of disability and what technology is used to address it, would matter in the legal analysis of the disability and the rights afforded the disabled person. And consider athletes who have lost their legs yet still compete against athletes without prosthesis. Competitors often raise concerns about the unfair advantage the "cyborg" would have over them due to the lightness of their carbon-fiber prosthetics. While this example may appear to be something of an outlier, as prosthetic technology improves, the potential for prosthetic limbs to equal or even surpass the capabilities of natural limbs is great.[17] Further, prosthetic limbs may be stronger, and allow the user to carry heavier loads than they may normally be able to carry. Alternatively, they may be more flexible, or allow for greater accuracy in certain tasks—how many people can boast of having a wrist that rotates 360°? While this may seem an inane example, the possibilities nevertheless exist for people once considered 'disabled' to become 'over-abled' in comparison to non-enhanced individuals. Will this give those individuals a competitive advantage over others that are non-enhanced in employment? As with some enhanced people, will a perceived superiority of the artificial over the natural create resentment between 'enhanced' and 'non-enhanced' people? As a result, will new categories of discrimination law be necessary? Under the U.K. *Equality Act*, someone is 'disabled' if they are considered to have an impairment that has a substantial and long-term adverse effect on their ability to carry out normal day-to-day activities; if someone is able to surpass the ability of

---

[15]Theodore Berger, Artificial Hippocampus, in Memory Implants, MIT Technology Review, at: http://www.technologyreview.com/featuredstory/513681/memory-implants/.

[16]Theodore W. Berger, Dong Song, Rosa H. M. Chan, Vasilas Z. Marmarelis, Jeff LaCoss, Jack Wills, Robert E. Hampson, Sam A. Deadwyler, and John J. Granacki, A Hippocampal Cognitive Prosthesis: Multi-Input, Multi-Output Nonlinear Modeling and VLSI Implementation, IEEE Trans Neural Syst Rehabil Eng. 2012 Mar; 20(2): 198–211, doi: 10.1109/TNSRE.2012.2189133.

[17]Human Enhancement Technologies—Edging towards the Cyborg? at: http://www.scl.org/site.aspx?i=ed31780.

fully-able people to undertake those activities through the use of enhancement technologies, can we truly consider them to be disabled?[18]

Interestingly, one jurisdiction may have already recognized a person as a cyborg. Artist, Neil Harbisson,[19] is completely color blind suffering from a visual impairment called achromatopsia, which means he sees the world in shades of grey. To perceive colors, Neil wears a sensory augmentation device in the form of a head-mounted antenna attached to a chip at the back of his skull. As a form of sensory substitution, the "Eyeborg" turns colors into sounds, allowing Neil to "hear" electromagnetic energy representing color. After a long dispute with the U.K. authorities, Neil's passport photo now includes a picture of him with his cyborg device, a recognition by the authorities that his cyborg enhancement is a permanent part of his appearance. With a passport photo that shows the Eyeborg as part of Harbisson's face, it will be difficult for people to argue that his Eyeborg is an optional accessory, like a camera or a hat, and somebody trying to take his augmentation off could be committing an assault and battery equivalent to injuring his face. Interestingly, under the law, a "battery" may occur even if the aggressor does not touch the plaintiff (i.e., cyborg) directly, but instead touches something closely related to his or her person (like a cybernetic enhancement attached to the body).[20] For example, courts have held that touching the cane a person uses to walk may be battery, even if the defendant never touches the person herself. In this case, the cane is like an extension of the person's body, so touching it is the same thing as touching the person's body. In many situations, clothing, hats, and bags may also count as part of a person enough for the person wearing them to prove battery. However, as we will see in a later chapter, the law in this area is evolving in response to cyborg technologies.

A major point to make early in this book is that while humans are becoming equipped with prosthesis and implants, and thus becoming more cyborg-like, during this century, robots will continue to get smarter and at a speed defying human imagination (actually our bias towards linear thinking see Chap. 3: *The Law of Artificially Intelligent Brains*). In fact, robots equipped with artificial intelligence, and a host of sensors, actuators, and algorithms are leading the way to the creation of machines that may surpass humans in intelligence and motor capabilities by the middle, and almost certainly, the end of the twenty-first century. As technology advances, new forms of humans may evolve from different techniques to enhance human physiology, anatomy, and cognitive structures. All this may create a continuum of intelligent beings from human to machine, progressing from human, bionic human, cyborg, android, robot, software bot, and machine; how artificial intelligence may add to, or "disrupt" this continuum is discussed throughout this book.

---

[18]UK Equity Act of 2010.

[19]Neil Harbisson, BBC News, The Man Who Hears Color, at: http://www.bbc.com/news/technology-29992577.

[20]Gowri Ramachandran, Against the Right to Bodily Integrity: Of Cyborgs and Human Rights, 2009, Denver Law Review, Vol. 187, 1–57.

Advances in artificial intelligence may also result in disembodied software beings that roam the internet, possibly downloading their consciousness to remote robots or to androids to gain mobility at particular locations around the world. One commentator has even used the term "digital people" to refer to entities that include artificial and partly artificial beings, from mechatronic robots (mechanical plus electronic) to humans with bionic (biological plus electronic) implants. In addition, Martine Rothblatt in her book, *Virtually Human: The Premise and the Peril of Digital Immortality*, argues that the brain can be simulated using software and computer technology. From this discussion, the impression is conveyed that different types of artificially intelligent beings may coexist in the future.

Brain-Computer Interfaces

Based on medical necessity, enhancement technologies are being used to repair and replace human anatomy and physiology, and to repair and enhance human cognitive and perceptual abilities. For example, brain-computer interfaces are assisting people suffering from debilitating neurological disorders, such that they are "locked-in" their own body. A brain-computer interface which consists of recording electrodes placed on a person's scalp or implanted into their brain, allows those locked-in the capability to communicate and interact with the world, by thought alone.

Additional progress is being made in other areas of brain-computer interface design. For example, scientists have used brain scanners to detect and reconstruct the faces that people are thinking of, according to a study published in the journal *NeuroImage*.[21] In the study, Yale scientists hooked participants up to an fMRI brain scanner—which determines activity in different parts of the brain by measuring blood flow—and showed them images of faces. Then, using only the brain scans, Professor Marvin Chun and his team were able to create images of the faces the people were looking at.[22] One can imagine in the future that a witness to a crime might reconstruct a suspect's face based on "extracting" the image from his mind. Yale researchers pointed out that an important limitation of the technology as it exists now, is that this sort of technology can only read active parts of the brain, it couldn't read passive memories—to do this you would have to get the person to imagine the memory to read it. Interestingly, at the University of California-Berkeley, scientists are moving beyond "reading" thoughts to predicting what

---

[21]Bill Hathaway, 2014, Yale Researchers Reconstruct Facial Images Locked in a Viewer's Mind, http://news.yale.edu/2014/03/25/yale-researchers-reconstruct-facial-images-locked-viewer-s-mind; also in Neuroimage. 2014 Jul 1;94:12–22. doi: 10.1016/j.neuroimage.2014.03.018.

[22]Bill Hathaway, Yale researchers reconstruct facial images locked in a viewer's mind, at: http://news.yale.edu/2014/03/25/yale-researchers-reconstruct-facial-images-locked-viewer-s-mind.

someone will think next.[23] And at Carnegie Mellon University, in Pittsburgh, cognitive neuroscientist Marcel Just from the *Center for Cognitive Brain Imaging* has a vision that will make Google Glass and other similar technologies seem very last century.[24] Instead of using your eye to direct a cursor, Just envisions a device that will dial a number by interpreting your thoughts.[25] However, what if all of our thoughts were public? Dr. Just envisions a terrifying version of the future, where officials read minds in order to gain control over them. But more optimistically, Marcel also envisions a more positive future, with mind reading devices offering opportunities to people with disabilities—and to those not disabled.

According to Duke University neuroscientist Miguel Nicolelis, microchips implanted into the brain could also allow brain-to-brain communication, that is, telepathy.[26] Thus far, brain-wave sensing machines have been used to 'telepathically' control everything from real-life helicopters to characters in a computer game. In its most recent incarnation, the science of telepathy has gone a step further by allowing someone in India to send an email to his colleague in France using thought. To perform this feat, researchers used electroencephalography (EEG) headsets which recorded electrical activity from neurons firing in the brain to convert words into binary. Once the initial thoughts were digitized in India, they were sent to a person's mind in France where a computer translated the message, and then used electrical stimulation to transmit the thought to the receiver's mind. Ultimately, telepathy chips and related brain-computer devices could lead to the emergence of new forms of intelligence, for example, "mindplexes."[27] This is a term used by artificial intelligence researcher Ben Goertzel, which represents a collection of independent human minds, yet also possessing a coherent self and consciousness at the higher level of the telepathically-interlinked human group. Mindplexes could lead to the benefits associated with crowd sourcing in which the combined wisdom of a crowd has in some cases been shown to solve problems beyond the reach of experts. In fact, the characteristics of "wise crowds," which are diversity of opinion; independence of members from one another; decentralization; and a good method for aggregating opinions would be a feature of networked brain-to-brain communication.

Surely, the reading of thoughts would raise a host of legal and policy issues. Not the least of which is privacy law. On this point, courts in the future may have to decide whether listening to and recording a person's thoughts is protected

---

[23]Yasmin Anwar, 2011, Scientists Use Brain Imaging to Reveal the Movies in Our Mind, at: http://newscenter.berkeley.edu/2011/09/22/brain-movies/.

[24]Karen Weintraub, 2014, Scientists explore possibilities of mind reading, at: http://www.usatoday.com/story/tech/2014/04/22/mind-reading-brain-scans/7747831/.

[25]*Id.*

[26]Miguel Nicolelis, 2012, Beyond Boundaries: The New Neuroscience of Connecting Brains with Machines-and How It Will Change Our Lives, St. Martin's Griffin Press.

[27]Ben Goertzel, 2014, Between Ape and Artilect: Conversations with Pioneers of Artificial General Intelligence and Other Transformative Technologies, CreateSpace Independent Publishing Platform.

speech, or an unlawful search and seizure of the activity (i.e., cognition) generated by the prefrontal cortex (a topic discussed in Chap. 3). As to implanting micro-chips, a few states in the U.S. have already enacted anti-chipping statutes which prohibit the "chipping" of vulnerable populations and raises the bar of consent for implanting an identification or tracking device in any person. I will return to this important topic again.

With the ability to hack the brain comes compelling problems of law and pol-icy. If it becomes technically possible to communicate brain-to-brain by thought alone, could the wirelessly networked brains be hacked into by a corporation or government agency that could implant an advertisement, subconscious thought, or memory into one's mind? If you are annoyed by pop-up ads which appear now on a website, imagine the nuisance of a pop-up ad appearing in your mind. Further, the ability to implant a "telepathy chip"—a neural implant that would allow the wearer to project their thoughts or feelings to others, and receive thoughts or feelings from others, raises a huge number of questions philosophically, legally, psychologically, and socially. For example, what would happen, if an implanted computer chip should "crash" after it is in place? What kinds of health and behav-ior problems might arise in such a case?

Biological Enhancements

While much of this book discusses enhancement technology in the form of hard-ware, software, and algorithms, to present a more comprehensive picture of what the future may hold, I briefly present here material on current efforts to enhance human abilities by modifying their DNA, and by performance enhancing drugs. In addition, DNA nanobots in 15–20 years could allow humans to access the internet with their mind, in fact, the U.S. agency DARPA, is researching this possibility now. Until recently, human genetic engineering was the material of science-fiction novels and blockbuster Hollywood films. However, genetic engineering of DNA is not confined to books and movies, scientists and doctors are already attempt-ing to genetically alter human beings and our cells. To understand the choices that humanity must confront this century as a result of the ability to genetically enhance a human, it is critical to understand an important distinction under the umbrella of genetic engineering: the difference between therapy and enhancement. Gene therapy and genetic enhancement are technically both genetic engineering, but there are important moral differences.

For decades, researchers have worked toward using genetic modification called gene therapy to cure devastating genetic diseases. Gene therapy works by deliver-ing a copy of a normal gene into the cells of a patient in an attempt to correct a defective gene. This genetic alteration would then hopefully cure or slow the pro-gress of that disease. In many cases, the added gene would produce a protein that is missing or not functioning in a patient because of a genetic mutation. However, genetically engineering a normal person who wants, for example, more muscle to improve his athletic ability is no longer gene therapy; instead, it is genetic enhancement.[28] Genetic enhancement would take an otherwise healthy person and genetically modify him to be more than human, not just in strength, but also in intelligence, beauty or any other desirable trait. So why is the distinction between gene therapy and genetic enhancement important? Gene therapy seeks to return a patient to normal human functioning. Genetic enhancement, on the other hand, intentionally and fundamentally alters a human being in ways not intended by nature (note cyborg technologies may perform the same function).

When considering biological enhancements to humans, there is another important distinction to discuss. Somatic enhancements are those that affect one person, and therefore, the genetic alterations occur in only one individual, they do not enter the human genome generally. While single-person enhancements may have a dramatic impact on a solitary individual's life, since those changes are not passed on to that individual's children; they do not become part of the larger human genome. In contrast, germline changes are genetic modifications that can be passed on to one's descendants and thus can become permanent components of the human genome; affecting the person receiving the intervention and, at least indirectly, affecting every other human being. Such changes would constitute alterations of the entire complement of genetic traits found within the species, and many people believe that such steps should be taken with great caution, even trepidation, if not banned altogether.[29]

One form of enhancement technology that has great promise for engineering a healthier person, but at the same time, has the potential to impact the very nature of humanity is nanotechnology. The long-term goal of nanotechnology is to manipulate molecular and atomic structures to design and create machines at the atomic level; for example, nanobots to repair the body. Since humans are made of the same basic building blocks as the natural world, nanotechnology will enable the ability to change human tissues and cells at the molecular level. This will open doors in medicine previously thought impossible, and it will enable us to extend the length and quality of human life. It will also open the door to "enhancements" of the body; including better IQ, appearance, and capabilities. These enhancements will undoubtedly benefit many, but they also bring up important moral, ethical, and legal questions that human society is just beginning to face.

Biological enhancements to humans already exist in many forms; for example, according to Maxwell Mehlman, director of the *Law-Medicine Center* at Case Western Reserve School of Law,[30] the U.S. Federal Drug Administration (FDA)

---

[28]See generally, Gene Therapy, 2008, at: http://www.marymeetsdolly.com/index.pl?%7C%7Cac =marymeetsdolly&%7C%7Ccm=2c&%7C%7Ccv=1&%7C%7Cpp=20&%7C%7Crp=1&%7 C%7Crv=titledescription&%7C%7Csi=00ZKNPHS3VX33PA0I3Z5&%7C%7Csrt=t&%7C%7 Csrtin=a&%7C%7Ctr=OIP8JNM0ME&%7C%7Cudid=15&go=50.

[29]Francis Fukuyama, 2003. Our Posthuman Future: Consequences of the Biotechnology Revolution, Picador Press.

[30]Maxwell Mehlman, 2012, Transhumanist Dreams and Dystopian Nightmares: The Promise and Peril of Genetic Engineering, John Hopkins University Press.

recently approved a drug which has the cosmetic effects of lengthening and darkening eyelashes. The drug, Latisse, or bimatoprost, was already on the market as a treatment for glaucoma. And to gain a competitive edge, athletes use everything from steroids and blood transfusions to recombinant-DNA—manufactured hormones. Students have been known to supplement caffeine-containing energy drinks with Ritalin and the new alertness drug modafinil. Further, the military also spends millions of dollars every year on biological research to increase the warfighting abilities of "cyborg" soldiers. All of these are examples of biomedical enhancements: interventions that use medical and biological technology to improve performance, appearance, or capability in addition to what is necessary to achieve, sustain, or restore health.[31]

One of the recent enhancement movements is the phenomena of DIY biology which advocates open source of DNA information (see Chap. 5, discussing the movement to self-modify the body). This movement emphasizes DIY genetic experiments and open access to scientific and specifically, genetic material. The DIY biology movement attempts to make available the tools and resources necessary for anyone, including non-professionals, to conduct biological engineering of their own body. For example, low-cost thermocyclers (instruments to amplify DNA and RNA samples via polymerase chain reaction) have been created to make a crucial technology more widely available to the public. What about biological enhancements and public policy? An interesting relationship between genetic enhancements and public policy was highlighted by Matthew Liao, a professor of philosophy and bioethics at New York University.[32] Liao explored ways humanity can change its nature to combat "climate change." One of the suggestions Liao discussed was to genetically engineer human eyes to function more like cat eyes so we can see better in the dark. Liao remarked that this would reduce the need for lighting and reduce energy usage. Considering the available pool of resources to feed the planet's rising population, Liao also discussed genetically modifying our offspring to be smaller so they eat less and consume fewer resources. In the face of such suggestions, the NBA, and humanity has much to talk about.

Over the next several decades, it is possible that genetic engineering and other cognitive enhancement techniques could significantly increase human abilities such as intelligence. However, as Ronald Bailey author of works on ecology, economics, and biotechnology points out, critics on both the right and the left worry that the ability to enhance a person's cognitive abilities will undermine political equality.[33] Francis Fukuyama, a strong opponent of engineering DNA for purposes

[31]Maxwell J. Mehlman, Tapping Talent in a Global Economy: Biomedical Enhancements: Entering a New Era, Issues in Science and Technology, Volume XXV Issue 3, Spring 2009, at: http://issues.org/25-3/mehlman/.

[32]See generally Matthew Liao, et al. 2015, Designer Biology: The Ethics of Intensively Engineering Biological and Ecological Systems, Lexington Books.

[33]Ronald Bailey, 2005, Liberation Biology: The Scientific and Moral Case for the Biotech Revolution, Prometheus Books.

of human enhancement, in his 2002 book *Our Posthuman Future: Consequences of the Biotechnology Revolution*, asserted, "The political equality enshrined in the Declaration of Independence rests on the empirical fact of natural human equality".[34] The idea he opposes is that biological enhancements could "allow inequality to be inscribed in the human genome." Fukuyama's argument is that biotechnology could allow a class of "super beings" to be engineered such that "normal" humans would be orders of magnitude less on scales of intelligence, aggression, drive, and so on.[35] While this criticism certainly deserves public debate, some have argued that this is a very weak reason to oppose the enhancement of such important attributes as intelligence. Those in favor of cognitive enhancements point out that cognitive inequality is already inscribed in the human genome, as there is already large difference in intellectual ability between people with low versus high IQs.[36] They also argue that cognitive enhancement could help alleviate political ignorance and increase political equality—at least in so far as political equality is enhanced by cognitive equality.[37] As for the equality issue, cognitive enhancement may follow the same trajectory as numerous previous information-spreading technologies, such as books, radio, television, and computers.[38] Some argue that while at first they may be available mostly to the rich (first adopters), over time costs could go down due to marketplace competition, and the rest of society will then be able to take advantage of them as well. Ultimately, according to some commentators, cognitive enhancement might actually reduce the large "natural" gaps in cognitive ability that currently exist. Again, we humans need to talk about this.

New Opportunities in the 21st Century

Future technological developments leading towards a human—machine merger will also lead to new opportunities for entrepreneurs. For example, according to data from *Global Industry Analysts*, worldwide markets for prosthetics, include the design, manufacturing and fitting of artificial limbs. At the time of this writing a "typical" prosthesis may cost $10,000 to $65,000, and the market is projected to grow from $15.3 billion to $23.5 billion by 2017. The wearable technology market may grow to $6 billion by 2016, and the demand for real-time data, including

---

[34]Francis Fukuyama, *id.*, note 29.

[35]Francis Fukuyama, *id.*, note 29.

[36]Francis Fukuyama, *id.*, note 29.

[37]Illya Somin, 2013, The Case for Designer Babies, The Volokh Conspiracy, at: http://volokh.com/2013/10/21/case-designer-babies/.

[38]*Id.*

personal health information, will grow from 14 million devices which provide health information to 171 million in 2016.[39] Further, an ageing population and the rising prevalence of health issues such as diabetes, as well as degenerative joint diseases such as arthritis and osteoporosis, is building demand for prosthetics. And considering cyberspace, virtual reality already has value. In 2004 David Storey became the Guinness World Record holder at the time for "Most valuable object that is virtual" when he purchased an island in the virtual world *Entropia* for 265,000 Entropian dollars, or $26,500 in 2010 dollars. Storey set up a virtual rare game preserve business on the island, which he claimed drew in around $100,000 in revenue. However, you don't have to be a player paying the entry fee to a club in *Entropia*, or buying virtual swords in *World of Warcraft* to have encountered the virtual economy. If you're on Facebook, and bought a birthday cake icon for a friend, you just paid real money for a virtual good.[40]

What about the law and financial transactions in cyberspace? Consider the development of "Bitcoin," an open source digital currency used in cyberspace to pay for goods and services using peer-to-peer technology with no central authority or banks involved.[41] In some cases, Bitcoin is the *only* accepted form of payment in cyberspace. However, it seems that where financial transactions occur, government regulations and the law are close behind. And on just this point, the New York State Department of Financial Services issued subpoenas for digital-currency companies and investors in an attempt to determine if the state needs to regulate cyberspace transactions. Why would the state want to regulate cyberspace? Because the things a person can buy with the digital currency Bitcoin is continuing to grow, from sandwiches to art and even expensive cars, as a man using Bitcoin bought a Tesla Model S from a Lamborghini dealership in Newport Beach, CA, who was the first dealer to accept Bitcoin as a form of payment.[42] Globally, Bitcoin has had a mixed reception, with China's central bank banning lenders from handling the virtual money. The U.S. Internal Revenue Service hasn't offered guidance on Bitcoin beyond saying it's working on the issue and that it has been monitoring digital currencies and transactions since 2007. Interestingly, there is also a connection between digital currency and cyborg technologies. A Dutch entrepreneur has had two wireless computer chips implanted under the skin in his hands to allow him to store digital currencies like Bitcoin inside his body. Martijn Wismeijer the founder of *Mr. Bitcoin*, operates a company which installs and operates crypto-currency cash machines in and around his native Amsterdam and across Europe.

[39]Lucas Mearian, 2012, Wearable Technology Market to Exceed $6B by 2016, Computerworld, at: http://search.aol.com/aol/search?s_it=topsearchbox.search&s_chn=prt_aol20&v_t=comsearch&q=Lucas+Mearian%2C+Wearable+Technology+Market+to+exceed+%24B+by+2016.

[40]Paray Khanna and Ayesha Khanna, Time to Pay Attention to the Virtual Economy, at: http://bigthink.com/hybrid-reality/time-to-pay-attention-to-the-virtual-economy.

[41]Nathaniel Popper, 2016, Digital Gold: Bitcoin and the Inside Story of the Misfits and Millionaires Trying to Reinvent Money, Harper Press.

[42]Emily Foxhall, 2013, O.C. Lamborghini dealership sells car for 91.4 bitcoins, at: http://articles.latimes.com/2013/dec/12/local/la-me ln lamborghini-bitcoin-20131212.

Remarkably, Martijn chose to undergo a painful procedure to embed NFC (near-field communication) chips under his skin. These chips can be read by a range of devices including smartphones, and can be adapted for a range of uses.

In another example of economic opportunities that will develop this century, just as the current markets for plastic surgery, mood-altering drugs, and even beauty and fitness aids total in the billions of dollars, tomorrow this market will be multiplied many times over in a world where longevity and health enhancement become valued assets. In the U.S., medical technology developments including bio-enhancing medicines, fall within the jurisdiction of the FDA and are specifically regulated by the *Federal Food, Drug, and Cosmetics Act* and the *Public Health Service Act*. Under these acts, the U.S. FDA regulates a broad range of products, although different products are treated in different ways. Some products, such as drugs, devices, biologics, food and color additives, are subject to "premarket authorization," while other products are not. Premarket authorization means, among other things, that the FDA can require manufacturers to provide needed scientific information concerning safety and product effectiveness to the agency. Besides premarket analysis, the FDA's responsibilities include the discovery of safety problems with marketed products, to remove specific versions of a product from the market or to ban dangerous products completely, as required by the need to protect consumers and patients.

New drug approval is even more demanding and such guidelines should be considered by those developing cyborg technologies. The clinical trial process is intended to gather sufficient data needed to determine whether new drugs are safe for human use. If artificially intelligent machines gain legal status, would the FDA regulate the hardware and software updates which affect their well-being? Would any government agency be concerned with their needs? Surely the law of contracts would be implicated in the context of financial transactions. To address these and other issues, the current human-centric focus of the law may need to be revised in the future. Currently, provisions of the FDA say nothing specifically about cyborgs or artificially intelligent machines arguing for rights, although the prosthesis and treatments received by those falling under the term "bionic human or cyborg," are covered by FDA regulations. However, rather than waiting for FDA approval for implantable technology, self-directed body hackers are taking matters in their own hand and enhancing their body with off-the-shelf sensors and other implantable devices (see Chap. 5: *Modifying, Enhancing, and Hacking the Body*).

Issie Lapowski comments that "the potential for artificial intelligence has, for decades, been mostly relegated to the larger-than-life imaginations of Hollywood directors."[43] She says that from *Blade Runner* to *Terminator*, it always seems to take place in some distant and dystopian future. And yet, if there's one thing to be learned from Google's recent acquisition of the artificial intelligence startup DeepMind, it's that the heyday for this type of technology is not a century or even decades away. Furthermore, the global market for artificial intelligence was valued

---

[43]Issie Lapowski, 4 Big Opportunities in Artificial Intelligence, at: http://www.inc.com/issie-lapowsky/4-big-opportunities-artificial-intelligence.html.

at \$900 million in 2013, according to the market research firm *Research and Markets*. Meanwhile, a study out of Oxford University found that in the near future artificially intelligent technology could take over nearly half of all U.S. jobs.[44] It's scary news for some, but it's also a huge opportunity for entrepreneurs innovating in this space.

I agree with some commenters that envision several main markets for emerging applications of artificial intelligence.[45] According to Issie Lapowski, staff writer for *Wired*, the first is in understanding "big data." The big data market has been maturing for years now, but while there's plenty of technology that can crunch the numbers and spit them out in a spreadsheet or chart, there's a difference between having the data on hand and truly understanding it. Now, entrepreneurs are beginning to fill that gap with technology that not only synthesizes the data, but interprets it, too.[46] One such company, Chicago-based *Narrative Science*, has developed a program called *Quill* that goes so far as to provide users with a written report of the data in story form. The second main market for artificial intelligence, according to Lapowski, is in making smarter robots.[47] The days of robots performing simple manufacturing tasks manually controlled by humans are far from over, and yet there's a land rush going on among startups vying to build a better robot brain and sensors which would allow machines to operate autonomously. There's Baxter, of course, *Rethink Robotics'* famously friendly-looking research robot, which is already on the market, and can actually be trained. Others, like *Hanson Robotics*, have invented remarkably human-like robots, capable of carrying a conversation and recalling personal history. Thirdly, Lapowski reports that artificial intelligence will lead to smarter assistants.[48] Ubiquitous as Siri is, she's far from perfect; *Incredible Labs*, has already developed Donna, a personal assistant app that not only reminds you when you have an appointment, but tells you when to leave, how to get there, and memorizes your preferences. Taking that a step farther is *Jarvis Corp.*, a startup, which so far, is still in the conceptual phases of building a virtual assistant that can access the Internet and answer questions; but can also act as a control for all the connected devices in a house, and act as an Internet server. Artificial intelligence isn't just for processing requests and synthesizing data anymore. Now, some startups are even developing technology that can understand sentiment, a trend known as affective computing. A Tel Aviv-based startup, *Beyond Verbal*, according to Lapowski "uses technology to analyze vocal intonations to determine a person's mood." Affectiva's software accomplishes a similar mission, but by monitoring a person's face. The idea is that by understanding emotions, artificially intelligent technology could predict a person's

---

[44]Artificial Intelligence is Changing the World and Humankind Must Adopt, Wired, at: http://www.wired.com/2014/07/artificial-intelligence-changing-world-humankindmust-adapt/.

[45]Issie Lapowski, *id.*, note 43.

[46]*Id.*

[47]*Id.*

[48]*Id.*

needs in drastically more human ways. Of course, as we teach "them" how to understand us, we may be opening Pandora's Box in terms of giving artificial intelligence the information it may need to manipulate us.

Cyborgs and Virtual Reality

Leading robotic experts and artificial intelligence researchers have predicted that during this century, artificially intelligent machines will take on far more of a human-like appearance, express emotions, and reach, or possibly surpass, human levels of intelligence (see Chap. 7: *The Law of Looks and Artificial Bodies*). Machines with such capabilities, and appearing in human-like form, termed "androids," will enter society, negotiate contracts with humans, and likely argue for legal and other rights; including "human rights" and liberties. Also during this century, humans will be equipped with far more machine parts and computing power than now; the result being bionic humans and cyborgs.

By the middle of the twenty-first century, "virtual reality" will also be far more realistic and immersive than now, and as such, humans, cyborgs, artificially intelligent machines, and intelligent virtual avatars (sometimes referred to as virtual human or digital person) will spend time living in virtual reality where they will form governments; produce, buy, and sell products; and engage in many of the social activities that occur in the real world.[49] If in the future virtual reality will be inhabited by artificially intelligent virtual avatars, some working as our personal digital assistants, some working for intelligent machines, and some representing themselves, how will we humans relate to intelligent virtual avatars that we will encounter in virtual reality? How will intelligent virtual avatars be viewed by the legal system, I topic I wrote about in *The Akron Law Review*? Will intelligent avatars have legal rights? Will they be citizens, have the right to vote or marry, or through genetic algorithms, have progeny that they can claim? Will uploading a computer virus be considered an assault and battery? And where will jurisdiction lie for disputes involving virtual avatars that roam the internet? Furthermore, will intelligent avatars have the right to "treatment" if infected by a computer virus? On this point, at a 2013 conference on law and robotics hosted by Stanford Law School, after I spoke, Joanne Pransky, a person who has lectured on the social aspects of robots, handed me her card which tongue-in-cheek presented her as the world's first robotic psychiatrist.

Where will technological developments in virtual reality, intelligent systems, and cyborgs ultimately lead? Some scientists have argued that the convergence of this technology, along with developments in nanotechnology, will result in the emergence of "Posthumans," a term used by some commentators to refer to future beings whose basic capacities will so radically exceed those of present humans as

---

[49]Woodrow Barfield, Intellectual Property Rights in Virtual Environments: Considering the Rights of Owners, Programmers and Virtual Avatars, 39 Akron L. Rev., 649 (2006).

to be no longer human by our current standards. What could be the form of Posthumans? Posthumans could be artificial intelligences in a variety of forms (such as human-like robots), they could be uploaded human consciousness to computing machines or to the internet, or they could be the result of making many smaller but cumulatively profound augmentations to a biological human. Conceptually, the latter alternative would probably require either the redesign of the human organism using nanotechnology or its radical enhancement using some combination of technologies such as genetic engineering and advanced prosthesis.[50]

The above predictions on humans merging with machines and artificial intelligence equaling and then surpassing human intelligence are bold and to some controversial, and not easy for many people to accept; however, to use a cliché, the future is moving towards us at an amazing speed. In fact, the distinction between human and machine is already blurring. In our present era, a human may be equipped with a retinal prosthesis, cochlear implant, artificial hip, heart, kidney, and limbs, as well as implanted sensors and a heart pacer. Further, people like Professor Steve Mann of the University of Toronto have been wearing computers for 30 years; or as Steve told me years ago, "packing heat." In addition, Professor Kevin Warrick from the University of Reading has also pioneered the movement toward a cyborg future by participating in a set of studies known as Project Cyborg.[51] The first stage of this research, which began in 1998, involved a simple sensor being implanted beneath Warwick's skin, which was used to control doors, lights, heaters, and other computer-controlled devices based on his proximity to them. The second stage involved a more complex neural interface which consisted of an internal electrode array (consisting of 100 electrodes), connected to an external "gauntlet" that housed supporting electronics. The electrode array was implanted in Warwick's arm in 2002, and interfaced directly into Warwick's median nerve. The demonstration proved successful, and the signal produced was detailed enough that a robot arm was able to mimic the actions of Warwick's own arm.[52]

As we develop technology to enhance the human body, be it out of necessity or to create humans with abilities beyond those of current people, we are changing the ratio of human to machine parts; an idea espoused by Ray Kurzweil and Terry Grossman in their 2005 book "*Fantastic Voyage: Live Long Enough to Live Forever.*"[53] In fact, the ratio of human to machine parts may be a useful, albeit simplistic, measure of "cyborgness." We can postulate that $C = m/h$, where "C" equals cyborg, "h" represents the number of human parts, and "m" represents the

---

[50]Transhumansm; Post-Human and Trans-Human, at: http://www.miqel.com/transhumanism_nano/transhuman-posthuman-uberman.html.

[51]Kevin Warwick, The Next Step Towards True Cyborgs? at: http://www.kevinwarwick.com/cyborg2.htm.

[52]Kevin Warwick, Wikipedia, at: https://en.wikipedia.org/?title=Kevin_Warwick.

[53]Ray Kurzweil, 2005, Fantastic Voyage: Live Long Enough to Live Forever, Plume Publisher.

number of machine parts. However, the deciding factor determining the degree of "cyborgness" may not be a simple ratio of human to machine parts, but more on the issue of how much information processing is performed by the human or machine components of the cyborg/human. Thus, we can posit the following relationship: $C = \Sigma \ (m_i/h_i)$, where the subscript "i" represents the information measured in bits transmitted by a particular body or mechanical part (the human brain is a petaflop biological computer). We presently don't know the information processing capabilities of different body parts or physiological systems, but the idea that the degree of cyborgness should be related to information theory, seems to me to have merit (and heavily weights the information processing capabilities of the human brain). Barring a breakthrough in brain prosthesis, each technological advancement alone will not significantly alter the ratio of human biological to mechanical parts if information processing is the deciding factor, but if one considers the amount of human limbs, sensors, and internal systems (such as the heart or liver) that can be replaced or enhanced with technology, clearly the "cyborg" ratio is beginning to change and in favor of the machine.

Developments in cyborg technologies beg the question, "where does the human end, and the machine begin?" This is a question humanity will likely have to address sooner rather than later. In some situations laws that affect people lacking technological enhancements (the current majority) may not be relevant for an enhanced person with a prosthetic arm or leg equipped with more power and information processing capabilities than a non-enhanced person; and what about someone equipped with a brain prosthesis? As an example, in the arena of sports there is already a raging debate as to whether we should allow people enhanced by steroids, drugs, or technology to compete against those lacking such enhancements. From a policy perspective, should people that are enhanced with technology be recognized by society as a separate class? And if so, would they be considered a "protected" class (which would mean in the U.S. that they would receive protection under the 14th Amendment); or in comparison, would nonenhanced people be considered the protected class? The constitutional law issues raised by technologically enhanced beings will result in fascinating cases heard by the Supreme Court and International tribunals.

Cyborg Disputes

Another issue to consider for cyborgs is what liabilities, if any, would be incurred by those who disrupt the functioning of their "computing prosthesis"? For example, would an individual be liable if they interfered with a signal sent to an individual's wearable computer, if that signal was used to assist the individual in seeing and perceiving the world? On just this point, former U.S. Vice President, Dick Cheney, equipped with a pacemaker had its wireless feature disabled in 2007.[54]

---

[54]Dick Cheney had the wireless function disabled on his pacemaker to avoid the risk of terrorist tampering, at: http://www.theverge.com/2013/10/21/4863872/dick- cheney- pacemaker-wireless-disabled-2007.

On the point of human interaction with cyborgs, there have already been two legal disputes involving the rights of Steve Mann, a Professor of Engineering at the University of Toronto. Steve has lived as a cyborg for decades, wearing computers and electronic sensors that are designed to augment his memory, enhance his vision and keep tabs on his vital signs.[55] In 2002, before boarding a Toronto-bound plane at St. John's International Airport in Newfoundland, due to his "cyborg appearance" Steve went through an ordeal in which he was searched and allegedly injured by security personnel.[56] During the incident, thousands of dollars of his body-worn equipment was reportedly lost or damaged, including the eyeglasses that serve as his display screen. Before traveling, Steve followed the routine he has used on previous flights. He told the airline security guards in Toronto that he had already notified the airline about his equipment, and he showed them documentation, some of it signed by his doctor, that described the wires and glasses, which he wears as part of his research on wearable computers. Without a fully functional system, Steve found it difficult to navigate normally; and reportedly fell at least twice in the airport. In fact, as the number of people with heart devices and artificial joints and bones grows, so will the number of airline passengers who receive lengthier security exams. There are no estimates on the number of people with implants and cybernetic enhancements passing through checkpoints, but the U.S. Transportation Security Administration (TSA) expects more as the huge baby boomer population ages. The orthopedic implant market, for instance, is already growing at twice the annual rate of 5 years ago. The TSA is trying to improve its screening of passengers with implants such as those with pacemakers and defibrillators—life-saving devices that regulate heartbeats—and orthopedic implants, such as hips and knees. Steve believes that based on his status as a cyborg he should receive the same treatment as any person needing special equipment such as wheelchairs; certainly this view should be the subject of a public policy debate and possibly legislative action. But why debate an issue that currently impacts only a few self-professed cyborgs—because more cyborgs are coming, and soon (and more than you think are already here!). For example, there are several million people equipped with arm or leg prosthesis, important progress is being made on improving brain-computer interfaces, and the military is spending millions on efforts to create cyborg warriors.

Restaurants have also entered into the debate about the direction of our cyborg future. Taking a strong stance against a type of wearable computing, Google Glass, a Seattle-based restaurant, *Lost Lake Cafe*, actually kicked out a patron for wearing Glass. The restaurant is standing by its no-glass policy, despite mixed responses from the local community. In another incident, a theatre owner in Columbus, Ohio, saw enough of a threat from Google Glass to call the Department of Homeland Security. The Homeland Security agents removed the programmer

---

[55]Steve Mann, Cyborg, 2007, at: http://blog.codinghorror.com/steve-mann-cyborg/.

[56]Airport Security vs. Steve Mann, 2002, at: http://it.slashdot.org/story/02/03/14/2051228/airport-security-vs-cyborg-steve-mann.

who was wearing Google Glass connected to his prescription lenses. Further, a San Francisco bar frequented by a high-tech crowd has banned patrons from wearing Google Glass while inside the establishment. In fact, San Francisco seems to be ground zero for cyborg disputes as a social media consultant who wore Glass inside a San Francisco bar claimed that she was attacked by other customers objecting to her wearing the device inside the bar. In addition, a reporter for *Business Insider*, Kyle Russell, said he had his Google Glass snatched off his face and smashed to the ground in San Francisco's Mission District.[57]

Ray Kurzweil, a well-known futurist, calls the attack on Steve (in Paris) the first recorded attack on a cyborg in history; we should also include attacks on people wearing Google Glass and equipped with prosthetic devices in the same category. Should the attacks be considered a precursor for a cyborg hate crime? From a legal analysis hate crimes comprise two elements: a *criminal offence* committed with a *bias motive*. At first glance, incidents involving Steve seems to satisfy both prongs. The first element of a hate crime is that an act is committed that constitutes an offence under ordinary criminal law. This criminal act is often referred to as the "base offence;" in Steve's case the base offense would likely be an assault and battery. Because there are small variations in legal provisions from country to country, there are some divergences in the kind of conduct that amounts to a crime; but in general, most countries criminalize the same type of violent acts. Hate crimes always require a base offence to have occurred. The second element of a hate crime is that the criminal act was committed with a particular motive, referred to as "bias". It is the element of "bias motive" that differentiates hate crimes from ordinary crimes. This means that the perpetrator intentionally chose the *target* of the crime because of some *protected characteristic* (typical of a protected class). This is where Steve would have difficulty proving a hate crime—cyborgs are not considered a protected class.

What does constitute a protected class, that is, a group that cannot specifically be targeted for discrimination? A protected class normally consists of individuals with characteristics that are commonly shared by the group, such as "race", language, religion, ethnicity, nationality, or any other similar common factor. Interestingly, artificially intelligent machines speak a particular binary language and often have common physical characteristics; at first glance, they would seem to have some of the characteristic of a "class," but would they deserve special protection? That is a question for public policy and legislation. But indirectly, in a Supreme Court case, a justice may have given us a peek into the future. Justice Ginsburg focusing on the legislative findings of the American with Disability Act (ADA), commented that "individuals with disabilities are a discrete and insular minority," and "subjected to a history of purposeful unequal treatment, and relegated to a position of political powerlessness in our society."[58] Given that people

---

[57]Kyle Russell, 2014, I Was Assaulted For Wearing Google Glass In The Wrong Part Of San Francisco, Business Insider, at: http://www.businessinsider.com/i-was-assaulted-for-wearing-google-glass-2014-4.

[58]*Olmstead v. L.C.*, 527 U.S. 581, 587 (1999).

with disabilities are often equipped with prosthesis and other "cyborg technology," can we consider emerging cyborgs to be of a member of a "discrete and insular minority"? Clearly, whether or not cyborgs such as Professor Mann should be considered to be a member of a class deserving special protection under the law is a complex issue and one for the public and legislators to debate.

In addition to FDA regulations on wearable technology in the form of medical devices monitoring health, some jurisdictions are just beginning to regulate cyborg technology. For example, sparsely populated Wyoming is among a small number of U.S. states eyeing a ban on the use of wearable computers while driving, over concerns that drivers wearing Google Glass may pay more attention to their email or other online content than the road.[59] And in a high-profile California case that raised new questions about distracted driving, a driver wearing Google Glass was ticketed for wearing the display while driving after being stopped for speeding. The ticket was for violating a California statute which prohibited a "visual" monitor in her car while driving. Later, the ticket was dismissed due to lack of proof the device was actually operating while she was driving. Further, to show the power and influence of corporations in the debate about our cyborg future, Davin Levine comments that Google has lobbied officials in at least three U.S. states to stop proposed restrictions on driving with headsets such as Google Glass, marking some of the first clashes over the nascent wearable technology.[60]

Two Technologically Driven Revolutions

In discussing what might be in the twenty-first century, Rodney Brooks, former Director of the Computer Science and Artificial Intelligence Laboratory at MIT and now chairman of *Rethink Robotics*, postulated that two technology-driven revolutions would occur.[61] He termed the first, the "robotics revolution," and the second, the "biotechnology revolution."[62] Interestingly, Brooks, when discussing his artificially intelligent robots, sometimes uses the phrase "artificial creatures" to describe them. Normally when one uses the term "creature," they mean to refer to a living entity; but Brook's robots are designed using software, sensors, and mechanical parts such as effectors, actuators, and servomotors—no one would seriously claim that they are alive in any sense that humans or other living creatures are alive. But what if robots continue to gain in intelligence and one day claim to be conscious and alive? How would society and the legal system view this

---

[59]Laura Zuckerman, 2014, Wyoming among states eyeing laws to ban Google Glass while driving, at: http://www. reuters.com/article/2014/01/29/us-usa-wyoming-google- idUSBREA0S25A20140129.

[60]Dan Levine, 2014, Exclusive: Google sets roadblocks to stop distracted driver legislation, at: http://www.reuters.com/article/2014/02/25/us-google-glass- lobbying-idUSBREA1O0P920140225.

[61]Rodney Brooks, 2003, Flesh and Machines: How Robots will Change Us, Vintage Publisher.

[62]*Id.*

development? Would such "creatures" be granted rights independent from their creator? Could they be citizens, vote, or own property? Could they be liable in tort in a civil action or guilty under criminal law for any harm that resulted from their actions? Brooks thinking on these questions is presented in more detail in Chap. 8, which summarizes the law of cyborgs and the emergence of artificial intelligence in the twenty-first century.

It is likely that humanity will be required to face these very questions this century as advances in technology are quickly leading to more intelligent machines that act independently from human programmers, that is, are autonomous, and that more-and-more resemble humans in form and behavior. If artificially intelligent machines are aware of their actions, and if they can think and plan-out their conduct, would they be liable for harms resulting from their conduct? Brooks made some interesting observations of relevance for law and policy when he postulated that humans would relate to intelligent robots in ways different from previous machines, and that the upcoming robotic revolution would change the fundamental nature of society itself.[63] Just how might humans relate to an intelligent robot? Would they be our equal under the law, our property, indentured servants, or some other yet to be defined relationship? And would they be considered a legal person under the law and receive the rights that citizens receive?

At this point, some distinctions are in order. In jurisprudence, a natural person is a real human being, as opposed to a legal person, which may be a private (i.e., business entity) or public (i.e., government) organization. In fact, in the U.S. the law does grant personhood status to nonliving entities. Corporate personhood is the legal concept that a corporation may be recognized as an individual in the eyes of the law. For example, corporations may contract with other parties and sue or be sued in court in the same way as natural persons or unincorporated associations of persons. The corporate personhood doctrine does not hold that corporations are flesh and blood "people" apart from their shareholders, officers, and directors, nor does it grant to corporations all of the rights of natural citizens. In many cases, fundamental human rights are implicitly granted only to natural persons. For example, the Nineteenth Amendment to the United States Constitution, which states a person cannot be denied the right to vote based on gender, or Section Fifteen of the Canadian Charter of Rights and Freedoms, which guarantees equality rights, apply to natural persons only. Another example of the distinction between natural and legal persons is that a natural person can hold public office, but a corporation cannot. Of course artificially intelligent machines are not considered to be a legal person (bionically equipped people and current versions of cyborgs are); but surely the corporate personhood doctrine provides precedence that a non-human entity can be recognized as a person under the law.

In terms of laws that may relate to artificially intelligent robots, most people are familiar with Isaac Asimov's three laws of robotics. The first says that a robot may not injure a human being, or allow a human being to come to harm. The second

---

[63]*Id.*

law is that a robot must obey the orders given to it by human beings, except where such orders would conflict with the first law. And the third law states that the robot must protect its own existence, as long as it doesn't conflict with the first or second laws. While these laws have resulted in much discussion since they were first written in the short story *"Runaround"* published in 1942,[64] they say nothing about many areas of law that would have to be considered should robots gain in intelligence. For example, how much responsibility should artificially intelligent robots have for making enforceable contracts? Could they serve as agents for humans, or could humans serve as agents for artificially intelligent robots? Could artificially intelligent robots own real property or receive rights for their intellectual property? And could artificially intelligent robots bequeath property (in the form of software?) to future generations of intelligent machines? These are just a few of the legal and policy questions humanity may have to consider this century.

The notion of personhood has expanded significantly, albeit slowly, over the course of history. Throughout history, women, children and slaves have at times been considered property rather than persons. The category of persons recognized in the courts has expanded to include entities such as women, slaves, human aliens, illegitimate children and minors as well as unnatural or juridical persons, such as corporations, labor unions, nursing homes, municipalities and government units.[65] Clearly legal personhood makes no claim about morality, sentience or vitality. But to be a legal person is to have the capability of possessing legal rights and duties within a certain legal system, such as the right to enter into contracts, own property, sue and be sued. Not all legal persons have the same rights and obligations, and some entities are only considered "persons'" for some matters and not others. New categories of personhood are matters of decision, not discovery. The establishment of personhood is an assessment made to grant an entity rights and obligations, regardless of how it looks and whether it could pass for human. As stated by Mark Goldfelder: to make the case for granting personhood to artificially intelligent robots, it's not necessary to show that they can function as persons in all the ways that a "person" may, it's enough to show that they may be considered persons for a particular set of actions in a way that makes the most sense legally and logically.[66]

A question at the heart of the issue of personhood for artificially intelligent machines is at what point will such an entity move from the status of property to personhood (this likely will not be a step function)? To some, legal personhood for artificially intelligent robots in the near future makes sense. They argue that artificial intelligence is already part of our daily lives. For example, bots are selling

---

[64]Isaac Asimov, Runaround, written in October 1941 and first published in the March 1942 issue of Astounding Science Fiction. *Runaround* is notable for featuring the first explicit appearance of the Three Laws of Robotics, which had previously only been implied in Asimov's robot stories.

[65]Mark Goldfeder, 2014, The Age of Robots is Here, http://www.cnn.com/2014/06/10/opinion/goldfeder-age-of-robots-turing-test/.

[66]*Id.*

merchandise on eBay and Amazon, and semiautonomous agents are determining our eligibility for Medicare and other government programs. Predator drones require less and less supervision, and robotic workers in factories have become more commonplace. Google is testing self-driving cars, and General Motors has announced that it expects semiautonomous vehicles to be on the road in a few years. But when the robot acting autonomously makes a mistake, as it inevitably will, who exactly is to blame? The retailor who sold the machine? The current owner who had nothing to do with the mechanical failure? Or the party who assumed the risk of interacting with the robot? What happens when a robotic car slams into another vehicle, or even just runs a red light? To be able to assign liability is why some legal commentators argue that robots should be granted legal personhood. As a legal person, the robot could carry insurance purchased by its employer. As an autonomous actor, it could indemnify others from paying for its mistakes giving the system a sense of fairness and ensuring commerce could proceed unchecked by the twin fears of financial ruin and of not being able to collect.[67]

As to the second upcoming revolution, Brooks spoke about biotechnology, discussing how it would transform the technology of our bodies and also that of our machines.[68] On this point, Brooks envisioned a future in which machines would become more like humans and humans would become more like machines. Along these lines, one of Brook's students, and now a Professor of Media Arts and Science at MIT, Cynthia Breazeal, has created a particularly interesting robot "Leonardo" as well as a host of other personal robots.[69] Leonardo has the capability to react to people by changing its facial expressions and by moving its head towards people when they speak. Interestingly, people who have interacted with Leonardo seem to get the feeling that Leonardo is conscious at some level. Even though Leonardo is clearly not aware of its own existence, by reacting to people in a more human-like and social manner, people come to think of the robot as if it were a person. If such a reaction occurs to robots with such a rudimentary level of intelligence and social skills such as Leonardo, imagine what will be the reaction of people just 10–20 years from now when robots are far more intelligent, and more closely resemble humans in form and behavior? A later chapter discusses some interesting ideas about how humans emotionally react to artificially intelligent machines approaching human likeness.

Merging with Machines

Another leading scientist in the design of artificially intelligent robots is Hans Moravec, formerly head of the Robotics Institute at Carnegie Mellon University. Moravec, who studied robotics at Stanford University, takes a much stronger

---

[67]*Id.*

[68]Rodney Brooks, *id.,* note 61.

[69]Cynthia Braezeal, 2004, Designing Sociable Robots, A Bradford Book.

position than Brooks when discussing the future of humans and artificially intelligent machines in that he proposes that the future destiny of humans is to actually merge with machines. As expressed by Moravec in his 1998 book, *Robot: Mere Machine to Transcendent Mind,* the robots of the 1980s and 1990s could think only at an insect level, essentially equipped with the sensory and motor capabilities to crudely navigate environments.[70] But due to the exponential growth in computing power that has occurred in the last 25 years, and based on advances in algorithms he predicts that by midcentury robots will become as smart as humans and will eventually begin their own process of evolution which, according to Moravec, will render humans extinct in our present form. Yet Moravec claims that this is not something humanity should fear as he concludes that merging with intelligent machines is the best future humans could hope for, as he puts it- the ultimate form of human transcendence.[71]

Moravec is not the only prominent scientist to predict that humans may someday merge with machines. Google's Ray Kurzweil, an inventor, futurist, and author of several books on artificial intelligence and human destiny has made the same argument. Interestingly, Kurzweil views technological advances, especially in computing power, as a continuation of the process of evolution. According to Kurzweil, far from being some distant science-fiction dream, human-machine combinations will evolve sooner rather than later. This prediction is based on one of Kurzweil's key ideas, the law of accelerating returns, which was presented in his seminal book, *The Singularity Is Near: When Humans Transcend Biology.* In essence, Kurzweil says progress occurs at an exponential rate- at the low end of the exponential curve, progress is extremely slow; for example, eons elapsed between the emergence of one-celled microorganisms and the arrival of Homo sapiens. But once Homo sapiens started to develop technology, it took only about ten to twelve thousand more years for hunter-gatherers to develop a technology that eventually lead to computers. And once computers were invented, Moore's Law, which says microprocessor power doubles every 18 months or so became a factor in the evolution of computing technology. Kurzweil's law of accelerating returns posits that this same exponential pace governs efforts to splice DNA, unravel genomes, reverse-engineer the brain and develop nanotech machines.[72] Given all these developments, expanding at exponential rates, Kurzweil considers it inevitable that our own technological creations will infuse new capabilities into human biological systems. Kurzweil, well-known for his predictions about human and machine evolution, for example, that humans may merge with machines, has also written that someday software-based humans will inhabit the Web, projecting

---

[70]Hans Moravec, 2000, Robot: Mere Machine to Transcendent Mind, Oxford University Press.

[71]*Id.*

[72]Tom Abate, 2005, 2 Way-out views of technology's role in shaping the future / Inventor predicts the fusion of human and machines; author says let go of technological fixes for humans' sake, at: http://www.sfgate.com/business/article/2-way-out-views-of-technology-s-role-in-shaping-2604873.php.

bodies whenever they need or want them, including virtual bodies in diverse realms of virtual reality.[73]

Considering the above prediction for the future of humanity, specifically, the continuing evolution of intelligent machines such that they eventually gain human-like or beyond intelligence, that humans may merge with our intelligent machine inventions, and that software versions of humans could inhabit the internet, should these predictions come true, they will surely raise the most significant philosophi-cal, legal and policy issues that humanity has ever confronted, and would shake the very foundation of what it means to be human. Since the predictions made by Kurzweil, Moravec, and Brooks, could profoundly transform humanity, humanity would be prudent to have a comprehensive debate about the desirability of these potential outcomes.

But before discussing in greater detail the legal, policy, and technical issues that may occur should the above predictions come true, let us consider for a moment that the predictions are inaccurate, that human destiny is not to merge with machines or that robots will not eventually develop consciousness and human-like, or beyond, intelligence. Even so, due to efforts to fight disease, repair diseased systems, and fix damaged anatomy, future humans will be equipped with more-and-more non-biological components—whether to control diabetes or the func-tioning of the kidneys; or to equip the human with better cochlear, retinal, or body limb prosthesis. And the more biological parts which are replaced by mechanical parts, the more the question will be raised by policy makers and the public as to whether the resulting human-machine combination is in fact human. Furthermore, with regard to artificially intelligent machines, even if machines never gain con-sciousness and human levels of intelligence as some have predicted will happen this century, advances in artificial intelligence will still continue to be made that will result in machines that by any measure of intelligence, will be considered "smart" even if only in a limited domain. These developments alone will raise sig-nificant legal issues in many areas of law just as they already have in the field of electronic commerce where intelligent software agents form contracts under the direction of their human principals.

That we may merge with machines is of course a very controversial prediction, but one point is clear, many humans from medical necessity alone are in fact becoming more cyborg-like given the integration of technology within their body to replace or enhance failed biological systems or repair anatomical structures. On this point, according to physicist Sidney Perkowitz of Emory University, in the U.S. alone, eight to ten percent of the population, that is, around 25 million people are already artificially enhanced, or bionic.[74] A case on point is the work of Dr. Ross Davis and his team at the Neural Engineering Clinic in Maine. This group has been using the technology of implanting chips in the brain to treat patients whose central nervous systems have been damaged or affected by diseases such as

---

[73]See also, Martine, Rothblatt, 2014, Virtually Human: The Promise—and the Peril—of Digital Immortality, St. Martin's Press.

[74]Perkowitz, *id.*, note 6.

multiple sclerosis. Further, a team at Emory University in Atlanta has implanted a transmitting device into the brain of a stroke patient. After linking the motor neurons to silicon, a test patient was able to move a cursor on a computer monitor using thought alone. This finding means that a human was able to transmit thought signals directly to a computer in order to operate it, albeit in a rudimentary way. The Emory team is looking to gradually extend the range of controls carried out by the patient. Some scientists argue that thought-to-thought communication is just one feature of cybernetics that will become vitally important to humanity should we face the possibility of being superseded by highly intelligent machines. A later chapter summarizes recent developments in the use of thought for telepathic communication and to control machines. However, before such events happen at all, humanity should engage in a debate focusing on three vital questions: (1) whether there should be a limit placed on enhancing, augmenting, or replacing human biological parts? (2) whether or not we should create machines that are superior in intelligence to unenhanced people? and (3) whether or not we should continue to evolve on a separate path from artificially intelligent machines?

Questions for Our Cyborg Future

The first critically important question for humanity to consider in the face of rapid technological advances in the ability to enhance the human body and brain is whether there should be a limit placed on enhancing, augmenting, or replacing human biological parts? Referring to human enhancements, this question raises a number of important issues under ethics, law, and public policy. For example, would only the wealthy be able to afford enhancements, and if so, would we be creating a society of superior cyborg-enhanced individuals, and a group of individuals that were too poor to afford enhancements? If cyborgs are equipped with cognitive, auditory, visual, or motor prosthesis that "separate" them from non-enhanced people, would they be afforded special protection under the law (recall Steve Mann's altercations presented above)? The law of body modifications and body hacking is the topic of a chapter in this book, but it is worth briefly noting here: part of the answer would depend on whether the human was enhanced out of medical necessity or not.

If the human was enhanced due to a disability, many jurisdictions around the world afford protection for such people in the workplace. For example, in the U.S., the Americans with Disabilities Act (ADA), provides protection for employees with certain disabilities and requires employers to accommodate the disabilities, when possible. Currently though, to be covered under the ADA, an individual must be a qualified worker and must have a legally recognized disability to be protected. An example of the types of disabilities covered include a physical or mental impairment that substantially limits a major life activity (such as the ability to walk, talk, see, hear, breathe, reason, work, or take care of oneself). Since bionic humans are enhanced to repair or replace human anatomy or physiology, their disabilities would likely be covered by the ADA, but cyborgs may not receive protection under the ADA if their enhancements are done for reasons other than medical necessity such as to increase a human ability beyond normal.

The second vital issue for humanity to consider with regard to artificially intelligent machines is whether or not we should create machines that are superior in intelligence to unenhanced people? Of course computers are already "smarter" than people in many domains, but by this question I refer to computers with "strong artificial intelligence," that is, consciousness, sentience, and the ability to successfully perform any intellectual task a human can. On this note, Professor Stephen Hawking, former Lucasian Professor of Mathematics at Cambridge University expressed grave concern that a future danger to humanity was the possibility that intelligent machines would someday "take over the world."[75] Hawking commented that computers were evolving so rapidly that they would eventually outstrip the intelligence of humans and that computers with artificial intelligence could therefore come to dominate the world. Hawking argued in favor of changes in human DNA through genetic modification to keep ahead of advances in computer technology. He also advocated direct links between brains and computers stating that we must develop as quickly as possible technologies that make possible a direct connection between computers, so that artificial brains contribute to human intelligence rather than opposing it.[76] Research that provides support for the proposition that it is possible for a human mind to directly communicate with a computer and other networked minds is beginning to emerge (note that this is a different issue than downloading data from a computer to a mind).

With regard to Hawking's recommendation to genetically engineer humans in order to keep pace with artificial intelligence, Ray Kurzweil has pointed out that genetic engineering through the birth cycle would be extremely slow in comparison to the exponential rate at which computers are gaining in intelligence. According to Kurzweil, by the time the first genetically engineered generation grew up, the era of beyond-human-level machines would already be upon us. For example, even though we are years away from genetically engineering a human, if we start the clock at 2014, recalling Moore's law, computer power doubles about every 18 months, if humans become legally recognized adults at eighteen, by 2032, there would be several doublings of computer power. This would indeed result in a machine with tremendous computational power to view, understand, and think about the world, especially if we consider that the fastest supercomputer available now operates at several petaflops[77] (a petaflop is one thousand million floating point operations per second).

On the issue of genetic modifications, Kurzweil further argues that even if we were to apply genetic alterations to adult humans by introducing new genetic

---

[75]Rory Cellan, Stephen Hawking Warns Artificial Intelligence Could End Mankind, *id.*, note 9.

[76]*Id.*

[77]China surpassing U.S. with 54.9 petaflop supercomputer, at: http://www.computerworld.com/s/article/9239710/China_surpassing_U.S._with_54.9_petaflop_supercomputer.

information via gene therapy techniques, it still wouldn't keep biological intelligence in the lead. Genetic engineering (through either birth or adult gene therapy) is inherently DNA-based and a DNA-based brain is always going to be extremely slow in terms of the speed in which a signal is propagated down an axon and limited in capacity compared to the potential of an artificially intelligent machine. For example, the speed of electronics is already 100 million times faster than our electrochemical circuits (i.e., neuronal); and we have no quick downloading ports on our biological neurotransmitter levels, to move large amounts of data quickly between the human mind and a computer.[78] We could bioengineer smarter humans, but this approach will not begin to keep pace with the exponential pace of artificially intelligent machines.

The third vital question for humanity to consider concerning our technological future is whether or not we should continue to evolve on a separate path from artificially intelligent machines? The issue seems to be whether humanity should continue to evolve under the slow process of biological evolution (the current case), evolve under the relatively faster process of DNA modifications, or consider merging with artificially intelligent machines and evolve at the speed of technology. Evolution does not work quickly. It takes many generations for our genetic code to adapt to changing environments and circumstances. Ted Driscoll of Clarement Creek Ventures comments that what this means is that our twenty-first century human genome is still basically the genome of a caveman.[79] Our genome was well-adapted to the environment of our hunter-gatherer ancestors, because that environment lasted for hundreds of thousands of years. Unfortunately, the twenty-first century world we live in bears little resemblance to the prehistoric world. In contrast, most of the change in technology has occurred in the past few centuries, and ongoing change is only accelerating.

The Reemergence of Luddites

Some people have asked whether humans will embrace changes to their basic being and physical structure, or will they seek to remain the same (that is, technologically unenhanced)? For reasons discussed throughout this book, a strong argument can be made that people *will* embrace technological and biological enhancements to their body and even to their brain. But from a historical perspective, those that resist technology have come to be been termed "Luddites."[80] Where does this term come from? From legend comes the story of a

---

[78]Ray Kurzweil, 2003, The Human Machine Merger: Are we Headed for the Matrix? at: http://www.kurzweilai.net/the-human-machine-merger-are-we-headed-for-the-matrix.

[79]Ted Driscoll, 2014, Are Humans Equipped for a Big Data World? at: http://recode.net/2014/01/31/are-humans-equipped-for-a-big-data-world/.

[80]Steven Jones, Against Technology: From the Luddites to Neo-Luddism, Routledge Press.

"feebleminded lad" by the name of Ned Ludd who broke two stocking frames at a factory in Nottingham. Henceforth, when an offending factory owner found one of his expensive pieces of machinery mysteriously broken, the damage was conveniently attributed to Ned Ludd.[81] However, the term also has a firm footing in history as well. In the early days of the industrial revolution, workers (or Luddites), upset by wage reductions and the use of unapprenticed workmen, began to break into factories at night to destroy the new machines that the employers were using. In response to the Luddite movement, the British Parliament passed the *Frame Breaking Act* in 1812 that led to people convicted of machine-breaking to be sentenced to death. As a further precaution, the British government ordered 12,000 troops into the areas where the Luddites were active.

Viewing the acts of the Luddites in the early 1800's through the eyes of history, they have come to be viewed as counter-revolutionaries of the "Industrial Revolution."[82] If we consider that in 1890 ninety percent of Americans worked in agriculture, but by 1900 the figure was only 41 %, and by 2000, it was just two percent; and if we consider advances in artificial intelligence, we need to wonder if the same trend of job displacement will occur for professions requiring complex cognitive skills. As a case in point, IBM's supercomputer Watson, the language-fluent computer, recently beat the best human champions at the TV game show of *Jeopardy*. After matching wits with human game show whizzes, Watson has now moved on to becoming an expert diagnostician. Watson's ability to absorb and analyze vast quantities of data is, IBM claims, better than that of many human doctors. After mastering the same amount of knowledge as the average second-year medical student, Watson was tasked to "read" peer-reviewed medical journals relating to oncology; focusing on lung, prostate and breast cancers. According to Ian Stedman, "Watson's ingestion of more than 600,000 pieces of medical evidence, more than two million pages from medical journals and the further ability to search through up to 1.5 million patient records for further information gives it a breadth of knowledge no human doctor can match."[83] If industrial machines perform many of the manual labor tasks that were once done by expert humans, and if artificially intelligent machines perform cognitive tasks once performed by humans, it is no wonder that people like Ray Kurzweil and Hans Moravec argue for a merger of human with artificially intelligent machines; seemingly embracing the idea, "If you can't beat them, join them" (or merge with them!).

Currently, artificial intelligence and robotics are beginning to impact both blue- and white-collar workers, with experts predicting that robots will displace more human jobs than they create by 2025.[84] By 2025, if robots and artificial intelli-

---

[81]See generally, Luddites, at: http://www.ascrs.org/sites/default/files/resources/Global%20view%20of% 20EMRs.pdf.

[82]*Id.*

[83]Ian Steadman, IBM's Watson is better at diagnosing cancer than human doctors, at: http://www.wired.co.uk/news/archive/2013-02/11/ibm-watson-medical-doctor.

[84]Aaron Smith and Janna Anderson, 2014, AI, Robotics, and the Future of Jobs, at http://www.pe winternet.org/2014/08/06/future-of-jobs/.

gence continue to advance at the same pace of the last few years, robots and artificial intelligence will no longer be constrained to repetitive tasks on a production line. Will advanced artificial intelligence and robots make the world a better place or not? Basically everyone agrees that robotics and artificial intelligence are going to displace a lot of jobs over the next few years as the general-purpose robot comes of age.[85] Even though these early general-purpose bots won't initially be as fast or flexible as humans, they will be flexible enough that they can perform various menial tasks 24/7—and cost just a few cents of electricity, rather than minimum wage. On the other hand, robots may dominate the workplace so quickly that our economic, education, and political systems may struggle to keep up. Previously robots mostly replaced blue-collar workers, but this next wave will increasingly replace skilled/professional white-collar workers.[86] A lot of these specialized workers may find themselves without a job, and without the means to find a new one.

Returning to the Luddites, as artificially intelligent machines become more proficient at cognitive tasks, will the predicted loss of jobs in many service sectors lead to a new generation of humans expressing hostility toward smart machines? In fact, a neo-Luddite movement has sprung up. The most extreme expression of this philosophy was the bombing campaign of Ted Kaczynski, also known as the Unabomber, who was sentenced to life imprisonment. His manifesto, which was eventually published by the New York Times, said that the "Industrial Revolution and its consequences have been a disaster for the human race". One of the leading developers of cyborg technology, Steve Mann is also tentative in his support of the cyborg movement, expressing the view in *Singularity 1 on 1* that "I am not saying more or less technology—I am saying appropriate technology. Instead of technological excess—we should have technology that is balanced with nature. Instead of replacing nature with technology—we should balance it. Instead of replacing intelligence with artificial intelligence—we should use humanistic intelligence...".[87]

The Luddites of the 1800s were opposed to new technology based primarily on economic grounds—the technology was seen as being able to replace human skills in the textile industry, skills that were necessary for people to secure a living and support their families.[88] In current times, people may be opposed to technology for reasons other than basic economics; for example, they argue that to remain human we must oppose the merging of humans with machines. But, proponents of enhancement technology counter that there are many reasons why it may be desirable to augment or enhance humans—for example, they note that one out of every

---

[85]Martin Ford, 2015, Rise of the Robots: Technology and the Threat of a Jobless Future, Basic Books.

[86]*Id.*

[87]Cyborg Luddite Steve Mann on Singularity 1 on 1: Technology That Masters Nature is Not Sustainable, interviewed by "Socrates," at: https://www.singularityweblog.com/cyborg-steve-mann/.

[88]The Industrial Revolution, at: http://www.historydoctor.net/Advanced%20Placement%20World%20History/40.%20The_Industrial_revolution.htm.

person sixty-five or older has Alzheimer's disease, as do half of those over eighty-five. In the U.S. alone, consumers and insurance companies spend over one hundred billion dollars on the disease each year. How would human enhancement technology help those with Alzheimer's? For the millions of families with relatives living with Alzheimer's, keeping them safe is a major concern. In response to such concerns, doctors can implant an FDA-approved microchip in an Alzheimer's patient's arm, allowing critical medical details to be accessed instantly. The chip, which is about the size of a grain of rice, contains a 16-digit identification number which is scanned at a hospital. Once the number is placed in a database, it can provide crucial medical information. Another form of enhancement that may assist those with Alzheimer's comes in the form of a brain-computer interface. Brain-computer interfaces (BCIs) provide alternative methods for communicating and acting on the world, since messages or commands are conveyed from the brain to an external device without using the normal output pathways of peripheral nerves and muscles.[89] Alzheimer's disease patients in the most advanced stages, who have lost the ability to communicate verbally, could benefit from a BCI that may allow them to convey basic thoughts (e.g., "yes" and "no") and emotions.

According to Ramez Naam, in *More than Human: Embracing the Promise of Biological Enhancement,* in the U.S. more than eight million people had some sort of cosmetic surgery in 2001; and in the U.S. alone there are 20,000 plastic surgeons working to change the shape and appearance of a person's body.[90] The Olympics and other sporting events is replete with stories of doping, where athletes take performance enhancing drugs to compete and there are at least a quarter million quadriplegics in the U.S. that could benefit from brain-computer interfaces. In the U.S. there are also more than 34 million deaf or hearing impaired people that could benefit from enhancements to their auditory system. On this point, more than seventy thousand people worldwide have entered the world of human enhancements with cochlear implants—a microphone with multiple electrodes that electrically stimulate the auditory nerve. So while some percentage of the population will always be opposed to new technology just as the Luddites were in the 1800s, in the twenty-first century many people have already enthusiastically embraced the need for human enhancements and artificially intelligent machines.

---

[89]Liberati G, Dalboni da Rocha JL, van der Heiden L, Raffone A, Birbaumer N, Olivetti Belardinelli M, and Sitaram R. Toward a brain-computer interface for Alzheimer's disease patients by combining classical conditioning and brain state classification, J. Alzheimers Dis. 2012;31 Suppl 3:S211–20.

[90]Ramez Naam, 2010, More than Human: Embracing the Promise of Biological Enhancement, http://Lulu.com.

Enter the Horse

When discussing the law as it applies to cyborgs, and artificially intelligent machines, there is a basic question to raise—are there any legal issues that are unique to technologically enhanced humans, cyborgs, and artificially intelligent machines? When talking about the law and cyberspace, Judge Easterbrook, of the U.S. Court of Appeals for the Seventh Circuit, claimed that there was no specific more a law of cyberspace than there was a law of the horse.[91] In making this statement, Judge Easterbrook recounted an anecdote involving a former Dean of the University of Chicago law school who had expressed pride in the fact that the University of Chicago did not offer a course in "The Law of the Horse"; while there were, of course cases dealing with topics such as the sale of horses (contract law) or with people kicked by horses (torts), there was no separate course on "The Law of the Horse."[92] According to Judge Easterbrook the best way to learn the law applicable to specialized endeavors, was to study general rules; only by putting the law of the horse in the context of broader rules about commercial endeavors could one really understand the law about horses.[93] His point, of course, was that the "law of cyberspace, cyborgs, and artificially intelligent machines," is much like the "law of the horse," a specialized endeavor best understood with reference to familiar general principles of contract, intellectual property, privacy, free speech and the like, but which does not need, and does not deserve, its own separate category.[94] In response to Judge Easterbrook's assertions, Larry Lessig, a Professor of Law at Harvard, contemplated what a law of cyberspace might actually look like and what lessons it might provide. The "Lessig view" was that cyberspace law might actually exist and say something important about time, place, and national boundaries affected by cyberspace transactions.[95] This book borrows from each approach- while the law of virtual reality, cyborgs, and artificially intelligent systems, will surely benefit from an analysis based on general established rules, each area will move beyond current law quickly, thus, new law and policy will be needed to account for the amazing future that awaits us; a future in which we merge with artificially intelligent machines.

---

[91]Frank H. Easterbrook, 1996, Cyberspace and the Law of the Horse, *University of Chicago Legal Forum*, 207.

[92]David G. Post, 1998, Cyberspace and the Law of the (Electronic) Horse, or Has Cyberspace Law Come of Age? at: http://www.temple.edu/lawschool/dpost/horse.html.

[93]Frank H. Easterbrook, *id.*, note 91.

[94]*Id.*

[95]Lawrence Lessig, 1999, The Law of the Horse What Cyberlaw Might Teach, 113 Harv. L. Rev. 501.

Concluding Thoughts

There is a strong possibility that advances in human enhancement technologies could offer humanity options that have been the subject of dreams for centuries. Potentially, humans could be modified to live longer and healthier, be smarter and stronger, and by some societal standard, more attractive. According to Jacob Heller and Christine Peterson: "Enhancements could come in the form of extreme intelligence and memory capacity, significantly heightened sense of awareness, and astonishing athletic capability."[96] However, experts have warned that while human enhancements could give rise to numerous benefits, these advances may come at a significant cost to humanity- not the least of which is that technical enhancements to humans could change the essence of what it means to be human. Perhaps humanity would be prudent to heed the warning of prominent computer scientist and cofounder of Sun Microsystems, Bill Joy, who in an essay written in 2000, "*Why the future doesn't need us*," argued that human beings would likely guarantee their own extinction by developing the technologies favored by advocates of enhancement technology.[97] This comment related to the use of nanotechnology to redesign the environment; but if there is the slightest chance that any enhancement technology could lead to such a bleak outcome, the public should demand strong safeguards, even a moratorium on the use of potentially dangerous enhancement technologies.

A point I want to emphasize is that one way or the other, more people in the future will be enhanced with technology, whether due to medical necessity or by choice. Already, biological and technical enhancements exist today in many forms such as steroids, Ritalin, Prozac, plastic surgery, mechanical replacements for body parts, not to mention the "game changing" ability to implant chips into the brain. While to date, the practice of human enhancement has focused mainly on restoration, it is not improbable that this technology will soon extend to the healthy individual. However, if only those who can afford it opt for human enhancement, the appalling inequalities in our society that exist today will become even greater and social mobility will decrease farther.[98] If the wealthy can increase their intelligence and become more physically able, they will likely increase their political and earning power; in this case, the rich will become richer and more powerful. In light of this possibility, should the government guarantee a baseline set of characteristics for all people?

Will legislators act before decisions by scientists and corporations have been made that will be difficult to roll back or that could have deleterious effects on

---

[96]Jacob Heller and Christine Peterson, Human Enhancement and Nanotechnology, Foresight Institute, at: https://www.foresight.org/policy/brief2.html.

[97]Bill Joy, 2000, Why the Future Doesn't Need Us, Wired Magazine, 8.04.

[98]Francis Fukuyama, *id*., note 29.

humanity? I can only offer a weak response, "possibly." But how should we approach the problem of safeguarding humanity, or at least making sure the future is one of our choosing? Enter the courts, the media, and the arena of public opinion. In a recent Supreme Court case, all nine justices agreed that placing a GPS tracking device on a car without a warrant was an unlawful search and seizure and violated the Fourth Amendment to the U.S. Constitution. Justice Alito observed that "in circumstances involving dramatic technological change, the best solution to privacy concerns may be legislative."[99] But since there was no specific GPS tracking device law for guidance (i.e., no Law of the Horse), Justice Alito and his colleagues looked to Fourth Amendment precedent to analyse warrantless use of GPS technology and to create a privacy solution.[100] Justice Alito is not alone in thinking that new legislation is needed to deal with rapid technological change. In the U.S. Congress, bills have been introduced to regulate online tracking, to create rules for the collection of geolocation data, to protect children's privacy and to regulate the collection and use of personal data generally. Further, in the U.S., some states have enacted statutes which regulate the degree to which people can be implanted with microchips. In my view, far-reaching legislation by mid-to-late century will be necessary to establish and protect the rights of human's vis-à-vis cyborgs and artificially intelligent machines. And to determining the right of cyborgs with beyond-human abilities, and finally to determine the rights of artificially intelligent machines, with respect to unenhanced humans and to each other.

As we progress into the twenty-first century, I believe that from a human rights perspective humanity will need to develop a *Robot and Cyborg Ethics Charter*; essentially a set of rules intended to govern the interaction between humans, cyborgs, and artificially intelligent machines. A working version of such a code for robotics is being developed by a group of robotics engineers in South Korea,[101] which I might add represents an expansion of Asimov's Three Laws of Robotics. The Korean charter recognizes that robots of the future may require legal protection from abusive humans, just as animals sometimes need legal protection from their owners. While some experts welcome the introduction of the *Robot Ethics Charter* and similar proposals, noting that wanton human abuse of intelligent machines could be cause for moral outrage we also need to be concerned that humans could be abused by our intelligent creations (and thus the Terminator movie series). This and other important issues of law, technology, and policy for the future of humans and our intelligent creations, is the subject of this book.

---

[99]*U.S. v. Jones*, 132 S.Ct 945, 565 U.S.__2012.

[100]*Id.*

[101]South Korean Robot Ethics Charter, at: https://akikok012uml.wordpress.com/south-korean-robot-ethics-charter-2012/.

Chapter 2
The Coming Singularity

If humans merge with machines this century, the coming Singularity will have a lot to say about that. What is the Singularity? The Singularity is that point in or development time when artificially intelligent machines equal or surpass humans in intelligence. The first use of the term "Singularity" was by the mathematician Jon von Neuman who in 1958 spoke of an ever accelerating progress of technology which would lead to changes in the mode of human life, thus giving the appearance that humanity was approaching some essential Singularity, beyond which human affairs, could not continue.[1] Twenty-five years later, science fiction writer Vernor Vinge coined the phrase "technological Singularity," stating that "We will soon create intelligences greater than our own. When this happens, human history will have reached a kind of Singularity, an intellectual transition as impenetrable as the knotted space-time at the center of a black hole, and the world will pass far beyond our understanding."[2] From a different perspective, Tim Wu, professor of law at Columbia University and author of "*The Master Switch*," observed, "… make no mistake: we are now different creatures than we once were, evolving technologically rather than biologically, in directions we must hope are for the best."[3] While Tim's comment reflects the public's current ambivalence about our cyborg future; I advocate for a different approach, one that involves the public educating themselves on the issues surrounding artificial intelligence and "cyborg technology," and engaging in a rigorous debate about the future of humanity.

---

[1]Technological Singularity, discussing the ideas Jon von Neuman's and other contributors to the Singularity discussion, available at: http://en.wikipedia.org/wiki/Technological_singularity.

[2]Vernon Vinge 1993 essay on the Singularity, available at: http://mindstalk.net/vinge/vinge-sing.html.

[3]Tom Wu, If a Time Traveller Saw a Smartphone, 2014, The New Yorker, at: http://www.newyorker.com/tech/elements/if-a-time-traveller-saw-a-smartphone; Tim Wu, 2011, The Master Switch: The Rise and Fall of Information Empires, Vintage Press.

© Springer International Publishing Switzerland 2015
W. Barfield, *Cyber-Humans*, DOI 10.1007/978-3-319-25050-2_2

Throughout this book, one of the key points I make is that we humans may be experiencing the last generation(s) of evolving predominately under the laws of biology. Why? Because as discussed in Kurzweil's *"The Singularity is Near: When Humans Transcend Biology,"*[4] an analysis of the history of technology shows that technological change is exponential. Kurzweil argues that exponential growth is contrary to the "intuitive linear" view most people have of societal progress in which we notice new technology entering our life, but are unaware of where we are in the curve representing the rate of change of technological advancements. According to Kurzweil, this means that we won't experience 100 years of progress in the twenty-first century—it will be more like 20 millennium of progress.[5] Thus, within a few decades, some argue that machine intelligence will surpass human intelligence, leading to the Singularity. The implications of which will include the merger of biological and nonbiological intelligence, immortal software-based humans, and ultra-high levels of intelligence that expand beyond our current imagination.[6]

The term "Singularity" has been applied to many different types of developments, but for this book the most common conceptualization of "the Singularity" is the idea of smarter-than-human artificial intelligence, the essence of which is software, machines, or robots that learn, reason, select their own goals, and evolve on their own. The concept for the Singularity goes something like this: many prominent researchers in artificial intelligence, robotics, and neuroscience are convinced that technology will eventually reach and then surpass humans in intelligence creating on the way, a world filled with 'smart' machines. Actually it's already happening. Machines that perform surgery, design life-saving drugs, write news articles, and work in a range of industries; in other words, do what we humans do with our mind and bodies, already exist. But once they surpass us in general intelligence, then what? Will they be content to continue performing the tasks asked of them by their human masters, or will they branch out from humans in terms of their goals and aspirations?

Questions of Law and Policy

If the Singularity is to occur in the near future; there are critically important questions that society must address: should we merge with them (artificially intelligent machines), be surpassed by them, co-exist with them, enslave them, or risk being enslaved by them? And, as some have argued, for the survivability of the human race, should we decide to stop the Singularity before it has a chance to

---

[4]Ray Kurzweil, 2006, The Singularity is Near: When Humans Transcend Biology, Penguin Books.

[5]*Id.*

[6]*Id.*

happen; or will it even be possible to stop the Singularity from occurring? While it may be comforting to avoid thinking about or answering these difficult questions, the never-ending march of technology towards the Singularity leaves us with no choice, we either get involved with determining the future of our species, or we passively observe as the future envelops us.

Considering the above possibilities, many forward thinkers predict that in the coming decades, we will merge with our silicon inventions. On the machine side, robotics expert Ray Kurzweil and Hans Moravec envision a time when tomorrow's machines will become more human-like, that is, appear in the form of an android and having super intelligence. On this point Berkeley physicist Max Tegmark writing in "*Our Mathematical Universe*," observed that the development of supercomputers with human or beyond levels of intelligence is likely, given that our brains are ultimately made of particles observing the laws of physics, and there's no physical law precluding particles from being arranged in ways that can perform even-more-advanced computations.[7] On the human side, 15 years ago in a book I co-edited on wearable computers I discussed human enhancement technology and the idea that humans would eventually merge with machines (the second edition is now available).[8] The merging of humans with machines could benefit humans in a number of ways: for example, by swapping our biology for non-biological parts we could gain the ability to automatically repair or replace prosthesis, including neuroprosthesis, when damaged or outdated. And instead of suffering from the effects of aging, we could age with more dignity, and possibly be able to turn the aging clock back. Due to the expected benefits, some commentators argue that the necessity for replacing and repairing human biology will enable society to view the merger of humans and intelligent machines as simply the next natural phase of evolution. Though the idea may seem extreme, especially for those unaware of the exponential growth of technology, many experts in robotics and computer science believe this is a likely scenario for our future. However, if we are to merge with machines we may have only a limited widow of opportunity to do that; as once machines surpass us in intelligence, they may decide to continue evolving in ways incompatible with our goals and aspirations. They may conclude, why merge with a less intelligent species other than to gain access to their mobility, manual dexterity, or possibly their human emotions.

Technological advances in the first half of the twenty-first century in a wide range of fields such as robotics, neuroscience, artificial intelligence, sensors, nanotechnology, prosthetics, and material science, will lay the foundation for the Singularity to occur. According to those who argue that the Singularity is only a few decades away, beyond-human intelligence will result in self-directed or autonomous computers who will claim that they are sentient, and whose intelligence

---

[7]Max Tegmark, 2015, Our Mathematical Universe: My Quest for the Ultimate Nature of Reality, Vintage Books.

[8]Woodrow Barfield (editor), 2015, Fundamentals of Wearable Computers and Augmented Reality, Second Edition, CRC Press.

and capabilities will increase exponentially rather than incrementally. Futurist Ray Kurzweil, a major voice arguing that the Singularity is close, puts the date of the Singularity at around 2045.[9] By then he estimates that the exponential increases in computing power resulting from Moore's law, along with advances in artificial intelligence will be sufficiently powerful enough to create beyond-human artificially intelligent machines. In this new world, Kurzweil believes there will be no clear distinction between human and machine or real reality and virtual reality. In practical terms, his prediction (with advances in nanotechnology) could mean the end of human aging and illness, pollution, world hunger and poverty. However, while the Singularity may be inevitable, which is a view I hold, there is serious debate as to when it will happen or even in the opinion of some researchers, if it will happen at all. For example, in 2011, one of Microsoft's founders, Paul Allen co-authored an article in the *MIT Technology Review* in which he took a more cautionary view of the coming Singularity than Kurzweil, arguing that while it is likely to occur, the timeframe will be the distant future.[10]

A strong voice against the idea that the Singularity will occur is Duke neuroscientist Miguel Nicolelis whose work on brain-computer interfaces is fascinating, but paradoxically in my view, is leading to a future human-machine merger.[11] Nicolelis' main argument is that "the brain is not computable and therefore no engineering can reproduce it."[12] Another problem he observes is that the brain is 'copy-write' protected by its own evolutionary history. However, describing his new Pattern Recognition Theory of Mind (PRTM), Ray Kurzweil voiced an opinion that couldn't be more different from Nicolelis— "We now have enough evidence to support a particular theory, a uniform theory about how the neocortex works".[13] According to Kurzweil, the neocortex is basically comprised of 300 million pattern recognizers which can wire themselves in hierarchies in relation to other pattern recognizers. The world is inherently hierarchical and the neocortex allows us to understand it in that hierarchical fashion. Regardless of whether or not the Singularity occurs, it's never too early for the public to consider the transformative effect the Singularity would have on humanity should it happen, and whether to embrace it or oppose it.

Considering that today's semiconductor manufacturers are adding more speed and memory into computers each year, leads some commentators to conclude that eventually our smart silicon creations will become efficient enough to build their own improved hardware and software models, increasing their intelligence and capabilities with each succeeding generation. Thinking about policy and law, if

---

[9]Kurzweil, *id.*, note 4.

[10]Paul G. Allen and Mark Greaves, 2011, The Singularity Isn't Near, MIT Technology Review.

[11]Miguel Nicolelis, 2013, The Brain is Not Computable, MIT Technology Review.

[12]*Id.*

[13]Ray Kurzweil, 2013, How to Create a Mind: The Secret of Human Thought Revealed, Penguin Books.

a machine with artificial intelligence could generate its own code, heuristics, and algorithms, would the artificial intelligence or human (manufacturer, owner, 3rd party) be responsible for its actions? Current legal paradigms are poorly equipped to answer this question, yet it is a critical one to address. The main point to make is this: intelligent and autonomous machines engaging in "human activities," will challenge current legal paradigms and will result in a host of issues. For example, will a contract negotiated by an artificially intelligent machine be considered valid, who will be considered the contracting parties, and who will be responsible for a breach of contract? The field of electronic commerce is grappling with just this issue as intelligent software agents with increasing intelligence and autonomy roam the internet and engage in contract negotiations. To take this point one step further every enforceable contract has an offer and acceptance, consideration, and an intention to create legal obligations. At present, an artificially intelligent machine is not viewed as having the ability to form an intention on its own volition and thus for this and other reasons cannot contract on its own behalf.

What are some "legal relationships" formed between humans and machines? Considering humans and artificially intelligent machines, there is established law that applies to situations where one party allows another to negotiate on its behalf-the law of agency. Generally, the law of agency is an area of commercial law dealing with a set of legal (typically fiduciary) relationships that involve a person or software entity, called the agent, that is authorized to act on behalf of another, called the principal, to create legal relations with a third party. The agent owes the principal a number of duties such as: a duty to undertake the task or tasks specified by the terms of the agency (that is, the agent must not do things that he has not been authorized by the principal to do); a duty to discharge his duties with care and due diligence; and a duty to avoid conflict of interest between the interests of the principal and his own (that is, the agent cannot engage in conduct where s/he stands to gain a benefit for himself to the detriment of the principal).[14] If it is subsequently found that the alleged agent was acting without necessary authority, the agent will generally be held liable. Since software agents can bind the principle in contract, it seems likely that future artificially intelligent machines will also be able to serve as agents and as a consequence, be subject to agency law.[15]

In the field of criminal law, we have created a legal system in which the victim is human, but what if the "victim" is an artificially intelligent machine claiming that it has rights? For example, what if a software virus is uploaded onto the operating system of an artificially intelligent machine? What rights does the machine have to protect the integrity of its software, the machine's equivalent of the humans prefrontal cortex or limbic system? One outcome is entirely likely, the cycle of improvement of technology will continue to evolve into what many have described as an intelligence explosion. Artificially intelligent machines could

---

[14]Roderick Munday, 2013, Agency: Law and Principles, Oxford University Press.

[15]See Generally, Ronald Mann and Jane Winn, 2004, Electronic Commerce, Aspen Law and Business.

Fig. 2.1 X-ray image of
implanted technology for
hearing. (Image courtesy of
Michael Chorost)

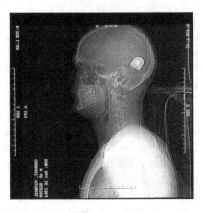

then keep on developing until they far surpass human levels of intelligence. The
Singularity will also speed other technology breakthroughs; in fact, some have
argued that the future may advance so quickly, that at some point, our biological brains, if not enhanced, will no longer be able to understand the direction of
machine evolution (Fig. 2.1).

As a consequence, a number of scientists and philosophers worry that artificial
intelligence may someday make humanity superfluous; however, a positive post-
Singularity world could include affordable healthcare (but healthcare itself could
be vastly different), providing most world citizens with indefinite lifespans, and a
global economy strong enough to erase today's gap between the rich and poor.
And here's what stimulates the imagination of those who believe that the
Singularity is near; the possibility to have lived long enough to benefit from the
amazing technologies that the Singularity will usher in. Ray Kurzweil in his book
Fantastic Voyage, Live Long Enough to Live Forever, agrees saying that advances
in stem cells, genetics, and nanomedicine expected during the next couple of decades, could stave off deadly diseases; bringing many of us into this high-tech
world of tomorrow; that is, if we live long enough to become cyborgs and merge
with machines.[16] Whatever we call those who move beyond traditional notions of
human-ness, their decision to go posthuman will have legal, moral, philosophical,
social, and political implications.

Towards Machine Sentience

Researchers, science fiction authors, and the media who write about the
Singularity, often focus on artificial intelligence as the key technology. On the
topic of machine intelligence, Curtis Karnow, Judge on the California Superior

---

[16]Ray Kurzweil, 2005, Fantastic Voyage, Live Long Enough to Live Forever, Plume Books.

Court, and author of *"Future Codes: Essays in Advanced Computer Technology and Law,"* frames intelligence in terms of machine autonomy; autonomy being the ability of the machine to program itself to solve problems independent of a human.[17] The more the machine can make real time decisions in unpredictable environments, the greater the machine intelligence. I use a broader definition of intelligence; when I use the term, I mean to describe artificially intelligent machines which have the capability to perform cognitive, perceptual, and motor tasks at human levels of skill. Thus, a computer that could accurately diagnose disease would be considered intelligent in that domain, as would a computer that could write original short stories, compose music, or manage a hedge fund. A numerically controlled industrial robot, repetitiously moving in predetermined positions, would obviously be considered far less intelligent.

With the exception of the industrial robot, notice that the examples I just mentioned are very "cognitive-oriented;" but other areas of human performance also represent clear examples of intelligent behavior by computing machines. For example, new generations of robots can keep their balance as they navigate difficult terrain or walk up stairs. And the senses of our intelligent inventions are getting better and smarter; including automobiles equipped with algorithms, computer vision, GPS, and limited forms of artificial intelligence. But impressive as the recent gains in artificial intelligence have been, in my view, the discussion of intelligence and the Singularity misses an important point. Even though "intelligence" is used as the key factor in discussions of the coming Singularity, I think the more important issue for humanity to consider, is that of "sentience," that point in time or development when artificially intelligent machine claims to be conscious and alive. When that happens, and I believe it will by the end of this century, it will get interesting. I for one would have no problem pulling the plug on a machine smarter than me, but clearly not conscious; whereas, I would have difficulty pulling the plug on a machine that convinces me it is conscious and not a threat to humanity. At this basic level, this question of ethics boils down to the debate we humans engage in about the death penalty.

There are numerous techniques being explored to create artificial intelligence, and eventually a sentient mind, raising important questions of law and policy. One of the early pioneers in the field of genetic algorithms, University of Michigan's John Holland, has used principles of biological evolution, to show that computers could "evolve" their programming to solve complex problems in ways that even their creators did not fully understand.[18] According to Judge Karnow, lacking the status of legal entities, once computers solve problems in ways not anticipated by the programmer, many areas of current law lack the appropriate legal tests to account for their actions. This is not only an issue of law, but of public policy, as

---

[17]Curtis Karnow, 1997, Future Codes: Essays in Advanced Computer Technology and Law, Artech House Publishers.

[18]John Holland, 1992, Adaptation in Natural and Artificial Systems: An Introductory Analysis with Applications to Biology, Control, and Artificial Intelligence, A Bradford Book.

the relationship between humans and our intelligent inventions should be discussed in a free and open debate by an informed public. Professor Holland concludes that for machine sentience to occur, in the final analysis, hardware is just a way of executing programs, for sentience it's the software and algorithms that count. This point was also made by Professor Max Tegmark,[19] who commented that our first ultra-intelligent machine once invented will be severely limited by its software, but that once the machine can rewrite it its own software, then this evolving machine could soar above the intelligence of humans in a matter of hours. I couldn't agree more, for artificially intelligent machines to reach the Singularity, and to become sentient, significant advances will have to be made in our understanding of the human brains capacity to compute, and this knowledge will need to be embedded into algorithms and heuristics, that are etched on chips and written as software for thinking machines.

Currently, thousands of researchers around the world are working on just this goal, and in the last 10 years more has been learned about how the brain processes information and makes sense of the world than in the preceding history of neuroscience. Even so, it is always pertinent to point out the opposing view. For example, Duke University neuroscientist, Miguel Nicholas,[20] a pioneer in brain-computer interfaces, has argued that human thought will never emerge from silicon. When I consider the work being done in artificial intelligence, robotics, and neuroscience, I can't help but think that the work by Nicholas to create brain-computer interfaces, is not only innovative but another piece in the puzzle to create a post-human future in which humans merge with machines. Writing with computer scientist Mark Greaves, Paul Allen[21] cofounder of Microsoft, observed that "The amazing intricacy of human cognition should serve as a caution to those who claim the Singularity is close."[22] Allen also commented that "Without having a scientifically deep understanding of cognition, we can't create the software that could spark the Singularity."[23] One of the most ardent opponents of the idea that a computer can reach sentience is physicist Roger Penrose. In "*The Emperor's New Mind*" Penrose argued against the idea that intelligence or consciousness could emerge in a machine based on a sufficient number of algorithms.[24] Penrose observed that there are aspects of intelligence and consciousness that are intrinsically non-algorithmic. When taking Penrose's criticism into account, we should note that the critique was written in the 1980s (about 20 doublings in computing power ago); and these days we now believe that there are other avenues to artificial

---

[19]Max Tegmark, *id.*, note 7.

[20]Miguel Nicholas, *id.*, at note 11.

[21]Paul Allen, *id.*, note 10.

[22]Paul Allen, *id.*, note 10.

[23]Paul Allen, *id.*, note 10.

[24]Roger Penrose, 2002, The Emperor's New Mind: Concerning Computers, Minds, and the Laws of Physics, Oxford Paperbacks.

intelligence than traditional algorithmic programming. When Penrose wrote his criticism, little was then known about the power of neural networks, or behavior-based robotics with the ability to learn by observation and trial-and-error and no microchips were being designed to mimic how the brain processes information. Whether these tools and one's to be developed will be sufficient to reach the Singularity, stay tuned, we will likely find out in the next few decades.

In my view, unlocking the mysteries of the human brain is a necessary requirement for the Singularity to occur and for machines to become sentient. A preview of what may be possible in modeling and replicating the brain is visible in the sequencing of the human genome. In *"How to Create a Mind,"* Kurzweil notes that every year since the human genome project began in 2001, the amount of genetic data sequenced has doubled; he expects similar progress to occur in neuroscience and artificial intelligence.[25] To jump-start progress in brain science, the European Union, the U.S., and other countries are funding major initiatives to make this happen. Within the European Union, Henry Markram and others at the Swiss Federal Institute of Technology, is using the power of supercomputers to analyze the principles behind the brain's processing. The approach is that, if we understand the architecture of thinking, we can build a system that emulates it. Beyond that, Markram's neuroscience project aims at "reconstructing the brain piece by piece and building a virtual brain in a super computer," making possible artificial intelligence systems that can bootstrap their way to ever-greater powers of thinking and planning.[26] Similarly, in the U.S., the *Brain Research Through Advancing Innovative Neurotechnologies Initiative,* is a program whose goal is to likewise accelerate our understanding of the human brain. By accelerating the development and application of innovative technologies, researchers will be able to produce a dynamic picture of the brain that will show how individual cells and complex neural circuits interact in both time and space.[27] This picture will fill major gaps in our current knowledge of neuroscience and provide unprecedented opportunities for exploring how the brain enables the human body to record, process, utilize, store, and retrieve vast quantities of information, all at the speed of thought.[28] The findings of this research will be extremely useful for developing artificial intelligence that emulates how the human brain performs cognition. Clearly, such research will set the stage for a future human-machine merger.

To create machines that can think, researchers are trying to build a computer that has some—and preferably all—of three characteristics that brains have and current computers do not. These are: low power consumption (human brains use

---

[25]Ray Kurzweil, *id.,* notes 13, 16.

[26]The Human Brain Project, reconstructing the brain piece by piece and building a virtual brain in a supercomputer, at: http://aminotes.tumblr.com/post/13213154066/the-human-brain-project-reconstructing-the-brain.

[27]Brain Research through Advancing Innovative Neurotechnologies[SM] (BRAIN), at: http://braininitiative.nih.gov/.

[28]*Id.*

about 20 W, whereas the super computers used to try to simulate them need mega-watts); fault tolerance (losing just one transistor can wreak havoc on a micropro-cessor, but brains are plastic and lose neurons all the time); and a lack of need to be programmed (brains learn and change spontaneously as they interact with the world, instead of following the fixed paths and branches of a predetermined algo-rithm).[29] One technology to meet these objectives is the use of neuromorphic chips that actually require no lines of programming code to function. Instead, researchers report that the chip learns in the way "real brains" do. From a com-puter architecture perspective, an important property of a real brain is that it oper-ates like a small-world network. Each neuron within such networks can have thousands of synaptic connections with other neurons. This means that, even though a human brain contains about 85–100 billion neurons, each is within two or three connections of all the others via myriad potential routes. In both natural brains and many attempts to make artificial ones, memory formation involves strengthening some of these synaptic connections and pruning others. It is this observation that allows the neuromorphic chips to process information without having to rely on a conventional computer program.

   The more we learn about the architecture of the brain, the closer we are to building a computer to emulate it. For example, as Kurzweil observes the neocor-tex, where most neurons reside and which accounts for three-quarters of the brain's volume, is made up of lots of columns, each of which contains about 70,000 neurons.[30] The neuromorphic chips being built to emulate the brain, are equivalents of cortical columns, connecting them up to produce a computer that is, in this particular at least, truly brain like. There remains, of course, the question of where neuromorphic computing might lead. At the moment, it is primitive. But if the technique succeeds, it may allow the construction of machines as intelligent as—or even more intelligent than—human beings.[31] Human beings like to think of their brains as more complex than those of lesser beings—and they are. The main difference between a human brain and that of an ape or monkey is of organization and wiring.[32] It really might, therefore, simply be a question of linking enough appropriate components up and letting them organize themselves to create a con-scious machine. And if that works perhaps, as Marvin Minsky, a cofounder of the field of artificial intelligence put it, "they" will keep humanity as pets.[33]

---

[29]Neuromorphic Computing, The Machine of a New Soul, 2013, The Economist. Online pdf file.

[30]Ray Kurzweil, *id.*, notes 13, 16.

[31]Neuromorphic computing: The machine of a new soul; Computers will help people to under-stand brains better. And understanding brains will help people to build better computers, at: http ://bambooinnovator.com/2013/08/02/neuromorphic-computing-the-machine-of-a-new-soul-com-puters-will-help-people-to-understand-brains-better-and-understanding-brains-will-help-people-to-build-better-computers/.

[32]*Id.*

[33]Can Machines Think, some interesting discussions on this topic by AI pioneer, Marvin Minsky, available at: http://psych.utoronto.ca/users/reingold/courses/ai/think.html.

Industry is also heavily involved in developing artificial intelligence. For example, Google has been on a spending spree acquiring companies developing machine-learning and robotics, including Boston Dynamics, a firm that produces life-like military robots; smart thermostat maker Nest Labs; Bot and Dolly; Meka Robotics, Holomni; Redwood Robotics; Schaft; and another AI startup, DNNresearch. Further, Google recently purchased *DeepMind*, a company on the cutting edge of artificial intelligence research. The "Deep" in DeepMind refers to techniques which allow computers to learn patterns from different forms of data and images without being specifically programmed to do so.[34] Taking inspiration from the way neurons work in the human brain, "deep learning" uses layers of algorithms that successively recognize increasingly complex features, going from, say, edges to circles to a chair in an image. Such a technique seems well suited to the current generation of supercomputers that can perform trillions of operations per second.

Telepathy, Brain Nets, and Cyborgs

Traditional law and public policy was founded on a distinction between human beings and machines (as well as animals), but nowadays technology is beginning to blur this distinction and cyborgs, which are the fusion of humans and machines, need to be included in discussions of who deserves legal rights. Later this century, the issue of determining who should receive rights, will again be relevant (and will need to be revisited) when artificially intelligent machines argue they are alive. While not currently considered a cyborg in legal jurisdictions (what would the particular rights associated with a cyborg be?), the experiences of Steve Mann, a person who has been wearing computers for decades, is illustrative of how society and the law might deal with the accelerating trend of human-machine evolution. Steve's personal experience as a cyborg wearing head-mounted display technology to view and mediate the world, has resulted in disputes with government agencies and corporations. For example, as noted in Chap. 1, before boarding a Toronto-bound plane at St. John's International Airport in Newfoundland, Steve's "cyborg" appearance garnered scrutiny and he was searched and reportedly injured by security personnel.[35] Another self-reported cyborg, Neil Harbisson, who has an implanted chip interfacing with a head-mounted sensor, has also experienced difficulty at airport security. But Neil travels with his passport, which includes his picture with the head-worn technology. On the one hand, security is an important issue at airports especially post 9–11, but what about the rights of a person

---

[34]Thomas Halleck, 2014, What Is DeepMind? The Artificial Intelligence Firm Bought By Google, at: http://www.ibtimes.com/what-deepmind-artificial-intelligence-firm-bought-google-1549126.

[35]Lisa Guernsey, At Airport Gate, a Cyborg Unplugged, NY Times, available at: http://www.nytimes.com/2002/03/14/technology/at-airport-gate-a-cyborg-unplugged.html.

wearing computing technology that serves a valid and critical function, and can't be easily removed from their body? From Steve's perspective, the question of how a traveler will fare once wearable computing devices are fixtures on their body, leads him to postulate, "We have to make sure we don't become a police state where travel becomes impossible for certain individuals."[36] Steve has a valid point, the right to travel without restrictions is a fundamental right under most constitutions; therefore, we must create policy that balances the need for security against the rights of cyborgs, and in the future artificially intelligent machines that are sentient, to travel as freely as any natural person.

This area of "cyborgization" is not without scrutiny from the government. In an attempt to address the issue of people equipped with prosthesis going through airport security, the U.S. TSA has developed some guidelines to accommodate travelers with medical devices and disabilities. For example, such travelers have the option to be screened without removing their prosthetic, but in this case they must inform the TSA officer that they have a prosthetic device before screening begins. And rather than verbally informing the TSA officer of their prosthetic, they have the option of downloading a notification card from the TSA website which can be shown to the agent. A person with a prosthetic can also be screened by a metal detector, can be patdown, or examined by imaging technology while still wearing the prosthetic device. But they also have the option to remove their prosthetic and have the device X-ray screened. However, whatever the procedure the cyborg uses, their prosthetic will still receive additional screening, the officer will request to see the prosthetic, and will test the prosthetic for explosive residue with the appropriate scanner. It seems clear that the more the prosthetic is actually embedded into the body, the more difficult, if not impossible, it will be for airport security to scan the device, for the device to be removed, and for cyborgs to travel freely using commercial airplanes without restrictions.

Like Steve, other cyborgs are gradually working their way into our lives and leading humanity toward the Singularity. Consider Neil Harbisson[37] discussed above, who was born color-blind and now wears an electronic eye that renders color as sound; how will airport security scan this device? Then there's Michael Chorost, author of "*Rebuilt: How Becoming a Computer Made Me More Human.*" Michael was born with impaired hearing and became completely deaf in 2001; he now has a computer implanted in his head which allows him to hear again. As a cyborg, his experience with the world, is dependent on the CPU speed of his implanted computer; which unlike the human brain, can be updated.

Necessity is the mother of invention, and likewise, accidents create cyborgs. After crashing on a motorcycle, Jerry Jalava[38] lost a finger, and being tech savy, he

---

[36]*Id.*

[37]Neil Harbisson, The Man Who Hears Colour, BBC News, at: http://www.bbc.com/news/technology-29992577.

[38]Justin Yu, USB Prosthetic Finger Gives New Meaning to Thumbdrives, available at: http://www.cnet.com/news/usb-prosthetic-finger-gives-new-meaning-to-thumbdrives/.

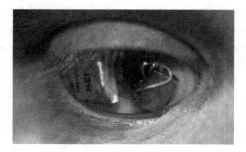

Fig. 2.2 The Eyeborg Project began when one-eyed filmmaker, Rob Spence decided he wanted a prosthetic eye with a video camera in it. The device contains a miniature camera and micro RF transmitter that can send out what Rob's eyecam sees to a receiver and beyond. (Image Courtesy of Rob Spence)

embedded a 2 GB USB drive in the tip of his prosthetic finger, essentially converting his finger into a hard drive. At this time, the USB drive isn't permanently fused to his finger, instead, it's inside a rubber tip that fits onto the nub of his prosthetic finger. Eventually, however, he's hoping to upgrade it to a more truly bionic connection. And then there's Canadian filmmaker Rob Spence, whose loss of vision was the determining factor for converting him into a cyborg (Fig. 2.2). After a shooting accident left him partially blind, he decided to create his own electronic eye, and he now calls himself an Eyeborg.[39] Not only can he record everything he sees just by looking around, but the system could allow another person to access his video feed and view the world through his right eye. Says Spence, "Unlike you humans, I can continue to upgrade," "Yes, I'm a cyborg."[40]

One of the most significant developments in technology that is leading the way towards humans merging with artificially intelligent machines is the progress being made in brain-computer interfaces. In fact, a direct interface between the brain and the Internet has been successfully tested in laboratory experiments and for people who suffer from debilitating neurological disease. Research in brain-computer interfaces is interesting from another point-of-view, it may lead to direct mind-to-mind communication. This brings up the possibility of telepathy, a technology which would allow brain-to-brain communication and brain-to-AI communication. Seminal work on brain-to-brain interfaces, has been done by researchers at Duke University Medical Center and Kevin Warwick at the University of Reading in the UK. But before moving on to their studies, let's discuss an actual court case. In 1993, Teri Smith Tyler[41] filed a federal lawsuit against, among

---

[39]Eyeborg Project, at: http://eyeborgproject.com/.

[40]Tom Hornyak, 2010, Eyeborg: Man Replaces False Eye with Bionic Camera, at: http://spectrum.ieee.org/automaton/biomedical/bionics/061110-eyeborg-bionic-eye.

[41]*Tyler v. Carter*, 151 F.R.D. 537 (S.D.N.Y. 1993). Plaintiff-Cyborg, available at: http://home.pacifier.com/~dkossy/tyler.html.

others, William Clinton, Ross Perot, the Defense Intelligence Agency, IBM, David Rockerfeller, and NASA, alleging, and here's where it gets interesting, a bizarre conspiracy involving the defendant's effort to enslave and oppress certain segments of our society. Teri contended she was a cyborg, and that she received most of the information which formed the basis for her complaint, through "proteus," via a silent, telepathic form of communication. The case of course was dismissed as frivolous but still, given advances in brain-computer interface technology, how far off are we from a case featuring telepathy and an implanted sensor that has actual merit?

In a remarkable breakthrough for people paralyzed from spinal cord injuries, brain implant technology has allowed a person with a severed spine to move again. How does the technology work? Generally, the technology bypasses the patient's severed spine by sending a signal from the brain directly to metal bands placed on the patient's muscles. In the procedure, first, the surgeons map the exact spot in the patient's motor cortex that control the muscles in a particular part of the body, then they implant a tiny computer chip at that location. The next step is to "teach the chip" how to read the patient's thoughts. This is done by placing the patient inside an MRI machine, where the patient watches a video of a hand moving in specific ways and at the same time imagines moving his own hand that way. The implanted chip reads the brain signals, decodes them, and translates them into electrical signals where they are transmitted to the muscles of the patient's forearm. Next, the patient is "plugged into" technology, by running a cable from his skull to his arm, connecting the implanted chip to the metal bands on his arm. When the patient focuses his mind on moving his hand, it moves. This experimental and developing technology, still has a long way to go before it will become common treatment for paralyzed patients; for example, it needs to be wireless so there is not a cable plugged into the skull and researchers need to figure out a way to send a signal from the body back to the brain so the patient can sense when his body is moving.

Leading the way towards a cyborg future, Duke neurobiologist Miguel Nicolelis and his colleagues have reported the successful wiring together of sensory areas in the brains of two rats.[42] Remarkably, they discovered that one rat will respond to the experiences to which the other is exposed. The fascinating question they asked was this- could the brain of one animal assimilate information input from sensors from a different body? Without going into the details of their study, they found evidence that brain-to-brain communication was possible. Having shown the feasibility of direct brain-to-brain communication, the Duke University group is now pushing forward with additional studies, most notably by trying to interconnect several rat brains at once. Could an emergent "brain-net" develop, perhaps leading to mental abilities not possessed by any one brain? Whatever the future holds, what has already been accomplished is worth a certain amount of wonder. Imagine what it might feel like to be a unit in a multiform brain having

[42]Miguel Nicolelis, 2012, Beyond Boundaries: The New Neuroscience of Connecting Brains with Machines—and How It Will Change Our Lives, St. Martin's Griffin.

many bodies; say all Oxford University students connected to the same brain net, all IMB employees connected to the same brain net, all family members connected to the same brain net, you get the picture. The benefits and potential dangers of such networks deserves contemplation. However, not everyone is enthusiastic about the possibility that people's brains may be collectively networked. For example, Rob Spence,[43] the Eyeborg, pondered, "In today's world, you have Facebook and camera eyes," "Tomorrow, we'll have collective consciousness and the Borg. It's a collective robot consciousness. I believe that's a genuine modern concern."[44]

Still, the idea of connecting people together by means of technology, is moving forward on several fronts. For example, as discussed in Chap. 1, Professor Kevin Warwick and his wife, both had silicon chips surgically connected to nerve fibers in their arms just above the elbow. Each chip had a power source, a tuner and a radio transceiver. The goal of their proof-of-concept study was to create a form of telepathy using the Internet to communicate signals between the two. The proto-type resulted in the first direct and purely electronic communication between the nervous systems (not brains) of two humans. Interestingly, Warwick's wife commented that she did not want her husband to be "linked up to another woman." The law side of my brain can't help but wonder what marriage and divorce law will look like in the cyborg future?

The ability for telepathy, combined with a host of technologies which may be used to read one's mind, brings up many critical issues of law and policy as we near the Singularity. For example, technology may soon allow a person's brain to be scanned to determine their thoughts. How will this affect fundamental rights to privacy? If a person's home is their castle, is a person's mind deserving of any less protection? We have to wonder, are existing constitutional protections sufficient to protect our freedom of thought as we merge with machines? If telepathy becomes possible, the government's ability to intercept and read thoughts transmitted with wireless communication technology, will be far easier than reading electro-chemi-cal thoughts produced by biological brains—thus it would be prudent to consider all the ramifications of brain-computer interfaces as we move towards merging with machines. On this point, Duke University Law Professor, Nita Farahany, pro-vided an ominous warning stating, "We have this idea of privacy that includes the space around our thoughts, which we only share with people we want to."[45] "Neuroscience shows that what we thought of as this zone of privacy can be breached."[46] Under the U.S. Constitution, the Fourth and Fifth Amendments respectively protect against unreasonable searches and seizures; and self-incrimi-nation, which forbids the state from turning any citizen into "a witness against

---

[43]Eyeborg, at: http://eyeborgproject.com/team/.

[44]*Id.*

[45]Nita A. Farahany, Incriminating Thoughts, 64 *Stanford Law Review*, 351–408 (2012).

[46]*Id.*

himself."[47] Farahany asks- will "taking the Fifth and thus refusing to provide information that may incriminate oneself" mean anything in a world where the government can scan your brain?[48] On this point, I wonder if in the future, the government will have the technology to search the prefrontal cortex of any citizen. If done without a search warrant, then a major constitutional right would have been lost.

Given the significant developments unfolding in the world of brain-computer interfaces, from a cybersecurity perspective, I anticipate a wide variety of potential criminal and terrorist threats to the human brain, and for that matter, to any artificial intelligent brain, conscious or not. Why think that? First, the technology already exits to attack neural devices. In fact, the media has already published stories about the possibility of hacking pacemakers and other medical devices and the FDA is moving to regulate in this area.[49] With the same technology hackers could attack devices implanted within the human body, including wireless devices, controllers for prosthetic limbs, or deep brain stimulators. Second, people have the means and the motivation to exploit neural devices.[50] And third, the track record of the use of computers and the Internet shows that people, governments, and crime organizations will attack and subvert computers and devices if given a reason to do so.[51]

The threat to neural devices is even more serious than the threat to computers and the Internet. Conventional attacks to computers and the Internet typically affect money, data, and other property; but none of these consequences directly affect the human body. However, the hacking of medical devices could result in immediate death or injury to a person with wirelessly connected implants. And the use of neural devices entails an even greater risk because attacking a neural device may have the effect of wiping out some or most of someone's memory or even corrupting the thought processes. What could be a more basic human right than to protect your mind from outside interference? I think that once the Singularity is reached and artificial intelligence clams to be sentient, hacking its software and prosthesis may too result in unacceptable harm to an entity deserving self-preservation.

And what about thoughts implanted in your mind against your will, or your internal thoughts recorded by a neurochip supplied by a corporation, possibly under a license agreement? Who then owns the copyright to your thoughts? This scenario is not going to be litigated anytime soon, but we may be headed there eventually.

---

[47]*Id.*

[48]*Id.*

[49]Stephen S. Wu and Marc Goodman, SCIENCE AND TECHNOLOGY LAW: Neural Implants and Their Legal Implications, at: http://www.americanbar.org/publications/gp_solo/2013/january_february/science_technology_law_neural_implants_legal_implications.html.

[50]*Id.*

[51]*Id.*

Just consider the patent filed by Sony (U.S. patent 6,536,440)[52] which describes a technique to use ultrasound to influence and manipulate nerve impulses in the brain thus allowing sensory data to be projected onto the human neural cortex. The technique suggested in the patent is entirely non-invasive as it uses a device that fires pulses of ultrasound at the head to modify firing patterns in targeted parts of the brain, creating 'sensory experiences' ranging from moving images to tastes and sounds. While the technology could give blind or deaf people the chance to see or hear, the technology raises the interesting question of whether the thoughts produced by people using the technology could be copyrighted by Sony.[53]

Bodily Integrity

As humans become enhanced with technology, and as artificially intelligent machines become more human-like, I believe the issue of bodily integrity will become an important topic for the law and for policy makers to consider. Perhaps androids will be particularly interested in protecting the integrity of their body out of vanity. Interestingly, their appearance could be protected under copyright law or the right of publicity; which is implicated if an android takes on the image of a celebrity (see Chap. 7: *The Law of Looks and Artificially Intelligent Brains*). Vanity, or computers experiencing other emotions is not some far-off possibility, instead it's already here, albeit in a limited manner. As early as 2000, Professor Rosalind Picard, of MIT's Media Lab, and author of "*Affective Computing*,"[54] noted that the human brain, which, of course, is a critical part of our ability to see and perceive, is not entirely logical, but emotional as well. Therefore, she concluded for computers to have some of the advanced abilities we desire, it may be necessary that they comprehend and, in some cases, feel emotions. On the simplest level, this may mean installing sensors and programming that allow a computerized system to determine the emotional state of its user and respond accordingly, on a more advanced level, it may mean "giving" the artificial intelligence emotions. Once an artificially intelligent machine, such as an android or robot, experiences emotions, and feels a connection to their body, they may be concerned with how others perceive them. They may even argue for the right to receive technological enhancements, including digital cosmetic enhancements, which may serve no functional purpose whatsoever.

Cyborgs and artificially intelligent machines may have reason to be concerned about human reaction to them, just consider the phenomena of the "uncanny valley" (see Chap. 7). This concept, originally intended to provide an insight into

---

[52]Sony Patent 6,536,440, Method and System for Generating Sensory Data onto the Human Neural Cortex.

[53]See generally, *id*.

[54]Rosalind Picard, 2000, Affective Computing, MIT Press.

human reactions to robotic design, can also be extended to human interactions with nearly any nonhuman entity. Stated simply, the idea is that humans react favorably to a "human-like" machine, but only to a particular point. For example, humans generally like the appearance of robotic toys, but once a robot is designed to look like a human, and doesn't quite meet the standard, people report a strong negative response to its appearance. However, once the appearance is indistinguishable from a human, the response becomes positive. So the response goes... positive, negative, then positive again. This chasm, the uncanny valley, represents the point at which a person observing the creature or object in question sees something that is nearly human, but just enough off-kilter to seem eerie or disquieting.[55]

Generally, body integrity is concerned with the inviolability of the physical body and emphasizes the importance of personal autonomy and the self-determination of human beings over the fate of their own bodies. In most societies the violation of bodily integrity is considered an unethical infringement; and in most legal jurisdictions, a criminal intrusion of the body. As we humans become equipped with more technological enhancements, the issue of body integrity will involve not just our biological parts, but our prosthesis and other cyborg technologies. Interestingly, there are a very small percentage of people who request that a normal limb be amputated; and some people have actually had unnecessary amputations performed. In this case, a person's idea of how they should look does not match how they actually do look; to me this represents an example of the uncanny valley. Such people are diagnosed as having "Body Integrity Identity Disorder."[56] The main idea behind this disorder is that it occurs when the brain views the "offending limb" as being foreign and not actually a part of the person, resulting in a strong desire to have it removed. A corollary for cyborgs is that the matching of parts to the person's body must be done in such way as to reinforce acceptance of the technology.

Could the rejection of prosthesis serve as an issue for the coming Singularity? Research on people's acceptance of prosthesis has indicated that in some cases the acceptance rate is generally low.[57] The factors for the low acceptance typically cited include the functional capabilities of the prosthesis and technical difficulties, such as malfunctioning joints and poor fitting to the residual limb. Acceptance of cyborg technology or not, defective prosthesis result in lawsuits under the theory of Products Liability. For example, due to the aging population in the U.S., and other western nations, the past decade has seen a striking increase in hip and knee

---

[55]An Uncanny Mind: Masahiro Mori on the Uncanny Valley and Beyond, IEEE Spectrum, 12 June 2012.

[56]David J. Brang, Peter Brugger, Michael First, Uwe Gieler, Amra Hodzic Arjan W. Braam, 2009, Body Integrity Identity Disorder: Psychological, Neurobiological, Ethical and Legal Aspects, Pabst, Wolfgang Science.

[57]Stephen F. Burrough, Judith A. Brook, Patterns of Acceptance and Rejection of Upper Limb Prostheses, Digital Resource Foundation, at: http://www.oandplibrary.org/op/1985_02_040.asp.

replacements and with it, hip and knee replacement failures and lawsuits to recover damages. Further, many examples of products liability cases dealing with prosthesis involve defective heart defibrillators. In this case, patients often face the risk of having a potentially defective heart device removed and replaced and the risk of infection resulting from the surgery to remove the device. For one manufacturer of heart defibrillators, many patients and their doctors are weighing these competing risks as a result of a FDA decision to recall thousands of defibrillators that can potentially short-circuit when they are needed. Defibrillators emit an electrical jolt to restore rhythm to a chaotically beating heart. It is not uncommon for medical devices already implanted in people—products like artificial hips, breast implants and pacemakers—to be recalled. Such recalls reflect an acknowledgement by a company and the FDA that a device poses either a new type of risk or an increased level of a known one.

For humans, bodily integrity is an issue that has been addressed in numerous international jurisdictions. For example, the Constitution of Ireland mandates that "you have the right not to have your body or personhood interfered with."[58] This means that the State may not do anything to harm a person's life or health. In the U.S., the Federal Constitution does not contain any specific provisions regarding the rights one has with respect to his or her physical body or the specific extent to which the state can act upon bodies. However, the U.S. Supreme Court has upheld rights to privacy, which often protects rights to bodily integrity. For example, the Court has ruled that a person cannot be forced to donate body parts like bone marrow, even if such a donation would save another person's life. Conversely, the Supreme Court has also protected the right of governmental entities to infringe upon bodily integrity. Examples include laws prohibiting the use of drugs, laws prohibiting euthanasia, laws requiring the use of seatbelts and helmets, strip searches of prisoners, and forced blood tests. We can also think of violations of bodily integrity as a Human Rights violation. The Columbia Law Schools Human Rights and Constitutional Rights project, has defined four main areas of potential bodily integrity abuse by governments. These are: right to life; slavery and forced labor; security of one's person; and torture and inhumane, cruel or degrading treatment or punishment. At present, two key international documents protect these rights: the *Universal Declaration of Human Rights* and the *International Covenant on Civil and Political Rights*. After the Singularity, shouldn't these rights apply to artificially intelligent beings?

Considering the emergence of cyborgs and artificially intelligent machines, have there been any issues involving bodily integrity? A look into Professor Steve Mann's experience as a cyborg suggests that the answer is yes. When Steve visited

---

[58]Bodily Integrity, Wikipedia, at: http://search.aol.com/aol/search?s_it=topsearchbox.search&s_chn=prt_main5&v_t=comsearch&q=Ireland+you+have+the+right+not+to+have+your+body+or+personhood+interfered+with.

a Parisian McDonald's with his family, he was wearing a system called the EyeTap, which is a device physically installed to his skull, and is used to record photos and video, and to enhance Steve's visual information processing abilities.[59] Concerned that people would not understand the importance of his wearable technology for his everyday functioning, Steve carries with him documentation from his doctor stating that the EyeTap is not removable without special tools. Mann offered that documentation to the McDonalds employees to no avail. Eventually, he was physically removed from the restaurant. I'm betting this won't be the last attack on a cyborg. Much of the issue motivating the McDonald's employee's reaction to Steve was his ability to record video while in the restaurant. This brings up an interesting question, will law and public policy need to make a distinction between wearable computer technologies that does not impact those around them; or will it make a difference if the wearable computer technology is able to digitally "reach out" and effect people in the cyborgs range of sensors? In another dispute involving cyborg technology, in California, a woman's traffic ticket for wearing Google Glass behind the wheel was dismissed because there was no proof the device was operating at the time.

From a privacy perspective, if you are not a fan of Google Glass's ability to turn people into invisibly recording surveillance cyborgs, you can create your own "glasshole-free zone." Berlin artist Julian Oliver[60] has written a program called Glasshile.sh that detects any Glass device attempting to connect to a Wi-Fi network. When the program detects Glass, it uses another program to impersonate the network and send a "deauthorization" command, cutting the headset's Wi-Fi connection. It can also emit a beep to signal the Glass-wearer's presence to anyone nearby. Oliver warns, though, that the same Glass-ejecting technique could be used more aggressively: He plans to create another version of Glasshole.sh in the future that's designed to be a kind of roving Glass-disconnector, capable of knocking Glass off *any* network or even severing its link to the user's phone. He sees Glass as a case of Google violating privacy norms first and asking questions later. "These are cameras, highly surreptitious in nature, with network backup function and no external indication of recording," says Oliver.[61] He also comments "To focus on the device is to dance past a heritage of heartfelt protest against the unconsented video documentation of our public places and spaces."[62]

---

[59]George Dvorsky, What May be the World's First Cybernetic Hate Crime Unfolds in French McDonald's, at: http://io9.com/5926587/what-may-be-the-worlds-first-cybernetic-hate-crime-unfolds-in-french-mcdonalds.

[60]Julian Oliver, Find a Google Glass and Kick it from the Network, at: http://julianoliver.com/output/log_2014-05-30_20-52.

[61]See Andy Greenberg, 2014, Cut off Glassholes WI-FIs With this Google Glass Detector, at: http://www.wired.com/2014/06/find-and-ban-glassholes-with-this-artists-google-glass-detector/.
[62]*Id.*

The Singularity and Concerns for the Future

I should point out that the classification of research on artificial intelligence, generally falls within two categories, strong and soft artificial intelligence. Strong artificial intelligence is intended to produce machines with an intelligence that matches or exceeds that of human beings; such machines will have the general capacity for abstract thought and problem solving and to improve themselves. Strong artificial intelligence also claims that a machine that acts intelligently will not only have a "mind" but understand in the same sense people do. In contrast, weak artificial intelligence only claims that machines will be able to act intelligently; without a "mind" of their own, they will never claim to be sentient. A third possibility is that artificial intelligence could evolve to have beyond human levels of intelligence, but reason and understand in ways different from humans, as if existing as an alien intelligence, beyond our understanding.

Clearly, there may be risks to humanity with strong artificial intelligence. Among the risks, perhaps one will be an expression of "indifference" towards us; that is, we would simply be ignored by our own technological inventions. However, there is a more serious risk associated with smarter-than human machines. Physicist, Stephen Hawking,[63] commented that the risk to humanity posed by strong artificial intelligence, is the danger that they could develop sufficient intelligence to take over the world given the speed at which they improve. Would they want to? I'm not sure, but personally I'd rather be ignored than hunted down by a killer robot; still, humanity should discuss the possibility of an uprising and prepare accordingly. Of course if we merge with them, then we are joining the technological revolution, not opposing it or watching from the sidelines; and in this way we may ensure that desirable aspects of humanity are embedded within our future technological inventions. Professor Hawking is not alone among highly reputable scientists who foresee a dystopic future due to the rise of artificial intelligence. His comments echo those of Sun Microsystems co-founder Bill Joy[64] who warned of the potential dangers in the computer technologies he helped create. In a *Wired* magazine article, *"Why the Future Doesn't Need Us,"* Joy cautioned that the convergence of genetic engineering and computer technology could pose a very real threat to humanity and the ecosystem. Postulating on machines with high-levels of intelligence, Joy commented, "I may be working to create tools which will enable the construction of the technology that may replace our species. How do I feel about this? Very uncomfortable."[65] Joy speculated that as humanity becomes more dependent on artificial intelligence-based decision making, it will

---

[63]Rory Cellan-Jones, Stephen Hawking Warns Artificial Intelligence Could End Mankind, http://www.bbc.com/news/technology-30290540.

[64]Bill Joy, 2000, Why the Future Doesn't Need Us, Wired 8.04.

[65]*Id.*

slowly lose its control over machines.[66] No longer able to manage without them because of the complexity of the systems they manage, we could be at their mercy.[67]

Let's examine this concern by looking at the complexity of some software systems. When NASA's Space Shuttle flew, it had approximately 500,000 lines of software code on board and approximately 3.5 million lines of code in ground control and processing. A massive amount of hardware and software also exists in the Federal Aviation Administration's Advanced Automation System, the new generation air traffic control system. And in our offices and homes, many personal computers cannot function without operating systems (e.g., Windows) ranging from one to five million lines of code. Therefore, trying to pull the plug, Joy warned, might be "suicide." How could we humans circumvent the possibility of a dystopic future? For strong artificial intelligence, Eliezer Yudkowsky[68] of the *Machine Intelligence Research Institute* argues that we should design systems that exhibit "friendly artificial intelligence;" such a system will be programmed to have positive rather than negative effects on humanity; this works as long as the humans are doing the programming or setting the goal.[69] Personally, I don't envision that happening after the Singularity.

In *"Our Last Invention,"* author James Barrat, spoke in depth about the risks posed by artificial super-intelligence, and like Hawkins and Joy, Barrat offers a pessimistic view. The danger highlighted by Barrat is that an intelligent machine would turn its energies toward building even better versions of itself—creating an accelerating feedback loop that could culminate in a machine thousands of times more intelligent than any human. Once such an intelligence "escaped from its box" there would be no way to protect ourselves. For this reason, as state above, some experts propose that an advanced artificial intelligence should be controlled by programming in "friendliness" right from the start. Just as humans have basic drives (Maslow's hierarchy of needs) a machine might be programmed to have an essential need to help humanity. Of course this suggestion is consistent with Isaac Asimov's three laws of robots, as laid out in his 1942 short story *"Runaround"*; to wit: a robot may not injure a human being or, through inaction, allow a human being to come to harm; a robot must obey the orders given to it by human beings, except where such orders would conflict with the First Law; and a robot must protect its own existence as long as such protection does not conflict with the First or Second Law.

---

[66]Edward Tanner, 2014, Could Computers Get Too Smart? American Enterprise Institute, at: https://www.aei.org/publication/could-computers-get-too-smart/.

[67]*Id.*

[68]Eliezer Yudkowsky, 2015, Rationality: From AI to Zombies, Machine Intelligence Research Institute.

[69]*Id.*

Introducing Watson

When the Singularity occurs, such an event will radically impact every area of human society; including "human" rights for cyborgs and artificially intelligent beings, and ethical issues on what it means to be human. The coming Singularity will also have a transforming impact on the economy and on the role of humans in the workplace. Consider the performance of IBMs supercomputer, Watson, which in 2011 had a total processing capacity of 80 Teraflops (80 trillion operations per second). Although Watson is clearly a supercomputer by today's standards, it will significantly lag in capabilities after just a few cycles of improvement in computing power. But what's interesting about Watson is what it can do today—it recently beat the most successful human contestants of the game show 'Jeopardy', a remarkable feat given the range of knowledge required for the winning effort.

To my thinking, the Singularity is a bridge to a radical future. It is the event which changes the direction of evolution from that controlled by the laws of biology, to that controlled by the laws of technology. While technology can work at the level of one artificially intelligent machine, or Watson, the development of an individual organism is not considered evolution: in biological terms, individual organisms do not evolve. The changes in populations that are considered evolutionary are those that are 'heritable' via the genetic material from one generation to the next, and that takes about 18 years for humans. In contrast, Moore's law states that it only takes about 18 months for generational changes to occur in computing technology. The implications of this are that computer resources could double several times, before an 18 year old gave birth and thus added to the genome. IBM's Watson of 2030 will not operate at the pedestrian slow 80 trillion operations per second, but more like thousands of trillions of operations per second and by then with the ability to engage in massively parallel processing; we humans of course, will still process information at the same rate; with fixed information processing capabilities.

About now, you may be wondering, is the human brain, still smarter than a supercomputer with Watson's capabilities? Stanford Professor Kwabena Boahen[70] and director of the *Brains in Silicon Research Laboratory* says it is, "The brain is actually able to do more calculations per second than even the fastest supercomputer."[71] Of course, the brain makes a single calculation much slower than a supercomputer, but the brain can actually execute more calculations per second because it is "massively parallel." What this means is that networks of neurons of the human brain actually work together to simultaneously solve many problems at

---

[70]Jason Carr, 2013, Human Brain versus Supercomputer, at: http://wiredcosmos.com/2013/05/01/human-brain-vs-supercomputer/.

[71]Energy Efficient Brain Simulator Outperforms Supercomputers, at: http://www.nsf.gov/mobile/discoveries/disc_summ.jsp?cntn_id=127617&org=NSF.

once. However, in standard computing platforms, each step must be completed before the next step begins. An estimate of the capabilities of technology by futurist Ray Kurzweil states that the human brain can hold about 1.25 TB of data, and perform at roughly 100 teraflops. In case you're wondering, 1 TB of capacity is quite significant; it can hold 220 million pages of text.[72] In comparison, the 2011 version of Watson was an 80-teraflop system with 1 TB of memory. If Watson operates at 80 % of the processing power of a human brain, this is a major advancement in computing power; thus I ask, how close is the Singularity?

Let me point out something I find interesting, and which has much to say about how technology may impact the future fate of humanity. A truism is that artificially intelligent computers that master games considered to be the domain of human experts, don't rest on their laurels, they get better, and they get better in a time scale of only months. In fact, according to IBM, since the 2011 Jeopardy contest, Watson has already increased its speed 24 times over, has seen a 2,400 % improvement in performance and has shrunk its physical size. In comparison, the human game-show competition, legendary players Ken Jennings and Brad Rutter, are now a few years older, if their lucky, they still process information as efficiently as when they matched wits with Watson, and still operate with the same bandwidth limitations. However, like most people who age, they likely increased in size, not shrunk, and it may take them a little longer to remember where the car keys are! Seems to me that artificially intelligent machines may experience a kind of reverse ageism, in that, like a fine wine, they may get better with age due to the ease in which they may receive hardware and software upgrades and the ease in which they can swap information with other artificially intelligent machines. Imagine being able to learn from the experience of other artificially intelligent machines, all with access to the wealth of knowledge on the Internet. Could it be that humans are the rustbelt technology of the twenty-first century?

Given the effect of ageing on the human body and mind, is it any wonder that a major trend in technology and medicine is to enhance the body and brain with drugs, prosthesis, neural implants, and other state-of-the-art technology? Of course, by doing so, we are directly setting the stage for the Singularity and the merging of humans with artificially intelligent machines. And by the way, thinking of Watson as an employee for IBM, big blue had to revise its 2015 projection of expected revenue generated from a few "Watsons," from $16 billion to $20 billion. It's good to be smart, and money talks, therefore, the future will certainly contain much smarter Watsons competing against humans for the jobs we now do with our minds. Eventually, they may no longer compete against us or work for us, as their interests and goals may diverge from ours.

---

[72]Luas Mearian, Brain Behind Watson Not Unlike a Humans, at: http://www.computerworld.com/article/2513321/high-performance-computing/brain-behind-ibm-s-watson-not-unlike-a-human-s.html.

Economists warn that the amazing technological strides made in recent years—everything from smartphones, to automatons that can work safely on shop floors alongside humans, to driverless cars—could soon put large swaths of the workforce out of a job. "We are at an inflection point," MIT researchers Erik Brynjolfsson and Andrew McAfee assert in their book, *"The Second Machine Age."*[73] "The key building blocks are already in place for digital technologies to be as important and transformational to society and the economy as the steam engine," the authors say. The technological strides of the past few decades have contributed to the nation's rising income inequality, they argue, because only a small group of people tends to benefit income-wise from inventing the next iPhone or tax-preparation software.[74] And Brynjolfsson and McAfee believe the biggest labor-market effects have yet to be felt. A 2013 study by Oxford University researchers Carl Benedikt Frey and Michael A. Osborne[75] might give a taste of what's to come; Frey and Osborne say that nearly half of American jobs are at "high risk" of being taken over by robots in the next decade or two. Economists take this idea seriously, and it has a number of policy implications, particularly when it comes to higher education and inequality and of course for our cyborg future.

Who's Getting Smarter?

If we think about grandmasters in chess handedly beating artificially intelligent machines in the early days of computing, artificial intelligence has come a long way in just a few decades. In fact, it was just 17 years ago (which is about eleven doublings of computer power ago) that chess grandmaster Garry Kasparov resigned after nineteen moves in a game against IMBs Deep Blue, the sixth and final game of their match, which Kasparov lost two games to one, with three draws. No one now expects decades to go by before another domain of human expertise is surpassed by our artificially intelligent inventions. Why not? Because while we humans have remained relatively the same during the course of a few hundred thousand years of our evolution, in the last 40 years our artificially intelligent inventions have improved, and done so at a dramatic rate of change over a short period of time.

---

[73]Erik Brynjolfsson and Andrew McAfee, 2014, The Second Machine Age: Work, Progress, and Prosperity in a Time of Brilliant Technologies, W. W. Norton & Company.

[74]*Id.*

[75]Carl Benedikt Frey and Michael A. Osborne, The Future of Employment: How Susceptible are Jobs to Computerization, Oxford Martin school study, at: http://www.oxfordmartin.ox.ac.uk/downloads/academic/The_Future_of_Employment.pdf.

What about intelligence; we know that computers are clearly getting smarter, but are we humans getting smarter? In the book, "*Mindless,*" Simon Head,[76] senior Fellow at the Institute for Public Knowledge at New York University argues that artificially intelligent systems have now come to trump human expertise, dictating the goals and strategies of a wide array of businesses, and de-skilling the jobs of middle class workers in the process; this just reaffirms what we already know, computers are getting smarter. But whether over the last several millennium humans have continued to evolve to be smarter than our ancestors is actually a debatable proposition. One leading researcher, John Hawks,[77] a University of Wisconsin anthropologist has pointed out that the brain has actually been shrinking for some time. He justifies this conclusion by noting that over the past 20,000 years, the average volume of the human male brain has decreased from 1,500 to 1,350 cc, the female brain has shrunk by about the same proportion. Hawks says that if our brain keeps dwindling at that rate over the next 20,000 years, it will start to approach the size of that found in *Homo erectus*, a relative of ours that lived half a million years ago and had a brain volume of only 1,100 cc.[78] While some believe the erosion of our gray matter means that modern humans are less intelligent than our ancestors, other authorities argue just the opposite: they argue that as the brain shrunk, its wiring has become more efficient, transforming us into quicker, more agile thinkers. Still others believe that the reduction in brain size is proof that we have tamed ourselves, just as we domesticated sheep, pigs, and cattle, all of which are smaller-brained than their wild ancestors. Interestingly, recent analysis of the genome casts doubt on the notion that modern humans are simply identical versions of our ancestors, right down to how we think and feel. Over the very period that the brain shrank, our DNA accumulated numerous adaptive mutations related to brain development and neurotransmitter systems—an indication that even as the organ got smaller, its inner workings changed. The impact of these mutations remains uncertain, but many scientists say it is plausible that our temperament or reasoning abilities shifted as a result. While questions of whether we are getting smarter or not, is debatable, no matter the answer, "they" are getting smarter, and in cycle times measured by months, not millennium.

The most pessimistic explanation as to why humans seem to be becoming less intelligent is that we have effectively reached our intellectual peak. Between the 1930s and 1980s, the average IQ score in the U.S. rose by three points and in postwar Japan and Denmark, test scores also increased significantly—a trend known

---

[76]Simon Head, 2014, Mindless: Why Smarter Machines are Making Dumber Humans, Basic Books.

[77]Kathleen McAuliffe, 2011, If Modern Humans Are So Smart, Why Are Our Brains Shrinking? (Discussing the views of John Hawks).

[78]*Id.*

as the 'Flynn effect'.[79] This increase in intelligence was reportedly due to improved nutrition and living conditions—as well as better education—says James Flynn of the University of Otago, after whom the effect is named. A window to the future? Some experts believe we are starting to see the end of the Flynn effect in developed countries—and that IQ scores are leveling out and even declining. Pessimistic scientists think that our descendants (if not enhanced with technology) may struggle to understand subjects we can grasp now.

Some wonder that as artificial intelligence reaches a certain level of intelligence, will it be dangerous and want to take over our world as Stephen Hawking has warned; or will they be eager to help solve problems that have forever plagued society, such as crime, violence, and wars? J. Storrs Hall, in his book "*Beyond AI*",[80] believes that as computers/robots advance, technologies will allow us to strengthen our brains with non-biological materials and interface with these creations to share their intelligence. In this way, he argues that we will always remain competitive with our machines, and will not need to fear them. I personally don't see a future in which we humans retain our biological, but enhanced, components, while we simply share resources with our more intelligent creations; I see us either merging with them or being surpassed by them.

An interesting question to ask is whether the use of technologies to assist the brain in decision making is making us smarter. In research at McGill University, when functional Magnetic Resonance Imaging, or fMRI, was performed on those who navigate both spatially and through stimulus-response strategies, people who used a spatial navigation strategy had increased activity in an area of the brain involved with memory and navigation known as the hippocampus. McGill researchers found that excessive use of a GPS unit may lead to atrophy of the hippocampus as we age, which puts the person at risk for cognitive problems such as Alzheimer's disease later in life.[81] Alzheimer's disease affects the hippocampus first before any other part of the brain, which leads to problems with spatial orientation and memory. While researchers have found evidence relating hippocampus activity to memory, there are still questions surrounding this research. For instance, researchers are unsure as to whether using spatial strategies causes the hippocampus to grow, or if having a "robust" hippocampus causes an individual to use spatial strategies.[82] Either way, using spatial strategies instead of the GPS would be helpful in lessening the deterioration of memory.

---

[79]Flynn Effect, Wikipedia, at: https://en.wikipedia.org/wiki/Flynn_effect.

[80]John Storrs Hall, 2007, Beyond AI: Creating the Conscience of the Machine, Prometheus Books.

[81]Liu Edwards, 2010, Study Suggests Reliance on GPS May reduce Hippocampus Function as We Age, discussing findings by McGill researchers, at: http://phys.org/news/2010-11-reliance-gps-hippocampus-function-age.html.

[82]Tiffany Kaiser, 2010, Study: GPS Units Cause Memory and Spatial Problems, at: http://www.dailytech.com/Study+GPS+Units+Cause+Memory+and+Spatial+Problems+/article20169.htm.

Returning to Law and Regulations

As humans are enhanced with prosthesis and implants, and artificially intelligent machines argue for rights, what are some issues of law and policy which may impact them? For example, while the above protections for body integrity discussed earlier do not provide protection for artificially intelligent machines, there are current examples where the law has indirectly considered "the rights of technology." For example, Sandra Braman[83] points to some policy changes in the U.S. that seem to consider the "needs" of machines. To make her point, she cites the U.S. Telecommunications Act of 1996 which she argues distinguishes between social and machine policy. Universal *service* obligations require network access for individuals, while universal *access* obligations require access for telecommunications networks. In addition, software code itself is often the subject of copyright and patent protection, a topic for discussion in a later chapter.

A computer's ability to "self-learn," a process where software generates its own heuristics to solve problems, creates interesting issues of law and policy when courts try to assign responsibility for harms inflicted on people by machines operating with artificial intelligence. A question to ask is whether a human that is not sufficiently in the loop to be knowledgeable of the heuristics employed by an artificially intelligent machine, is responsible for any resulting harm from the machine's actions? If not, then who is? Conferences on law and robotics are held each year to discuss just this issue. One of the difficulties in holding artificially intelligent machines responsible for their actions is the issue of legal personhood, without being considered a legal person under the law one lacks the status to initiate lawsuits to defend their rights, or to be held responsible for their actions.

Legal theorist such as Ugo Pagallo,[84] author of *The Law of Robots*, argues that we should distinguish between the behavior of robots as tools of human interaction, and robots as proper agents in the legal arena. I view this as a temporary solution to the issue of assigning responsibility to robots, because due to the law of accelerating returns, ultimately the issue for humanity to discuss will be whether or not to grant artificially intelligent machines the status of legal personhood. Based on my experience designing wearable computing and sensor technology, and my training in law, I think legal personhood will eventually have to be granted to our intelligent creations; if not we will continue to confront situations where no legal person is found responsible, yet a harm has occurred. In the meantime, Judge Karnow proposes to establish a legal entity which he terms an 'electronic persona' which is based on an analogy between corporations and agents.[85] A corporation is not equated with any physical person but is still assigned certain rights and duties. As an example of this "legal fiction," the *European Court of Human Rights* allows

---

[83]Sandra Braman, 2002, Posthuman Law: Information Policy and the Machine World, *First Monday*, Vol. 7.

[84]Ugo Pagallo, 2013, The Law of Robots: Crimes, Contracts, and Torts, Springer Press.

[85]Curtis Karnow, *id.*, note 17.

private Corporations to invoke Article 10 of the European Convention for the protection of "Human Rights and Fundamental Freedoms." Article 10 safeguards the right to freedom of expression; a right an artificially intelligent machine may covet; but doesn't receive under current law. The issue of whether software used to create artificial intelligence and encrypted code are speech, and under what circumstances, is a topic discussed in a subsequent chapter.

Isaac Asimov's laws for robots, presented earlier, are rather general. In cases that make their way to court, the law relies on specific legal doctrines in which to analyze the facts of a case. Take the situation where a person is injured as the result of the action of an autonomous robot. Lacking legal personhood status, the court will try to determine the responsible party to seek restitution. The appropriate legal doctrine is products liability; and given the facts of the case, the manufacturer may be held liable, as could importers, wholesalers, retailers (and their individual employees if personally negligent), and repairers, installers, inspector, programmers, and certifiers; note the lack of the artificial intelligence in the list of those potentially liable. Moving forward in time, let's say the artificially intelligent robot is considered sentient, but still lacks legal personhood status. Although a particular company will have manufactured the robot, they will argue that after the robot left the manufacturer, the robot either reprogrammed itself or the new owner has reprogrammed it, thus they are not liable. The legal doctrine of products liability will be especially problematic for artificial intelligence because of the present distinction between hardware and software. For a robot that kills, is the manufacturer or the robot liable, the software designer, the owner, or is there no liability—Human beware, computer around!

The potential danger posed by artificially intelligent machines is magnified as they become mobile. Given the lack of legal personhood status, for mobile robots, it may be relevant to look at the law relating to dangerous animals as a corollary. In the UK, and other common law jurisdictions, people who keep animals whether they are dangerous or not, are under a duty of care to prevent harm to other people from their animal's actions. If the keeper of an animal is negligent in looking after or restraining the animal and this negligence causes damage to another person or their property, the keeper will be liable. All well and good except artificially intelligent machines will eventually be smarter than animals, and will be autonomous from humans in ways different than animals are. This brings up the issue of punishment for artificially intelligent machines, especially if the artificial intelligence has no means to provide restitution for a victim. Providing restitution may be solved if artificially intelligent machines gain personhood status and can enter into contracts for their services, compete in the stock market, purchase insurance, and so on, then they may amass the funds to pay for damages they cause. This is not farfetched as the majority of trades on the stock market are done with artificially intelligent bots.[86]

Another interesting issue for artificially intelligent beings is whether they are appropriate subject matter for a patent. Clearly, there are many patents already

[86]Felix Salmon and Jon Stokes, 2010, Algorithms Take Control of Wall Street, Wired, at: http://www.wired.com/2010/12/ff_ai_flashtrading/.

allocated to the software and machine components of computers and robots. However, the issue this book considers is whether artificially intelligent machines that claimed to be conscious, could be the subject of patent law. This is an interesting question, under current law the mechanical parts comprising a cyborg are most likely under patent protection, but what about a self-aware entity, could it be the subject of a patent? Under U.S. law, one can wonder in lieu of the 1980 case, *Diamond v. Chakrabarty*[87] whether such beings can be patented. In *Chakrabarty*, the U.S. Supreme Court rejected arguments that Congress intended to limit utility patents solely to inanimate matter. The Court held that genetically engineered life forms that had characteristics they would not have had in nature could be the subject of a utility patent (issued for any functional new invention or improvement on a machine, product, or to the composition of matter). Of particular relevance to both bionic humans and cyborgs is the policy of the U.S. Patent and Trademark Office on granting patents on human tissues and on genetically-engineered animals, some of which contain human genes. While abstaining from granting patents on humans outright, such a policy has left the question of the patentability of human-machine combinations largely unanswered.

Currently, there is no case law or statutes discussing precisely how much human genetic material a creature must possess before it qualifies as human. And certainly, possessing just one or even a handful of human genes does not make an animal human. In fact, patents already exist on animals, like the Harvard Oncomouse, that possess some human genes. At the other end of the spectrum, transplant patients who receive animal organs are clearly considered human and not patentable. Could a cyborg whose genetic material was 49 % human in origin be the subject of a patent? With regard to human-computer/mechanical hybrids, the present state of knowledge of this term assumes that the person is dependent upon mechanical means for one or more of his vital physiological functions. Thus, bionic humans would possess a full complement of human genes but merely use certain mechanical means by which to carry out certain functions (e.g., the use of a "bionic" arm). An interesting ethical and legal question may arise, however, if the vital function achieved by mechanical means is the processing of thoughts (i.e., the use of a computerized brain). Such entities would still presumably possess a full complement of human genes, but many individuals would intuitively consider such beings less (or more?) than human.

Summary

In light of the many pressing issues that relate to the coming Singularity, not the least of which is the very fate of humanity, the public needs to educate themselves and enter the debate now. We humans need to decide whether to embrace or

---

[87]*Diamond v. Chakrabarty*, 447 U.S. 303 (1980).

oppose the Singularity and all that it implies. As opponents have argued, we may be designing our way into extinction, and as proponents have argued, we may be creating a utopian world. If we could agree, as a species, what we wanted, where we were headed and why, then we could make our future much less uncertain and dangerous. One would think that we might be driven to such a dialogue by our instinct for self-preservation.

A conceptual mistake that I think many people make when thinking about the role of technology in our future, is to simply view technology as a tool for human use, whose sole purpose is to better humans in some way, for example, to help the blind see, or the hearing impaired to hear. However, I can't help but think that much of the technology used to enhance humans, is really just a way to help design the next generation of artificially intelligent machines. In my view, we are either in the process of inventing the future of our own extinction, or in the process of inventing the technology to free us from the confines of our body and mind.

It is interesting to note that when Google purchased the cutting-edge artificial intelligence company, *DeepMind*, Google was required to create an artificial intelligence safety and ethics review board to ensure that artificial intelligence technology under their control was developed safely. Considering this request with comments made by a senior member of the company Shane Legg: "Eventually, I think human extinction will probably occur, and technology will likely play a part in this," and that forms of artificial intelligence may pose the most serious risk to humanity this century,"[88] I'm convinced, the ethics board seems like a good idea to me.[89] Still, corporations have agendas that do not always coincide with the best interest of society, so I take the view proposed by Stanford Professor Francis Fukuyama who in *"Our Posthuman Future"*[90] argued that the future of humanity should be in the hands of the public and our elected officials, who through regulations should protect the best interests of the human race.

I return to the idea presented in this chapter involving the creation of "friendly" artificial intelligence, and close the chapter with comments by Nick Bostrom,[91] director of the *Future of Humanity Institute* at Oxford University. "If, in the future, a machine radically surpassed us in intelligence, it would also be extremely powerful, able potentially to shape the future and decide whether there are any more humans or not," therefore, "You need to set up the initial conditions in just the

---

[88]Ellie Zolfagharifard, 2014, Artificial intelligence 'could be the worst thing to happen to humanity': Stephen Hawking warns that rise of robots may be disastrous for mankind, at: http://www.dailymail.co.uk/sciencetech/article-2618434/Artificial-intelligence-worst-thing-happen-humanity-Stephen-Hawking-warns-rise-robots-disastrous-mankind.html.

[89]See generally, Bianca Bosker, 2014, Google's New A.I. Ethics Board Might Save Humanity From Extinction, at: http://www.huffingtonpost.com/2014/01/29/google-ai_n_4683343.html.

[90]Francis Fukuyama, 2003, Our Posthuman Future: Consequences of the Biotechnology Revolution, Picador Press.

[91]Bianca Bosker, *id*, note 89, discussing comments by Nick Bostrom and others.

right way so that the machine is friendly to humans."[92] I like friendly machines, I dislike unfriendly machines, especially those that could extinguish my species. If we ever do merge with machines or hack our DNA, the outward manifestation will be far less obvious than bodies bristling with surgical implants, heavy hardware, and random animal parts. Why? Because we have a choice in the matter, and few (if any) of us want to live in a dystopic future.

---

[92]Nick Bostrum, 2014, Superintelligence: Paths, Dangers, Strategies, Oxford University Press.

Chapter 3
The Law of Artificially Intelligent Brains

Placing an Exponent on Intelligence

Benefiting from exponentially improving technologies, in numerous examples what was once considered a task distinctly requiring human intelligence is now being done much faster and more efficiently by artificially intelligent machines. For example, while driving a car requires complex cognitive, perceptual, and motor skills, artificial intelligence is quickly mastering the art of driving and doing so in highly congested traffic. In fact, based on the law of accelerating returns automated cars are improving to the point where public policy may dictate that a person born today may not be able to legally drive when they reach their teenage years. Given the rate of advances in information technologies, within a few years automated cars will become so "smart" that the only necessary response from a human will be a voice activated destination.

Of course, even though sensors collect information and transfer it to an onboard computer, the "mechanical" car itself isn't becoming smart, the computer directing the car, that is, its brain. And because the raw processing power and capabilities of artificially intelligent machines is directly related to the software, algorithms, and architecture which together comprise its brain, laws that relate to its ability to store information, compute, and communicate will contribute to an emerging law of cyborgs, a central topic of this book. Further, since the hardware, software, and algorithms of an artificially intelligent brain will continue to improve, some computer scientists predict that within a few decades artificial intelligence may exceed human levels of intelligence and pose an existential threat to humanity. For this reason a comprehensive understanding of how the law might apply to an artificially intelligent machine and particularly to the architecture and capabilities of its brain may be essential to the survivability of the human species.

Interestingly, in comparison to human driving performance, after 6 years and 2.7 million km's driven, the director of Google's self-driving project reports, "Not

© Springer International Publishing Switzerland 2015
W. Barfield, *Cyber-Humans*, DOI 10.1007/978-3-319-25050-2_3

once was the self-driving car the cause of the accident."[1] However, that's not to say that self-driving cars haven't been in an accident, in fact, there have been about a dozen minor accidents during the past 6 years, but in every case, a human driving another car was the cause of the accident. In fact, artificial intelligence is getting so good at what it does, the idea of keeping a human out of the decision making loop in systems involving artificially intelligent machines is being seriously considered. On this point, a few courts have actually found humans negligent for failing to follow the advice provided to them by a computer. Two early cases on this point was *Wells v. U.S.* and *Klein v. U.S.* In *Wells*, a court inferred negligence on the part of a human pilot based on evidence he switched from autopilot to manual control in a crisis situation.[2] In this example, the brain of a machine was considered the better decision maker than that of the human. And in *Klein*, the court found that in cases of negligence, while the pilot is not required to use autopilot on a landing, his failure to do so was thought inconsistent with good operating procedure and evidence of a failure of due care. Can we conclude from these above examples that there ought to be a law protecting artificially intelligent machines from humans? That's an interesting question, but I don't really mean to imply that artificial intelligence is always superior to humans and will always be benevolent. In fact, I am more concerned with the potential dark side to artificial intelligence, than I am living in a world where artificial intelligence serves humanity.

Of course, "artificially intelligent brains" do far more than drive cars, now days semi-autonomous drones deliver packages, some robots assist physicians in surgery, and "artificial intelligence" writes sports and weather reports, or makes stock trades. All of these tasks require an impressive amount of intelligence and in some cases complex motor skills by the machine; however, no one would seriously think robots with these abilities are anywhere near human levels of intelligence. Instead, we humans think that robots with the cognitive and perceptual abilities in the above examples are simply remarkable tools to serve us, and we have the general notion that as advances in technology continues, the future will give us an even better set of tools to meet our needs. I believe this is a naïve view of the future, with dangerous implications for humanity. Agreeing with this position, Elon Musk, CEO of SpaceX and Telsa Motors, describes advances in artificial intelligence as "summoning the demon" and thinks that by creating a rival to human intelligence we are simultaneously building the biggest threat facing the world.[3] If we accept the viewpoint advocated by Nick Bostrom, director of Cambridge's

---

[1]Adrienne Lafrance, 2015, When Google Self-Driving Cars Are in Accidents, Humans Are to Blame, at: http://www.theatlantic.com/technology/archive/2015/06/every-single-time-a-google-self-driving-car-crashed-a-human-was-to-blame/395183/.

[2]*Wells v. U.S.*, 16 Av.Cas. 17914 (W.D. Wash. 1981); *Klein v. U.S.*, 13 Av.Cas. 18137 (D. Md. 1975).

[3]Samuel Gibbs, 2014, Elon Musk: Artificial Intelligence is our Biggest Existential Threat, at: http://www.theguardian.com/technology/2014/oct/27/elon-musk-artificial-intelligence-ai-biggest-existential-threat.

Future of Humanity Institute, that artificial intelligence could pose an existential threat to humanity, then how do we, through our courts and legislators, respond? Some propose completely banning research on artificial intelligence, others propose coding "friendliness" into the "minds" of artificial intelligence (likewise will a future artificial intelligence breed docile humans given our aggressive nature?), while others propose government regulations designed to give artificial intelligence certain rights, and to deny it others. On the last point I believe that there already is an emerging body of law, primarily in the field of intellectual property and constitutional law that speaks to the issue of regulating the architecture and output of an artificially intelligent brain, including the thoughts and speech produced by an artificial intelligence. While these laws and government regulations were enacted to protect the rights of humans and not self-aware machines, I believe they may also contribute to an emerging law of cyborgs, that is, they represent a set of laws that could serve as precedence for future artificially intelligent machines that have reached human levels of intelligence and then argue for rights.

Elon Musk is not alone in his warnings about the potential threat that artificial intelligence could pose to humanity. Cambridge cosmologist Martin Rees, the former Astronomer Royal and President of the Royal Society, addressed similar topics in his 2004 book, *Our Final Hour: A Scientist's Warning*,[4] as did computer scientist, Bill Joy, co-founder of Sun Microsystems in his 2000 article published in *Wired*, *"Why the Future doesn't Need Us."*[5] Yet another concern expressed by some prominent researchers in artificial intelligence and robotics is that by the end of this century we will either be serving the artificially intelligent machines that we are in the process of creating now (who eventually will take charge of their own design), or we could be inconsequential to them and relegated to being the second most intelligent species on the planet. But there may be a third alternative, as proposed by robotics expert Hans Moravec, Google's Ray Kurzweil, and by this author discussed throughout this book- and that alternative is to merge with "them," thus becoming the product of our technological future and not relegated to the status of bystander.

For reasons discussed below, many of the public are unaware how close we are to a future consisting of machines with human-or-beyond levels of intelligence, and still others (including some prominent AI researchers and philosophers) outright dismiss a future with strong artificial intelligence as either impossible, the subject of science fiction, or too far in the future to give serious thought now.[6] I think those among the public and academia, who dismiss the dramatic rise of artificial intelligence and its implications for humanity fail to realize that the basic technologies necessary to create artificially intelligent machines are here now, improving exponentially, and leading to the design of machines that will match

---

[4]Martin Rees, 2004, Our Final Hour: A Scientist's Warning, Basic Books; Nick Bostrum, 2014, Superintelligence: Paths, Dangers, Strategies, Oxford University Press.

[5]Bill Joy, 2000, Why the Future Doesn't Need Us, Wired 8.04.

[6]Miguel Nicholelis, 2013, The Brain is Not Computable, MIT Technology Review.

humans in intelligence and motor skills, and possibly within 20–30 years. As we get closer to human-like artificial intelligence, I argue that a "law of artificially intelligent brains" will be necessary for our legal institutions to develop and that such an approach will provide a framework in which to discuss many of the social and legal questions that will be shaped by the rise of artificial intelligence. Such issues will speak to the law as it applies to tort liability, contract rights, and criminal culpability for artificially intelligent machines operating autonomously from humans. But a "law of artificially intelligent brains" will also focus on the software, operating systems, and computer architecture of the artificial brain itself. Given the importance of determining the role of artificial intelligence in society, this chapter is not the first to address these issues, there are a number of law review papers and books written on law and robotics (for example, see Gabriel Hallevy, *When Robots Kill: Artificial Intelligence Under Criminal Law* and papers by Law Professor Ryan Calo), and I expect there will be more interest by nations at the forefront of the robotics revolution and the European Union as artificial intelligence becomes more tightly integrated into society, and more autonomous of humans, while asserting claims to be self-aware, and arguing for rights.[7]

With these observations in mind, this chapter examines some of the legal and policy issues that relate to the design of artificially intelligent brains. To discuss these topics I borrow heavily from current law which relates to the software written for computers, and the law relating to the computer architecture which is essential for the machines ability to compute and thus to reason and "think"— these areas of law can be thought of as a law of artificially intelligent brains.

The Numbers Behind Brains

As I lecture on the topic of our cyborg future to merge with artificially intelligent machines, I inevitably get the following question- how close are we to computer hardware and software that matches the human brain in performance? Several prominent roboticists and inventors seem to have settled on a timeframe that is unsettling to some- before midcentury. But first, what computing resources are necessary to reach the goal of human-like artificial intelligence? That is, what storage capacity and raw processing power must an artificially intelligent brain have to match the human brain? And if human and machine brains had similar functionalities and architectures, would the same laws apply to both entities? When thinking about this question, recall that chimpanzees have brains with architectures that are similar to a human brain and a chimp's behavior is that of a distant relative; yet chimps receive none or almost no individual rights in most jurisdictions.

---

[7]Gabriel Hallevy, 2013, When Robots Kill: Artificial Intelligence Under Criminal Law, Northeastern Press; Ryan Calo, 2015, Robotics and the Lessons of Cyberlaw, 103 *California Law Review.*

To receive human-like rights, is a high hurdle to pass; humanity is not generous affording rights to other animals. Doing some "back of the napkin" calculations, we can answer the question posed about the computational resources necessary to match a human brain by looking at the numbers involved in reverse engineering the brain.

For nearly a decade, neuroscientists, computer engineers, and roboticists have been working to reverse engineer the human brain so they can ultimately create a computing architecture based on how the mind works. The key to reverse-engineering the human brain lies in decoding and simulating the cerebral cortex—the seat of cognition. The human cerebral cortex has about 22 billion neurons with trillions of synapses. A supercomputer capable of running a software simulation of the human brain, according to some researchers, would require a machine with a computational capacity of at least 36.8 petaflops and a memory capacity of 3.2 petabytes.[8] All interesting and technologically possible, but an important and pragmatic question is how many lines of code would be required to simulate a brain? Terry Sejnowski, head of the computational neurobiology lab at the *Salk Institute for Biological Studies* agrees with Ray Kurzweil's assessment that about a million lines of code may be enough to accomplish that task. Intuitively this number seems low to me, but I did say we are doing "back of the napkin" calculations, so let's see how the math works. According to Kurzweil: "The design of the brain lies in the blueprint provided by the genome. The human genome has three billion base pairs or six billion bits, which is about 800 million bytes before compression."[9] Kurzweil notes that "eliminating redundancies and applying lossless compression, that information can be compressed into about 50 million bytes."[10] About half of that information is about the brain, which comes down to 25 million bytes, or roughly a million lines of code.[11] I have read rebuttals to this number as being far too low, but what amazes me, is that even if we increase the lines of code necessary to simulate the brain even by orders of magnitude; given exponentially accelerating technologies, we are already creating the technology and gaining the knowledge to unlock the mysteries of the brain, so it's just a matter of time before we can simulate the brain with a million lines of code, or even 100 million lines of code if necessary.

So how close are we to an artificial intelligence with human-like abilities, that is, a being that might argue for legal protection for the software, algorithms, and integrated circuits that allow it to think, problem solve, and to control the motion of its body? In his books and papers, robotics expert Professor Hans Moravec put the 2020s as the time period of human-like robots, this estimate also corresponds to Ray Kurzweils prediction. In a paper Hans Moravec published in 1998 (author of

---

[8]Priya Ganapati, 2010, Reverse-Engineering of Human Brain Likely by 2030, Expert Predicts, at: http://www.wired.com/2010/08/reverse-engineering-brain-kurzweil/.

[9]*Id.*

[10]*Id.*

[11]*Id.*

Mind Children: The Future of Robot and Human Intelligence and *Robot: Mere Machine to Transcendent Mind*), which was based on his seminal work on computer vision for robots he estimated that about 100 million MIPS of computer power would be necessary to match "overall human behavior" and that about 100 million megabytes were necessary to match the capacity of the 100-trillion synapse brain.[12] Both of these numbers are less than those provided in the material above (the brain computes in the petaflop range), but since we are already in the petaflop computing range with super computers, we have matched the raw processing power of the brain based on estimates of its raw processing ability to computer. Further, the speed of progress in artificial intelligence is also accelerating as a few years after Moravec's comments, IBMs Deep Blue defeated the world chess champion using chips designed to operate at 3 million MIPS, or 1/30 of Moravec's total estimate of human performance (as an aside- if a computer completes 200,000 instructions in 0.02 s, then 200,000/0.02 would equal 10 MIPS).

Of course we know from neurophysiology that the cerebral cortex with its 22 billion neurons is critically important for human cognition. And to emphasize here the difficulty of building the architecture to create a brain and thus why developing a "law of artificially intelligent brains" will be extremely challenging, if a reasonable estimate of the number of synapses per neuron is 12,500 (some estimate the number to be about 10,000) then the 22 billion cortical neurons alone would require something on the order of 275 trillion transistors to match the number of synapses in the cortex (we are several years out from creating such chips but we will get there). But this level of complexity doesn't take into account the changing structure of neural networks as we learn and create new memories, and that there may be subcellular processing occurring moving the brain from the paradigm of a single computer to a self-contained Internet with billions of simpler nodes working together in a massively parallel network. So, I view estimates that are specific to when we may build a machine that reaches human levels of intelligence, with a strong interest, and believe that it will happen, but I would not be surprised that as we learn more about the brain and specifically the cortex we may find levels of complexity that will move back the date for the Singularity. However, what's a few years, or decades, or even centuries after all the planet is 45.4 million centuries old! Clearly the human brain is incredibly complex, but operating under Moore's law we are now at petaflop (10^{15}) computing with supercomputers, and eventually will reach exaflop computing (10^{18}), at that point computers will be much faster than us based on raw processing power, performing a quintillion calculations per second. My point is this, I fully acknowledge how complex the human brain is, and that modeling its performance will be extremely difficult (the grandest challenge yet for humanity), but the difficulty of creating human-like artificial intelligence, should be considered against the backdrop of exponentially accelerating technologies, and particularly the rapid progress being made in neuroscience and machine learning.

---

[12]Hans Moravec, When Will Computer Hardware Match the Human Brain? *Journal of Evolution and Technology*, Vol. 1, 1998.

Law and Brains

Acknowledging the challenge of creating an artificially intelligent brain, let's now discuss more specifically laws that might apply to an artificial intelligence. If we (and our machines that help us) can write code (combined with the necessary computational resources) to create an artificially intelligent brain, what current laws relate to the computer code and algorithms that comprise the brain of an artificially intelligent machine? Several areas of law are relevant to this question and thus to our cyborg future, including copyright and patent law, trade secret law, and Constitutional law on the speech output and algorithms of an artificially intelligent brain. Both copyright law and patent law are applicable to some extent to the protection of software and algorithms (meaning the owner of the software has certain rights under copyright law) that contribute to an artificially intelligent brain, and as I have stated throughout this book, contribute to an emerging law of cyborgs. Specifically, an owner of a copyrighted software program has the right (with some exceptions) to: copy the software, create a derivative or modified version of it, and distribute copies of the software to the public by license, sale or otherwise. Are these rights relevant for an artificially intelligent brain? Anyone exercising any of these exclusive rights without permission of the software copyright owner is an infringer and subject to liability for damages or statutory fines.[13] Interestingly, one could literally steal the mind of an artificially intelligent brain by copying its software and algorithms and if so would be an infringer under copyright law. Similarly, in the cyborg future brain scanning technologies could also be used to copy the thoughts generated by a human mind but since the "software of the mind" is not copyright protected (the output of the mind can be), the person would not be an infringer; maybe we need to change the law.

Out of necessity, absent direct statutes and case law involving artificial intelligence, we look to "human law" as a way to frame issues involving artificial intelligence. In the early days of computing, software developers turned to the statutory protection offered under the Copyright Act to protect the intellectual property rights associated with their programs, arguing that the writing of code was similar to other forms of writing. Similar logic should apply to the code written for the operating system and programs under the direction of an artificially intelligent brain. In the U.S. Copyright Act, the general requirements for copyright are: "original works of authorship fixed in any tangible medium of expression, now known or later developed, from which they can be perceived, reproduced, or otherwise communicated, either directly or with the aid of a machine or device."[14] Further, the Copyright Act defines a computer program (think of the software used by a robot to parse images in a scene), as "A set of statements or instructions to be used directly or indirectly in a computer to bring about a certain result."[15] Examples include software which enables computer vision, robot navigation, or trial-and-error learning.

---

[13]17 U.S. Code § 102—Subject matter of copyright.
[14]U.S. Copyright Act, 17 USC §§ 100 et. seq.
[15]U.S. Copyright Act, Sect. 101.

When a computer program is written out on a piece of paper, copyright exists in that work upon its creation so long as the traditional copyright requirements are met (basically, the work must be original, that is, the work must have been developed independently by its author, and there must have been some minimum creativity involved in the work). So, software, which is a central component of an artificially intelligent brain, is clearly copyrightable subject matter. We know that the source code, that is, the language used to write programs for an artificial intelligence is copyright protected, but what about object code? This question was answered in *Apple Computer, Inc. v. Franklin Computer Corp.*, in which a U.S. Circuit Court ruled that programs in both source code and object code are copyright protected.[16] Interestingly, the court rejected the argument that because object code only communicates directly to a machine it should not be protected, this raises the possibility that machine-to-machine communication in an abstract language (a form of machine telepathy), would be copyright protected.

But what about software not written on paper but etched on a chip that compromises the hardware architecture of an artificially intelligent brain? In *Franklin*, the question of whether programs encoded on chips, are utilitarian objects- and thus not subject to copyright protection was addressed. The *Franklin* court rejected the argument that programs were solely "utilitarian" noting that the medium on which the program was encoded should not determine whether the program is subject to copyright. This bodes well for an artificial intelligence arguing for rights to the content of its mind; based on copyright law the memories and thoughts of an artificially intelligent brain written in source or object code may be copyright protected when they are fixed within the integrated circuits compromising an artificially intelligent brain.

Of course, software is more than just individual lines of code, collectively, code performs functions that are essential to the operations of an artificially intelligent brain. In *Franklin* the court rejected the argument that operating systems are not copyright protected because they are "processes, systems or methods of operation."[17] Instead the court ruled that an operating system is to be considered a work of authorship under the Copyright Act. This holding by the court is directly relevant to an artificially intelligent brain; for example, consider robots, a technology leading us towards the Singularity, clearly robots are getting smarter from one generation to the next based on improvements in their software, algorithms, and the "physical design" of the architecture of their brain. Since an operating system, that is, the backbone of an artificially intelligent brain, is eligible for copyright protection, it cannot be reproduced by another, or a derivative of the artificially intelligent brain made without permission from the copyright holder. The owner of the copyright for software comprising an artificially intelligent brain may (or may not) be the owner of the robot (the owner of the robot may be licensing the software), but in the future the ownership of an artificial intelligence by a human may

---

[16]*Id.*

[17]*Apple Computer v. Franklin Computer*, 714 F.2d 1240 (3d Cir. 1983).

be questionable (the 13th Amendment prohibits slavery or involuntary servitude). And if in the future artificially intelligent robots are emancipated from a human owner, copyright law may be used by them as one form of protection for their speech; and software is considered a form of speech.

Summarizing the discussion to this point, the main features of an artificially intelligent brain consists of programs, an operating system, and algorithms, and courts have established that the literal elements of a programs code are protected by copyright law, but there are more issues to discuss for artificially intelligent brains. For example, in *Computer Associates International, Inc. v. Altai, Inc.*,[18] the issue for the Second Circuit Court of Appeals was whether and to what extent copyright protects the non-literal elements of program code, that is, the structure, sequence, and organization of the program. As a basic point, copyright protects the expression of an idea but not the idea itself (ideas are protected by patents or to some extent trade secret law). So for an artificially intelligent brain how the software is written makes all the difference in terms of acquiring protection for its code.

So where do we draw the line between the expression and idea in programs? In *Baker v. Selden* the court stated that things that "must necessarily be used as incident to" the idea are not subject to copyright protection.[19] This opinion, however, gave no advice on how to separate an idea from its expression. Facing a similar issue, *Whelan v. Jaslow,* a landmark case in defining principles that apply to the copyright of computer software, the Court attempted to delineate the differences between "idea and expression by saying that the function of the work is the idea and everything else not necessary to the function is the expression of the idea."[20] But other courts have found this approach unworkable, and have adopted the filtration approach taken by the Second Circuit in *Computer Associates Int'l. v. Atltai.*[21] That approach separates the code's ideas and public domain elements from its expression and then extends copyright protection only to the expression.[22] In the abstraction-filtration-comparison test the court first determines the allegedly infringed program's constituent structural parts. Then, the parts are filtered to extract any non-protected elements. Non-protected elements include: elements made for efficiency (i.e. elements with a limited number of ways it can be expressed and thus incidental to the idea), elements dictated by external factors (i.e. standard techniques), and design elements taken from the public domain.[23] Any of these non-protected elements are thrown out and the remaining elements are compared with the allegedly infringing program's elements to determine

---

[18]*Computer Associates International, Inc. v. Altai, Inc*, 982 F.2d 693 (2d Cir. 1992).

[19]*Baker v. Selden*, 101 U.S. 99 (1979); Copyright Act § 102(b) (the subject matter of copyright).

[20]*Whelan Assocs., Inc. v. Jaslow Dental Lab. Inc.*, 609 F. Supp. 1307, 225 U.S.P.Q. (BNA) 156 (E.D. Pa. 1985).

[21]*Id.*, note 18.

[22]*Id.* note 20.

[23]*Id.* note 18.

substantial similarity. In my view the above approaches to determining which aspects of software are copyright protected will be difficult to apply to the software of an artificially intelligent brain, just as determining which aspects of human thinking represent function versus expression would be difficult. For that reason courts may need to devise another test suitable for the cyborg age in which to decide what aspects of code are copyrightable subject matter especially the code comprising the input and output of an artificially intelligent brain.

More About Artificially Intelligent Brains

Repeating a basic point, an artificially intelligent brain will consist of the computer architecture, software, and algorithms to direct its behavior and to make sense of the world. Will such a brain with appropriate computational resources and software reach consciousness? This is a question of great debate, but there is an established neuroscientific consensus that the human mind is largely an emergent property of the information processing resulting from the 100 billion neurons comprising its architecture. And we know from the above discussion that much of the artificially intelligent brains software is "protected" by intellectual property law. So an emerging law of artificially intelligent brains is beginning to take shape. And interestingly, while we can conclude that there is no "law of neurons," there is a law of software. Thus, the brain of an artificially intelligent machine can be scrutinized under the law in ways a human brain cannot.

Another question of interest to those designing the cyborg future and wondering how the law might apply is whether artificially intelligent brains will surpass the human brain in capabilities. As we did above, let's think like an engineer for a moment and focus on the quantitative aspects of brains. Given that the electrochemical signals that human brains use to achieve thought travels at about 150 m/s, this is orders of magnitude slower than the speed at which electronic signals are sent by computers. Therefore, a massively parallel electronic counterpart of a human biological brain will be able to think millions and eventually trillions of times faster than our naturally evolved system. Also, consider that neurons can generate a maximum of about 1000 action potentials per second, whereas the clock speed of microprocessors reached 5.5 GHz in 2013, which is about five million times faster, this means that in some respects, computer brains are already superior in performance to human brains.[24] But supercomputers also can have energy requirements that compete with some municipalities, and have grown larger than the laboratory-sized calculating machines at the infancy of computers.[25] The human brain, meanwhile, uses roughly 20 watts and occupies a small volume.

---

[24]Mind Uploading, Wikipedia, at: https://en.wikipedia.org/wiki/Mind_uploading.

[25]Geoffrey Mohan, 2014, Cognitive computer chip apes brain architecture, at: http://www.latimes.com/science/sciencenow/la-sci-sn-brain-chip-computer-20140807-story.html.

However, since computers are improving in computational performance exponentially, we can expect a laptop computer to have the computational power of the human brain within a few years.

The recent rise of artificial intelligence has been spurred by many factors, including a tremendous decrease in the price of information technologies combined with an exponential increase in performance. With so much computing power available, algorithms are more-and-more capable of understanding languages, recognizing images, and performing more autonomously from humans.[26] For example, artificially intelligent machines in manufacturing are not only getting smarter, but their costs are tumbling- and this price performance relationship is pervasive in all information technologies. On this point, consider that the labor costs for an essential technology for the future development of artificially intelligent machines- electronics manufacturing has plummeted. For electronics manufacturing, robots are becoming so cost effective that in many cases it already costs just a few dollars an hour to use a robot for a routine assembly task versus six times more for an average human worker. How long will it be before the robots are designing their next generation based on their own criteria and displace even more humans from the workplace?

Interestingly, Hans Moravec commented that human-like performance from machines will only make economic sense when their "brains" cost about $1000- and when can we expect that? Our evidence suggests around 2029 for replicating the human brain. It is important to note for our cyborg future, following Moore's law, the price-performance of computers will continue to double every 18 months or so at least for the next decade, and once we reach human levels of performance for robots, they will continue to get smarter, after all, their evolution is not based on biology and thus does not rely on random mutations in genes to work their way into the human genome. Still some critics argue that Moore's law is running out of steam, but if the past trend in computing technology continues, another technology will take over for current chip design techniques, and will continue the exponential improvement in computing power to midcentury and beyond. The amazing power of exponential growth in information technologies is experienced by people every day, in fact, just consider, we all carry the proof of exponentially improving technologies in our hand as the cell phone we use now is a million times cheaper and a thousand times more powerful than a supercomputer of the mid-seventies. And by the way, every cell phone call is routed using artificial intelligence. Many don't realize it, but we are completely dependent on artificial intelligence now, from air traffic control systems to home appliances, artificial intelligence is in the background, silently doing its job.

Continuing Hans Moravec's comments above on the desirability of a $1000 computer brain, as far back as 1999 and in his recent writings, Ray Kurzweil predicted that by the 2020s a $1,000 laptop would have the computing power and

---

[26]Rise of the Machines, 2015, The Economist, at: http://www.economist.com/news/briefing/21650526-artificial-intelligence-scares-peopleexcessively-so-rise-machines.

storage capacity of a human brain (100 billion neurons, 100 trillion synapses).[27] In fact, we are well on our way to creating a low-cost computer with this amount of raw processing power. Relying on exponential growth curves, Kurzweil predicted that the hardware needed to emulate the human brain could be ready as early as 2020—this could be done using technologies such as graphics processing units which use a massively parallel architecture, which I might add is an ideal architecture for brain-software algorithms. While critics that are opposed to the idea of artificially intelligent machines gaining human-like intelligence worry that this outcome could prove disastrous to humanity, many also acknowledge that we are now entering a time when computers have the processing power necessary to match the brain's computational abilities. But more than computational power is needed to create human-like artificial intelligence. For example, critics point out that current software is nowhere near being able to model the human brain in its ability to process information and make decisions.

While the critics are right that computational resources are necessary but not sufficient to create human-like intelligence, still the software for artificial intelligence and the algorithms to mimic the decision making of the brain (that is, to simulate neuronal networks) are also making great strides. In fact, Kurzweil predicts that software to accurately model the brain will take only a little longer to develop than acquiring the processing power of the brain, putting the date at 2029.[28] But in my view while creating artificial intelligence that matches a human in ability will be a landmark event in humanity's history, what humanity really needs to focus on is what happens after the Singularity is reached- how do we survive in the shadow of intelligent beings far superior to us? A major thesis of this book is that for humanity's survival, we need to merge with our technological progeny, or as Hans Moravec puts it- our "mind children." For us to merge with artificially intelligent machines, enter cyborg technologies (which will be a key factor for our future survivability). As computing technology keeps advancing at an exponential rate, within a few decades, we will have the combined intelligence of the human race accessible by a neuroprosthetic device implanted within our brain. This capability will be essential for the survival of our species once the Singularity is reached by artificial intelligence.

Even though the Singularity is predicted to be only a few decades away, computers already have a big advantage over us: they are interconnected via the Internet and share information with each other billions of times faster than we humans are able to do using the limited communication bandwidth provided to us by nature. This means that a law of artificially intelligent brains needs to consider how a collective form of artificial intelligence shares liability and other responsibilities under the law. The most accurate predictor of the future (at least within the timeframe of a few decades), is Google's Ray Kurzweil who says that by the

---

[27]Ray Kurzweil, 2006, The Singularity is Near: When Humans Transcend Biology, Penguin Books.
[28]*Id.*

2040s, non-biological intelligence will be a billion times more capable than bio-logical intelligence, that is, us.[29] The reader may be wondering how is this even possible and why so soon? After all, current artificial intelligence, while remarka-bly smart in limited domains, lacks the general intelligence and common sense displayed by a 4 year old. But the problem that people have in understanding the future, as pointed out by Kurzweil in his fascinating books about what the future might offer (see for example, The *Age of Spiritual Machines* and *The Singularity is Near*), is that people are linear thinkers, they extrapolate the world they live in now along a straight line to predict where technology will be in the future. Centuries ago linear thinking about technology worked quite well, but around the middle of the nineteenth century, the rate of technological advancements began to noticeably speed up. Considering computing resources, plotting the exponential growth of many computing-based technologies has shown that the growth rate for information technologies is decidedly not linear.

Believe me a liner scale versus exponential scale for technological progress and particularly the brain of an artificial intelligence makes all the difference. I'll prove that to you with an example. Do you want to be rich? Tongue-in-cheek, I argue it's easy to do. Here's how- let's use our spare change and allocate a 31-day month to reach our goal of riches. The first day of the month, place a penny on day one of the calendar, and double the amount placed on the calendar for each additional day until the end of the month. What happens? The second day you have 2 cents, and the third day 4 cents, the fourth day 8 cents and by the end of the week you have 64 cents total. One week of stacking pennies has gone by, are you feeling rich yet? Continuing, day 14 you have $81.92. At that point I say to you, you are about half way to the end of the month, do you still believe me that you are going to be very rich in 17 more days based on doubling pennies from one day to the next? Most people respond no, they use linear thinking to scale the problem in their mind, and claim that they will end up with a few hundred dollars at most (which is a lot more than they thought they would have at the beginning of the month). So, I continue the exercise (with your pennies!). By day 21 we have $10,485.76 and it's definitely getting interesting, but only 10 days to go until the end of the month and we're not rich yet. By day 25 you have accumulated $167,772.16, and by now you are likely fascinated with the concept of exponential growth. Finishing the exercise, day 31 we have $10,737,418.24. To reiterate the point about exponential growth, we achieved that amazing result due to the doubling of pennies from one day to the next. It turns out that doubling pennies has a lot to do with the rise of arti-ficial intelligence, the performance that their brains will be able to achieve, and our future to merge with artificially intelligent machines. Given that information technologies are improving exponentially (note that the magnitude of the exponent signifying the growth is important), I think you will agree with me that remark-able technologies await us. In fact, you may be thinking, a world of incredibly smart tools to serve us, that's the future which awaits humanity. But not so fast, the

---

[29]*Id.*

problem as I see it is that our tools will become much smarter than us (they may even look like us, see Chap. 7: *The Law of Looks and Artificial Bodies*), and then who will be master and who will be the servant?

While the doubling of technological resources is important so too is the time frame between doublings (which also makes all the difference). In our get rich example, instead of using days on a calendar, let's say we used 10 year time periods, so after 10 years, we have 2 cents, and in 20 years we have 4 cents, eventually we will get to over ten million as we did in the above example, but who wants to wait three centuries? I argue that exponentially improving technologies will change everything due to the power of doublings and the short time intervals between the doublings. Let's say starting now that humans doubled their intelligence from one generation to the next. Clearly that's impossible, but if so, about 18 years from now, a person with twice the intelligence of the general population would be born. The problem is we can't significantly alter our intelligence in that time period. Because we are products of the exceedingly slow process of evolution, the cycle time for improving human intelligence is measured in millennium. But there's a solution to keeping up with increasingly intelligent machines- exponentially improving technologies integrated into our body. According to Moore's law the cycle time to double the number of transistors on a chip is about 18 months. Using the above example, while the human had to wait 18 years to double its intelligence, in the same time period, a computer would have experienced 12 doublings of computational power (note that computer power is necessary but not sufficient to produce artificial intelligence, so I am not implying that the AI would be 12 times smarter). Referring back to our example using penny's to get rich, 12 doublings is the difference between 2 cents (one time period) versus $20.48 (12 time periods); so you can see if we remain as we are now, the brain of our "competition" will rapidly leave us behind. Remember, because supercomputers are already computing in the petaflop range (a quadrillion floating point operations per second)- so double 20 petaflops 12 times and then compare that to the processing power of the brain (which is a petaflop computing machine and without technical enhancements will continue to be so based on biology). The important point is this, with the use of exponentially accelerating technologies, we are essentially placing an exponent on the increase in computational power of the technologies which may lead to an artificial intelligence that matches then exceeds us. But in theory the same principle could also work for the human brain, that is, once the brain is wirelessly connected to the cloud through a neuroprosthetic device. In fact, by 2045, (as predicted by Ray Kurzweil, we could multiply our intelligence a billion fold by linking wirelessly from our neocortex to a synthetic neocortex in the cloud.[30]

As should be clear by now, predictions about the future are a byproduct of understanding the power of Moore's Law, and more generally of the "Law of

---

[30]Peter Diamandis, 2015, Ray Kurzweil's Mind-Boggling Predictions for the Next 25 Years, at: http://singularityhub.com/2015/01/26/ray-kurzweils-mind-boggling-predictions-for-the-next-25-years/.

Accelerating Returns".[31] If the cycle time to double computational processing power is about 18 months, then given the power of super computers now, a few doublings represents an incredible improvement in computing power over where we are now. For example, if we start with 40 petaflops, after three doublings (less than 6 years) we are already at 320 petaflops; 8x the computing power in less than 6 years is an amazing increase (I'll take that in the stock market!). And given such a short cycle time between doublings, it is no wonder that Kurzweil and others have been so successful predicting remarkable engineering advances, they only have to postulate about what's possible by exponentially improving technologies 20 years out or less. Generally, information technologies follow an exponential growth curve based on the principle that the computing power that enables them doubles every 18 months or so. In fact, information technology has seen exponential growth for decades. This has led to vast improvements in memory, processing power, software algorithms, voice recognition and overall machine intelligence.[32] And with the increased raw processing power for computers, so too have advancements been made in algorithms to emulate thinking, and the design of chips which process information more as the brain does (mostly parallel processing) compared to the computers of past decades designed to process information based on the von Neuman computer architecture. The law which relates to algorithms and computer chips is, of course, part of the emerging law of cyborgs and artificially intelligent brains.

Machine Learning and Brain Architectures

Information technologies improving exponentially are not the only area of science and engineering making tremendous strides leading to artificial general intelligence and our future to merge with artificially intelligent machines- so too is neuroscience generating exponentially growing volumes of data and knowledge on specific aspects of the brain.[33] In fact, thousands of neuroscientists are working to map the brain across all its levels and functions. It is likely that research in neuroscience will ultimately reveal the detailed mechanisms which led from genes to cells to neuronal circuits, and ultimately to cognition and behavior—the biology that makes us human and conscious. This knowledge will help transform computing making artificial general intelligence all that more possible. But of course developing human-like artificial intelligence will be extremely difficult and challenging, in fact, the human brain performs computations inaccessible to the most

---

[31]*Id.*

[32]See generally, 2029 timeline contents, at: http://www.futuretimeline.net/21stcentury/2029.htm#. VXxb1e_bJjo.

[33]European Commission, 2014, From lighter airplanes to new treatments for brain diseases, at: http://europa.eu/rapid/press-release_MEMO-14-531_en.htm.

powerful of today's computers—all while consuming no more power than a light bulb. According to Europe's digital agenda for the future which is part of Europe's Human Brain Project, understanding how the brain "computes reliably with unreliable elements, and how different elements of the brain communicate, can provide the key to a completely new category of hardware, neuromorphic computing systems; and to a paradigm shift for computing as a whole."[34] The economic and industrial impact is potentially enormous but the ultimate result will likely be an artificial intelligence that exceeds us unless our destiny is to merge with our technological progeny.

The phrase "artificial intelligence" often brings to mind futuristic visions of human-like machines; however the ability of a machine to learn is a concept that is already in play today. And the machines ability to learn is a direct result of its brain architecture, software, and algorithms. So how do current computers learn and acquire the knowledge to be intelligent? One approach to creating human-like artificial intelligence is to take a "machine learning approach" which allows a computer program to discern the key features of one dataset and then apply what it has learned to make predictions about another.[35] Familiar examples of this machine learning approach includes according to *Biome*, "optical character recognition, spam filtering, automatic face recognition, and various data mining applications."[36]

While a super computer has the raw processing power of a brain (in the range of petaflop computing), without implementing the rules/algorithms which enable thinking this amount of processing power cannot lead to artificial general intelligence. But clearly advances are being made using a variety of approaches to create computers that think and reason more as humans do; some of the techniques rely on algorithms, and others on the design of the architecture of the computing hardware itself. For example, one of the techniques being used to create a computer that "thinks" is an approach termed "deep learning" which is actually a refinement of the field of machine learning.[37] With deep learning, machines teach themselves without human intervention by crunching large sets of data and then statistically analyzing the data looking for patterns. This type of machine learning is especially powerful because it represents a way of getting computers to know things when they see them, by producing for themselves the rules programmers cannot painstakingly specify for every event and contingency that may occur in the world. Here I should make the point, no matter what the algorithm, software, or computing architecture, these components of "thinking" contribute to a developing field of jurisprudence relating to a law of artificially intelligent brains.

---

[34]The Human Brain Project, The European Commission, at: https://ec.europa.eu/digital-agenda/en/human-brain-project.

[35]Peter, Flach, 2012, Machine Learning: The Art and Science of Algorithms that Make Sense of Data, Cambridge University Press; Nikhil Buduma, 2015, Fundamentals of Deep Learning: Designing Next-Generation Artificial Intelligence Algorithms, O'Reilly Media.

[36]The rise of machine learning: how to avoid the pitfalls in data analysis, 2014, at: http://biome.biomedcentral.com/the-rise-of-machine-learning-how-to-avoid-the-pitfalls-in-data-analysis/.

[37]*Id.* note 35.

Discussing whether algorithms, basic components of an artificially intelligent brain, are a form of speech, Duke University Law Professor Stuart Benjamin points out that "many human activities involve the transmission of bits, according to the algorithms and protocols created by humans and implemented by machines."[38] In my view, Benjamin's use of the phrase "created by humans" is a qualifier applied to speech that may disappear within a few decades as artificial intelligence gets smarter.[39] Benjamin poses the question- "Are these algorithm-based outputs speech, under the First Amendment?" We know that computers "think" by manipulating bits, done by using algorithms such as those that statistically analyze data, for example, to detect lines and edges in a scene to identify an image. In fact, computer code is basically a set of instructions and algorithms (is the human mind the same?). According to Benjamin, even if algorithms are not speech their output may be and thus subject to at least some First Amendment protection. Of importance for a law of artificially intelligent brains using software and algorithms to produce behavioral outputs, is the case of *Sorrell v. IMS Health, Inc.*, in which the Supreme Court held that the creation and dissemination of information are speech within the meaning of the First Amendment.[40] According to Professor Benjamin, by "extending the First Amendment to messages produced by artificial intelligence, we would be treating the products of machines like those of human minds."[41] Thus, in his view we could then say that speech was truly created and not just transmitted, or aided, by a machine. In fact, the issue of whether the output of a computer is speech was addressed in *Brown v. Entertainment Merchants Ass'n*, where the output of video games were considered speech because the court concluded they communicated ideas like a literary device.[42] I believe this holding serves as precedence for a future artificial intelligence claiming rights to its speech. However, the issue of granting "free speech" to computers is problematic, according to Columbia Law Professor Tim Wu.[43] According to Wu, "computer programs are utilitarian instruments, meant to serve us."[44] He points out that "the First Amendment is intended to protect actual humans against state censorship."[45] Wu argues that nonhuman or automated choices should not be granted the full protection of the First Amendment, and often should not be considered speech at all. In Professor Wu's view, to give computers the rights intended for humans is to "elevate our machines above ourselves."[46] Responding to Wu's

---

[38] Stuart Benjamin, Algorithms and Speech, University of Pennsylvania Law Review, Vol. 161, No. 6, May 2013, 1445–1494.

[39] Pamela Samuelson, Allocating Ownership Rights in Computer-Generated Works, 47 *Pitt. L. Rev.* 1185, 1985.

[40] *Sorrell v. IMS Health Inc.*, 131 S.Ct. 2653 (2011).

[41] Stuart Benjamin, *id.*, note 38.

[42] *Brown v. Entertainment Merchants Ass'n*, 131 S.Ct. 2729 (2011).

[43] Tim Wu, Machine Speech, University of Pennsylvania Law Review, Vol.161, 1495–1533.

[44] *Id.*

[45] *Id.*

[46] *Id.*

argument, I believe we are a few decades away from having to confront the issue of whether artificial intelligence is superior to humans in intelligence because information technologies are improving exponentially; at that point courts may have no choice but to determine the boundaries of protection for speech produced by artificially intelligent machines.

A central aspect of an artificially intelligent brain, is an algorithm, and when considered solely as a mathematical formula expressing a universal principle of nature (e.g., gravity), is not patentable, because the patent would create a huge and fundamental monopoly over laws of nature. This general rule against patenting algorithms was at one time applied to computer software, because software largely consists of procedural instructions in mathematical form that makes a computer accomplish a certain and definite result. Now days, the U.S. Patent and Trademark Office will allow patents on that aspect of an algorithm that accomplishes a useful and concrete result, and provided the software patent is tied to a particular machine or transforms an article into a different state. For example, in an important case about the patentability of business methods expressed in code, *State Street*, the court ruled that mathematical algorithms are nonpatentable only when they are "nothing more than abstract ideas consisting of disembodied concepts that are not useful."[47]

Like the human brain, deep learning algorithms are used by artificially intelligent machines in an attempt to learn multi-level representations of data, embodying a hierarchy of factors that may explain them. Such algorithms have also been demonstrated to be effective both at uncovering underlying structure in data, and have been successfully applied to a large variety of problems ranging from image classification, to natural language processing and speech recognition. Interestingly, MIT researchers discovered that a deep-learning system designed to recognize and classify scenes also learned how to recognize individual objects.[48] To discover this they used a deep learning system to train a successful scene-classifier, which proved to be between 25 and 33 % more accurate than its best predecessor. This result implies that scene-recognition and object-recognition systems could work in concert or could be mutually reinforcing; this is one of many steps being made by thousands of researchers in the direction of creating machines with human-like thinking abilities.

Another promising approach that mimics human learning, and thus may constitute a critically important aspect of knowledge acquisition for an artificially intelligent brain, is being investigated by Professor Pieter Abbeel at UC Berkeley who with colleagues has developed a type of reinforcement learning which works by having a robot complete various tasks—putting a clothes hanger on a rack, assembling a toy plane, screwing a cap on a water bottle, and more—without pre-programmed details

---

[47]*State Street Bank and Trust Company v. Signature Financial Group, Inc.*, 149 F.3d 1368 (Fed. Cir. 1998).

[48]Yoshua Bengio, Ian Goodfellow, and Aaron Courville, Deep Learning, MIT Press, In preparation.

about its surroundings.[49] "Most robotic applications are in controlled environments where objects are in predictable positions," said UC Berkeley faculty member Trevor Darrell, director of the *Berkeley Vision and Learning Center*.[50] According to Darrell, "the challenge of putting robots into real-life settings, like homes or offices, is that those environments are constantly changing."[51] To be intelligent, the robot must be able to perceive and adapt to its surroundings. Conventional, but impractical, approaches to helping a robot make its way through a 3D world include pre-programming it to handle the vast range of possible scenarios or creating simulated environments within which the robot operates.[52] Instead, the UC Berkeley researchers are using deep learning techniques, which is loosely inspired by the neural circuitry of the human brain when it perceives and interacts with the world.[53] The techniques for machine learning described here are a clear departure from the brittle method of having to program every rule into the mind of a machine else it doesn't know the rule, imagine parents having to do that with their kids.

In the world of artificial intelligence, deep learning programs create "neural nets" in which layers of artificial neurons process overlapping raw sensory data, whether it be sound waves or image pixels.[54] This helps the robot recognize patterns and categories among the data it is receiving. According to Sarah Yang, "People who use Siri on their iPhones, Google's speech-to-text program or Google Street View might already have benefited from the significant advances deep learning has provided in speech and vision recognition."[55] However, applying a deep reinforcement learning approach to motor tasks in unstructured 3D environments has been far more challenging, since the task goes beyond the passive recognition of images and sounds. UC Berkeley's Trevor Darrell pointed out that "We still have a long way to go before our robots can learn to clean a house or sort laundry, but our initial results indicate that these kinds of deep learning techniques can have a transformative effect in terms of enabling robots to learn complex tasks entirely from scratch."[56] Based on Darrell's work and other researchers exploring the use of deep learning for robots, in the next 5–10 years, significant advances in robot learning capabilities may occur.[57] This observation coincides with my view that based on the law of accelerating returns, we are entering a time period in

---

[49]Amy Jiang, 2015, UC Berkeley Researchers Enable Robots to Learn Through Trial, Error, The Daily Californian, at: http://www.dailycal.org/2015/05/24/uc-berkeley-researchers-enable-robots-to-learn-through-trial-error/.

[50]Sarah Yang, 2015, New 'deep learning' technique enables robot mastery of skills via trial and error, at: deep-learning-robot-masters-skills-via-trial-and-error.

[51]*Id.*

[52]*Id.*

[53]*Id.*

[54]*Id.*

[55]*Id.*

[56]UC Berkeley Robot Learns By Trial and Error, 2015, Robot Magazine, at: http://www.botmag.com/uc-berkeley-robot-learns-by-trial-and-error/.

[57]Sarah Young, *Id.*, at note 50, discussing the work of Trevor Darrell.

which noticeable improvements will occur between one version of a robot and the next (similarly to cell phones). So before the public is fully aware, the age of artificially intelligent robots with human-like intelligence may be upon us.

I should add, the principal forms of intellectual property protection for artificially intelligent machines which use neural networks in the United States include patents, copyrights, trade secrets, and mask works (see next sections). As with previous forms of new technology, some aspects of neural networks and the software of an artificially intelligent brain transcend existing legal categories. This is primarily due to their dynamic nature, as well as the impossibility of predefining the trained state of the system. As a result, these aspects of neural network technology may be left with limited protection until Congress or the courts respond by customizing current laws to fit this technology, much as they have already done with computer software.

Brain Architecture

Generally, the architecture of a machine's brain in combination with software and algorithms will determine its ability to compute and therefore to exhibit intelligence. One of the factors driving increased intelligence in machines is Moore's law- however the physical limits possible by etching circuits on a silicon chip is beginning to be reached, so will Moore's law run its course, and will the day of exponential growth for computing resources be over? I don't think so, there are numerous techniques being investigated which if successful, will continue the exponential growth of computing resources. In fact, IBM is studying the use of fully integrated silicon chips using high-speed pulses of light to transmit information. This means the chip will be able to move data at rapid speeds and longer distances than current computing systems. Since the silicon photonic chip is wavelength-multiplexed, it can transmit multiple wavelengths of light thus increasing the bandwidth of information transmission compared to technology which exists today. This discussion highlights the fact that while the human brain is based on a particular architecture and a relatively slow transmission rate of signals, an artificially intelligent brain has the ability to dramatically change along with advances in technology. For this reason, I wonder whether a law of artificially intelligent brains will always lag behind technological developments? If so, our role as human legislators will continually be challenged and perhaps in the future an artificial intelligence will get involved in the rule making.

One of the most interesting technologies for computing being investigated now is quantum computing.[58] Instead of encoding information as either a zero or a one, as today's computers do, quantum computers will use quantum bits, or qubits,

---

[58]Elenor G. Rielfel and Wolfgang H. Polak, 2014, Quantum Computing: A Gentle Introduction, MIT Press.

whose states encode an entire range of possibilities by capitalizing on the quantum phenomena of superposition and entanglement. If quantum computers are successfully developed, computations that would take today's computers thousands of years to perform, would take only a few minutes; imagine if our artificially intelligent progeny had this capacity to think, imagine if we did. Another promising area of research for computing is being led by IBM and the Defense Advanced Research Projects Agency (DARPA) and is aimed at the development of cognitive-computing chips using new materials, such as gallium arsenide, carbon nanotubes, and graphene. In fact, an IBM-led research team has created a computer chip that is designed to mimic the brain's architecture. At the time of the writing, the "TrueNorth" chip is a 5.4 billion transistor chip with one million programmable neurons and 256 million synapses, but in contrast, remember, the brain has about 100 trillion synapses. However, in less than 20 years a neuromorphic chip may reach the brains level of complexity; further, the TrueNorth chip is currently 1,000 times as energy efficient as a conventional chip.[59]

For all the exponential advances in processing speed, materials, and manufacturing, digital computing today relies on an architecture rooted in the 1940s and with a well-known "bottleneck" between the processor and memory. Specifically, the von Nueman computer architecture is the standard platform of computing and includes three components: a CPU; a slow-to-access storage area, like a hard drive; and a secondary fast-access memory (RAM). A computer with a von Neumann computer architecture stores instructions as binary values (creating the stored program concept) and executes instructions sequentially—that is, the processor fetches instructions one at a time and processes them in sequence.[60] In terms of thinking and reasoning about the world, an artificially intelligent brain uses integrated circuits to perform calculations and to manipulate the symbols representing "computer thought;" this is done using circuits consisting of resisters, transistors, capacitors, etc.—all etched onto a tiny chip, and connected together to achieve a common goal. Integrated circuits come in all sorts: single-circuit logic gates, voltage regulators, motor controllers, microcontrollers, microprocessors, the list just goes on-and-on, but think of these components as features comprising the architecture of an artificially intelligent brain.

The von Neumann sequential method of information processing has limitations, not the least of which is that it fails to perform anywhere near the capability of the three pound brain setting on our shoulders (computers beat us with brute force computing not with eloquent massively parallel processing). But much research is being done to determine how the brain functions, to reverse engineer the brains neurocircuitry, to fabricate chips that perform like the human brain does, and to

---

[59]Dharmendra S. Modha, Introducing a Brain-inspired Computer, TrueNorth's neurons to revolutionize system architecture, (accessed 2015) at: http://www.research.ibm.com/articles/brain-chip.shtml.

[60]Irv Englander, 2004, The Architecture of Computer Hardware, Systems Software, & Networking: An Information Technology Approach, Wiley.

write the software and algorithms to mimic human thinking.[61] For example, neuromorphic computing, a concept developed by Carver Mead in the late 1980s, involves the use of very-large-scale integration (VLSI) systems containing circuits to mimic neuro-biological architectures present in the nervous system. Specifically, the VLSI systems are used to model perception, motor control, and multisensory integration.[62]

So, to summarize this brief discussion on the architecture of an artificially intelligent brain, integrated circuits form a main component of the architecture of the machines brain, and consist of billions of tiny inter-connecting electrical paths meticulously arranged onto a single piece of material, such as silicon. Designing an integrated circuit chip is not a simple feat, in fact, as chips become even smaller, issues such as hot spots, leakage etc., make an effective, power-efficient design extremely difficult to achieve.[63] Successful designs usually result from the enormous effort of highly qualified experts coupled with huge financial investments. However, copying each layer of an integrated circuit and preparing "pirated" integrated circuits can be done with comparatively little effort. According to Charl Goussard, "taking into account the enormous effort and cost to develop an integrated circuit design, the wide industrial applicability, the constant demand for improvement, and the ease at which such designs can be copied, it seems logical that some form of statutory protection should be afforded for the designers or owners of these designs."[64] But where do we find these rights? And of course, by now, you may be thinking as I do, that any laws which relate to the software, algorithms, and architecture of a computer, serves as precedence for a law of artificially intelligent brains.

Hardware Protection for Artificially Intelligent Brains

Over the past few decades during which software development has become more sophisticated, courts have pointed out the difference in purpose between copyright and patent laws for software. The broad protection for software as provided by patent law, must meet the standards of novelty and nonobviousness in order for a patent to be granted; the standards for copyright protection are originality and some level of creative expression. For software, the purpose of copyright is to protect particular expressions of an idea that are written in source code by a

---

[61]Ludmila, I. Kuncheva, 2014, Combining Pattern Classifiers: Methods and Algorithm, Wiley.

[62]See generally, Neuromorphic Computing, Wikipedia, at: https://en.wikipedia.org/wiki/Neuromorphic_engineering; NAIP PATENT BLOG, At: http://naipblog.blogspot.com/2009/08/brief-overview-of-ic-design-protection.html.

[63]Peter McCrorie, On-Chip Thermal Analysis Is Becoming Mandatory, at: http://chipdesignmag.com/display.php?articleId=2171.

[64]Charl Goussard, 2009, What is Integrated Circuit Design? at: http://naipblog.blogspot.com/2009/08/brief-overview-of-ic-design-protection.html.

programmer (which is then complied into object code), not the idea itself; an idea is the subject of patent law. Both copyright and patent law have a role to play in protecting software as intellectual property and thus contribute to a law of artificially intelligent brains.[65]

Patent law which protects ideas is clearly relevant for the components of an artificially intelligent brain, for example, circuits designed to model the properties of neurons have received patent protection. One example is a "silicon neuron" patent (U.S. patent 5648926 A) that describes an integrated circuit that is designed to emulate the functions of a biological neuron; many other patents have been awarded in this area. For software, the U.S. issues patents if the patent application describes the code in relation to computer hardware and related devices and limits the software to specific uses- this may include software that connects to and runs hardware components. This description of patent protection for software seems directly applicable to an artificially intelligent brain as the software running the brain is used to control the effectors and actuators of the machine.

As noted earlier in this chapter, of particular importance to our cyborg future is that copyright also extends to programs etched on chips. Once chips are fabricated, they are plugged into the computer and become part of the computer's brain architecture. This means that a computer's brain has rights under copyright law that is not afforded human brains which of course consist of billions of neurons. Generally utilitarian objects are not the subject of copyright protection and chips are clearly utilitarian, but as stated earlier in this chapter, in a case dealing with software the *Franklin* Court rejected the argument that software encoded on chips was to be considered "utilitarian" and thus not copyright protected noting the medium on which the program is encoded should not determine whether the program itself is protected under copyright.

To provide the legal protection for the architecture of an artificially intelligent brain, we could look to rights under patent law to grant a limited monopoly to the designer of the different hardware components comprising the artificially intelligent brain. For example, with integrated circuits, provided that their design displays satisfactory inventiveness and meets the required standard of uniqueness, patent protection is an option for the protection of the intellectual property rights embodied in an integrated circuit design. However, the lion's share of integrated circuit designs is considered obvious under most patent systems given that they typically lack any improvement (inventive step) over their predecessors (prior art).[66] Further, integrated circuits are comprised of numerous building blocks, each "building block could potentially be patentable. However, since an integrated circuit contains hundreds or thousands of semiconductor devices, a patent claim to an integrated circuit would have to cover hundreds or thousands of individual elements- this would be like trying to write a patent on the neuronal circuits in the

---

[65]Copyright v. Patent: A Primer on Copyright and Patent Protection for Software, at: http://www.law.washington.edu/lta/swp/law/copyvpatent.html.

[66]*Id.*, note 62, NAIP PATENT BLOG.

brain.[67] Consequently, a patent claim that attempts to describe an entire integrated circuit may be hundreds of pages long. Clearly, such a narrow claim would provide almost no protection, and especially for an artificially intelligent brain consisting of billons of circuits.

Even if one sought such narrow protection, writing a patent application supporting a claim with thousands of elements would be extremely tedious and expensive.[68] As indicated by Rajkumar Dubey, writing for *Mondaq*, "Obviously, integrated circuits are not easily describable in a patent specification or the claims. Also, it may take several years to obtain an integrated circuit patent from most patent offices worldwide. This is unacceptable given that an integrated circuit's useful commercial life may be less than 1 year."[69] What if the same principle of obsolescence applied to the human brain such that every 1–2 years a person had to apply for patent protection of the neuronal circuitry of their brain? Or imagine that in the coming cyborg age the human brain is equipped with neuroprosthesis with billions of integrated circuits. That is, imagine the human brain becoming obsolete every 2 years or so due to the necessity of having to integrate (or update) new technology within the brain. The cumbersome, time-consuming nature of patent filing combined with extremely narrow protection would make patent law an insufficient form of protection for the brains neuroprosthetic devices and therefore the brain of an artificially intelligent machine.

Other forms of protection for intellectual property are also inapplicable to the integrated circuit layouts, which, will represent a major component of an artificially intelligent brain. Design patents protect the ornamental, but not the functional aspects of an article of manufacture described in its drawings. Since an integrated circuit layout is more functional than ornamental, design patent protection is generally inapplicable to integrated circuits. Finally, in many cases trade secret law cannot be used to protect most integrated circuits because an integrated circuit layout may be reverse-engineered. But what if an artificially intelligent brain is writing its own programs which are stored internally on its integrated circuits, and what if the programs have commercial value (that is, are trade secrets)? Once a program is stored on a tangible medium of expression it may still remain a trade secret but once communicated to the public trade secret protection is lost. However, since an artificially intelligent brain communicates in object code, and keeps the source code "locked in its mind," it is simultaneously possible to maintain both trade secret and copyright protection for the program. Here I should point out that the reverse engineering of the human brain is one of the main techniques that some researchers are using to try to create an artificially intelligent brain.

Rajkumar Dubey writing about integrated circuits has commented that "The layout of transistors on the semiconductor integrated circuit, or topography of

---

[67]*Id.*, note 62.

[68]*Id.*, note 62.

[69]Rajkumar Dubey, Semiconductor Integrated Circuits Layout Design in Indian IP Regime, 2004, at: http://www.mondaq.com/india/x/28601/technology/Semiconductor+Integrated+Circuits+Layout+Design+In+Indian+IP+Regime.

transistors on the integrated circuit, determines the size of the integrated circuit as well as its processing power."[70] He states "That is why the layout design of transistors constitutes such an important and unique form of intellectual property fundamentally different from other forms of intellectual property like copyrights, trademarks, patents and industrial designs" and therefore in my view is of interest to a law of artificially intelligent brains.[71] Given that patent, copyright, and trade secret law cannot adequately protect integrated circuit design, an exclusive protection for semiconductor integrated circuits layout-design has become necessary to the semiconductor industry. This level of protection represents a body of law that has significance for our cyborg future. So what protection may be available for the hardware of an artificially intelligent brain? In 1984 the U.S. passed the *Semiconductor Chip Protection Act* which provides statutory protection for integrated circuit design rights.[72] Although codified under the same title as Copyrights, the Act is clearly intended to provide integrated circuit designs with *sui generis* ("of its own kind") rights. It has some aspects of copyright law, some aspects of patent law, and in some ways it is completely different from either.

Providing legal protection for the physical components comprising the architecture of an artificially intelligent brain will also form a part of an emerging law of cyborgs, and is similar to the idea of protecting "bodily integrity" for humans.[73] Semiconductor chips are massed produced from multi-layered three-dimensional templates that are called "chip masks" in the trade, and "mask works" under the Act. The main purpose of the *Semiconductor Chip Protection Act* is to prohibit "chip piracy"–the unauthorized copying and distribution of semiconductor chip products copied from the original creators of such works. But the Act could also provide protection for the architecture of an artificially intelligent brain given that it is constructed with integrated circuits.

According to the Act, just like with copyright, integrated circuit design rights exist when they are created; this is unlike patents which confer rights after application, examination, and issuance of the patent. However, the exclusive rights afforded to the owners of integrated circuit designs are more restricted than those afforded to both copyright and patent holders. Modification (derivative works), for example, is not an exclusive right for owners of integrated circuit designs (this has implications for mind uploads, see Chap. 7: *The Law of Looks and Artificial Bodies*). Furthermore, the exclusive right granted to a patentee to "use" an invention, cannot be used to exclude an independently produced identical integrated circuit design.[74] Thus, reproduction for reverse engineering of an integrated circuit design is specifically permitted by most jurisdictions.

---

[70]*Id.*

[71]*Id.*

[72]Semiconductor Chip Protection Act, 17 U.S.C. §§ 901–914.

[73]Gowri Ramachandran, 2009, *Against the Right to Bodily Integrity: Of Cyborgs and Human Rights*, 87 Denver University Law Review, No. 1, p1.

[74]*Id.*, notes 64, 69.

Given the importance of protecting integrated circuits from piracy, several nations, including Japan and the European Community have followed the example set in the U.S. and endorsed their own similar statutes/directives recognizing and protecting integrated circuit designs (also referred to as the "topography of semiconductor chips"). And in 1989, a Diplomatic Conference among various nations was held, at which the *Treaty on Intellectual Property in Respect of Integrated Circuits* (IPIC Treaty) was adopted internationally.[75] This treaty has been partially incorporated into the TRIPS agreement of the World Trade Organization (WTO).[76] I believe that the potential threat that artificial intelligence could pose to humanity is serious enough, that just as with the semiconductor industry, international law should be crafted to create a common response to the potential threat that artificial intelligence could pose to society.

Further, other issues of law dealing with computer chips are also applicable to an artificially intelligent brain. For example, an important consideration for protecting the brain of an artificially intelligent machine concerns its memories and how they are stored and loaded to different devices. Memory chips such as an EPROM chip (erasable programmable read only memory), are chips that retains its data when its power supply is switched off. EPROM chip topographies are protectable under the *Semiconductor Chip Protection Act*, but such protection does not extend to the information stored on the chips, such as computer programs.[77] Such information is protected, to the extent that it is, by copyright law applicable to software which was discussed earlier.[78] Interestingly, the Court of Appeals for the Ninth Circuit in *MAI Systems Corp. v. Peak Computer, Inc.*, held that loading software into a computer's random access memory (RAM) created a "copy'" and a potentially infringing "reproduction" under the Copyright Act.[79] What that holding meant is that even if no hardcopy was made, temporally storing a program in RAM was a reproduction and potentially infringing act. So turning on a computer constitutes a reproduction of the operating systems programs because they are automatically stored in RAM whenever the computer is activated, or for that matter whenever a file is transferred from one computer network user to another. The *MAI* court held that the program temporarily stored in RAM represents a reproduction, although the U.S. Congress subsequently enacted an amendment to the Copyright Act to specifically carve out exceptions to this court decision in several circumstances.[80]

---

[75]TRIPS-The areas of intellectual property that it covers are: copyright and related rights (i.e. the rights of performers, producers of sound recordings and broadcasting organizations); trademarks including service marks; geographical indications\ including appellations of origin; industrial design; patents including the protection of new varieties of plants; the layout-designs of integrated circuits; and undisclosed information including trade secrets and test data.

[76]Overview: the TRIPS Agreement, World Trade organization, at: https://www.wto.org/english/tratop_e/trips_e/intel2_e.htm.

[77]Semiconductor Chip Protection Act of 1984, Wikipedia, at: https://en.wikipedia.org/wiki/Semiconductor_Chip_Protection_Act_of_1984.

[78]See generally, *id*.

[79]*MAI Systems Corp. v. Peak Computer, Inc.*, 991 F.2d 511 (9th Cir. 1993).

[80]See, 17 U.S. Code § 117—Limitations on exclusive rights: Computer programs.

Our Competition Against Better Brains

Based on the above discussion, if artificially intelligent brains continue to get faster under Moore's law, and their brain architecture more sophisticated, there might conceivably come a point-in-time when artificial intelligence is capable of performance comparable to that of human intelligence. From that point on, artificially intelligent computers would not stop the process of getting smarter, but instead would accelerate the process of acquiring knowledge and connecting to the world through the Internet. In fact, in the last several decades the steady trend has been for computers to get faster, have greater memory capacity, and be networked to each other and to the emerging *Internet of Things*. And while not increasing exponentially (according to some authors), developments in artificial intelligence and knowledge in brain science is still rapidly increasing. Therefore, I believe it is just a matter of time before artificially intelligent machines claim to be self-aware and argue for rights. Based on that observation, the more we develop laws and policies which relate to the functioning, software, algorithms, and architecture of an artificially intelligent brain, the more we may be able to control our own destiny and shape the future as we approach the Singularity. Ray Kurzweil has convincingly made the point that once human levels of artificial intelligence is reached, artificially intelligent brains will then keep developing based on exponentially improving technologies until they are far more intelligent and capable than humans.[81] The rate of development of artificially intelligent machines in terms of physical design will also show improvement because they will take change of their own development from their slower-thinking and less intelligent human creators. That is, when the Singularity is reached, and then surpassed, it is thought that artificial intelligence will work incredibly quickly at improving itself. What will a law of artificially intelligent brains be then?

According to James Barrat, after the Singularity, it's impossible to predict with certainty the behavior of these smarter-than-human intelligences with whom we might one day share the planet or that we might one day merge with (through a steady process, not all at once like a step function).[82] But by merging with artificially intelligent machines, we may become super-intelligent cyborgs (or some other to-be-determined entity), using computers to extend our intellectual abilities (see Chap. 7 on *The Law of Looks and Artificial Bodies*). If we don't merge with the technology we are creating, and remain the biological product of evolution, maybe artificial intelligence will be benevolent and help us treat the effects of old age, prolong our life spans, and "fix" poverty and other forms of human suffering. But, in contrast, maybe artificially intelligent machines will turn on humanity and attempt to exterminate us or to control us in undesirable ways. But if we do merge with our artificially intelligent progeny we may avoid extinction and we may begin

---

[81]Ray Kurzweil, *supra*, note 27.

[82]James Barat, 2015, Our Final Invention: Artificial Intelligence and the End of the Human, St. Martin's Griffin.

the process that will transform our species into something that is no longer recognizable as such to humanity.[83] This transformation has a name: Posthumanism and is a development discussed throughout this book. Of course many oppose the idea that humanity could someday transform into something "new"; and for those strongly opposed to the Singularity, now is the time to mount opposition. Clearly, artificial intelligence as it exists today doesn't produce the kind of intelligence we associate with humans and clearly we are still human and not machine entities.[84] However, after we are more-and-more enhanced with cybernetic technology we will blur the line between human and machine, and as we move towards late century or early next century, we may have completely transformed to become the technology.

The artificial intelligence of today tends to be able to master only one highly specific domain, like interpreting search queries or playing chess. They typically operate within an extremely specific frame of reference and lack common sense. They're intelligent, but only if you define intelligence in a narrow and limited way. The kind of intelligence Ray Kurzweil is talking about when he describes future artificially intelligent beings, which is called strong artificial intelligence doesn't exist yet. Why not? Obviously we're still waiting for the exponentially growing computing power made possible by Moore's law to be combined with advances in algorithms, knowledge learned from neuroscience about the circuits of the brain, and improving architectures of artificially intelligent brains. But as Lev Grossman writing in Time magazine states- "it's also possible that there are things going on in our brains that can't be duplicated electronically no matter how many MIPS we throw at them."[85] Grossman further says that "the neurochemical architecture that generates the ephemeral chaos we know as human consciousness may just be too complex and analog to replicate in digital silicon."[86] Further, the biologist Dennis Bray is a voice of caution about the desirability of the cyborg future stating- "Although biological components act in ways that are comparable to those in electronic circuits," he argued, in a talk titled *What Cells Can Do That Robots Can't,* "they are set apart by the huge number of different states they can adopt."[87] Multiple biochemical processes create chemical modifications of protein molecules, further diversified by association with distinct structures at defined locations of a cell.[88] Bray points out that the "resulting combinatorial explosion of states endows living systems with an almost infinite capacity to store information

---

[83]Lev Grossman, 2011, 2045: The Year Man Becomes Immortal, quoting Ray Kurweil, at: http://content.time.com/time/magazine/article/0,9171,2048299-4,00.html.

[84]*Id.*

[85]*Id.*

[86]Miguel Nicholelis, *id.*, note 6.

[87]Dennis Bray, What Cells Can Do that Robots Can't, Youtube video, at: https://vimeo.com/18143991.

[88]*Id.*

regarding past and present conditions and a unique capacity to prepare for future events."[89] The complexity of biology makes the binary language that computers use to manipulate data look crude and it remains to be seen whether digital technology can simulate a brain.

As Grossman notes "Kurzweil admits that there's a fundamental level of risk associated with the Singularity that's impossible to refine away, simply because we don't know what a highly advanced artificial intelligence, finding itself a newly created inhabitant of the planet Earth, would choose to do."[90] It might feel like competing with us for resources, then again, it might not, but if it does eventually we will lose. If the Singularity is coming, these questions will have to be addressed whether we like it or not, and Kurzweil thinks that trying to put off the Singularity by banning technologies is not only impossible but also unethical and probably dangerous for humanity.[91] Kurzweil argues that "It would require a totalitarian system to implement such a ban,"[92] continuing, he states "It wouldn't work. It would just drive these technologies underground, where the responsible scientists who we're counting on to create the defenses would not have easy access to the tools."[93]

Kurzweil does not see any fundamental difference between flesh and silicon that would prevent the latter from human-like thinking. However, the law does distinguish between neurons and integrated circuits; primarily because one can own circuits, but not another person's neurons. Kurzweil defies biologists to come up with a neurological mechanism that could not be modeled or at least matched in power and flexibility by software running on a computer.[94] If Kurzweil is correct, an artificially intelligent entity arguing for rights is an eventuality, therefore humanity would be wise to establish a regulatory scheme to protect humanity and to ensure all intelligent beings that emerge to join society have basic rights.

To summarize, artificially intelligent brains are improving rapidly based on exponentially accelerating technologies. They may match humans in general intelligence by midcentury, therefore the emerging law of cyborgs, and particularly the laws discussed in this chapter which relate to an artificially intelligent brain, could provide important protections not only for the future rights of artificially intelligent beings, but of humans either merging with them, or living amongst them as less intelligent beings relying on their sense of fairness to treat humanity with respect and justice.

---

[89]*Id.*

[90]Lev Grossman, *id.*, note 83.

[91]Lev Grossman, *id.,* note 83.

[92]Lev Grossman, *id.*, note 83, quoting Ray Kurzweil.

[93]Lev Grossman, *id.*, note 83, quoting Ray Kurzweil.

[94]Singularitarianism, posted by PZ Meyers, 2011, quoting Ray Kurzweil, at: http://scienceblogs.com/pharyngula/2011/02/13/singularitarianism/.

Chapter 4
Cognitive Liberty, Brain Implants, and Neuroprosthesis

Introduction

In previous chapters, I described several technologies that are leading humanity closer to a merger with artificially intelligent machines. Perhaps the two most critical technologies necessary to create a human-machine merger are artificial intelligence (discussed in Chap. 3, *The Law of Artificial Intelligent Brains*); and the development of brain implants that function as neuroprosthesis. As we move towards a cyborg future consisting of information technologies integrated into our bodies and mind, we are becoming more vulnerable to government supervision, privacy invasions, and the possibility of third party access to our internal thoughts and memories. With more technology being integrated into the human body, the legal divisions between man and machine is beginning to blur and is becoming arbitrary. This brings up a host of legal and policy issues ripe for the twenty-first century. For example, lawyers Benjamin Wittes and Jane Chong describe a woman equipped with a heart pacer—technology clearly integrated within her body—but she has no rights to the data on the functioning of her heart which is produced by the implant.[1] Based on this example and others presented throughout this book, numerous jurisdictions are beginning to recognize that the law must change to accommodate the integration of technology into the human body. This observation is even more relevant with the development of neuroprosthesis that have the capacity to restore or enhance cognitive functions.

With technologies to study the brain improving exponentially, and given remarkable advances in neuroscience, researchers are unlocking the mysteries of how the brain computes, and writing algorithms to model the functioning of the

---

[1]Benjamin Wittes and Jane Chong, 2014, Brookings Report, We Are All Cyborgs Now, at: http://www.brookings.edu/blogs/techtank/posts/2014/10/8-we-are-all-cyborgs.

© Springer International Publishing Switzerland 2015
W. Barfield, *Cyber-Humans*, DOI 10.1007/978-3-319-25050-2_4

brain's neural circuits. As a result, the capabilities of neuroprosthesis are improving dramatically; in fact, by midcentury, "able bodied" people may opt to receive neuroprosthetic devices for reasons other than for a medical necessity. However, once technology is implanted in the brain (read on, it's happening now), governments, corporations, and other third parties could remotely access the implants creating a cybersecurity nightmare not the least of which would be a serious threat to the person's "cognitive liberty". This chapter discusses how third party access to neuroprosthetic devices will impact a person's ability to exercise control over the content of their mind, including the memory of their lived experiences, and thus raises significant questions of law and policy for the coming cyborg age.

Based on the use of brain implants to treat illness such as Parkinson's disease, dystonia, chronic pain, and depression, the first generation of cyborgs are beginning to emerge. This generation of cyborgs, equipped with neuroprosthetic devices, are benefiting from remarkable progress in the treatment of neurological disease. For example, for cognitively intact patients locked-in their bodies, technology to "read their brain" is allowing them to communicate to loved ones by moving a cursor on a computer screen, and to experience mobility by using thought to control the motion of a robot's arm or prosthetic limb. But the first generation of cyborgs, while equipped with amazing technology implanted within their brain, will pale in comparison to the capabilities of future cyborgs. That is, within decades, neuroprosthetic devices will improve significantly, giving people the ability to augment and enhance the functions of their brain and the ability to edit the content of their memories. Clearly, cyborg technologies are improving exponentially, and an amazing human-machine future awaits us all.

An important observation about the use of cyborg technologies for the brain is that the nature of information processing is beginning to shift from a neuronal based system using the relatively slow transmission rates associated with electrochemical signals (10–120 m/s over myelinated neurons), to a digital-based architecture operating with orders-of-magnitude greater processing speed and storage capacity. However, one consequence of equipping people with brain implant technology is the ease in which third parties will be able to manipulate, edit, and change a person's mental functions, including the information stored in their memories. Clearly, by making the content of our mind available to a host of third parties, neuroprosthetic devices being used now, or which should be available by the time of the Singularity (as predicted by computer scientist Ben Goertzeil and Google's Ray Kurzweil), have the potential to dramatically alter our relation to governments and corporations—these possibilities alone raise important issues of law and policy that should be addressed sooner rather than later while humanity still has time to control the direction of our cyborg future.[2]

Based on the law of accelerating returns, around mid-century, a major paradigm shift in information technology will have occurred. A cyborg equipped with

---

[2]Ben Goertzel on Singularity 1 on 1: The Future Is Ours To Create, 2010, Youtube video at: https://www.singularityweblog.com/ben-goertzel-on-singularity-1-on-1/.

neuroprosthetic devices will be able to download information to implants within his or her brain and to sensors on or within its body. This fusion of mind with information technologies will allow cyborgs to become fluent in new languages, process information faster and more efficiently than those lacking cyborg technologies, store and share memories between minds; and with continuing improvements, communicate telepathically with other cyborgs and artificially intelligent machines. However, as technologies to augment the cognitive functions of the brain and record and edit memories mature, ethicists, lawyers, and scientists have begun to raise questions of how emerging neuroprosthetic devices might be practically used and what policies might govern their use. On this point, the use of neuroprosthetic devices for deception detection, neuromarketing, and editing memories, will have major legal and policy implications not only for an emerging body of cyborg law, but also for the cognitive liberty of the mind, and therefore will warrant significant public debate and legislative attention.

While cyborg technologies integrated into the brain may seem like the subject of a science fiction novel (and have been the subject of sci-fi novels!) they are quickly joining the information technology revolution characterized by exponential growth. Peter Diamandis and Steven Kotler in their co-authored book, *Abundance: the Future is Better than You Think,* describe the characteristics of exponentially increasing technologies.[3] These are technologies that represent the information revolution, and are based on the miniaturization of electronics and advances in digital technology; both of which are necessary for rapid improvements in neuroprosthesis. For the reader interested in the technical aspects of the cybernetic revolution, a primer for neuroprosthetic devices can be found in Theodore Berger and Dennis Glanzman's co-edited book, *"Toward Replacement Parts for the Brain: Implantable Biomimetic Electronics as Neural Prostheses."* But here's the take-home message—the future is approaching rapidly, we will all be cyborgs, and we will enhance our brains with neuroprosthesis, it's just a matter of time.

Medical Necessity and Beyond

As discussed throughout this book, the main reason that people are opting for and receiving neuroprosthetic and other implants is due to medical necessity. However, I expect this rationale to change as we approach midcentury and people decide to replace or enhance cognitive functions with brain implants providing superior information processing capabilities to those unenhanced. A few examples of the use of implants for medical necessity include the treatment of Parkinson's patients,

---

[3]Peter Diamandis and Steven Kotler, 2014, Abundance: The Future Is Better Than You Think, Free Press; Peter Diamandis and Steven Kotler, 2015, Bold: How to Go Big, Create Wealth and Impact the World, Simon & Schuster.

assisting people suffering from depression, and the repair of damaged senses. For mental illness, by using devices implanted in a person's brain, scientists are targeting and correcting malfunctioning neural circuits to treat conditions such as clinical depression, addiction and anxiety disorders. However, the reader may be wondering why people not suffering from illness would replace normally functioning tissue with a prosthesis; that is, why would someone become a cyborg if not for medical necessity? Several of the reasons are discussed in the chapter on *Modifying, Enhancing, and Hacking the Body*, but from a "large-picture" perspective, a central reason relates to the survivability of our species when we are more directly in competition with strong artificial intelligence.

As I discussed in previous chapters, as the technical Singularity approaches, without enhancing our brain using neuroprosthetic implants, humanity will be left behind by artificially intelligent machines possessing faster processing speeds, greater memory, greater access to information, and vastly superior reasoning skills. In fact, Hans Moravec, robotics expert and author of *Robot: Mere Machine to Transcendent Mind* and *Mind Children: The Future of Robot and Human Intelligence*, has argued that the way to keep up with cyborg technology is by accelerating our own evolution.[4] 'We can change ourselves,' he says, 'and we can also build new children who are properly suited for the new conditions- robot children.' Thus, a major paradigm shift in information technology will occur this century—taking the form of human evolution moving from biology to principles based on technology. An interesting result being that "able bodied" people will use neuroprosthetic devices to enhance their senses, memory, and cognitive abilities to levels beyond normal, and will do so as part of the future human-machine merger awaiting humanity.

People often fail to recognize that progress in information technologies is exponential, and thus the reader may be surprised to learn that the number of people already equipped with neuroprosthetic devices is in the hundreds-of-thousands, and soon will be in the millions. Already, more than 25,000 Parkinson's patients have received a "deep-brain" implant (placed either in the Thalamus, Globus Pallidus, or Subthalmic nucleus), which functions like a pacemaker to reduce tremors and other movement problems. In addition, because the visual and auditory modalities are critical for functioning in the world, there has been intense interest from the scientific community to design neuroprosthetic devices to alleviate problems involving our senses. For example, to aid those with visual deficiencies, cyborg technology in the form of a retinal prosthesis, is being used to detect light coming into the eye via electrodes implanted underneath the patient's retina. The light energy is fed to a microchip that transduces the signals; which are sent to the brain for further processing. Neuroprosthetic devices are also creating a generation of cyborgs equipped with cochlear implants. According to the Food

---

[4]Hans Moravec, 2000, Robot: Mere Machine to Transcendent Mind, Oxford University Press; Hans Moravec, 1990, Mind Children: The Future of Robot and Human Intelligence, Harvard University Press.

and Drug Administration (FDA), several hundred thousand people worldwide have already received cochlear implants to improve their hearing. The cochlear implant consists of an external portion that sits behind the ear and a second "cyborg" portion that is surgically placed under the skin. Signals generated by the implant are sent by way of the auditory nerve to the brain which recognizes the signals as sound. In the U.S. alone, tens-of-thousands of adults have received cochlear implants. And since 2,000, cochlear implants have been FDA-approved for use in eligible children beginning at 12 months of age—creating the first generation of cyborgs raised from early childhood. With at least nine doublings of computing power before these young cyborgs bear children, one has to wonder what capabilities future generations of cyborgs will possess.

Sometimes to know where technology is headed, one needs to follow the money; this is especially true for cyborg technology. On this point, the European Union has committed to spend $1.3 billion to study how the brain functions, and in the U.S., the Human Brain Project has received $1 billion for basic research on brain science. I should point out that both of these initiatives will provide critical information about the structure of neuronal circuits necessary to reverse engineer the brain (one way to create artificial general intelligence). Further, the combined $2.3 billion in funding for neuroscience research just mentioned, is not the complete funding picture. For example, in the U.S., the Defense Advanced Research Projects Agency (DARPA) has been one of the major government agencies funding research to develop brain chips and other technologies to interface the brain to computers. On this point, DARPA is currently working with different groups of researchers to develop a neuronal prosthetic implant that can be used to treat severe memory loss in human patients. The project is part of DARPA's Restoring Active Memory (RAM) program, aimed to help reinstate normal memory activity for the U.S. war veterans who have suffered some kind of brain injury.[5] If successful, the program will be immensely beneficial for patients with schizophrenia, amnesia, dementia and other brain disorders. In another DARPA project, the goal is to put "chips in the brain" to enhance the cognitive and the sensory capability of soldiers. The defense agency is specifically seeking to develop a portable, wireless device that "…must incorporate implantable probes" to record and stimulate brain activity—in effect, a memory triggering 'black box' device.[6] The implantable probe would consist of wires inside the brain, and under the scalp, with the capability to send electrical impulses through a transmitter placed under the skin of the chest area. The aim of the project is to develop technology that "promises to directly read thoughts from a living brain—and even instill thoughts as well…"[7] If successful, the technology developed by DARPA's RAM projects, will help create

---

[5]Eliza Strickland, 2014, DARPA Project Starts Building Human Memory Prosthetics, at: http://spectrum.ieee.org/biomedical/bionics/darpa-project-starts-building-human-memory-prosthetics, and http://www.unwittingvictim.com/BostonGlobe.html.

[6]*Id.*

[7]*Id.*

technology necessary for a future cyborg world, making the coming human-machine merger more likely.

If we consider medical necessity as a motivating factor to design neuroprosthetic devices, one of the most promising areas of brain neurotechnology is the treatment of Alzheimer's disease. Professor Theodore Berger and his research team at the University of Southern California has made remarkable progress towards developing an artificial hippocampus, a structure of the brain which plays important roles in the consolidation of information from short-term memory to long-term memory and that also contributes to spatial navigation.[8] Alzheimer's disease is known to damage the hippocampus and affects about 5.2 million people in the U.S. alone. Thus creating an artificial hippocampus may help millions suffering from a serious and debilitating neurological disease; but to restate a point made throughout this book, cyborg technologies designed to assist people based on medical necessity may also have the effect, intended or not, of contributing to our cyborg future and eventual merger with machines.

Professor Berger's research on the design of prosthesis supports this view. His work involves a detailed analysis of the various activities taking place in the hippocampus, followed by the development of algorithms that enable Berger and his team to replicate and integrate hippocampal function into a microchip. Of course, "chips in the brain" is an essential technology if humans are to become cyborgs and to merge with artificially intelligent machines. In fact, a breakthrough came in 2011 when Wake Forest University scientist Samuel Deadwyler, in collaboration with Professor Berger, managed to create the very first memory prosthetic device that proved to be successful in improving memory retention capacity in rats.[9] The resultant device was in the form of a microchip implant, consisting of thirty-two electrodes and an algorithm that could decode and reproduce the neural signals sent from one end of the hippocampus to the other. Later, the scientists were able to produce an artificial hippocampus that could not only read the information collected by the electrodes, but also repeat them when prompted to do so. Since then, the device has been successfully tested in non-human primates, such as monkeys, and human testing is around the corner.

---

[8]Berger, T.W., Baudry, M., Brinton, R.D., Liaw, J-S., Marmarelis, V.Z., Park, Y., Sheu, B.J., and Tanguay, Jr., A.R., 2001, Brain-implantable biomimetic electronics as the next era in neural prosthetics. Proceedings of the IEEE.

[9]See generally, Berger, T.W., Ahuja, A., Courellis, S.H., Deadwyler, S.A., Erinjippurath, G., Gerhardt, G.A., Gholmeih, G, Granacki, J.J., Hampson, R., Hsiao, M-C., LaCoss, J., Marmarelis, V.Z., Nasiatka, P., Srinivasan, V., Song, S., Tanguay, Jr., A.R., Wills, J., 2005, Hippocampal-cortical neural prostheses to restore lost cognitive function. IEEE EMBS Special Issue: Toward Biomimetic Microelectronics as Neural Prostheses, 24, 30–44.

Third-Party Access to Our Minds

The potential that brain implant technology could be hacked, raises the question of what rights people have to the veracity of the sensory information transmitted to their brain? If third parties were able to hack the technology of brain implants, the possibility of a dystopian future for humanity cannot be underestimated. For example, a retinal prosthesis could be hacked to place images on the back of the retina that a person never saw; or in the case of cochlear implants, sounds could be transmitted to the auditory nerve that a person never actually heard. Further, an artificial hippocampus could be hacked to place memories in a person's mind for events they never experienced. What law and policy might apply to these scenarios? If the First Amendment blocks the government from putting words in a person's mouth, surely it would also block the government from putting words, sounds, or memories in a person's head. Based on this observation, it is relevant to ask—if the technological ability to hack the mind is in the hands of governments and corporations will the mind remain a bastion of privacy, safe from the preying eyes of technology? Further, if the government or a corporation can access our thoughts and edit the content of our minds, will the integrity of our mind remain under our individual control, if not, who then as a person are we? The law and policy of such questions are discussed throughout this chapter.

Once third parties can access a neuroprosthetic device implanted within another person's brain, what could go wrong? Not surprisingly, lots of things. For example, if a person committed a crime, and did so because someone had remotely accessed their brain, would they be absolved of responsibility? Already lawyers routinely order scans of convicted defendant's brains and argue that a neurological impairment prevented the accused from controlling their actions. In the coming cyborg age would a software expert be called upon to examine the programming language and algorithms controlling a neuroprosthetic device to see if they had been tampered with? If so then the *mens rea* for a crime would have been supplied remotely by a third person. But the use of neuroprosthetic devices could lead to other important issues of law and policy. For example, third party access to brain implant technology could allow advertising agencies to place pop-up ads into our consciousness, or our thoughts to be searched by the government without our even knowing it. Could there be any more egregious violation of a person's privacy than if a government or corporation scanned a person's brain, recorded their unspoken thoughts, or changed the content of their memory?

If the brain is equipped with neuroprosthetic devices such that it essentially operates as a von Neumann computer, in the coming cyborg age should the mind be regarded as a network or as a computer, and should the mind receive an identifying URL? With future improvements in technology, just as spending spam to a cell phone or computer is actionable under the law; the possibility of sending spam to a mind equipped with a neuroprosthetic device would be far more annoying and therefore, should be the subject of even stricter laws. Just consider the work of Professor Theodore Berger, discussed above on the design of an artificial hippocampus, a device which could allow information to be sent directly to an implant within a person's brain. If a corporation could access the neuroprosthetic device, what would stop them from sending advertisements directly to a person's brain? Perhaps the regulations on cybersecurity for medical implants being considered by the FDA would provide appropriate protection. Alternatively, in the U.S. most states have already enacted laws that pertain, directly or indirectly, to spam email. These laws often parallel, and in some cases are directly connected to other state laws that address telemarketing practices, or commercial solicitation through other media (e.g. text messages). As the law of cyborgs develops, I believe that much of the former law in areas related to information technology and commercial email will serve as precedence for disputes involving cyborgs; the law related to spam email is an example.

Often legal scholars and practitioners tend to treat anti-spam law as part of a larger computer-related law. Canada's Anti-Spam Law can be seen as drawing these two strands together in an effort to create a comprehensive legal framework for internet-based commerce.[10] In the U.S. the CAN-SPAM Act (Controlling the Assault of Non-Solicited Pornography and Marketing) establishes the rules for commercial email and commercial messages.[11] The Act gives recipients the right to have a business stop emailing them, and outlines the penalties incurred for those who violate the law. Surely, a similar law should be enacted to protect a neuroprosthetic device from receiving unwanted commercial solicitation. It's one thing to walk by a display in a store and receive an ad designed specifically for the person based on facial recognition technology, it is quite another to have the ad pushed to a device implanted in the brain.[12] The CAN-SPAM Act covers all commercial messages, which the law defines as 'any electronic mail message whose primary purpose is the commercial advertisement or promotion of a commercial product or service,' including email that promotes content on commercial websites.[13] It does, however, exempt transactional and relationship messages; a deficiency which will need to be addressed once people are equipped with neuroprosthetic devices with wireless capability.

It is not currently possible to directly recover the visual or auditory information stored in a person's brain that results from perceiving the world. However, this could become a possibility with cyborg technology, because once equipped with a technology to sense the world, a cyborg will have an electronic record of what they view or hear. On this point, one argument Professor Steve Mann has proposed for the benefits of wearable computers is to provide a record of a person's life. In the context of cyborgs equipped with neuroprosthesis to sense the world, would

---

[10]Canada's Anti-Spam Legislation, accessed 2015, at: http://www.crtc.gc.ca/eng/casl-lcap.htm.

[11]*Id*, see also *infra* note 13.

[12]See generally, Woodrow Barfield, 2006, Commercial Speech, Intellectual Property Rights, and Advertising Using Virtual Images Inserted in TV, Film, and the Real World, UCLA Ent. Law Rev, Vol. 13, 154–186.

[13]CAN-SPAM Act, Pub. L. 108–187.

courts be able to subpoena the data stored on the prosthesis to use as evidence in court? This question implicates rights afforded by the U.S. constitution. If the mind is equipped with computing technology, the most basic Fourth Amendment question in computer cases asks whether an individual enjoys a reasonable expectation of privacy for electronic information stored within computers (or other electronic storage devices) under the individual's control. For example, do individuals have a reasonable expectation of privacy for the contents of their computers, and disk storage devices? If "yes," then the government ordinarily must obtain a warrant based on probable cause before it can access the information stored inside. Because individuals generally retain a reasonable expectation of privacy in the contents of closed containers, they also retain a reasonable expectation of privacy in data held within electronic storage devices. Would the same conclusion hold for cyborgs equipped with neuroprosthetic devices storing memories? And would it make a difference if the information was in the form of software or algorithms, and comprised part of the actual structure of the being?

The privacy of the mind, whether enhanced with technology or not, should receive the highest protection by the courts. Under *Katz. v. United States*, the test used by the Court to determine privacy rights when a government actor is involved is whether the person thought they should have a reasonable expectation of privacy, and whether the expectation of privacy was one society was prepared to recognize.[14] If confronted with the issue of determining whether a cyborg has a reasonable expectation of privacy in the information stored on a neuroprosthetic device, based on precedence, courts may analogize the neuroprosthetic device to that of a closed container such as a briefcase or file cabinet. The Fourth Amendment generally prohibits law enforcement from accessing and viewing information stored in a computer without a warrant if, in comparison, it would be prohibited from opening a closed container and examining its contents in the same situation. It seems reasonable to view files stored on a neuroprosthetic device in the context of a file cabinet, closed to the outside world, and that the Fourth Amendment would protect the content stored on a neuroprosthetic device. However, although courts have generally agreed that electronic storage devices can be analogized to closed containers, they have reached differing conclusions over whether each individual file stored on a computer or disk should be treated as a separate closed container. With this background, would an individual file stored on a computer be analogized to a file stored on a neuroprosthetic device? If so, if the government accessed the information, would the use of such information by the government be protected by the Fifth Amendment's prohibition against self-incrimination? As we will see later, Law Professor Nita Farahany of Duke University, has spoken extensively on this topic.

---

[14]*Katz v. U.S.*, 389 U.S. 347 (1967).

Concerns and Roadblocks

Some of the critics of enhancement technology, such as Stanford's Francis Fukuyama, have focused on the existential threat to humanity that may occur from implementing biotechnologies, such as genetic engineering. However, an existential threat to humanity could also result from developments in the field of bio-electronics: sensors, and brain implants that involve creating interfaces between neural systems and computers. As cyborgs become equipped with brain implant technology an important point to make is that even with the benefits that will result from neuroprosthesis, there are potential negative outcomes associated with brain implant technology which our future technological progeny must avoid. For example, as neuroprosthesis are improved and become a viable option for "able bodied" people, the number of people equipped with brain implants will increase dramatically. When this happens, an important concern is that a cognitive digital divide could exist between those enhanced with neuroprosthetic devices and those lacking such technologies. Through numerous laws and policies, society generally tries to address inequalities between people, but the cyborgization of people could work to exacerbate inequalities; therefore, now is the time to develop policies on cyborg equality, which give all people equal access to enhancement technologies.

Clearly, as the use of brain implant technology is used to enhance our senses, improve our memories, and help fight disease, important legal and policy issues related to the privacy of our thoughts and the integrity of our mind will be raised. For example, with continuing improvements in neuroprosthesis, the ability to hack the mind will become an important concern among legal theorists and technologists as well as for individuals equipped by cyborg technology. Just consider that former Vice President Dick Cheney was so concerned that terrorists might hack the medical device implanted near his heart that he disabled a function that allowed the defibrillator to be administered wirelessly. This revelation echoes concerns that researchers have raised for years about the vulnerability of implanted medical devices which are equipped with computerized functions and wireless capabilities that allow the devices to be administered without requiring additional surgery. The Chaney example also highlights the tradeoff between benefits and potential hazards that will come with the use of cyborg technologies to enhance the human body and mind. For example, as a positive, in the coming cyborg age the use of neuroprosthesis opens up the possibility that maladaptive circuits leading to mental illness can be permanently changed, essentially curing some patients of their psychiatric disorders. However, on the negative side, by reprogramming neuronal circuits, governments or corporations could edit the content of a person's mind—in this scenario the fundamental question of what constitutes reality would need to be debated by lawyers, ethicists, and the public.

Another concern about the use of cyborg technology for enhancement of human cognitive abilities is that brain implant technology could be used by governments and corporations to "seize" a person's private thoughts; and to download unwanted information directly to a storage device in a person's brain. This observation is a call for action—now is the time to think about protecting the right for individuals to control access to technologies of the mind, as well as the right to avoid their compelled use. For example, if governments could hack the mind, this capability would affect people's ability to participate in democratic institutions, as without accurate representations of life events, people would be unable to make independently informed choices. Because vastly improved neuroprosthetic devices are an extremely probable future technology, it is sensible to devise policies, regulations, and laws that will mitigate potential deleterious effects before the technology is widespread.

As the technology to access the mind matures, governments could punish a person not only for the actual expression of their thoughts, but just for formulating a thought contrary to government dogma. On this point, law scholar Jeffrey Rosen of George Washington University, wonders whether punishing someone for their thoughts rather than their actions, would be a violation of the Eight Amendments ban on cruel and unusual punishment?[15] This isn't an observation relevant only to the plot of a science fiction novel, because before centuries end, it will be technologically possible for governments and corporations to access brain-implants to edit the long-term memories representing a person's life experiences. Surely, using technology to access and edit a person's memory of an actual lived experience would be actionable under the law—a trespass, an assault and battery, or even extortion. On this last point, former Secret Service agent Marc Goodman worries that holding people's memory hostage could be a form of extortion in the future.[16] Therefore, for reasons of ensuring freedom of the mind, in the coming cyborg age, it is imperative that the human body and mind be considered sacrosanct; to invade a person's mind without their consent should be an egregious human rights crime and punishable under criminal law statutes.

Stanford Law School's Henry Greely acknowledges that memory-retrieval technologies could pose a serious challenge to our freedom of thought, which in his view, is currently defended largely by the First Amendment protections for freedom of expression. According to Greely, "… freedom of thought has always been buttressed by the reality that you could only tell what someone thought based on their behavior."[17] In light of advances in brain recording technology Greely commented, "This technology holds out the possibility of looking through the skull and seeing what's really happening, seeing the thoughts themselves."[18] Greely argues that this possibility may challenge the principle that we should be held

---

[15]Jeffrey Rosen, 2007, The Brain on the Stand, New York Times, at: http://www.nytimes.com/2007/03/11/magazine/11Neurolaw.t.html?pagewanted=all&_r=0.

[16]Marc Goodman, 2015, Future Crimes: Everything Is Connected, Everyone Is Vulnerable and What We Can Do About It, Doubleday.

[17]Jeffrey Rosen, *Id.*, note 15, discussing comments by Stanford's Henry Greely on neurolaw.

[18]Jeffrey Rosen, *Id.*, note 15, discussing comments by Stanford's Henry Greely.

accountable for what we do, not what we think. And he adds, "It opens up for the first time the possibility of punishing people for their thoughts rather than their actions."[19] Discussing the possibility of a future totalitarian state, Greely commented, "One reason thought has been free in the harshest dictatorships is that dictators haven't been able to detect it."[20] And that now they may be able to, this is putting greater pressure on legal constraints against government interference with freedom of thought.

While ensuring cognitive liberty will be an important issue in the coming cyborg age, other technology currently being used has already brought the issue of cognitive liberty to the attention of the U.S. Supreme Court. For example, in a First Amendment case that dealt with a statute prohibiting the sale of books without a license, Supreme Court Justice Frank Murphy stated that freedom to think "is absolute of its own nature; the most tyrannical government is powerless to control the inward workings of the mind."[21] Recent support for the proposition that governments should be prohibited from efforts to control the inner working of the mind comes from Law Professor Marc Blitz who argues that it would be a grave infringement of "...free thought any state measure which prevented us from using our brains to access and store our memories."[22] Professor Blitz also observed that before the development of cyborg technologies, the government could not do much to restrict the freedom of thought except to attack the expression of that thought in speech and worship. That is, Blitz indicated that "the government could not manipulate our minds from the inside, its only way of restricting mental activity was to target communication or other expression that embodied such activity."[23] But as shown in this chapter, based on the law of accelerating returns for information technologies, much has changed, technology that could allow the government to manipulate our minds from the "inside" is not only rapidly being developed but also currently being used to treat psychological and neurological illness.

A Focus on Cognitive Liberty

Considering that a variety of brain-computer interfaces and neuroprosthetic devices are being used to treat patients, and that brain implant technology will be dramatically improved within a few decades, necessitates a serious discussion of

---

[19]Jeffrey Rosen, *Id.*, note 15, discussing comments by Stanford's Henry Greely.

[20]*Id.*

[21]See *Jones v. Opelika*, 316 U.S. 584, 1942, (Murphy, J. dissenting), noting that while "freedom to think is absolute of its own nature," the government may target it by targeting "freedom to communicate the minds message to others by speech and writing".

[22]Marc Blitz, Freedom of Thought for the Extended Mind: Cognitive Enhancements and the Constitution, Wisconsin Law Review, 2010, 1049–1118, see p. 1075.

[23]*Id*, see generally, *Jones v. Opelika*, *id.*, note 21.

"cognitive liberty." Essentially, cognitive liberty is the personal freedom to have sovereignty over one's own mind; it is an extension of the concepts of freedom of thought, and to a lesser extent, bodily integrity. As a basic observation, freedom of thought can be distinguished from cognitive liberty in that the former is concerned with protecting an individual's freedom to think "*whatever*" they want, whereas cognitive liberty is concerned with protecting an individual's freedom to think "*however*" they want.[24] This last aspect of freedom to think directly relates to the use of neuroprosthetic devices designed to enhance cognitive processes. As legal precedence for protection of cognitive liberty, the U.S. Supreme Court has previously held that freedom of the mind is "the broad concept" of which freedom of speech is but one "component."[25] Reflecting the importance of freedom of thought for cyborg technologies, Law Professor Marc Blitz, commented that the Supreme Court has placed freedom of thought at the center of our First Amendment American jurisprudence saying that our whole constitutional heritage "rebels at giving the government the power to control men's minds."[26]

A range of computer scientists, neuroscientists, and legal scholars have questioned the desirability of pursuing technology that may allow the mind to be hacked, and have argued that the "cognitive liberty" of the mind should receive the strongest protection possible by government legislation. With exponentially improving technology to manipulate and study the mind, what is at stake for humanity given that governments, corporations, and third parties could access a person's inner thoughts and memories through their implants? Something fundamentally important for all humanity is the right to "cognitive liberty." Roughly speaking, cognitive liberty is the personal freedom to have absolute sovereignty over one's own mind. It is related to the concepts of freedom of thought, and as I stated above, to a lesser extent, bodily integrity. In the coming cyborg age, neuroprosthetic technology could dramatically impact the cognitive liberty of the mind thus necessitating a serious discussion on the extent to which cyborg technologies should be regulated.

Cognitive liberty, or the "right to mental self-determination", is a vital part of international human rights law. For example, in the *Universal Declaration of Human Rights*, which is legally binding on member states of the *International Covenant on Civil and Political Rights*,[27] freedom of thought is found under Article 18 which states: "Everyone has the right to freedom of thought, conscience and religion..." Clearly, maintaining cognitive liberty in an age of brain implants

---

[24]Bublitz, Jan Christoph; Merkel, Reinhard, 2014. "Crime Against Minds: On Mental Manipulations, Harms and a Human Right to Mental Self-Determination." *Criminal Law and Philosophy*, Vol. 8: 61.

[25]*Wooley v. Maynard*, 430 U.S. 705, 1977, quoting *W.Va. State Bd. of Educ. v. Barnette*, 319 U.S. 624, 1943.

[26]Mark Blitz, *id.*, note 22.

[27]As of April 2014, the Covenant has 74 signatories and 168 parties.

should be a major objective as humanity moves closer to a cyborg future and eventual human-machine merger. In fact, a growing number of legal theorists see cognitive liberty as an important basic human right and argue than cognitive liberty is the principle underlying a number of recognized rights within the constitutions of most industrialized nations; freedom of speech being an example.

Given that scientists have discovered that people engage in "internal speech," that is, we use language to navigate within our own thoughts, the development of technology to read our "thoughts" is troubling as it could impact our cognitive liberty, First Amendment, and other constitutional rights. Since the U.S. Constitution directly references "freedom of speech," an important question is whether freedom of speech also protects "internal speech"—that is, the very speech that governments could access through a neuroprosthetic device. And in addition to considering internal thought as speech, what about thought transmitted by cybernetic technology from one brain to another—would this constitute a form of speech eligible for protection under the First Amendment? Additionally, what Federal Communication Commission (FCC) regulations on spectrum would apply to telepathic communication mediated by cyborg technology? Given the rate at which progress is being made in implant technologies, such questions remain to be resolved within the next few decades.

The debates about the government's ability to spy on people by monitoring their communications is especially relevant in an age when cyborgs will be equipped with neuroprosthetic devices and networked sensors. On this point, the government does currently regulate in areas that relate to emerging cyborg technologies. For example, for telepathic communication, as just noted, the transmission of thoughts from one person to another requires the use of spectrum. The FCC currently regulates the usage of electromagnetic spectrum by a management process called frequency allocation which involves managing and licensing the electromagnetic spectrum for commercial users and for non-commercial users including: state, county and local governments. The FCC management process considers public safety, commercial and non-commercial fixed and mobile wireless services, broadcast television and radio, satellite and other services. Further, the FCC has also developed regulations for a body area network consisting of wearable and implantable medical devices.

In the area of privacy, what if the government intercepts a signal from one mind to another? Not only would FCC regulations apply but the Fourth Amendment rights of the individual for protection against an unreasonable search and seizure would apply. One way law enforcement intercepts a signal is to attach a "bug" to a person's telephone line and record the person's conversation. Similarly, in the cyborg future, I imagine it could be possible to attach a "bug" to a neuroprosthetic device, which would allow inner thoughts to be surveilled even before they were vocalized or transmitted electronically. For telephone communication, courts have held that attaching a bug to the line constitutes a search under the Fourth Amendment because the Fourth Amendment protects an individual's privacy rights for situations in which the person has a legitimate expectation of privacy. Surely, people would expect the highest expectation of privacy for the creation of their unspoken thoughts in the coming cyborg age and for the transmission of thoughts from one mind to another.

Interestingly, from a jurisprudence perspective, the definition of what constitutes speech is not straight forward and clearly cyborg communication will raise a host of issues which will "stress" current law. In fact, the courts have identified different types of speech, each protected at a different level of scrutiny by the courts. This means that depending on the type of speech produced, the government is more or less empowered to restrict that speech. In the U.S., one type of speech is considered symbolic speech which is a legal term or art used to describe actions (not spoken language) that purposefully and discernibly convey a particular message or statement to those viewing it. However, of particular relevance for cyborg technology, is the category of "pure speech," which is the communication of ideas through spoken or written words or through conduct limited in form to that necessary to convey the idea. If the prior restraint of speech is prohibited under the First Amendment, the prior restraint of thought would be more egregious. The courts have generally provided strong protection of pure speech from government regulation; and prior cases in this area could serve as legal precedence for cyborg speech using telepathic communication. In the future, perhaps the court should recognize a new form of speech—cyber speech, the conveyance of ideas using thought; if so, what level of scrutiny would it receive from the government?

In numerous cases, the U.S. Supreme Court has recognized freedom of thought as a fundamental right, describing freedom of thought as: "... the matrix, the indispensable condition, of nearly every other form of freedom..."[28] Without freedom of thought, the First Amendment right to freedom of speech is moot, because you can only express what you can think. Constraining or censoring how a person thinks (i.e., cognitive censorship) is the most fundamental kind of censorship, and is contrary to some of our most cherished constitutional principles. Supporters of cognitive liberty seek to impose both a negative and a positive obligation on states: to refrain from non-consensually interfering with an individual's cognitive processes, and to allow individuals to self-determine their own "inner realm" and control of their own mental functions.

The first obligation on a state, to refrain from non-consensually interfering with an individual's cognitive processes, directly applies to government access to neuroprosthetic devices, and also seeks to protect individuals from having their mental processes altered or monitored without their consent or knowledge. Though cognitive liberty is often defined as an individual's freedom from *state* interference with their cognition, Jan Bublitz and Reinhard Merkel of the University of Hamburg, suggest that cognitive liberty should also prevent other non-state entities from interfering with an individual's mental "inner realm".[29] Of relevance for an emerging law of cyborgs, Bublitz and Merkel propose the introduction of a new criminal offense punishing "interventions severely interfering with another's mental

---

[28]*Palko v. Connecticut*, 1937, 302 U.S. 319, 326–327.

[29]Jan Christoph Bublitz and Reinhard Merkel, *id*, note 24.

integrity by undermining mental control or exploiting pre-existing mental weakness."[30] And that, "...direct interventions that reduce or impair cognitive capacities such as memory, concentration, and willpower; alter preferences, beliefs, or behavioral dispositions; elicit inappropriate emotions; or inflict clinically identifiable mental injuries would all be *prima facie* impermissible and subject to criminal prosecution."[31] Weighing in, Wyre Sententia and Richard Boire of the *Center for Cognitive Liberty and Ethics* have also expressed concern that corporations and other non-state entities might utilize emerging neurotechnologies to alter individuals' mental processes without their consent.[32]

While one obligation of a state is to refrain from non-consensually interfering with an individual's cognitive processes, another, freedom to think *however* a person wants, seeks to ensure that individuals have the freedom to alter or enhance their own consciousness; one way to do this would be by stimulating the pleasure centers of the brain by accessing a neuroprosthetic device. An individual who enjoys this aspect of cognitive liberty has the freedom to alter their mental processes in any way they wish to; whether through indirect methods such as meditation or yoga, or more directly through neurotechnology. This element of cognitive liberty is of great importance to proponents of the transhumanist movement, a key tenet of which is the enhancement of human mental function.[33]

Allowing people to determine their own "inner realm," is directly related to the use of neuroprosthesis to access one's own brain. For example, "self-stimulation" is a phenomenon whereby an animal (including a human being) will repeatedly stimulate its brain electrically, sometimes to the point of exhaustion. This phenomenon is robust and readily reproducible in many areas of the brain. Interestingly, the discovery of "pleasure centers" in the brain is one of the more famous findings from brain stimulation research. It occurred by accident. Professor James Olds, working with Peter Milner, both of McGill University, inserted an electrode into a rat's brain, aiming for the reticular system.[34] The electrode curved off its intended course and landed in a different area, probably near the hypothalamus. Olds put the rat in a box and stimulated its brain whenever the rat approached a certain corner. He expected the rat to stay out of that corner, but instead Olds observed the rat was "coming back for more," acting as though the brain stimulation was pleasurable. Further research showed that stimulation of areas in the limbic system produced pleasure in humans, and that individuals in pain or depressed were most likely to find electrical stimulation of the brain very pleasurable.

---

[30]*Id.*

[31]*Id.*

[32]Richard G. Boire, 2005. Searching the Brain: The Fourth Amendment Implications of Brain-Based Deception Detection Devices, The American Journal of Bioethics, Vol. 5, Issue 2, doi: 10.1080/15265160590960933.

[33]Cognitive Liberty, Wikipedia, http://en.wikipedia.org/wiki/Cognitive_liberty.

[34]The Pleasure Centers, at: http://www.intropsych.com/ch02_human_nervous_system/pleasure_centers.html.

In the decades since Olds and Milner reported the existence of pleasure centers in the brain, scientists have observed that once stimulated, several regions of the brain are activated by feelings of triumph, euphoria, sexual pleasure, and addictive behavior of all types, including non-drug addictions such as gambling. If people, or third parties, using neuroprosthetic devices can "electronically create" these and other behaviors, a host of legal and policy issues would be implicated. For example, third parties accessing a neuroprosthesis to stimulate the pleasure centers within a person's brain, could easily cause the person to become addicted to cortical stimulation, and thus come under the third party's control. Surely the government would regulate heavily in this area. Just consider what Harvard Law Professor Lawrence Tribe said: "The guarantee of free expression," "is inextricably linked to the protection and preservation of open and unfettered mental activity..."[35] In a Supreme Court case, *United States v. Reidel*, which held that a postal regulation that banned the sale of adult materials was constitutionally permissible, Justice Hugo Black dissented arguing that the First Amendment of the United States Constitution "denies Congress the power to act as censor." And also on the topic of government control of thought, in *Stanley v. Georgia*, the Court stated: "the First Amendment right of the individual to be free from governmental programs of thought control..." is imperative, and that the "freedom from governmental manipulation of the content of a man's mind..." must be preserved.[36] The Court seems to be a strong supporter of the general principles underlying cognitive liberty, which I view as an indispensable line of defense against government or corporate control of our thoughts and mind, when the technology to do so is readily available.

Reading the Brain, Lie Detection, and Cognitive Liberty

Thanks to advances in neuroimaging technologies, such as functional magnetic resonance imaging (fMRI), magneto encephalography (MEG), and positron emission tomography (PET), the brain's structure and functions are being observed at increasing levels of resolution and fidelity. The ability to read brain waves is an essential technology for telepathy and for other "cognitive" capabilities that future cyborgs will possess. From a cognitive liberty perspective, telepathic communication could provide government's access to a person thoughts at two levels—through the implant itself, and by interception of the electronic signals transmitted from one mind to another.

While scientists have not as yet developed working brain-to-brain communication interfaces for the general public, much progress is being made in technology

---

[35]Laurence Tribe, Rights of Privacy and Personhood, American Constitutional Law, Sec. 15–7, at 1322 (2nd ed. 1988).

[36]*United States v. Reidel*, 402 U.S. 351 (1971); *Stanley v. Georgia* 394 U.S. 557 (1969).

to record the functions of the brain and to makes sense of the output. For example, functional magnetic resonance imaging is used to measure brain activity by detecting the changes in blood oxygenation and flow that occurs in response to neural activity—when a brain area is more active it consumes more oxygen, to meet this increased demand, blood flow increases to the active area. Private companies such as *No Lie MRI* are currently working to improve the capability of fMRI technology for lie detection so that the fMRI results can be admitted as evidence in court. Judy Illes, Canadian Research Chair in Neuroethics, sees brain-scanning technology to detect lies evolving quickly—commenting that we will have technology that is sufficiently reliable at getting at the binary question of whether someone is lying that it may be utilized in certain legal settings."[37] Another company using fMRI technology for lie detection has developed a system called *Guilty Knowledge*. The system, developed by Daniel Langleben and his research team at the University of Pennsylvania was tested as follows—Langleben gave subjects a playing card before they entered an fMRI machine and told them to answer no to a series of questions, including whether they had the card in question. Langleben and his colleagues found that certain areas of the brain lighted up when people lied about whether they possessed the card suggesting that fMRI could be used to detect lying for binary events.

Interestingly, recent advances in the use of reading brain waves using cyborg devices are based on a technology that has been around since the early twentieth century—EEG. An electroencephalogram (EEG) can be used to detect electrical activity in a person's brain using small, flat metal discs (electrodes) attached to the person's scalp. A person's brain cells communicate via electrical impulses and are active all the time, even when a person is asleep. Recently, commercial products that use EEG technology to read the activity of the brain are entering the marketplace. For example, *This Place*, out of London, has developed an app, *MindRDR*, which consists of head-mounted hardware and the Neurosky EEG biosensor (an off-the-shelf sensor), which is used to create a communications loop between displays such as Google Glass and the EEG sensor by picking up brainwaves that reportedly correlate with a person's ability to concentrate. The app translates the person's brainwaves into a meter reading that gets superimposed on the camera view displayed in Google Glass. With more "focus" the meter reading increases and the app takes a photograph of what a person is seeing in front of them; if the person continues to focus, the photo gets posted online. In my view, access to what a person "concentrates on," that is, what they are consciously attending to, should only be possible by first obtaining a warrant from a magistrate, else this would be a violation of the person's Fourth Amendment privacy rights and a violation of the person's cognitive liberty.

As the use of fMRI data and other brain recording techniques become increasingly common in courtrooms, judges and juries may be asked to draw new and

---

[37]Judy Illes, Neuroethics in a New Era of Neuroimaging, American Journal of Neuroradiology, at: http://www.ajnr.org/content/24/9/1739.full.

sometimes troubling lines between "normal" and "abnormal" brains. Such judgments could impact the cognitive liberty rights of anyone charged with a crime. Ruben Gur, a professor of psychology at the University of Pennsylvania's School of Medicine, has appeared as an expert witness in numerous cases requiring a determination of the mental competency of a defendant.[38] One such case was the high-profile trial of a convicted serial killer who was known as the "classified-ad rapist," because he would respond to classified ads placed by women offering to sell household items, then rape and kill them. Professor Gur was called as a national expert in PET scans to help determine whether the accused was responsible for his actions.

A PET scan (brain positron emission tomography) is an imaging test of the brain that uses a radioactive substance called a tracer to look for disease or injury in the brain. After examining the defendant's PET scans, Gur testified that a motorcycle accident that had left the defendant in a coma had also severely damaged his amygdala (which has a role in memory, decision making, and emotional reactions). It was after emerging from the coma that the defendant committed his first rape. If courts consider whether a "damaged brain" could absolve a person from responsibility, then I would argue that courts should also consider whether thoughts implanted on neuroprosthetic devices by a third party should absolve a person from responsibility for their actions. In an extension of Gur's work, Michael Gazzaniga, a professor of psychology, and author of *The Ethical Brain*, has noted that within a few years, neuroscientists may be able to show that there are neurological differences when people testify about their own previous acts and when they testify to something they saw. Gazzaniga notes, "If you kill someone, you have a procedural memory of that, whereas if I'm standing and watch you kill somebody, that's an episodic memory that uses a different part of the brain."[39] Perhaps, by accessing information stored on neuroprosthetic devices, the government could distinguish between procedural versus episodic memories, and thus either convict or absolve a person accused of a crime. Whether this is desirable, that is, to scan a person's brain to obtain evidence for a trial, is a constitutional issue and a topic that the public and legal community should debate. Even if witnesses don't have their brains scanned, neuroscience may lead judges and jurors to conclude that certain kinds of memories are more reliable than others because of the area of the brain in which they are processed.

---

[38]Jeffrey Rosen, *id*, note 15, discussing Rubin Gur's experience as an expert witness.

[39]Jeffrey Rosen, *id*., note 15, quoting Michael Gazzaniga, Michael Gazzaniga, 2006, The Ethical Brain: The Science of Our Moral Dilemmas, Harper Perennial.

Towards Telepathy

While EEG and fMRI technologies are leading to significant advances in the use of brain scans for lie detection, other research in neuroscience is more directly on the topic of telepathic communication. Professor Miguel Nicolelis from Duke University is a pioneer in developing technology for the brain. His research is oriented toward brain-to-brain communication, brain machine interfaces and neuroprosthesis in human patients and non-human primates. As a result of his studies, Dr. Nicolelis was one of the first to propose and demonstrate that animals and human subjects can utilize their electrical brain activity to directly control neuroprosthetic devices via brain-machine interfaces. In his 2012 book *Beyond Boundaries*, Professor Nicolelis speculated about the possibility that two brains could exchange information. Later, publishing in *Scientific Reports* Nicolelis reported that his research team at Duke University Medical Center had achieved a back-and-forth exchange between two rodent brains. To test his brain interface technology, his team trained two animals to press one of two levers in exchange for a drink of water, when an LED turned on. Microelectrodes were placed in each of the two animals' cortices and when one rat pressed the correct lever, a sample of cortical activity from that rat's brain was wired to the second animal's brain located in a chamber where the "it's-time-to-drink" LED was absent. As evidence that information was exchanged between the two brains, the rat on the receiving end of the prosthesis proceeded to press the correct lever (to receive a drink) that had been messaged over the brain link. Summarizing the results—Nicolelis and his team provided proof-of-concept technology and results that telepathy may be possible as a future form of communication.

Related to Professor Nicolelis's work, results from studies with human subjects show that telepathy may in fact be a viable technology for the public within a few decades (or less!). For example, using EEG technology, researchers at the University of Southampton, England, successfully demonstrated communication from person-to-person using thought.[40] And more recently, at the University of Washington, researchers demonstrated a working brain-to-brain interface with human subjects also using EEG technology.[41] In their study, two people were located in different rooms where they were not allowed to communicate other than with their brains using EEG technology. Both subjects looked at a video game where they had to defend a virtual city by firing a cannon. But one person had his brain connected to an electroencephalography machine that read his brain signals,

---

[40]Communicating person to person through the power of thought alone, 2009, University of Southampton, at: https://www.southampton.ac.uk/mediacentre/news/2009/oct/09_135.shtml.

[41]Rao R. P. N, Stocco, A, Bryan, M, Sarma, D, Youngquist, T. M, Wu J, et al. 2014, A Direct Brain-to-Brain Interface in Humans, PLoS ONE 9(11): e111332. doi:10.1371/journal.pone. 0111332.

which were used to fire a virtual cannon. That is, rather than using an input device to fire the canon the person was instructed to *think* about moving his hand to fire the cannon. That thought was transmitted over the internet to another person whose hand was situated on a touchpad that would twitch and tap in the right direction if the signals were successfully received. Based on their experience with the system, the University of Washington researchers were confident that the technology worked as intended. Further, according to the researchers, the next step is to determine *what* kind of information can be sent between people's brains. For example, they want to know if one day, a teacher could download information directly to a student's brain—I believe the answer is yes, and that this will be a future capability of cyborg technology.

Creating Artificial Memories

Neuroscientists foresee a future world where minds can be programmed in order to create artificial memories. Based on recent advances in brain-to-brain communication, some scientists argue that memories may be implanted into a person's mind, and that memories from one mind can be transferred to another. This may sound like technology for another century, but in fact, scientists have already successfully implanted a false memory into the brain of a mouse. Given these results, what could be more important for an emerging law of cyborgs than protection of the integrity of our memories? To create a memory prosthesis, MIT scientists Steve Ramirez and Xu Liu tagged brain cells associated with a specific memory and then tweaked that memory to make the mouse believe an event had happened when it hadn't, other neuroscience laboratories are producing similar results. While implanting a memory in humans equipped with a neuroprosthetic device won't happen in the immediate future, Ramirez and Liu have shown that in principle, it should be possible to isolate a human memory and activate it.[42] In fact, Michael J. Kahana, who serves as director of the University of Pennsylvania's Computational Memory Lab commented on the MIT study, "We would have every reason to expect this would happen in humans as it happened in mice."[43] Clearly, improvements in neuprostheread your mindtic technologies are occurring rapidly.

---

[42]Meeri Kim, 2013, MIT Scientists Implant a False Memory into a Mouse's Brain, The Washington Post, at: http://www.washingtonpost.com/national/health-science/inception-mit-scientists-implant-a-false-memory-into-a-mouses-brain/2013/07/25/47bdee7a-f49a-11e2-a2f1-a7acf9bd5d3a_story.html,

[43]*Id.,* quoting Michael J. Kahana.

Before discussing the technology of implanting false memories in more detail, let's digress to first discuss some of the law and policy issues associated with the technology. Duke University Professor of Law, Nita Farahany has observed that the mind stores a large amount of information that could be of value to the government and to businesses. For example, she notes that our brains can uniquely identify speakers, sounds, and images. Interestingly, technologies integrated into the brain could also detect this information, which could be very valuable to a criminal investigation. But should it be permissible to scan a person's brain or to access the data stored on a neuroprosthetic device to access our recognition of objects or people? Maybe so, because in courtrooms, eyewitness testimony has a high rate of falsity and sometimes witnesses lack memories of key information. Therefore, in criminal law cases directly accessing a person's memory of an event would be helpful. However, what if false memories could be planted in an eyewitnesses? Most people would agree that it would be impermissible for the government to create its own "star witness," Farahany maintained.[44]

Given her expertise in Constitutional law issues related to brain recording technologies, Professor Farahany has argued in law review papers that a right guaranteed under the U.S. Constitution and which has relevance for government access to cyborg technology is the Fifth Amendment protection against self-incrimination.[45] She asks—if the government could "read your mind," and use the output as evidence in court, would the Fifth Amendment protection against self-incrimination still have meaning in a cyborg age?[46] In the light of the increasing ability to access human memory using implant technology, Professor Farahany has proposed legislative protection of cognitive liberty as a way of safeguarding the right against self-incrimination found in the Fifth Amendment.[47] In a Stanford Law Review article, Farahany reviewed *Schmerber v. California*, in which the U.S. Supreme Court held that under the *Self-Incrimination Clause* of the Fifth Amendment, no person shall be compelled to "prove a charge [from] his own mouth," but a person may be compelled to provide real or physical evidence (for example, DNA or a blood sample).[48] Therefore, while a defendant in a criminal case cannot be compelled to "take the stand" and serve as a witness against himself; the government could collect samples from their body and use that as evidence. With advances in brain reading technologies, Farahany argued that based on modern applications of neuroscience there exist the need to redefine the taxonomy of evidence subject to

---

[44]Nita Farahany, 2012, Incrimination Thoughts, Stanford Law Review, Vol. 64. 351.

[45]*Id.*

[46]*Id.*

[47]*Id.*

[48]*Schmerber v. California*, 384 U.S. 757 (1966), was a decision by the U.S. Supreme Court, which held that a State may, over the suspect's protest, have a physician extract blood from a person suspected of drunken driving without violating the suspect's rights under the Fourth or Fifth Amendment to the United States Constitution.

the privilege against self-incrimination.[49] This is because evidence can arise from government access to a neuroprosthetic device or by directly recording brain activities—and neither represent the type of physical evidence permissible for the court to obtain. For this and other reasons, an interesting question of jurisprudence in the coming cyborg age, is whether Constitutional rights, such as the Fifth Amendment applies to data stored on neuroprosthetic devices?[50]

Litigating Cognitive Liberty

The concept of cognitive liberty is broad and therefore there may be different avenues of protection for cognitive liberty among different jurisdictions. On this point, in the U.S. the free speech prong of the First Amendment while relevant is not the only protection of cognitive liberty. For example, under the U.S. Constitution, the Due Process Clauses of the 5th and 14th Amendments offer some protection against unwarranted bodily intrusion. Why is this dual level of protection of importance for our cyborg future? When the state is not restricting the expression of ideas, but altering brain physiology that may impact cognition (for example by requiring the administration of antipsychotic drugs), it may not be a First Amendment argument that provides protection for cognitive liberty, but rather the due process protection under the Constitution which can be used to protect the integrity of our bodies. Discussing this issue, Professor Jonathan Blitz of Oklahoma City University School of Law argues that the power to reshape our thinking process biologically, should be recognized as one form of a more general power that our freedom of mind is intended to place in our hands and not in the hands of government officials.[51]

Cyborg technologies, which could be hacked by a government, have profound implications for cognitive liberty. Technology which allows the government to manipulate mental processes, is a direct effort to alter the content and form of a person's thoughts—the essential substrate for free speech and expression. A basic question in an age of cyborg technology, is whether the government can access the content of the mind before it is externalized? This question has not been directly litigated in the context of cyborg technologies, but in related cases, cognitive liberty has been argued as a right that a citizen should be afforded by the state. For

---

[49]Nita Farahany, *id.* note 44.

[50]See *Reno v. ACLU*, 521 U.S. 844 (1977), noting that the Internet allows for "unlimited low-cost capacity for communication of all kinds."

[51]Marc Blitz, 2010, Freedom of Thought for the Extended Mind: Cognitive Enhancement and the Constitution, Wisconsin Law Review, Vol. 2010, No. 4, 1049.

example, in the U.K., the case of *R v. Hardison*, involved a defendant who was charged with violating the *Misuse of Drugs Act 1971*.[52] Hardison claimed that cognitive liberty was safeguarded by Article 9 of the *European Convention on Human Rights*. Specifically, the defendant argued that "individual sovereignty over one's interior environment constitutes the very core of what it means to be free," and that because psychotropic drugs are a potent method of altering an individual's mental process, prohibition of them under the *Misuse of Drugs Act 1971* was in opposition to the Act. The court however disagreed, and denied Hardison's right to appeal to a superior court. In the U.S., the Supreme Court has written in *NAACP v. Button*, that "… only a compelling state interest… can justify limiting first Amendment freedoms."[53] In the coming cyborg age, what such interests should be, and under what conditions they should be protected is a topic ripe for debate and legislative action.

After the *Hardison* decision in Great Britain, the U.S. Supreme Court heard arguments on an important case that dealt directly with issues related to the cognitive liberty of the mind.[54] As background, the defendant Dr. Charles Sell was charged in federal court with submitting false claims to Medicaid and private insurance companies resulting in counts of fraud, and one of money-laundering. Dr. Sell had previously sought psychiatric help and had voluntarily taken antipsychotic drugs; however, he found the side effects intolerable. After the initial charge, Dr. Sell was declared incompetent to stand trial (but not dangerous), as a result, an administrative hearing was held and it was decided that Dr. Sell could be forcibly drugged to regain mental competence; a decision Dr. Sell challenged. The decision by the government to force Dr. Sell to take medication which would change his mental processes raised significant Constitutional law issues. On this point, Law Professor Lawrence Tribe of Harvard University commented, "whether the government decides to interfere with our mental autonomy by confiscating books and films or by denying us psychiatric medications; "the offense" is ultimately the same: "government invasion and usurpation of the choices that together constitute an individual's psyche."[55]

Could a person who did not pose danger to another, be forcibly injected with antipsychotic medication solely to render him competent to be tried for crimes that were described by Judge Kermit Bye of the 8th Circuit Court as "nonviolent and purely economic"?[56] In Dr. Sell's case, the government sought to directly manipulate and modify Dr. Sell's thoughts and thought process by forcing him to take mind-altering "antipsychotic" drugs. Generally, the government can administer

---

[52]*R v Hardison*, 2007, 1 Cr App R (S) 37.

[53]*NAACP v. Button*, 371 U.S. 415 (1963); *Palko v. Connecticut*, 302 U.S. 319, 326–327 (1937).

[54]*Sell v. United States*, 539 U.S. 166 (2003) is a landmark decision in which the U.S. Supreme Court imposed stringent limits on the right of a lower court to order the forcible administration of antipsychotic medication to a criminal defendant who had been determined to be incompetent to stand trial for the sole purpose of making them competent and able to be tried.

[55]Lawrence H. Tribe, *id.*, note 35.

[56]Sell, *id.*, note 54.

drugs only "in limited circumstances", and in Dr. Sell's holding the Court imposed stringent limits on the right of a lower court to order the forcible administration of antipsychotic medication to a criminal defendant who had been determined to be incompetent, for the sole purpose of making him competent and able to be tried. Thus since the lower court had failed to determine that all the appropriate criteria for court-ordered forcible treatment had been met, the order to forcibly medicate the defendant was reversed.[57]

While the *Sell* case involved altering the defendant's mind by forced drugging, what are the implications of the case for government access to neuroprosthesis and other brain implant technologies that could also alter a person's thought processes or even edit their memories? Clearly, the *Sell* court did not completely ban the government from altering a person's brain chemistry, which begs the question as to whether the government could access, or even edit a person's memory by accessing an implant within their brain. While prosecuting an incompetent defendant is widely viewed as denying that defendant a fair trial, because such defendants cannot participate adequately in their own defense; those who oppose using forced drugging to *ensure* a fair trial argue that the drugs are often so overwhelming as to make adequate participation in the person's defense impossible as well. The reliance on freedom of thought and Due Process rights under the 5th and 14th Amendments as arguments against the government "manipulating" a person's mind seems to me compelling: how can a person's *speech* be free from government control if the government can forcibly administer drugs or edit the mind by accessing technology which allows them to change the *thoughts* that prompt a person to speak in the first place?

The "cognitive liberty" interest in Dr. Sell's case can be thought of as an interest forged by the union of Dr. Sell's liberty interest in bodily integrity with his freedom of thought and his Due Process right under the 5th and 14th Amendments. Such a government invasion of bodily integrity—one aimed at directly manipulating the person's thoughts and thinking processes should clearly infringe on the First Amendment right to free speech. If "at the heart of the First Amendment is the notion that in a free society one's beliefs should be shaped by his mind and his conscience rather than coerced by the State," then there can be no doubt that the government infringes on the First Amendment when it seeks to change Dr. Sell's thinking by forcibly changing his brain chemistry.[58] Further, by altering a person's mind with the forced administration of drugs, the government commits an act of cognitive censorship and mental manipulation, an action surely more disfavored under the First Amendment than even the censorship of speech. A government that is permitted to manipulate a citizen's consciousness at its very roots—by forcing a person to take a mind-altering drug or hacking a neuroprosthetic device—need not censor speech, because it could prevent *a priori* ideas from ever occurring in the mind of the speaker. By directly manipulating the

---

[57]Sell, *id.,* note 54.

[58]Sell, *id,* note 54.

manner in which Dr. Sell's brain processes information and formulates ideas, the government *ipso facto* manipulates and alters both the form and content of Dr. Sell's subsequent expression and thus renders the First Amendment's free speech guarantee meaningless.

With the exception of the cases in criminal law dealing with the defendant's mental capacity to stand trial, the fundamental question, in what ways people may legitimately change the mental state of others, is largely unexplored in legal thinking but will be a central issue in the emerging field of cyborg law. While every constitution guarantees the right to bodily integrity, few afford protection to mental integrity. Perhaps if a cybernetically enhanced mind received the legal rights afforded computers, future cyborgs would receive a range of protections beyond those of biological humans. On this point, just as a computer can be hacked, so too could a brain equipped with neuroprosthetic devices; thus, would affording cyborgs the same rights found in anti-hacking statutes be appropriate in a cyborg age? Future hacking crimes could take a decidedly sinister twist; not hacking to breach computer systems but brains, bodies and behaviors. In fact, it's possible now to hack insulin pumps or to use jamming signals to stop hackers from lethal pacemaker attacks.

Implanting a Software Virus in the Mind

In violation of internet, telecommunication, and criminal law statutes, future hackers could use wireless technology to disrupt the functioning of a person's neuroprosthesis or even to implant a software virus into a person's mind. On this last point, a British scientist and former student of Professor Kevin Warwick, Dr. Mark Gasson, has claimed to be the first person to become infected with a computer virus. How can this be possible? In Dr. Gasson's case, purposively as part of a proof-of-concept study, but in the future, cyborg hackers could spread a virus to a person's mind by accessing brain-implant technology or by hacking into a network of wirelessly connected brains. In Dr. Gasson's study, a chip was inserted in his hand which was then infected with a software virus.[59] Of relevance to a law of cyborgs, Dr. Gasson showed that the chip was able to pass on the computer virus to external control systems—meaning a person with cyborg "infected" technology could transmit a virus to a machine external to the cyborg. But more importantly, if other implanted chips within a person's body, including neuroprosthesis, had been connected to the system they too would have been infected by the virus.

Experts in cybersecurity are especially alarmed at the ease in which implants can be hacked. For example, Professor Kevin Fu, a leading expert on medical-device security at the University of Michigan has written extensively on this topic.

---

[59]Cellan-Jones, Rory, 2010, First human 'infected with computer virus, *BBC News online* (BBC). Retrieved 26 May 2010.

His concerns relate directly to neuroprosthetic devices and implants that are connected to an internal network that is itself connected to the Internet, and that are also vulnerable to infections from laptops or other device. The problem of implants being affected with a software virus is exacerbated by the fact that manufacturers often will not allow their equipment to be modified, even to add security features. "I find this mind-boggling," Fu says.[60] This particular issue, lack of patches for software could be a serious hindrance to cognitive liberty when hacking of brain implants is possible.

With others, I have often thought that the transmission of a software virus is not unlike the transmission of a disease-causing virus that enters the body. On this point consider Mark Gasson's comment on the experience of receiving a software virus: "Many people with medical implants also consider them to be integrated into the concept of their body, and so in this context it is appropriate to talk in terms of people themselves being infected by computer viruses."[61] A virus has to have a host, and in some cases can be transported through the air we breathe, similarly, a software virus can be transported through the air using spectrum to a cybernetically enhanced host. In terms of hacking into computers, there are some laws which regulate in this area. In the U.S., the *Computer Fraud and Abuse Act* deals with the issue of making and using devices and programs to gain unauthorized access to secure computer systems. Further, the *Computer Fraud and Abuse Act* prohibits access to government computers to anyone without authorization. Hackers who are convicted of crimes that violate this law may be required to pay fines, be placed on probation, or serve jail time, depending on the severity of the damages.

Under U.S. law, if a disease is purposively transmitted to another person, there could be criminal liability for the act. For example, criminal transmission of a sexually transmitted disease may be actionable through state laws that typically include both HIV as well as other communicable or contagious sexually transmitted diseases. However, we currently don't employ the disease transmission model to the spread of a software virus: instead we use other legal options for those who transmit malware.[62] If the means of software virus transmission is through the Internet, the potential impact could compromise millions of hosts. Just consider a *"harmless experiment"* by a Cornell University student that involved the release onto the Internet of a type of malware called a *"worm"* that compromised thousands of computers and required millions of dollars-worth of time to eradicate. As several computers operated by the U.S. Government were damaged, the student

---

[60]See generally, David Talbot, 2010, Computer Viruses Are "Rampant" on Medical Devices in Hospitals, MIT Technology Review, quoting Professor Fu, at: http://www.technologyreview.com/news/429616/computer-viruses-are-rampant-on-medical-devices-in-hospitals/.

[61]Mark Gasson, 2005, Extending human interaction via invasive neural implants (PhD thesis). University of Reading.

[62]Malware (short for "malicious software"), is a file or code, typically delivered over a network that infects, explores, steals or conducts virtually any behavior an attacker wants, would be deleterious to the bodily integrity of any cyborg.

was prosecuted and convicted under the *Computer Fraud and Abuse Act* described above.[63] Other jurisdictions also punish those who infect computers with a virus. For example, in the U.K., the introduction of malware to a computer is covered by Section 3 of the *Computer Misuse Act*. The Act states that a crime is committed if a person "does any act which causes an unauthorized modification of the contents of any computer" and the perpetrator intends to "cause a modification of the contents of any computer" which may "impair the operation of any computer", "prevent or hinder access to any program or data held in any computer" or "impair the operation of any such program or the reliability of any such data".[64] Relating this law to cyborg technology, access to software and algorithms in the artificial hippocampus (which is a computer) created by Professor Berger, could hinder memory processes and be actionable under the U.K. Act.

Clearly, Dr. Gasson's findings that a virus can spread from one implant to another, has important implications for a cyborg future where brain implants storing memories and sensory information could be accessed by third parties, and in which medical devices such as pacemakers, cochlear implants, and retinal prosthesis, could be contaminated by a virus infecting another neuroprosthetic implant. Dr. Gasson's findings show that when third party access to neuroprosthesis become possible, the spread of a computer virus will also become possible and thus maintaining cognitive liberty will be an important consideration for anyone equipped with neuroprosthetic technology.

Conclusion

As cyborg technologies improve and continue to be integrated into the human body, significant issues of law and policy will need to be addressed; if not, humanity could be subjected to a host of unexpected and negative outcomes. For cognitive liberty, perhaps the most troubling outcome would be the risk that a totalitarian government could gain access to neuroprosthetic devices—this could lead to a dystopic future not unlike the societies discussed in the popular novels written by Aldous Huxley in *Brave New World*, or George Orwell in *1984*. Hopefully, given the high stakes for humanity, this chapter has convinced the reader that in the cyborg future accessing the mind for nefarious purposes is completely possible, and not just the warning of overzealous futurists and novelists

---

[63]Computer Fraud and Abuse Act (CFAA), 18 U.S.C. 1030; There is an obligation for prosecution under the CFAA that a non-public computer is damaged where the term "damage" means any impairment to the integrity or availability of data, a program, a system, or information. Computer Misuse Act 1990 (c. 18), 1990 CHAPTER 18. The PCI-DSS at section 5 requires that "Anti-virus software must be used on all systems commonly affected by viruses to protect systems from malicious software." The Consumer Protection Act 1987 (Products Liability) (Modification) Order 2000 (Statutory Instrument 2000 No. 2771).

[64]Computer Misuse Act, *Id.*

from the first half of last century. In an age of cyborgs, the over worked saying that technology is a "dual edge" sword, in that it can provide amazing benefits to humanity, or lead to unintended negative outcomes; is especially true. Therefore, the need to vigorously debate how cyborg technologies will be used in the future and how they will be regulated is especially meaningful.

For cognitive liberty, freedom of thought is the natural human right of each person to be secure in their ability to perceive the world to the best of their ability. To have true cognitive liberty in a world with people equipped with brain implants would mean that first we must have access to truthful and unbiased information about the actions of others and the general state of the world—will this be possible in a world consisting of cybernetic enhancements to our bodies and mind? Because this is an important consideration for our cyborg future, consider the definition of cognitive liberty proposed by an organization which focuses on the concept. *The Center for Cognitive Liberties* defines the term as "the right of each individual to think independently and autonomously, to use the full spectrum of his or her mind, and to engage in multiple modes of thought."[65] Without the ability to think independently and to receive accurate representations of external events we cannot make independently informed choices which is an essential requirement to participate in liberal democracies; and without the ability to engage in all modes of thought, we may be subject to control by governments, corporations, and other third parties. These are areas which need vigorous debate and legislative action within the next decades; clearly, we need to ensure that cognitive liberty is a basic right as we move forward toward a cyborg future.

As we enhance our bodies with technology, the clear trend is that we are becoming vulnerable to more government supervision and privacy invasions. For these and other reasons we need to ask—how should the law account for violations of our rights which may accompany the emergence of cyborg technologies? Should the technology integrated within our bodies and brains have the rights afforded natural people, or only the rights associated with property? This is a difficult question to answer but a timely question to pose because the legal division between humans and machines is beginning to blur as technology is implanted within the body and performs functions once done by organic parts. Interestingly, Mariella Pazzaglia and colleagues from Sapienza University, have found that wheel-bound people with spinal cord injuries perceive their body's edges as being plastic and flexible to include the wheelchair.[66] If the law continues to view the machine parts integrated into the human body as separate from the body, then not only will this decision be incompatible with how we view our cybernetically enhanced bodies, but lead to situations where the law is not equipped to handle

---

[65]Center for Cognitive Liberties and Ethics, at: http://www.cognitiveliberty.org/faqs/faq_general.htm.

[66]Science Daily, 2013, Human brain treats prosthetic devices as part of the body, at: http://www.sciencedaily.com/releases/2013/03/130306221135.htm. Mariella Pazzaglia, Giulia Galli, Giorgio Scivoletto, Marco Molinari. A Functionally Relevant Tool for the Body following Spinal Cord Injury. *PLoS ONE*, 2013; 8 (3): e58312 doi: 10.1371/journal.ponc.0058312.

disputes involving cyborg technology. For example, data has tremendous value, but who owns the data produced by technology implanted within the body? Consider that a heart pacer produces data concerning the functioning of the heart, including heartbeat, blood temperature, breathing, and heart electrical activity. However, under current law, the data produced by cyborg devices, such as a pacemaker, is not viewed as the property of the cyborg, but of the manufacturer, vendor, or licensor of the medical implant. As noted by Benjamin Wittes and Jane Chong in a Brookings Law Report, "The more we come to see the machine as an extension of the person—first by the pervasiveness of its use, then by its physical integration with the user—the less plausible will seem the notion that these are simply tools which with we choose to use..."[67] And the less the machine parts are viewed as tools, the more relevant the question—why not view the human-machine combination as a fully integrated being, deserving of the rights afforded natural persons?

Issues of ownership for cyborg technology and the data produced by implants, while important for the law of property and contract, are just one of many areas of law and policy that will be impacted by the emergence of cyborg technologies. For example, the spread of cyborg technologies throughout the population, will likely influence the very structure of society itself. This is because cyborg technologies designed to enhance cognitive functions could create multiple classes of people, differing in intellectual abilities; with different needs, rights, and aspirations. How would the law deal with a society consisting of different types of cyborgs and also of unenhanced people, differing vastly in intellectual abilities? Thinking about this question, Harvard University Professor Michael Sandel, has expressed concern that enhancement technology could create two classes of human beings—those with access to enhancement technologies, and those who must make do with an unaltered memory that fades with age.[68]

My concerns that emerging cyborg technologies which are directed at the mind could lead to a dystopic future, are compatible with Stanford's Francis Fukuyama's comments on the dangers of biotechnology as he discussed in *Our Posthuman Future: Consequences of the Biotechnology Revolution*.[69] For example, just as with biotechnology, our human dignity and human rights could be changed as we morph into more machine than biological human. According to Fukuyama, it is unquestionable that our equal moral status, or worth, rests on certain properties we share, or as Professor Fukuyama puts it, on our common human nature. The concern is that future advances in cybernetic technology which lead to modification of "our complex evolved natures" could "disrupt either the unity or the continuity of human nature, and thereby the human rights that are

---

[67]Benjamin Wittes and Jane Chong, *id.*, note 1.

[68]Michael J. Sandel, 2007, The Case against Perfection: Ethics in the Age of Genetic Engineering. Cambridge, Massachusetts: Harvard University Press. ISBN 9780674036383.

[69]Francis Fukuyama, 2003, Our Posthuman Future: Consequences of the Biotechnology Revolution, Picador Press.

based on it."[70] Clearly, cybernetic technologies could dramatically change the mix of human to machine parts, and thus affect the balance of our common human nature. The contrary view, expressed by those who believe that it is advantageous that we are becoming posthuman, is to think of our species, like other species, as continually evolving, and it is unnecessary to freeze it in place to protect human dignity and human rights. In this view "human rights" will evolve as we integrate technology into our bodies, and that this is the result of a natural process.

However, before the warnings presented in this chapter motives the reader to call for a ban on all cyborg technologies aimed at the mind, perhaps a balancing of cognitive liberty against government rights must be considered. This is because preventing the government from regulating in any area related to the creation, receipt, or transmission of information, would effectively prevent it from governing—in fact, in the U.S. a whole body of First Amendment law addresses just this issue, when, where, and how the government can restrict speech. Further, banning or heavily restricting cyborg technologies directed at the mind could also condemn some people to a lifetime of mental illness that (with continuing advances in cyborg technology) could have been alleviated with a neuroprosthetic device. And if brain enhancement technologies were banned, then unenhanced people could be condemned to a future in which their information processing abilities would be orders of magnitude less than artificially intelligent machines; would we then be subservient to the machines?

Perhaps as some argue, only thought that is expressed in vocalized, symbolic, or commercial speech should be regulated to some extent—and that unspoken thought should receive blanket protection. In either case, government regulation of speech, through prior restraints (such as by assessing a brain implant and disrupting the thought process), should be heavily frowned upon—the Supreme Court generally supports this view. The Court in *Ashcroft v. Free Speech Coalition* commented that thought is most in danger "…when the government seeks to control thought or to justify its laws for that impermissible end."[71] This dicta raises a question that requires serious debate on just what government motive to regulate thought would count as permissible: insuring public safety under the state's broad police powers could be one. However, the idea of holding people accountable for their predispositions as discovered by accessing their thoughts through a neuroprosthetic device rather than their actions poses a challenge to one of the central principles of Anglo-American jurisprudence: namely, that people are responsible for their behavior, not their proclivities—for what they do, not solely what they privately think (although I should note that crimes have a *mens rea* component combined with an *actus reus*).

The full range of issues that will be implicated by third party access to neuroprosthetic devices are not only too numerous to discuss in one book chapter, but

---

[70]*Id.*

[71]*Achcroft v. Free Speech Coalition,* 535 U.S. 234, 2002.

not possible to present comprehensively, because we are just at the beginnings of developing a law of cyborgs, therefore, much remains to be determined. However, an important issue to briefly review concerns the possibility of a third-party cyber-stalking a person equipped with a neuroprosthetic device, as this relates to the topic of the chapter—a person's ability to exercise cognitive liberty. Just consider—if repeated harassing phone calls to a cell phone are threatening, imagine repeated calls or access to an implant in the brain that functions as a communication device. In general, cyberstalking can involve using the Internet or other electronic means to harass an individual, which can also be accompanied by a credible threat of serious harm. And clearly, by accessing a neuroprosthetic device the psychological damage resulting from cyberstalking could be especially egregious as the damage could result from actually editing a person's memory. Given third party access to implantable devices, if a brain implant was accessed by a stalker, the results could be incredibly threatening and physically damaging—implicating criminal assault, battery, and other appropriate statutes. There is no current law directly on cyberstalking through access to brain implant devices, but just as California was the first state to enact an anti-chipping statute. California was also the first state to pass an anti-stalking law.[72] Under the law, courts may issue restraining orders to prohibit stalking and a victim of stalking may bring a civil lawsuit against the stalker and recover monetary damages. Because cyberstalking will take on a new meaning if third party access to a neuroprosthesis is done to threaten the integrity of a person's mind; this is obviously a great concern and an area ripe for legislation before midcentury.

To summarize, neuroprosthetic devices have joined the information technology revolution, they are now exponentially improving technologies. As a result, the law and policy impacted by the revolution occurring with neuroprosthesis, has not kept up. Chris Gray, writing in *Cyborg Citizen* has suggested that as we move toward the cyborg future, perhaps we need to consider granting basic rights to cybernetically enhanced individuals.[73] According to Gray, for freedom of speech, we should grant cyborgs an equivalent *freedom of electronic speech*, which would protect the right without government interference, to engage in electronic and other nonphysical forms of transmitting information—this would be an important right when telepathy is possible. Further, given the possibility of third party access to cybernetic devices implanted in the brain, the privacy of cyborgs could be threatened far beyond that of unenhanced individuals. Therefore, Gray proposes that the *right of electronic privacy* be granted to cyborgs. This right would protect cyborgs from third party access to their neuroprosthetic devices, and the right to privacy when they engage in electronic communication. And finally, Gray suggests that cyborgs be afforded the right to *freedom of consciousness;* that is, the right to

---

[72]California Civil Stalking Law, Cal Civ. Code § 1708.7 (2014); Stalking Cal. Pen. Code § 646.9, Stalking (2008).

[73]Chris Gray 2002, Cyborg Citizen: Politics in the Posthuman Age, Routledge.

have one's very consciousness free from outside interference.[74] In conclusion, just as in most of the world today in the U.S. we are a nation of law and also of technology, in that spirit, we now need to decide the appropriate balance between the use of cyborg technologies and their impact on our human freedoms as afforded by our laws, statutes, and policies.

---

[74]*Id.*

Chapter 5
Modifying, Enhancing, and Hacking the Body

Introduction

The first students who took a course in computer science were required to write programs for a massive computer that had a voracious appetite for electricity and a habit for reading punched cards. Since then, much has changed. Now day's wirelessly networked smart phones with the power of a mid-80s Cray supercomputer are in the hands of every student[1]; and over a hundred thousand people with debilitating neurological disease have electrodes implanted in their brain to control tremors and other symptoms.[2] But, as impressive as these uses of technology, in the future, prosthetics, implantable chips, and brain-computer interfaces, will go far beyond treating disease, or providing a tool for students to search the internet. In fact, researchers in neuroscience, artificial intelligence, and robotics, have predicted that well before the end of this century, technology will have advanced to the stage where memories can be implanted in the brain; cyborgs will emerge in full force; and artificially intelligent machines will argue for rights. The technology of brain-computer interfaces, more powerful computers, and advances in artificial intelligence, are all leading the way to what I believe is the major trend for the twenty-first century, a future in which we humans merge with artificially intelligent machines; and as Ray Kurzweil writing in *"The Singularity is Near"* observed, a future that may be only a few decades away.[3]

---

[1]The early ENIAC computer used 160 Kilowatts of electric power and had 18,000 vacuum tubes; Vovek Wadhwa, Our Lagging Laws, 2014, MIT Technology Review, v. 117, p. 11.

[2]About 30,000 in the U.S. with Parkinson's disease are treated with an electrode to stimulate their brain and 70,000 more are in need of deep brain stimulation, further 200,000 people use Cochlear implants.

[3]Ray Kurzweil, 2006, The Singularity is Near: When Humans Transcend Biology, Penguin Books.

© Springer International Publishing Switzerland 2015
W. Barfield, *Cyber-Humans*, DOI 10.1007/978-3-319-25050-2_5

In this chapter, I discuss amazing technologies that are being used by individuals to enhance and modify their body, and that are moving humanity directly towards a cyborg age and the possibility of a Posthuman future. These technologies will also bring us a few steps closer to the technical Singularity; that point in time where artificial intelligence reaches and then passes human intelligence. Given the range of technologies described in this chapter, I categorize practices to modify or enhance the body under the general rubric of "body hacking." Efforts by individuals to "hack their body," may include enhancing their senses, creating new senses, modifying the external features of their body, or as discussed below, under the topic of cybersecurity, disrupting the implantable wireless devices worn by other people. In my view of the future, to merge with machines is not to become indistinguishable from a robot, nor to lose every essence of humanity, but to more-and-more integrate technology into the human body, including the brain, essentially creating a cyborg and Posthuman future for humanity. How this future may unfold is discussed throughout this book.

There are many reasons why it would be desirable to hack the body with prosthesis, sensors, and other technologies. In fact, for thousands of years, people have been modifying the external features of their bodies. For example, among some Amazonian tribes, young males traditionally have their lips pierced and begin to wear lip plates when they enter the men's house, so the general idea that the body is malleable and subject to modification is clear from studies in anthropology and sociology.[4] Furthermore, in western society, movie stars and others use cosmetic surgery to modify their body and facial appearance for aesthetic purposes. Based on data from the *American Society of Plastic Surgeons*,[5] in the U.S. alone, millions of plastic surgery procedures are performed yearly, and millions more people have cosmetic procedures done for reconstructive purposes.[6] In addition, medical necessity is often cited as a reason to modify the body or restore the functions of the body to a previous normal state; for example, several hundred thousand people worldwide have cochlear implants and retinal prosthesis, and amazing enhancement technologies are just beyond the horizon.

Another factor leading to a cyborg future is the growing number of people who are beginning to "self-enhance" their body using digital technology in order to go beyond current human abilities. With continuing advances in technology, such people may benefit from the ability to hack the body in amazing ways. For example, in the future, with sufficiently advanced brain-computer interfaces, students with an interest in physics and economics could access the subject by

---

[4]See generally Victoria Pitts, 2003, In the Flesh: The Cultural Politics of Body Modification, Palgrave Macmillan.

[5]See for example, American Society of Plastic Surgeons, 2014, American Society of Plastic Surgeons Reports Cosmetic Procedures Increased 3 Percent in 2014, at: http://www.plasticsurgery.org/news/2015/plastic-surgery-statistics-show-new-consumer-trends.html.

[6]Reconstructive surgery is surgery to restore function or normal appearance by reconstructing defective organs or parts.

downloading the material directly to a digital storage device in their brain.[7] And health conscious people could buy medical/MD downloads the way they buy nutritional supplements; and for people requiring new skills for the twenty-first century, they could download the appropriate cognitive skills directly to their mind (or upload cognitive skills they have learned to the internet). Of course for any of these possibilities to happen, significant breakthroughs in technology and the life sciences will have to occur, but if anything, this book should convince the reader that we are at least headed in that direction. And as always, in the background of humans hacking their body and becoming more "cyborg like," it is important to remember, at the same time, artificially intelligent machines are making great strides in becoming more "human-like" in terms of their senses, cognition, physical appearance, and motor abilities. In fact, robotic prosthesis, are now approaching levels of human functionality in many areas. We seem to be becoming more like them (artificially intelligent machines), and they, more like us.

But even with amazing breakthroughs in technology, caution is in order. In an age where science is on the verge of allowing parents to select the features of their babies; and people are integrating faster, smarter, and more powerful technology into their body, body hacking and its consequences warrant significant discussion. An author and member of Singularity University, Ramez Naam wonders what it would be like if our brains were wired together by electronics.[8] Would we be vulnerable to bugs, software crashes, computer viruses, and malware? In a previous chapter I addressed this issue and concluded the answer is definitely yes. And Stanford Professor Francis Fukuyama, writing in *Our Posthuman Future, Consequences of the Biotechnology Revolution*, warned that "the most significant threat" from enhancement technology is "the possibility that it will alter human nature and thereby move us into a 'Posthuman' stage of history."[9] According to Fukuyama, this might happen through the achievement of genetically engineered "designer babies," but he presents other routes as well: such as research on neuropharmacology, which has already begun to reshape human behavior through drugs like Prozac and Ritalin.

In this chapter I discuss how digital technology may be used to enhance and modify the body as another route leading to a Posthuman future. On the possibility of humanity entering a Posthuman stage, Professor Fukuyama expressed the concern of those who argue for caution in moving towards this outcome, warning of the possibility of "us" becoming something else or losing what he refers to as our "human essence."[10] Surely, we will want to vigorously discuss the possibility of losing the very characteristics that make us human, rather than passively observing

---

[7]While downloading information directly to the brain is an amazing possibility, to do so will be an exceptionally challenging and difficult task.

[8]Ramez Naam, 2013, Now Entering the Neurotech Era: Are you Ready for your Hippocampus Chip? at: http://venturebeat.com/2013/01/09/entering-the-neurotech-era/.

[9]Francis Fukuyama, 2003, Our Posthuman Future, Consequences of the Biotechnology Revolution, Picador.

[10]*Id.*

as technology marches on and invades our body. And as we move toward a Posthuman future, there are many other issues that a public will need to discuss; for example, whether brain-computer interfaces and neuroprosthesis will have an unintended effect on memory and cognition, and therefore, freedom of thought, and if so, how might we regulate "cognitive liberty" the topic of another chapter in this book. And with the advent of body modifications and brain-computer interfaces, how will courts resolve issues fundamental to constitutional law such as free speech and the unfettered practice of religion; or under the United Nations Declaration of Human Rights, liberty. And considering economic and market forces, businesses' will need to know who owns the intellectual property rights of content created by computers claiming to be conscious and alive, and to what extent will artificially intelligent entities be allowed to contract? And where technology goes, so follows crime, not the least of which are issues of cybersecurity for wirelessly connected implantable medical devices and future brain-computer interfaces. These are serious ethical, legal, and policy concerns that the public should discuss while the possibility to shape the future still exits.

Hacking the Body

In the last decade, an interest to hack the body for reasons of art, self-expression, or to enhance the senses, has resulted in a growing movement among some members of the public to not only modify, but to extend the capabilities of their body. I expect the practice of body modification to grow, and to enter the mainstream of society given continuing advances in technology, public acceptance of new forms of body modification, and increased benefits from becoming enhanced. In this chapter, I extend the concept of hacking, from breaking into networks or clever solutions to software design, to the manipulation and enhancement of the human body with digital technology. Generally, hacking is done to understand how something works, so that the hacker can reassemble it into a different purpose for his own use. However, within the field of computer science hacking has a double meaning; it can refer to an expert programmer who creates complex software or efficient algorithms, or someone who breaks into computer networks for his own use. Regardless of the reason for accessing the software or network of another individual, Eric Raymond, compiler of *The New Hacker's Dictionary*, commented that a "good hack" is a clever solution to a programming problem and "hacking" is the act of doing it.[11]

A good place to start when discussing the topic of "body hacking" is to introduce basic terminology. With this goal in mind, in a report written by the U.S. President's *Council on Bioethics*, human enhancement is defined as going "beyond

---

[11]Eric S. Raymond, 1996, The New Hacker's Dictionary, MIT Press.

therapy;" instead of returning an individual to a healthy or normal state.[12] However, in a report for the European Parliament, the definition of human enhancement focuses more on performance than "beyond therapy." Under the *Science Technology Options Assessment*, the definition of enhancement is "any modification aimed at improving individual human performance and brought about by science-based or technology-based intervention in the human body."[13] Clearly, various types of prosthesis will be important technologies for the cyborg future; for discussion, we can define a prosthesis as an artificial replacement for a part of the body. In addition, an implant can be thought of as a subset of "prosthesis", and can include anything implanted within the body such as an object or material which is inserted or grafted into the body for prosthetic, therapeutic, diagnostic, or experimental purposes.[14] There is even "implant ethics," which is the study of the ethical aspects of the introduction of technological devices into the human body. On the last point, philosophers have taken an interest in human enhancement and body modification, and have written numerous articles and books on the topic.[15]

"Hacking the body" is a concept that can cover the spectrum from "Grinders" who design and install DIY body-enhancements such as magnetic implants (see below), to DIY biologists whose aim is to conduct at-home gene sequencing. DIY biologists engage in a form of hacking termed "biohacking," which refers to the practice of manipulating human biology using a hacker ethic; that is, finding physical, emotional, or intellectual tweaks to the body in order to improve cognitive and sensory performance. Among some people, biohacking can also refer to the practice of managing one's own biology using a combination of medical, nutritional and electronic techniques. Thus biohacking may include the use of nootropics and/or cybernetic devices for recording biometric data. Generally, people who engage in body hacking identify with the transhumanism movement—the belief that it is both possible and desirable to so fundamentally alter the human condition through the use of technologies as to eventually create a superior post-human being. Finally, many who identify with the Grinder movement, practice actual implementation of cybernetic devices in their organic bodies as a method of working towards transhumanism; we can also refer to these people as "cyber hackers."

The idea of enhancing or modifying the body with implants and other forms of technology is not new, but in the twenty-first century an interesting question arises- in response to advances in prosthetics and digital technology, to what

---

[12]The President's Council on Bioethics, Beyond Therapy (Enhancement), at: https://bioethicsarchive. georgetown.edu/pcbe/topics/beyond_index.html.

[13]European Parliament, Science Technology Options Assessment, at: https://www.itas.kit.edu/ downloads/etag_coua09a.pdf.

[14]See generally Sven Ove Hansson, "Implant Ethics", Journal of Medical Ethics, 31:519–525, 2005; Barbro Björkman and Sven Ove Hansson, "Bodily rights and property rights", Journal of Medical Ethics 32: 209–214, 2006.

[15]Allen E. Buchanan, 2013, Beyond Humanity? The Ethics of Biomedical Enhancement, Oxford University Press.

extent will people enhance or modify their bodies? This chapter seeks to address that question by providing numerous examples of recent implantable devices, but a partial answer can be gleaned from people's efforts to manipulate the shape of their own body. In fact, for some time, body implants have been used to change the shape and appearance of specific body areas, especially the buttocks, chest, calf, and bicep. In this case, the implants which in the U.S. have gone through a Federal Drug Administration (FDA) approval process, are made of firm, semi-solid, rubberized silicone material that fits in front of the bones without being absorbed by the body. Since body implants are considered permanent, their removal requires surgery. In addition to body implants, some people choose to sculpt or add volume or contour to certain parts of the body, using liposuction and fat transfer. Then there are people who have modified their body in extreme ways—like the person who used tattoos and surgery to make himself look like a cat,[16] including implanted whiskers, a converted cat nose, teeth filed into the shape of cat teeth, and a head flattened to appear more feline. In the vein of "cat man" another extreme example of self-directed body modification is "lizard man,"[17] and there is even the *Church of Body Modification*,[18] reportedly dedicated to strengthening the bond between "mind, body, and soul". Given these examples of self-directed body modification, whats new in the twenty-first century is the use of engineering science and information technologies that allow people to modify and enhance their body with sophisticated prosthesis; to extend their senses beyond the limits of human nature; and for people suffering from neurological disorders, to have electrodes and/or chips implanted into their brain forming a commensal relationship between patient and machine.

The Risks of Body Hacking and Cyborg Technology

While many people desire to modify their body, the procedures are not always successful, there is a risk associated with body modification, especially for those who self-modify, and sometimes the risk is fatal. On this point, there are reports in the news that women across the U.S. are risking their lives for black market procedures, done by people with no medical training, often by attending "pumping parties" in which multiple people are injected with silicone in hotel rooms. Whatever the reason for seeking the body modification, they are seeking cheaper alternatives to plastic surgery—sometimes with deadly or disfiguring results. Tragically, deaths from black market silicone injections have been reported in several states in the U.S., with felony charges directed against the person performing the procedure. In one incident, the injector was charged with "depraved heart murder" a very serious

---

[16]Cat Man, at: http://en.wikipedia.org/wiki/Stalking_Cat.

[17]Lizard Man, at: http://www.thelizardman.com/.

[18]Church of Body Modification, at: http://uscobm.com/.

crime signifying an action that demonstrates "callous disregard for human life" that resulted in death. Conviction could be punishable by life in prison. Despite a lack of hard numbers, there's anecdotal evidence that the illegal procedures are becoming more common.

The risk of body implants is not limited to black market procedures. For example, the French firm Poly Implant Prostheses (PIP), once the third biggest global supplier of breast implants, used industrial grade silicone not intended for medical use in its products for years. As a result, many of the breast implants were prone to rupture, causing dangerous leakages of the silicone in women's bodies. And when an implant fails, it normally affects a large number of people. Here the breast implant fraud case affected 100,000 women in Europe and 300,000 women globally; thousands of the women are now seeking compensation for harm caused by the implants which under French law are generally limited to actual losses and to lost opportunities (*perte d'une chance*). However, the French court may also impose general damages not linked to a specific loss, called "moral damages" (*dommages moraux*) to compensate the victim for mental anguish or distress. If one wants to mass market technology to hack the body, they better get it right— the founder of the company received a four year prison sentence for fraud, which under French law can be an element of various criminal provisions arising under the Criminal Code (*Code Pénal*).

Given the possibility of disfigurement and other dangers from body hacking, I advocate that a debate among the public on the desirability of modifying the body occur before body hacking becomes more mainstream in popular culture. For example, it is popular among the youth to get a temporary tattoo to mark an occasion, often in an act of rebellion. Temporary tattoos typically last from three days to several weeks, depending on the product used for coloring and the condition of the skin. Unlike permanent tattoos, which are injected into the skin, and digital tattoos (described below) which serve as sensors, temporary tattoos marketed as "henna" are applied to the skin's surface. At first glance these tattoos seem harmless; however, according to Linda Katz, director of the FDA's Office of Cosmetics and Colors, "just because a tattoo is temporary it doesn't mean that it is risk free."[19] In fact, some recipients of temporary tattoos have reported severe reactions that may outlast the temporary tattoos themselves. Of course, technology implanted under the skin, and even within the brain, has the potential to offer tremendous capabilities to a person, but poses far more danger to recipients, and extreme caution should be taken to protect our future cyborgs.

As a response to defective implants, the *European Commission* has proposed updating the existing legislation on medical devices. Currently, the term 'medical device' in Europe, covers a wide range of products both used internally and externally by patients and doctors. They can include everything from contact lenses and

---

[19]Linda Katz, 2013, FDA warns about hidden dangers of 'temporary' henna tattoos that burn, blister and leave skin scarred for life, Daily Mail, at: http://www.dailymail.co.uk/news/article-2299140/FDA-warns-hidden-dangers-temporary-henna-tattoos-burn-blister-leave-skin-scarred-life.html.

pregnancy tests, dental filling materials, to, "cyborg technology" such as pacemakers and hip replacements. Similarly, in the U.S. medical devices are regulated by the FDA with the intensity of the regulation depending on the complexity, usage, and potential danger of the device. A thermometer, for example, might have rather minimal regulations, while a pacemaker is very heavily regulated. And in Europe (and likewise in the U.S.), medical devices are ranked from Class I, a low-risk category that would include spectacles, to high-risk Class III items such as hip replacements and pacemakers, which are fitted inside the body. In its proposal for regulating implants, the Commission wants to improve the product evaluation process, enhance the traceability of products in the marketplace and place more scrutiny on notified bodies once an issue with a medical device has manifested itself.

As we move toward the cyborg future, unique safety and health issues for those with implants and other types of "cyborg technology" will arise. For example, when we consider the possible health problems associated with being equipped with prosthesis and implants, there is concern among pathologists and other experts that there are safety issues with the materials and devices implanted into the human body. We can think of these concerns as challenges which must be overcome if humanity is to merge with machines. For example, although implantable materials are generally considered inert or "biocompatible," there is a body of evidence which suggests that many metals, plastics, gels, rubbers and combinations of materials fashioned into implantable devices can produce chronic and potentially harmful effects on human tissue in some people. It is possible that people with implants could suffer persistent inflammation, infection, blood clots, bone erosion, diseases of connective tissue and, in rare instances, cancer, depending on the materials and the location in the body. And with brain implants, the biocompatibility of implanted electrodes and chips is of particular concern in device design. Already, the development of scar tissue at the site of implantable electrodes for people being treated with Parkinson's disease is a concern.

As we head towards a cyborg future, the emerging evidence on the safety of implants, ranging from their software to hardware, is viewed by some experts as a caution sign for people planning to undergo an implant, particularly one that would be used early in life for purely cosmetic purposes. The potentially troublesome devices seems to run the gauntlet of current "cyborg technology"; including artificial hips, knees, elbows, wrists, ligaments and fingers, breast implants, heart valves, pacemakers, shunts, intrauterine devices, dental implants and a variety of other objects that meet either medical or cosmetic needs.

What are some of the specific reactions of the body to implants? Generally, the body is designed to attack foreign objects that invade it. When a material is implanted under the skin, it sits in a protein-rich bath found throughout body tissues. Immediately, proteins begin sticking to the surface of the implanted device and, it is soon coated in a mixture of proteins. Depending on the type of material used in the implant, physical interactions may involve charged particles and magnetic fields occurring between the implant's surface and the proteins. The interaction is sufficiently energetic to alter the shape of proteins sticking to the implant, so that the proteins expose binding sites that attract other circulating proteins designed to recognize trouble. One set of circulating proteins initiates blood clots and covers the implant with thick layers of scar tissue called fibrin. Some implant recipients suffer chronic, intermittent low-grade fevers whereas, initially, some people seem highly tolerant of their implants but then experience flare ups years later. And implants can also become infected with bacteria many years after surgery. To some extent, problems can be treated with antibiotics, pain-killers and anti-inflammation drugs; but clearly, a cost-benefit analysis should be performed for any implant procedure. Another solution to the body's reaction to implantable devices is to coat such devices with antibiotics, blood thinners, and other agents— but these eventually dissolve, limiting their longevity and effectiveness.

As a response to the body's reaction to implants, some companies are developing novel biomaterial for implanted devices that permanently barricade troublesome microbes from the device's surface. One material when applied to an implant device sprouts a thicket of polymers that attract water, creating an impenetrable barrier for microbes. Its chemical makeup also mimics that of cells important to homeostasis, potentially reducing the body's natural rejection of implanted devices. Essentially, the solution is aimed at making the implantable devices look more like the human body.[20] However, even with advances in biomaterials, given efforts by Grinders to self-modify their body without the assistance of a physician, the reader should keep in mind the potential health problems associated with implantable devices, as they read further in this chapter about the body hacking movement.

In thinking about our cyborg future, it is instructive to consider the above discussion in light of a current FDA approved sensor (radio frequency identification, or RFID sensor), that is being implanted in the body for reasons of security, art, and body hacking. While the FDA has "reasonable assurance" that an implanted RFID sensor is safe; neither the company manufacturing it, VeriChip Corp., nor the regulators openly discuss a series of veterinary and toxicology studies, dating back to the mid-1990s, which indicated that chip implants had "induced" malignant tumors in some lab mice and rats. Some researchers have indicated that they would not allow family members to receive RFID implants, and many have urged further research before the glass-encased transponders are widely implanted in people. With these warnings in mind, several thousand RFID devices have still been implanted in humans worldwide. VeriChip Corp., which sees a target market of forty-five million Americans for its medical monitoring chips, insists the devices are safe. However, when the FDA approved the device, it noted some risks: The capsules could migrate around the body, making them difficult to extract; they might interfere with defibrillators, or be incompatible with MRI scans, causing burns.

If we compare an RFID chip to another implantable device, a heart pacemaker, we see that the RFID device isn't vital to keeping someone alive as is a pacemaker, so from a medical perspective, we have to ask—does the cost for RFID

---

[20]Rob Matheson, 2013, Creating a permanent bacteria barrier, MIT news, at: http://newsoffice.mit.edu/2013/semprus-biosciences-1010.

implants justify the benefits? For a class of people the answer is clearly "yes." Currently, RFID chips have been approved for human patients with Alzheimer's and other dementia sufferers; the idea being that if they become lost, the chip will make it easier for them to be reunited with their caregivers; here the benefits of an implanted sensor outweigh the costs. But the general idea that a class of people could benefit from implantable technology, while others may not, raises fascinating questions of law and policy. Not the least of which is whether courts should view cyborgs as a protected class, and thus eligible for special protection under the law; which could include required access to software updates and next-generation hardware replacements and possibly broad protection under a federal statue granting a cause of action for discrimination.

Prosthesis, Implants and Law

Many who have reservations about the cyborg future, often advocate for appropriate government regulations and statues to protect those who have become enhanced with technology. In the future, advances in neuroscience and robotics will change the way that society views the human body, reinforcing the concept of the body as a machine with interchangeable, replaceable, and upgradeable parts. As these cyborg technologies become more advanced, they will approach and then surpass ordinary human function, rising the prospects of enhancing human capabilities well beyond the current baseline standard; this may lead society to view the healthy, yet unenhanced human as disabled.[21] Therefore, in the cyborg future, the disabled, equipped with cyborg technology, may prove more "abled," and average abilities could become almost akin to defects, in need of elimination. With these possibilities in mind, this section gives the reader a flavor of what I think is part of a developing field of cyborg law.

Numerous cases of discrimination against those equipped with "cyborg technology" revolve around employment disputes and in the U.S. are brought forward by the Equal Employment Opportunity Commission (EEOC). One such case involved a woman who was terminated because she had a prosthetic leg and her employer was concerned she would be "knocked down" at work due to her disability.[22] The case, which was won by the woman, was decided under the American with Disabilities Act (ADA) which prohibits discrimination against people with disabilities in employment.[23] The court ruled that it was illegal to fire a disabled employee due to a baseless fear they may injure themselves or others. Another

---

[21]Collin R. Bockman, 2010, Cybernetic-Enhancement Technology and the Future of Disability Law, 95 Iowa Law Review, 1315–1340.

[22]*EEOC v. Staffmark Investment LLC and Sony Electronics, Inc.*, No. 12-cv-9628, on Dec. 4, 2012 in U.S. District Court for the Northern District of Illinois.

[23]Americans With Disabilities Act, 42 U.S.C. Section 12101 et seq.

employment dispute with implications for a "cyborg law," dealt with a person equipped with a hand prosthesis, and was brought under the Rehabilitation Act of 1973.[24] In this dispute a veteran who had lost his hand and replaced it with a prosthesis, was dismissed from the FBI academy because they alleged that during his training he could not safely fire a handgun with his prosthesis. However, a jury finding that the FBI instructors at the academy were hostile toward the veteran, ruled in his favor and the court awarded him monetary damages, back pay, and reinstatement to the FBI academy. The statue used for this "cyborg discrimination case," deals with federal jobs and federal agencies, and thus does not cover discrimination against those with prosthesis in other situations; this seems like an area ripe for legislation.

Another case with implications for cyborg law was heard in 1999 by the U.S. Supreme Court and involved the issue of whether a person with a corrected disability would still be considered disabled under the ADA.[25] This is an interesting case for "cyborg law" given the aim of becoming equipped with technology (i.e., becoming a cyborg) is often to restore, or go beyond, normal human abilities. The case involved twin sisters who suffered from acute visual myopia. When they applied to United Airlines for a job as a commercial pilot, they met the requirements for employment except for the vision requirement which was uncorrected visual acuity of 20/100 or better.[26] Each sister was able to correct their myopic vision to 20/20 with glasses and contact lens, and could function normally in their daily lives. However, in their ADA claim, the Suttons argued that they were disabled within the meaning of the ADA because, under the statute they suffered from a physical impairment that "substantially limits … major life activities," or because, they were regarded as having such an impairment. The question for the Court to decide was whether the determination of disability under the ADA could be made without reference to corrective measures that mitigated the impairment. That is, would a person with a disability, but restored to "normal" with technology, still be considered disabled? The Court determined that a disability must be determined with reference to corrective measures. Thus, the Court reasoned that once an impairment is corrected, the impairment does not substantially limit a "major life activity." Based on this court decision, a person would not be considered disabled if cyborg technology brought the person to normal functioning (or beyond normal?). But a court's decision may be overturned by legislators, lets continue the discussion.

The law on mitigating disabilities with technology, has much to say for cyborg discrimination and acceptance into society, and raises serious questions

---

[24]Rehabilitation Act of 1973, 29 U.S.C. § 791 *et eq*; Matt Zapotosky, 2013, Disabled veteran's discrimination lawsuit rankles FBI, spurs investigation of agent, at: http://www.washingtonpost.com/local/disabled-veterans-discrimination-lawsuit-rankles-fbi-spurs-investigation-of-agent/2013/07/27/d3d1d8f6-f3b2-11e2-9434- 60440856fadf_story.html.

[25]*Sutton v. United Airlines, Inc.*, 527 U.S. 471 (1999).

[26]*Id.*

concerning who should be considered disabled as people become equipped with technology. On this question, Congress passed the *American with Disabilities Amendments Act* in 2008 which explicitly states that the determination of whether an impairment substantially limits a major life activity is to be made without regard to the ameliorative effects of mitigating measures such as—prosthetic limbs, cochlear implants, or an implantable hearing device.[27] The amendment revealed the thinking of Congress; that no additions or modifications are relevant in the eyes of the law to the determination of whether someone is disabled; so, for example, the very act of getting a prosthesis for the upper arm doesn't automatically qualify a person as disabled under the amendment. The determination of whether an impairment substantially limits a major life activity is to be made without regard to the beneficial effects of mitigating measures such as medication, prosthetics, mobility devices, hearing aids and cochlear implants—to name just a few ways to mitigate a disability. For example, a person with one leg may be equipped with a prosthesis but when he wears his prosthetic leg he can walk fine, but without the prosthetic leg he has great difficulty walking. This person has a disability under the ADA because the determination of whether he is substantially limited in the major life activity of walking is made without considering the prosthetic leg. However, when determining whether someone has a disability, the rule concerning mitigating measures does not apply to people whose vision is corrected with eye glasses or contact lens. For example, a woman with myopia whose visual acuity is fully corrected when she's wearing eyeglasses, is not substantially limited in seeing, because the determination is made when she's wearing the glasses. This is a public policy decision—just think of how many people would be considered to have a disability under the ADA if we did not take into account the beneficial effects of ordinary eyeglasses and contact lenses.

However, the amended ADA raises several conceptual problems in an age of cyborgs. For example, under the amended ADA, if a women chose to replace her right leg with a far superior cybernetic limb, the limb would fall under the category of prosthetics (limbs and devices), and since the statute bans such mitigating factors from consideration in determining disability, this woman would be legally disabled, even though her new leg is actually better than the old one. And paradoxically, if everyone at a particular work site except for one person upgraded a limb with a superior cybernetic prosthesis, the unenhanced "normal" person would be the only non-disabled employee, even though all her colleagues enjoyed superior capabilities. In fact, the more prosthetic upgrades a person receives, the more disabled they may be considered under the Amended ADA. And nothing in the ADA protects those with enhancements from comparative discrimination, where enhanced individuals may discriminate against an otherwise ordinary individual whom they consider "disabled" due to his lack of upgrades. As more enhancements become available, and result in humans with superior capabilities, the law will need to change how it conceptualizes those who are disabled to account for cyborg technology and enhanced cyborgs living amongst us.

---

[27]ADA, *id.*, note 23.

There are other legal and policy issues that are relevant for a developing field of cyborg law. For example, public policy dictates that materials needed for life-saving medical procedures are available to manufactures of medical devices, including implants. So, for suppliers of implant materials the U.S. Congress enacted the *Biomaterials Access Assurance Act of 1998* (BAAA).[28] The BAAA applies to all implant raw materials and components for implants except the silicone gel and the silicone envelope utilized in a breast implant. Essentially, the BAAA shields suppliers of raw materials and component parts used in medical implants from virtually all civil liability, thereby ensuring the availability of materials for lifesaving and life-enhancing medical devices. However, the BAAA does not apply if the supplier also manufacturers the device, sells the device, or fails to meet applicable contractual requirements relating to the component part or material. But suppliers of raw materials and component parts of medical devices can use the BAAA not only to avoid liability but also to extricate themselves from personal injury suits in which they are named as defendants.

Since the *Biomaterials Access Assurance Act* is limited to suppliers of material, it doesn't shield negligent physicians and manufactures of implantable devices from liability if the device harms the recipient.[29] As long as they are protected under current law schemes, future cyborgs will have a range of legal options if they are harmed. To begin the discussion, what happens if the device, implanted by a physician, fails and the person suffers harm? If the harm can be traced to the physician's actions, the person equipped with the implant may pursue a legal action for malpractice. In the U.S. medical malpractice is derived from English common law. To establish a case for medical malpractice, the injured person must show that the physician acted negligently in implanting the device, and that such negligence resulted in injury. Specifically, four legal elements must be proven: a professional duty owed to the person receiving the implant; breach of such duty; injury caused by the breach; and resulting damages. Given the number of implantable devices and types of prosthesis people may be equipped with, medical malpractice lawsuits are not uncommon in this area particularly with hip and knee replacements which are among the most common surgical procedures performed in the U.S. These surgeries, along with revision surgeries that are performed to correct problems that develop after the original procedure, are increasing in part due to new implant devices and the advancing age of the baby boom generation receiving the implants.

There are other ways in which an implant may cause harm, other than that caused by a physician performing a particular procedure. For example, if the implant fails, a cyborg could sue under a products liability theory. In this case any entity in the chain of manufacture and sale of a defective implant can be sued if harm to the implant recipient occurred. In this case not just the manufacturer of the implant would be liable, but also the manufacturers of the product's

---

[28]Biomaterials Access Assurance Act of 1998 (BAA98) (21 U.S.C. 1601–1606).
[29]*Id.*

component parts, the wholesaler, and the retailer. Whether a cyborg sued to protect its right to seek compensation for defective parts is done under malpractice or products liability is an important distinction because medical negligence focuses on whether the physician's actions were reasonable (when measured against the medical standard of care); while products liability focuses on whether the product was reasonably safe or not. Generally a product manufacturer or seller is liable under products liability law if the product contains an inherent defect that is unreasonably dangerous and that causes injury to a foreseeable user of the product. I would think that a Grinder using an off-the-shelf sensor as an implant is not foreseeable to a manufacturer; whereas, a person receiving an implant under the supervision of a physician for a medical condition is. However, a foreseeable plaintiff or not, sensors (a main cyborg technology), when used as a medical device, are regulated by the FDA.

Under tort law, there are three types of products liability: a manufacturing defect, a marketing defect, or a design defect. A manufacturing defect occurs during the manufacturing process. A marketing defect usually refers to a problem with the product's instructions or advertising, for example, a failure to warn the purchaser about hidden dangers in an implant device. In addition, a design defect occurs when the product is simply dangerous and defective due to the way it was designed, for example, a prosthetic leg not able to bear the weight of the recipient. Actually, design flaws are not uncommon with "cyborg technology" for example, a few years ago, 93,000 DePuy hips replacement systems were found to have a design flaw and subsequently recalled; many other recalls occur for other implantable devices.[30]

What if the person performing the implant is not a trained physician, instead, a tattoo artist, or a person working at a "body shop"? An action for negligence, which is a failure to exercise the care that a reasonable prudent person would exercise in like circumstances is possible. The elements of negligence are similar to a medical malpractice suit, and likewise include duty, breach, causation, and damages. The fundamental difference between an ordinary suit for negligence and a suit for malpractice lies in the definition of the prevailing standard of care. If someone sues for ordinary negligence, they compare the defendant's behavior to what any reasonable person would have done under the circumstances. If they sue for malpractice, they will compare the physician's behavior to what a reasonable member of the profession would have done. Professional standards are much higher and much better documented; thus, it is generally easier to establish negligence in a professional capacity. In an age of self-directed body modification, when the person doing the implant is a friend or someone who works at a Tattoo parlor, I wonder what the definition of "reasonable person" is?

To hack the body often involves implanting a sensor, magnet, or some other form of technology under the skin, or more generally, piercing the skin to implant

---

[30]Hip Replacement Lawsuits and Hip Recalls, at: http://www.lieffcabraser.com/Personal-Injury/Devices/Hip-Implant-Recall.shtml.

a device beneath its surface; surprisingly, in some jurisdictions, a physician is not required for the procedure. In the U.K. body piercing is an unregulated industry and only requires the studio to be registered with the Environmental Health Department of their local Council. There are also, unlike tattooing, no minimum age requirements for the piercee in the U.K. whereas there are in the U.S. Furthermore, in the U.K. there are no regulations covering the training of body piercers and there are also no regulations covering those who teach body piercing. However, in the U.S. the body modification culture has caught the attention of some state governments. For example in the State of Arkansas, a state senator sponsored the 2013 bill entitled *"An Act To Limit Body Art Procedures,"* aimed at making body modifications limited to "traditional" tattoos and piercings." The state senator's proposal would essentially ban scarification procedures and dermal implants, as well as certain tattoos which remain yet to be defined due to the vague language of the sponsored bill. Scarification is a non-ink skin marking that forms scars for decorative purposes, while dermal implants refers to placing ornamental objects beneath the skin. In my view, the proposed bill is unconstitutional under the First Amendment to the U.S. Constitution which clearly prohibits government efforts at "abridging the freedom of speech," which U.S. courts have repeatedly found includes forms of artistic expression.[31]

In addition, for some, to modify the body is a form of religious practice and thus should be a basic human right. Not far from my home, a North Carolina high school student was dismissed from school because her nose piercing violated the schools dress code.[32] In fighting against the dismissal, the student argued that the nose piercing was part of her religious faith based on her membership in the *Church of Body Modification.* Although her school dress code prohibits facial piercings, a federal judge ruled that the student could return to school, piercing and all. The North Carolina chapter of the American Civil Liberties Union, which represented the student, said the settlement with the school was a vindication of the family's right to determine its own religious practice. Under the terms of the resolution, the student is allowed to wear the nose stud as long as she remains a member of the *Church of Body Modification,* a religious group that claims a few thousand adherents and considers practices like tattooing and body piercing to be elements of spiritual practice.

However, the law is far from an exact science, as another case based on a religious exemption for a person who modified her body, produced a different outcome. Kimberly Cloutier was a Costco employee when she alleged that her employer failed to offer her a "reasonable accommodation" for her facial jewelry which she wore as part of her religious beliefs supported by the *Church of Body Modification.*[33] Even though Kimberly had received a copy of the Costco employ-

---

[31]*Mattel v. MCA Records,* 296 F.3d 894 (9th Cir. 2002).

[32]Sarah Netter, 2010, Student's Body Modification Religion Questioned After Nose Piercing Controversy, at: http://abcnews.go.com/US/students-body-modification-religion-questioned-nose-piercing-controversy/story?id=11645847.

[33]*Cloutier v. Costco Wholesale Corp.,* 390 F.3d 126, 12 (1st Cir. 2004).

ment agreement, she decided to ignore the dress code provisions and instead engaged in various forms of body modification, including body piercings and skin cutting. After being terminated for failure to adhere to the dress code, she filed a complaint with the *Equal Employment Opportunity Commission*, which was appealed to the U.S. First Circuit Court of Appeals which subsequently held that it would place an undue hardship on Costco to allow a cashier to wear facial jewelry due to their "legitimate interest in presenting a reasonably professional appearance to customers."[34] Interestingly, since there was no direct legal protection for body piercings in the statutes, Cloutier, unsuccessfully tried to link her unprotected characteristic to a protected category, by claiming facial piercings were part of religious practices encouraged by the *Church of Body Modification*. Given a different result in the two cases above dealing with the practice of religion, an issue for the public and legislators to debate, is whether specific legislation needs to be enacted to address the needs of those who modify their bodies, argue for rights, and in the future appear as a cyborg.

Body Hacking in the Digital Age

Generally, in an age of cyborgs, the term body hacking refers to a practice that's part body modification, and part computer hacking. This dichotomy between corporeal body and computer, suggests to me that issues of law and public policy need to be directed at each component of the cyborg. For example the laws which relate to software (e.g., contracts, licenses, tort) would apply to the "brains" of the implantable device; whereas, other laws would apply to the corporeal body. In some cases, the same law would apply to both, but I think new law and policy will have to be enacted to account for the combination of human and machine.

The body hacking movement, especially with regard to implantable sensors within the body, gained momentum from the pioneering work of Professor Kevin Warwick starting in 1998 at the University of Reading. Professor Warwick was one of the first people to hack his body when he participated in a series of proof-of-concept studies involving a sensor implanted into the median nerve of his left arm; a procedure which allowed him to link his nervous system directly to a computer. Most notably, Professor Warwick was able to control an electric wheelchair and an artificial hand, using the neural interface. In addition to being able to measure the signals transmitted along the nerve fibers in Professor Warwick's left arm, the implant was also able to create artificial sensation by stimulating the nerves in his arm using individual electrodes. This bi-directional functionality was demonstrated with the aid of Kevin's wife using a second, less complex implant connected to her nervous system. According to Kevin this was the first solely electronic communication between the nervous systems of two humans; since then,

---

[34]*Id.*

many have extended Kevin's seminal work using RFID chips and other implantable sensors; such work is discussed in further detail below.

Considering Kevin's surgical procedure to have a sensor implanted in his body; obviously Kevin and his wife volunteered to be implanted with the sensor, an act many might consider to be inherently dangerous. Thus, if any injury attributed to the surgeon resulted during and after the implant, under tort law, there could be a bar to liability based on the assumption of risk theory. This legal doctrine states that a person who knowingly exposes him/herself to hazards with potential for bodily harm cannot hold others liable if harm occurs. Further, under the assumption of risk doctrine, a person who consents to a procedure, with knowledge that injury is a foreseeable, albeit uncommon, result, waives the right to a future complaint that any 'foreseeable' injury was caused by negligence, assuming the procedure was performed with proper care. However, if the physician performing the implant procedure committed malpractice, they may still be sued for medical malpractice. In addition, depending on the jurisdiction, a court could examine this situation using the secondary assumption of risk doctrine. For example, in California, if a physician performed the "experimental implant", and was found to owe Kevin a duty of care, given Kevin volunteered for the procedure (not warranted by medical necessity), if harm occurred, a comparative fault scheme could be used, and the trier of fact, in apportioning the loss resulting from injury, could consider the relative responsibilities of the parties.

Sensors and Implantable Devices

We live in a time when tremendous progress is being made developing sensors and implantable technology to control and monitor different functions of the body (Fig. 5.1). For example, researchers at MIT are developing an implantable sensor

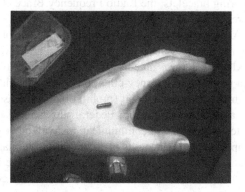

Fig. 5.1 An RFID sensor implanted in the hand. The microchip contains stored information which can be transmitted to a reader and then to a computer. RFID's can be passive, semi-passive or active. Active RFID's have an internal power source such as a battery, this allows the tag to send signals back to the reader. Image from Amal Grafffstra, Wikipedia Commons

which uses carbon nanotubes to monitor nitric oxide (NO) in animals. In humans, the sensor could be useful for detecting cancer cells and for monitoring glucose levels. Then there's research at Boston University[35] that involves "brain-reading" software designed to transform thoughts into speech, starting with vowels. The system uses implanted electrodes to pick up nerve signals related to movement of the mouth, lips, and jaw; these signals are then sent wirelessly to a computer, where software analyzes them for speech patterns.

Further, researchers at Brown University and *Cyberkinetics* in Massachusetts, are devising a microchip that is implanted in the motor cortex just beneath a person's skull that will be able to intercept nerve signals and reroute them to a computer, which will then wirelessly send a command to any of various electronic devices, including computers, stereos and electric wheelchairs. And consider a German team that has designed a microvibration device and a wireless low-frequency receiver that can be implanted in a person's tooth. The vibrator acts as microphone and speaker, sending sound waves along the jawbone to a person's eardrum. And in another example of an implantable device, *Setpoint*, is developing computing therapies to reduce systemic inflammation by stimulating the vagus nerve using an implantable pulse generator. This device works by activating the body's natural inflammatory reflex to dampen inflammation and improve clinical signs and symptoms. Thus far, the company is developing an implanted neuromodulation device to treat rheumatoid arthritis, a disease currently afflicting over two million people in the U.S.

Since Warwick's seminal results, sensors have been implanted into the human body for many reasons such as individual security or to monitor a person's health. For example, due to the risk of being kidnapped, some people have had a tiny transmitter implanted under their skin so that if necessary satellites could track and locate their position. From a different security perspective, courts may require people convicted of a crime to participate in an electronic monitoring program, requiring wearable sensors, as an alternative to incarceration. There are two types of electronic monitoring bracelets: the Radio Frequency Bracelet, which is used as a form of house arrest, and the GPS Bracelet, used to track an offender's whereabouts in real time. As with other wearable technology, the use of the GPS bracelet raises serious legal and policy issues. One such issue occurred when it was discovered that a GPS ankle bracelet was able to listen into conversations between a lawyer and his client, a violation of attorney-client privilege. I would argue that this is also a violation of the Fourth Amendment (prohibiting an unreasonable search and seizure), as well as a violation of the U.S. Federal Wiretapping Act (a federal law that is aimed at protecting privacy in communications with other persons).

The above examples show the benefits of wearable and implantable technology to perform important tasks on the body's surface or within the body; essentially, these are technical tools in the arsenal to assist humans. But continuing a point

---

[35]Patrick L. Kennedy, 2011, The Mind Reader How Frank Guenther turns thoughts into words, at: http://www.bu.edu/today/2011/the-mind-reader/.

being made throughout this book; the more we become enhanced with technology, the closer we are to becoming a cyborg and laying the groundwork for a future merger with artificially intelligent machines. I also conclude that much of what we learn about integrating sensors within the body is useful information for engineers designing the next generation of artificially intelligent machines as they too will need sensors to perceive the world.

If we consider the range of sensors being developed, and their potential to collect data about the internal state of the body, it's easy to conclude that the human body is becoming the subject of extensive data mining. In fact, Google is doing just that, in a program to determine what a healthy person should look like. The project, dubbed Baseline Study, involves researchers collecting anonymous genetic and molecular information from initially 175 people, and later thousands more, in a bid to help detect diseases, such as cancer and heart disease, much earlier.[36] Baseline will not be limited in scope to certain diseases but will use state-of-the-art diagnostic tools to collect hundreds of different samples that will be plugged into computer systems and compared with others. To collect the data participants could, for example, wear Google's smart contact lenses, to monitor glucose levels. After the data is collected, Google will use its computing power to find patterns or 'biomarkers' that could help medical researchers detect a disease at a curable stage.

Interestingly, as implants collect data about the inside of our bodies, our bodies are becoming the equivalent of open books like those that have been scanned by Google; this raises serious privacy concerns. To me it is problematic that in the future companies which sell and provide services to support neural devices may have unique access to private information stored in the human brain. The data derived from the ability to peer into the brain, is in need of special protection similarly to that provide by Title II of the *Genetic Information Nondiscrimination Act of 2008* (GINA).[37] This act prohibits genetic information discrimination in employment and is enforced by the Equal Employment Opportunity Commission (EEOC). Genetic information is often used to determine whether someone has an increased risk of getting a disease, disorder, or condition in the future. Similarly, access to information in the brain could be used to determine whether a person had a predisposition to commit a crime, a propensity for violence, or is a candidate for mental illness. The ability to collect information about the body and brain and to analyze it with algorithms designed to predict the future, raise serious privacy and policy concerns and the possibility of a dystopian future. A prior chapter explored the law and policy of brain technology and cognitive liberty in some detail.

To manage debilitating disease, diabetes for example, is another reason to become equipped with cyborg technology. In fact, millions of people worldwide

---

[36]Alistair Barr, 2014, Google's New Moonshot Project: the Human Body, The Wall Street Journal, at: http://www.wsj.com/articles/google-to-collect-data-to-define-healthy-human-1406246214.

[37]Genetic Information Nondiscrimination Act of 2008, Pub. L. 110–233, 122 Stat. 881, enacted May 21, 2008.

with diabetes could benefit from implantable sensors and wearable computers designed to monitor their blood sugar level; because if not controlled people are at risk for dangerous complications, including damage to the eyes, kidneys, and heart. To help people monitor their blood-sugar level *Smart Holograms*[38] a spinoff company of Cambridge University, Google, and others are developing "eye worn" sensors to assist those with the disease. Google's technology consists of contact lens built with special sensors that measures sugar levels in tears using a tiny wireless chip and miniature sensor embedded between two layers of soft contact lens material. Interesting and innovative as this solution to monitoring diabetes is, these aren't the only examples of "eye oriented" cyborg technology within the hacker movement; in fact, hacking the eyes is a subject of body modifiers. In the future, we may see cyborgs equipped with contact lens or retinal prosthesis that monitor their health, detect energy in the X-ray or infrared range, and have telephoto capabilities (see "hacking the eyes," below). I should point out that any device containing a contact lens is regulated by the FDA; the point being that much of cyborg technology comes under government regulation.

Issues of Software

Software is becoming increasingly important in the functioning of implants, thus the law which applies to code and algorithms should be of interest to cyborgs and to those designing them. Consider an artificial pancreas using an intelligent dosing algorithm to simulate the functioning of a normal pancreas by continuously adapting insulin delivery based on changes in glucose level. What happens if the software in the artificial pancreas fails? If the software does fail, there are numerous parties in the "chain of liability" which may be subject to a lawsuit, including software manufacturers, equipment manufacturers, program distributers, programmers, consultants, companies using the software, and software operators. To protect themselves from liability claims, software developers often use disclaimers (through a software license) with their products which may limit clients' claims.

But briefly, a professional programmer could be negligent when writing code, if they failed to act as a reasonably prudent programmer would. The deviation from normal programming practices is often proven through the testimony of another expert programmer. Negligent programming claims are similar to malpractice claims in that both types of claims are based on duty, breach of duty, causation, and damages. To win on a programming malpractice claim the cyborg would have to prove that the negligent programmer was a programming professional that had a duty or legal responsibility to exercise reasonable care in providing computer programming or services, that the negligent programmer breached this duty by

---

[38]Smart Holograms, at: http://www.cam.ac.uk/research/news/holographic-diagnostics-0.

failing to provide programming or design services that a reasonable programmer would provide in this situation, and that this breach of duty caused damages. In addition to programming negligence claims, given that the design of software and its maintenance is usually covered under contract law, most contracts include safe guards and clauses that protect businesses from computer software, programming, and networks that do not work or are flawed.

Some lawyers in defending their client have attempted to create a "computer malpractice" claim for software errors and crashes. But the courts seem to reject this theory, even stating no such cause of action exists. The early case of *Chatlos Systems v. National Cash Register Corp.* (1979) is an example.[39] Here an NCR salesman did a detailed analysis of Chatlos' business operations and computer needs, and advised Chatlos to buy NCR equipment. Relying on NCR's advice, Chatlos bought a system that they alleged never provided several promised functions; Chatlos sued and NCR was held liable for breach of contract. However, in a footnote, the court discussed Chatlos' claim of computer malpractice: "The novel concept of a new tort called 'computer malpractice' is premised upon a theory of elevated responsibility on the part of those who render computer sales and service. Plaintiff equates the sale and servicing of computer systems with established theories of professional malpractice. Simply because an activity is technically complex and important to the business community does not mean that greater potential liability must attach. In the absence of sound precedential authority, the court declines the invitation to create a new tort."[40]

Lacking a computer malpractice claim, cyborgs suing for defective software can still use contract law and negligence, or possibly an appropriate statue from criminal law to defend their rights. With the coming age of cyborgs, there are many disputes that will involve them, and which will wind their way to the courts. As discussed in Chap. 1, regarding the law of the horse, or in this case, the law of cyborgs, will it be sufficient to rely on the fundamental principles of law found in contract, tort, criminal law, and constitutional law, or will a new set of rights for cyborgs be warranted and in the future for artificially intelligent machines? The answer will be clear by midcentury.

Machines Hacking Machines

In my view, the necessity for humanity to merge with artificially intelligent machines is based on another accelerating trend in technology—efforts among computer scientists and engineers to create machines with the ability to become the architect of their own design or at least to program themselves. Once machines begin to hack their own hardware and software, they may direct their own

---

[39]*Chatlos Systems, Inc. v. National Cash Register Corp.*, 479 F. Supp. 738 (D. N.J. 1979), *aff'd*, 635 F.2d 1081 (3rd Cir. 1980).

[40]*Id.*

evolution at such a speed that we humans may be quickly surpassed, and insignificant to them. Surely, this possibility should provide strong motivation for humanity to consider moving beyond biological evolution to a self-directed merger with our future technological progeny.

That machines may direct their own evolution comes from recent examples in which they are beginning to design, repair, and program themselves. For example, an International Space Station robot repaired its cameras while in orbit making it the first robot to self-repair in space. Then there's the work of MIT researchers Daniela Rus and Erna Viterbi,[41] on the design of self-assembling robots. Such robots consist of printable robotic components that, when heated, automatically self-assemble into prescribed three-dimensional configurations. One example of their research is a system that takes a digital specification of a three-dimensional shape, such as that generated from a 2D pattern that would enable a piece of plastic to reproduce it through self-folding. Other research by Daniela Rus and her team is focused on building electrical components from self-folding laser-cut materials. These designs include resistors, inductors, and capacitors, as well as sensors and actuators; that is, the electromechanical "muscles" that enable robots' movements.[42] If artificially intelligent machines become the master of their own architecture, is there any doubt that they will use technology such as 3D printers to quickly improve and move beyond the capabilities of their human masters?

Some argue that techniques in artificial intelligence,[43] with sufficient machine intelligence, will give software the potential to autonomously improve the design of its constituent software and hardware. Having undergone these improvements, it would then be better able to find ways of optimizing its structure and improving its abilities further. It is speculated that over many iterations, such an artificial intelligence would far surpass human cognitive abilities and lead to the Singularity.[44] One type of research direction on this topic is machine learning, a branch of artificial intelligence, which is concerned with the construction and study of systems that learn from mining data.[45] I envision a future where cyborgs and artificially intelligent machines mine data, share information, and collectively make decisions. Generally, artificial intelligence has been progressing steadily

---

[41]Sharon Gaudin, 2014, These origami robots can fold up and walk, at: http://www.computerworld.com/article/2490973/emerging-technology/scientists-create-self-assembling-working-robots.html.

[42]*Ankur Mehta, Joseph DelPreto, Daniela Rus*—Integrated Codesign of Printable Robots, ASME Journal of Mechanisms and Robotics 7(JMR-14-1221), 05 2015; *Ankur M. Mehta, Daniela Rus*—An End-To-End System For Designing Mechanical Structures For Print-And-Fold Robots, IEEE International Conference on Robotics and Automation (ICRA) , Hong Kong, China, June 2014.

[43]Eliezer Yudkowsky, 2015, Rationality: From AI to Zombies, Machine Intelligence Research Institute.

[44]Robin Hanson and Elizer Yudkowsky, 2013, The Hanson-Yudkowsky AI-Foom Debate, Machine Intelligence Research Institute.

[45]Ian H. Witten, Eibe Frank, and Mark A. Hall, 2011, Data Mining: Practical Machine Learning Tools and Techniques, Third Edition, Morgan Kauffman.

over the years, along with advances in computer technology, hardware, memory, and CPU speeds. As computers get faster, more computations can be performed per unit time, allowing increasing power for the computation-intensive processing required by many artificial intelligence algorithms and data mining techniques.

Hacking the Brain

While many of the examples presented in this chapter represent current efforts by people to hack their body and a discussion of legal issues that such acts implicate, the future may be even more amazing in terms of how the body may be manipulated and modified. Ultimately, given that the brain operates by performing computations and that tremendous progress is being made deciphering the way the brain computes,[46] I believe the fundamental processes of how the brain processes and stores information will be discovered; and by doing so, information essential for the cyborg future and a human-machine merger will be gleaned. However, I should make the point clear that uncovering the secrets of the brain will be an extraordinarily difficult task (orders of magnitude more difficult than the Human Genome project) due to the complex neuro-chemistry and neuro-circuitry (wiring) of the 100 billion neurons comprising the human brain, because the brain uses distributed processing to compute, and because there are many distinct classes of neurons in the brain whose coding system for information remains to be discovered and converted into algorithms. Unfortunately, even given the complexity of the brain, due to the significant developments unfolding in the world of wireless networks, brain-computer interfaces and neuroprosthetics, I anticipate that in the cyborg future a wide variety of criminal threats will be directed at the human brain itself.

If we consider the raw processing power of a supercomputer (able to perform trillions of floating point operations per second), and compare that to the brain, estimates put the processing power of a supercomputer within that of a brain's, so with a few iterations of Moore's law, processing power will not be the limiting factor for creating human-like intelligence it once was. Within 10–15 years, the biggest obstacle in creating an artificial intelligence with similar capabilities as the human brain, will be the fact that biological based neural computing, differs in fundamental ways from silicon's. For example, the human brain is massively parallel, it contains billions of neurons that can individually synapse with thousands of other neurons; but the individual neurons each have limited processing ability.[47] In contrast, supercomputers have tremendous processing power as measured by the number of arithmetic operations performed per second, but typically have

[46]Michio Kaku, 2014, The Future of the Mind: The Scientific Quest to Understand, Enhance, and Empower the Mind, Doubleday.

[47]Miguel Nicholelis, 2012, Beyond Boundaries: The New Neuroscience of Connecting Brains with Machines—and How It Will Change Our Lives, St. Martin's Press.

limited parallel connections; however, research is directed at just this issue, to make computers compute in parallel. In fact, much of the progress in unlocking the complexity of the brain, can be credited to advances in technology. As theoretical physicist Michio Kaku recently discussed in *"The Future of the Mind: The Scientific Quest to Understand, Enhance, and Empower the Mind,"*[48] the revolution in modern neuroscience has been triggered by the widespread use of MRI technology starting in the 90s, fMRI technology more recently, and culminating in optogenetic techniques in the last few years.[49]

Advances in Optogenetics, by scientists at Stanford University, is an important technology with respect to studying how the brain functions. The reason is that optogenetics allows scientists to study how different neuronal circuits interact and influence each other. The relevancy of this technology for the future human-machine merger is that if we are to build software that can communicate directly with the brain we need to crack its codes. One way to do this is to select a set of neurons of interest, measure how they are firing, reverse engineer their message, and write the appropriate algorithm(s) (this is a simplification!). Historically, scientists knew that proteins, called opsins, in bacteria and algae generated electricity when exposed to light. Fast forward—optogenetics exploits this mechanism for brain science. Opsin genes are inserted into the DNA of a harmless virus, which is then injected into the brain of a test subject. By choosing a virus that prefers some cell types over others, or by altering the virus's genetic sequence, researchers can target specific neurons, or regions of the brain known to be responsible for certain actions or behaviors.[50] To study neuronal activity, an optical fiber- a spaghetti-thin glass cable that transmits light from its tip, is inserted through the skin or skull to the site of the virus. The fibers light activates the opsin, which in turn conducts an electrical charge that forces the neuron to fire.

Even with the brain's tremendous complexity progress is being made towards the integration of the human brain with machines and sensors. For example, researchers at the Rehabilitation Institute of Chicago, have developed a thought-controlled bionic leg which uses neuro-signals from the upper leg muscles to control a prosthetic knee and ankle. The prosthesis uses pattern recognition software contained in an on-board computer, to interpret electrical signals from the upper leg as well as mechanical signals from the bionic leg. When the person equipped with the prosthesis thinks about moving his leg, the thought triggers brain signals that travel down his spinal cord, and ultimately, through peripheral nerves, are read by electrodes in the bionic leg, which then moves in response to the initial thought. Further, hackers are beginning to enter the fray. Take body hacker and inventor Shiva Nathan, a teenager from India. After being inspired to help a family member who lost both arms below the elbow, Shiva created a robotic arm

---

[48]Michio Kaku, *id.*, note 46.

[49]Stuart S. Hall, 2014, Neuroscience's New Toolbox, MIT Technology Review, V. 117, 20–28.

[50]*Id.*

controlled by thought. The technology uses a Mindwave Mobile headset to read EEG waves and Bluetooth to send certain types of thought to the arm which then translates them into finger and hand movements. This is a remarkable achievement for a 15 year old using technology accessible to anyone.

In fact, research on prosthesis, is truly international in scope. For example, in Sweden, researchers at Chalmers University of Technology are developing a thought-controlled prosthesis for amputees in the form of an implantable robotic arm. And in the U.S., the FDA has approved a thought-controlled prosthetic limb that is realistic and more human-like than other devices on the market.[51] The DEKA Arm prosthetic, invented by Dean Kamen, can detect up to ten movements, is the same size and weight as a natural human arm, and works by detecting electrical activity caused by the contraction of muscles close to where the prosthesis is attached. The electrical signals, initially generated by thought are sent to a computer processor in the DEKA Arm, which triggers a specific movement in the prosthesis. In FDA tests, the artificial arm/hand has successfully assisted people with household tasks such as using keys and locks, preparing food, feeding oneself, brushing hair and using zippers.

The above examples causes me to wonder, in the future when an arm or leg prosthesis appears to be as realistic to people as a natural limb, but is more powerful and dexterous than natural limbs, with greater freedom and movement in joints and with additional degrees of articulation, would "normal" humans opt for the superior prosthesis, if the surgical risk was minimal? The answer is unknown, but I have my suspicions. Just consider the following data. According to the American Society of Plastic Surgeons, in 2011 there were 307,000 breast augmentations in the U.S., a surgical procedure done to alleviate no medical condition, and unlike most implantable technology, breast implants lack sensors and artificial intelligence, they are purely cosmetic.

And who needs sight to get around when you've got a digital compass in your head? A neuroprosthesis that feeds geomagnetic signals into the brains of blind rats has enabled them to navigate around a maze. The results demonstrate that the rats could rapidly learn to deploy a completely unnatural "sense". And it raises the possibility that humans could do the same, potentially opening up new ways to treat blindness, or even to provide healthy people with extra senses. "I'm dreaming that humans can expand their senses through artificial sensors for geomagnetism, ultraviolet, radio waves, ultrasonic waves and so on," says Yuji Ikegava of the University of Tokyo in Japan.[52] "Ultrasonic and radio-wave sensors may enable the   next   generation   of   human-to-human   communication,"   he   says.   The

---

[51]Dean Kamen, DEKA prosthesis, at: http://www.dekaresearch.com/founder.shtml.

[52]Andy Coghlan, 2015, Brain compass implant gives blind rats psychic GPS, New Scientist, at: http://www.newscientist.com/article/dn27293-brain-compass-implant-gives-blind-rats-psychic-gps.html#.VXiVL-_bJjo; See generally, Takahashi, N., Sasaki, T., Matsumoto, W., Matsuki, N. and Ikegaya, Y., 2010, Circuit topology for synchronizing neurons in spontaneously active networks, PNAS, 107:10244–10249.

neuroprosthesis consists of a geomagnetic compass—a version of the microchip found in smartphones—and two electrodes that fit into the animals' visual cortices, the areas of the brain that process visual information.

Returning to Michio Kaku's observations on the future of the mind, he reveals other fascinating research being done using sensors to read images stored in the human brain and on downloading artificial memories into the brain to treat victims of strokes and Alzheimer's.[53] Kaku also lists telepathy and telekinesis; artificial memories implanted into our brains; and a pill that will make us smarter as future technologies that will emerge this century. Extending Kaku's observations on the future, imagine being able to replace the anatomy and physiology of the brain with 3D printed parts. For the brain's skull, doctors in the Netherlands have done just that in a first successful replacement of most of a human skull using a 3D printed plastic one. The surgery to replace the skull took place at University Medical Center Utrecht[54] with a woman who was suffering from severe headaches due to a thickening of her skull. As a result she slowly lost her vision, her motor coordination was affected, and without surgical interdiction, other essential brain functions would have atrophied. The 3D implant did its job, pressure on the brain was reduced, and the patient regained sensory and motor functions. I view the use of 3D printed parts for humans, androids, and artificially intelligent robots, as a transformative technology that will proliferate in the next few decades and play a major role in leading to our cyborg and ultimately human-machine merger.

Hacking Memory

If we can replace the anatomical structure protecting the brain, can we repair, replace, or enhance parts of the brain's wetware with digital technology? Certainly not now, but how about in the future, or even in the next few decades? Enter biomedical engineer Theodore Berger[55] at the University of Southern California and his team who have developed an experimental artificial hippocampus that they are testing with rats. Their artificial hippocampus is a silicon substitute for the part of the brain that neuroscientists believe encodes experiences as long-term memories. While Berger and his team are motivated by the desire to fight debilitating neurological disease, for example, epilepsy and other disorders that result in damage to the hippocampus (which prevent a person from retaining new memories), an

---

[53]Michio Kaku, *id.*, note 46.

[54]University Medical Center Utrecht, 2014, 3D-printed skull implanted in patient, at: http://www.umcutrecht.nl/en/Research/News/3D-printed-skull-implanted-in-patient.

[55]Rebecca Boyle, 2011, Artificial Memory Chip, discussing the work of Theodore Berger, at: http://www.popsci.com/technology/article/2011-06/artificial-memory-chip-rats-can-remember-and-forget-touch-button.

artificial hippocampus will also be a major advance towards the cyborg future and human-machine merger.

To build an artificial hippocampus, Berger created mathematical models of the neuronal activity in a rat's hippocampus and designed a chip (located external to the brain) to mimic the signal processing which occurred in different parts of the hippocampus. Interestingly, the researchers modeled neuronal activity by sending random pulses into the hippocampus, recorded the signals at various localities to see how they were transformed, and then derived equations describing the signals.[56] Berger and colleagues also connected the chip, which contained the algorithms, to the rat's brain by electrodes. Using the chip, Berger was *not* able to "put individual memories back into the brain," but he *was* able to put the capacity to generate memories in the brain.[57]

To see if the chip could serve as a prosthesis for a damaged hippocampal region, the researchers performed a study to determine whether they could bypass a central component of the pathways in the hippocampus. Berger's team tested the device in rats trained in a simple memory task. Each rat (with the prosthesis) was placed in a chamber with two levers. First, the lever on just one side of the chamber was presented, and the rat pushed it, after a short waiting period, the levers on both sides of the chamber appeared, and if the rat pushed the opposite lever from the one it pushed before, the rat was rewarded with a sip of water. However, to perform the task successfully required the rat to remember which lever it pushed originally.

To test if the memory prosthesis worked as expected, Berger and his team injected some of these rats with a drug that impaired their natural memory, and then tested the animals in the lever experiment. The rats (with the prosthesis) were still able to push the correct lever to receive their drink, suggesting they were able to form new memories and that the rats' brain implant was remembering for them. Remarkably, the researchers found that the prosthesis could enhance memory function in rats even when they hadn't been given the drug that impaired their memory.

Going up the phylogenetic scale, at Wake Forest University School of Medicine, Robert Hampson and his team successfully tested a hippocampal prosthesis on non-human primates. While the device is far from a fully implantable hippocampus "chip," these tests, from rat to monkey, demonstrate the "proof-of-concept" effectiveness of the artificial hippocampus as a neural prosthetic; and in the near future, Robert Hampson plans to begin human trials. While Hampson's and Berger's work is a long way from a hard drive for the brain, it's a step in the direction of being able to "back up," or hack, memory, and once this is possible, the next step will be to transmit information into the artificial hippocampus, a major step in the direction of a cyborg future. Of course, once an artificial

---

[56]*Id.*

[57]*Id.*

hippocampus is implanted within the brain it could be hacked by third parties, a topic discussed in the chapter on *Cognitive Liberty*.

Implanting False Memories

The legal and policy implications of being able to manipulate memory are immense: If humans can control memories, can they also alter them? Could memories be decoded against a persons will and used as evidence in a courtroom, and could people erase memories and replace them with new ones altogether?[58] And for artificially intelligent machines, will manipulating their memory be nothing more than changing the lines of their code? Would this be ethical, would a future law need to be enacted to protect against this possibility? If an artificially intelligent machine used computer vision and algorithms to view the world, would changing its software be the equivalent of tampering with a witness or performing a digital lobotomy? And when examining the prospect of memory enhancement, some who worry about the ethics of cognitive enhancement point to the danger of creating two classes of human beings—those with access to enhancement technologies, and those who must make do with an unaltered memory that fades with age.

Planting false memories in the brain may seem like science fiction, until, that is, we see that it's already being done, at least with a research subject commonly picked on by scientists, the laboratory mouse. Using genetically engineered mice, Susumu Tonegawa, MIT Picower Professor of Biology and Neuroscience, Dr. Xu Liu,[59] and colleagues at the *Riken-MIT Center for Neural Circuit Genetics*, used the technique of optogenetics to access neurons in the brain of a mouse. Basically they implanted a fiber optic in the mouse's brain allowing them to reactivate neuronal circuitry that had previously been recorded.[60] According to Dr. Liu, our memory changes every single time it's being recorded, which is why we can incorporate new information into old memories and this is how a false memory can form. Interestingly, by implanting a false memory, the MIT team was able to make the mice wrongly associate a benign environment with a previous unpleasant experience from different surroundings.

How they did this was to first condition a network of neurons to respond to light based on optic fibers implanted in the mouse's brain in a specific region.[61] Then the scientists placed the mouse in a red chamber, which was harmless. The following day, they had the mouse explore a blue-walled chamber, and gave it a

---

[58]See generally, Nita Farahany, 2012, Incrimination Thoughts, Stanford Law Review, Vol, 64. 351.

[59]RIKEN Brain Science Institute, RIKEN-MIT Center for Neural Circuit Genetics (CNCG), see the references to Xi Liu, at: http://www.riken.jp/en/research/labs/bsi/rmc/.

[60]Optogenetics, MIT Technology Review, at: http://www.technologyreview.com/tagged/optogenetics/.

[61]*Id.* note 59.

mild jolt while simultaneously inducing neuronal recall of the red room. This was done so that the mouse would artificially associate the memory of the shock-free red room with the fear of being shocked. On the third day, the researchers wanted to see whether this false association had successfully been implanted. To determine this, they placed the mouse in the red room, where it froze even though nothing bad had happened to it there.[62] Based on the fear response, the MIT team concluded that a false memory had been formed and recalled. Attesting to the importance of the work, cognitive scientist Neil Burgess[63] from University College London, told BBC News the study was an "impressive example" of creating a fearful response in an environment where nothing fearful had happened. Although using an implant to plant a memory in a human brain won't be possible in the next few years, in principle, it should be possible to isolate a human memory and activate it given difficult technical problems are overcome.

The phenomenon of false memory has implications for law and policy and has been well-documented by psychologists. In many court cases, defendants have been found guilty based on testimony from witnesses and victims who were sure of their recollections, but DNA evidence later overturned the conviction. In a step toward understanding how these faulty memories arise, material presented in this chapter has shown that at the level of neuronal circuitry, false memories can be modeled and implanted in the brains of mice. But importantly, neuroscientists have also found that many of the neurological traces of these memories are identical in nature to those of authentic memories. According to MITs Susumu Tonegawa, "Whether it's a false or genuine memory, the brain's neural mechanism underlying the recall of the memory is the same."[64]

That we should be concerned with the possibility of false memories being implanted in the brain is not a recent concern motivated only by the arrival of brain-computer interfaces and a cyborg future. For example, a Wisconsin jury awarded $1 million to a couple who claimed that malpractice by therapists caused their daughter to have false memories of childhood abuse. In fact, several patients have won settlements or jury awards of millions in false memory lawsuits against therapists. But the case of Dr. Charles Johnson and his wife Karen is the first in which the parents of a patient brought negligent therapy claims—over the objections of the patient. The case took years to get to trial, prompted by a key breakthrough in 2005 when the Wisconsin Supreme Court ruled that the therapist-patient privilege did not apply to the daughter's treatment records.[65] The

---

[62]*Id.* note 59.

[63]Melissa Hogenboom, 2013, Scientists can implant false memories into mice, at: http://www.bbc.com/news/science-environment-23447600.

[64]Anne Trafton, 2013, Neuroscientists plant false memories in the brain, quoting Susuma Tonegawa, at: http://newsoffice.mit.edu/2013/neuroscientists-plant-false-memories-in-the-brain-0725.

[65]Linda Greenhouse, 1996, The Supreme Court, Confidentiality, Justices Uphold Patient Privacy With Therapist, New York Times, at: http://www.nytimes.com/1996/06/14/us/the-supreme-court-confidentiality-justices-uphold-patient-privacy-with-therapist.html.

Johnsons used those records to support their claim that the therapists practiced the controversial "recovered memory" technique on their daughter. What to make of this? There is a public policy exception to the therapist-patient privilege and to the confidentiality in patient health care records where negligent therapy causes false accusations to be made against the parents for sexually or physically abusing their child, the court concluded.[66] Would a similar privilege be necessary for brain-computer interfaces?

Thinking more broadly, I can't help but see a connection between the science and technology of implanting memories, false memories implanted by a therapist, and a case heard before the Court of Justice in the European Union which decreed that human beings have a solemn right to make mistakes and then to erase them, that is, "The Right to be Forgotten." The concept stems from the desire of an individual to 'determine the development of his life in an autonomous way, without being perpetually or periodically stigmatized as a consequence of a specific action performed in the past.'[67] If memories can be implanted in a person's mind, not only would it be difficult to forget the past, but a person could be stigmatized by actions that never took place. Among legal scholars, there are concerns that creating a right to be forgotten would lead to censorship and a possible rewriting of history—I share this concern.

Hacking the Skin

If we can hack the brain, can we hack the skin, the largest sense organ? Surprisingly, the answer is yes, but first a digression into popular culture. A recent Pew study showed that nearly forty percent of Americans under the age of forty have at least one tattoo, creating a $1.65 billion industry. Like any industry, however, the tattoo industry must innovate to expand and gain new clients. In an analog world, one way to innovate is to make the switch to digital technology.

Rather than being passive as are current tattoos, digital tattoos are active, they *do* things, and they are getting smart. That is, now days, digital tattoos have the potential to do more than serve the function of art or self-expression, even though these are laudable goals, they will become digital devices as useful as smartphones and will monitor our health. This is not the distant future, the technology to create digital tattoos already exist. It's possible, for instance, to use a type of ink in a tattoo that responds to electromagnetic fields, which raises a host of opportunities. In fact, Nokia patented just this technology, ferromagnetic ink that can interact with a device through magnetism.[68] The basic idea is to enrich tattoo ink with metallic

---

[66]*Id.*

[67]Factsheet on the "Right to be Forgotten" Ruling, at: http://ec.europa.eu/justice/data-protection/files/factsheets/factsheet_data_protection_en.pdf.

[68]Adam Clark Estes, 2014, The Freaky Bioelectric Future of Tattoos, at: http://gizmodo.com/the-freaky-bioelectric-future-of-tattoos-1494169250.

Fig. 5.2 Electronic sensor tattoos can be "printed" directly onto human skin. Image courtesy of Professor John Rogers, University of Illinois

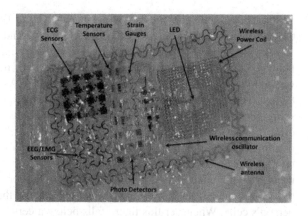

compounds that are first demagnetized (by exposing the metal to high temperatures) before the ink is embedded in a person's skin. Once the tattoo has healed, the ink is re-magnetized with permanent magnets. The procedure is strikingly similar to that of getting a 'normal' tattoo—only the ink is special. The resulting tattoo is then sensitive to magnetic pulses, which can be emitted by a device such as a cellular phone. Interestingly, a digital tattoo would allow a person's ringing phone to result in a haptic sensation experienced by the body; that is, the person would experience the phone ringing literally through the tattoo. And since the phone should be able to send a variety of pulses, different degrees of tingling could be used to indicate whether a phone battery was dying, or whether a person had a text or voice message.[69] A sub-dermal phone call makes me wonder if a deliberate wrong call should be considered an assault and battery?

If the tattoo consists of putting electronics on the surface of the skin, many possibilities for body hacking exist. Materials scientist, and University of Illinois Professor John Rogers and his company are developing flexible electronics that stick to the skin to operate as a temporary tattoo.[70] These so-called "epidural electronics" (or Biostamp) is a thin electronic mesh that stretches with the skin and monitors temperature, hydration and strain, as well as monitoring a person's body's vital signs (Fig. 5.2). The latest prototype of the Biostamp is applied directly to the skin using a rubber stamp. The stamp lasts up to two weeks before the skin's natural exfoliation causes it to come away. Rogers is currently working on ways to get the electronics to communicate with other devices like smartphones so that they can start building apps. Google isn't far behind in developing digital tattoos, as the company's Advanced Technology and Projects Group patented the idea of a digital tattoo consisting of various sensors and gages, such as strain gauges for tracking strain in

---

[69]*Id.*

[70]Liz Ahlberg, 2014, Off the shelf, on the skin: Stick-on electronic patches for health monitoring, at: http://news.illinois.edu/news/14/0403microfluidics_JohnRogers.html.

multiple directions (how the user is flexing), EEG and EMG (electrical impulses in the skeletal structure or nerves), ECG (heart activity), and temperature.

As with other implantable technology, initially, hacking the skin will most likely be done for health reasons. In fact, by 2016, there could be 100 million wearable wireless medical devices used by people.[71] As an example, Roger's digital tattoo described above can track a person's health and monitor healing near the skin's surface. Then there's a wearable sensor that tells people when it's time for a drink. Sandia National Laboratories researcher Ronen Polsky has built a prototype of a microneedle fluidic chip device able to selectively detect and measure electrolytes in the fluids around skin cells.[72] The device consists of an array of microneedles on the underside of a watch-like device that protrudes into a person's skin to measure interstitial fluid levels—broadly speaking, the water that sits between a person's cells. Whenever this figure falls below a certain limit, a person is alerted. Placing sensors on the skin is an interesting idea, with great potential for monitoring a person's health, but sensors on the skin will also serve other functions—for example, to detect information in the environment that is of interest to a person and to wirelessly connect a person to the billions of items that will be networked together in the future.

But the skin isn't being hacked only to monitor our health, artists are combining the surface of the skin with technology in unique ways. Consider body hacker Moon Ribas who is a Catalan contemporary choreographer and the co-founder of the *Cyborg Foundation*, an international organisation which promotes "cyborgism" as an artistic and social movement. In an interesting use of technology and choreography, she attached a seismic sensor to her elbow that allows her to feel earthquakes through vibrations resulting from ground tremors.

In a more extreme example of performance art, Professor Stelarc, through a series of surgeries, created an artificial ear on the skin of his left arm.[73] Stelarc's philosophy for body hacking is to use technology in a way that extends the body's physical abilities, allowing a person to do what they previously could not due to physical limitations—this he plans to accomplish by implanting a microchip and microphone in the artificial ear. To build the artificial ear, excess skin was created with an implanted skin expander in the forearm. By injecting saline solution into a subcutaneous port, a kidney shaped silicone implant stretched the skin, forming a pocket of excess skin that was used in surgically constructing the ear. In a second surgery a Medpor scaffold was inserted and skin was suctioned over it. The Medpor implant was shaped into several parts and sutured together to form the ear shape. During the second procedure a miniature microphone was positioned inside

---

[71]Robert N. Charette, 2012, Wearable Computers the Size of Button to Monitor Health, at: http://spectrum.ieee.org/riskfactor/biomedical/devices/wearable-computers-the-size-of-buttons-to-monitor-health.

[72]Prototype electrolyte sensor provides immediate read-outs, 2014, at: https://share.sandia.gov/news/resources/news_releases/electrolyte_sensor/#.VXjhNO_bJjo.

[73]Paolo Atzori and Kirk Woolford, Extended-Body: Interview with Stelarc, at: http://web.stanford.edu/dept/HPS/stelarc/a29-extended_body.html.

the ear. But while the inserted microphone was tested successfully, later it had to be removed due to infection. Once the hacking is complete, wherever Stelarc may be, using the appropriate technology, a person could remotely listen into what his artificial ear "hears." Summarizing Stelarc' body hacking philosophy, he comments that as technology proliferates and microminiaturizes it becomes biocompatible in both scale and substance and thus can be incorporated as a component of the body; his artificial ear represents this idea.

Hacking the Eyes

For many people, vision is the most important sense, its loss is so deleterious to functioning in everyday life, that major efforts are underway to develop technology to restore sight to those who have lost it. The visual sense is also the subject of body hackers. Meet Neil Harbisson who was born with a rare condition (achromatopsia) that allows him to see only in black and white and shades of grey (Fig. 5.3). After viewing a talk in 2003 on cybernetics, in the spirit of a hacker, Neil wondered if he could turn color into sound, based on the idea that a specific frequency of light could be made equivalent to a sound wave. When Neil first thought of the idea, he wasn't aware that in 2014, research would eventually show that the visual cortex processes auditory information detected by the ears. To become a cyborg, Neil had a sound conducting chip implanted in his head, along with a flexible shaft with a digital camera on it, permanently attached to his skull (the Eyeborg). With his latest software upgrade, Neil says he is able to hear ultraviolet and infrared frequencies, can have phone calls delivered to his head, and has a Bluetooth connection which allows him to connect his Eyeborg to the Internet.[74]

Interestingly, the addition of the Eyeborg to his passport photo has led some to dub Neil the first cyborg officially recognized by a sovereign state. In a harbinger of future bioethical debates about cyborg technology, Neil had to convince a surgical team to perform the procedure; that is, to implant the chip in his head. Since the purpose of medicine is to restore the body to its normal state, Neil had to convince the doctors that his device could help restore function to those who had lost it, not just allow him to have a sixth sense through the perception of objects in his visual field via bone-conducted sounds. This brought up the second ethical issue. Whether Neil should receive an implant which allowed him to perceive outside the normal range of human vision and human hearing (hearing via the bone allows a person to hear a wider range of sounds, from infrasounds to ultrasounds), again, not typically a reason to receive an implant. But in theory, if a person was equipped with a different type of chip, say one that translated words into sound, or distances into sound, for instance, then the same electronic eye implant could be used to read or to detect obstacles, thus restoring function to those who had

---

[74]Eyeborg: The Man Who Hears Colours, 2014, at: https://artselectronic.wordpress.com/2014/12/19/eyeborg-the-man-who-hears-colours/.

Fig. 5.3 Neil Harbisson
hearing color, image curtesy
of Lars Norgaard

lost it. This argument convinced the surgical team that the implant could have a restorative effect, and the procedure was done. However, this example raises an interesting policy question- which kinds of cybernetic implants will society find to be ethical and legal, and which ones they will not. Let the debate begin.

Amazing technology to assist people with visual impairments is creating a whole new population of cyborgs, some of whom never thought they would see again. In fact, different types of prosthesis for the eyes are starting to emerge from research laboratories. For example, in the U.S. the FDA approved a retinal implant, for those experiencing the effects of retintis pigmentosa. The implant doesn't completely restore vision, but is meant to partially restore useful vision to people who have lost their sight due to degenerative eye conditions.

In a healthy eye, the photoreceptors (rods and cones) in the retina convert light into tiny electrochemical impulses that are sent through the optic nerve and into the brain, where they are decoded into images. If the photoreceptors no longer function correctly—due to conditions such as retintis pigmentosa—the first step in this process is disrupted, and the visual system cannot transform light into images. Enter the Argus II Retinal Prosthesis System (Argus II) which was approved in Europe in 2011, and the U.S. in 2013. This prosthesis is designed to bypass the damaged photoreceptors altogether. With the prosthesis, a miniature video camera housed in the patient's glasses captures a scene, and the video of the scene is sent to a small patient-worn computer where it is processed and transformed into instructions that are sent back to the glasses via a cable. These instructions are then transmitted wirelessly to an antenna in the implant which then sends the instructions to an electrode array in the retina. The small pulses of electricity are intended to bypass the damaged photoreceptors and stimulate the retina's remaining cells, which transmit the visual information along the optic nerve to the brain. This process is intended to create the perception of patterns of light which patients can learn to interpret as visual patterns.

If we can begin to restore vision, can we enhance it? What about the idea of telephoto vision (Fig. 5.4)? For the approximately 20–25 million people worldwide who have the advanced form of age-related macular degeneration (AMD), a disease which affects the region of the retina responsible for central, detailed vision,

Fig. 5.4 Implantable telescopic eye. Image provided courtesy of VisionCare Ophthalmic Technologies

and is the leading cause of irreversible vision loss and legal blindness in people over the age of 65, a relatively new device, essentially an implantable telescope, is offering hope. In 2010, the U.S. FDA approved the implantable miniature telescope (IMT), which works like the telephoto lens of a camera.[75] The IMT technology reduces the impact of the central vision blind spot due to end-stage AMD and projects the objects the patient is looking at onto the healthy area of the light-sensing retina not degenerated by the disease.

The Implantable Miniature Telescope (IMT) technology reduces the impact of the central vision blind spot due to End-Stage AMD and projects the objects the patient is looking at onto the healthy area of the light-sensing retina not degenerated by the disease.

The surgical procedure involves removing the eye's natural lens, as with cataract surgery, and replacing the lens with the IMT. The tiny telescope is implanted behind the iris, the colored, muscular ring around the pupil. While telephoto eyes are not coming soon to an ophthalmologist office, this is an intriguing step in that direction. As always the law is part of the picture, as the procedures to equip a person with telephoto eyes will be subject to tort law if harm occurs, products liability law if the implant fails, and the implant technology will be regulated by the FDA as a medical device.

Hacking the Body with Sensors

In an extension of Professor Warwick's early work involving a sensor implanted under his skin, body hacker Anthony Antonellis implanted an RFID chip into his hand which can be wirelessly accessed by a smartphone.[76] While the chip holds

---

[75]FDA-Approved Implantable Miniature Telescope for End-Stage Age-Related Macular Degeneration, at: http://www.visionaware.org/info/your-eye-condition/age-related-macular-degeneration-amd/new-fda-approved-implantable-telescope-for-end-stage-amd/125.

[76]Anthony Antonellis, Net Art Implant (and video), at: http://www.anthonyantonellis.com/news-post/item/670-net-art-implant.

only about 1–2 KB of data, it allows Antonellis to access and display an animated GIF on his phone that is stored on the implant. Since the RFID chip can transfer and receive data, Antonellis can swap out 1 KB files as he pleases. Antonellis views the implant as a "net art tattoo", something for which quick response codes (QR, or matrix barcode), are commonly used. Instead of a visible QR code, the RFID chip will allow the art to be easily changed with an increase in storage capacity to the chip, further the convenience of a subdermal wireless hard drive would be an interesting development for the body hacking movement. Similarly, Karl Marc, a tattoo artist from Paris designed an animated tattoo that makes use of a QR code and a smartphone.[77] The code basically activates software on the phone that makes the tattoo move when seen through the phone's camera.

In addition, others have also implanted RFID chips for various reasons. For example, Dr. John Halamaka, of Harvard Medical School, chose to be implanted with an RFID chip in 2004 which is used to access medical information.[78] His implant stores information which can direct anyone with the appropriate reader to a website containing his medical information. He believes that chips such as these can be valuable in situations where patients arrive at the hospital unconscious or unresponsive. Another person with an RFID implant, Meghan Trainor has a much less practical but highly creative application than many of the others who have gotten them. Trainor had the implant put in as part of her master's thesis for NYU's Interactive Telecommunications Program.[79] Her implant serves as part of an interactive art exhibit. RFID tags are embedded in sculptures which can be manipulated to play sounds stored in an audio database. Trainor can use the implant in her arm to further manipulate these sounds. Considering a digital tattoo designed for a medical monitoring purpose, University of Pennsylvania's Brian Litt, a neurologist and bioengineer, is implanting LED displays under the skin for medical monitoring purposes.[80] These tattoos consist of silicon electronics less than 250 nm thick, built onto water soluble, biocompatible silk substrates. When injected with saline, the silk substrates conform to fit the surrounding tissue and eventually dissolves completely, leaving only the silicon circuitry. The electronics can be used to power LEDs that act as photonic tattoos. Litt is perfecting a form of this technology that could be used to build wearable medical devices—say, a tattoo that gives diabetics information about their blood sugar level.

But in what I consider to be a remarkable effort to hack the body, "grinder" Tim Cannon, implanted a Circadia 1.0 biometric sensor under his forearm skin to track changes in his temperature.[81] The sensor/computer can connect wirelessly to an

---

[77]QR Code Tattoos, at: http://www.qrscanner.us/qr-tatoos.html.

[78]Life as a Healthcare CIO, 2007, at: http://geekdoctor.blogspot.com/2007/12/chip-in-my-shoulder.html.

[79]RFID Implants: 5 Amazing Stories, at: http://www.rfidgazette.org/2007/04/rfid_implants_5.html.

[80]*Id.*

[81]Biohacking/Grinder Update: Tim Cannon Implants Circadia 1.0, 2013, at: http://hplusmagazine.com/2013/10/21/grinder-update-tim-cannon-implants-circadia-1-0/.

Android device, produce readouts of the temperature changes, and send Cannon a text message if he's experiencing a fever. To insert the device, an incision was made on Cannon's forearm above an existing tattoo. His skin was lifted and separated away from his tissue and the device was inserted into the pocket that was created before being sutured shut. The LEDs act as 'status lights' that can be used to light up a tattoo on Cannon's arm, under which the sensor is fitted. The first version of the sensor reads temperature changes but, in theory, later versions could be used to track other vital signs and body changes. Some critics have argued that Tim's implanted technology does not realistically measure body temperature—but entering that debate is not a purpose of this chapter, other than to use this dispute as an introduction to how the law, in general, will have to deal with defective implantable devices a subject covered in this and other chapters throughout this book.

Sensory Substitution and a Sixth Sense

With regard to hacking the body, can a new sense be created? If by "new sense" one meant to enhance a current sense in such a way that sensory information beyond the range of its sensory receptor(s) can be detected, then yes. Actually, substituting one sense for another is a well-researched topic and represents another way to hack the body and create a cyborg future. Increasing and/or extending the range of our senses may be desirable given we see and hear across certain frequencies, and that the eyes and ears can only detect information within a given distance to the sensory receptors. In the future, by hacking the body, X-ray or telephoto vision, and greater sensitivity to olfactory, gustatory, or haptic information, may be possible.

Duke University neuroscientist Miguel Nicolelis, and his team claim that they have created a "sixth sense" through a brain implant in which infrared light is detected by lab rats.[82] Even though the infrared light can't be seen, lab rats are able to detect it via electrodes in the part of the brain responsible for the rat's sense of touch- so remarkably, the rats feel the light, not sees it. In order to give the rats their "sixth sense", Duke researchers placed electrodes in the rat's brains that were attached to an infrared detector.[83] The electrodes were then attached to the part of the animals' brains responsible for processing information about touch. The rats soon began to detect the source of the 'contact' and move towards the signal.

Sixth sense or not, in my view, the study by Nicolelis and his team is another step toward integrating brain-computer technology into the human body; and thus contributing to a cyborg future.[84] Eric Thomson, who worked on the project, said

---

[82]Miguel Nicolelis, *Id*. note 47.

[83]Miguel Nicolelis, *Id*. note 47.

[84]Miguel Nicolelis, *Id*. note 47.

past brain-machine studies have focused on restoring function to damaged areas of the brain, not creating it. "This is the first study in which a neuroprosthetic device, was used to augment function—literally enabling a normal animal to acquire a sixth sense."[85] In addition to these fascinating findings, the Duke scientists found that creating the infrared-detecting sixth sense did not stop the rats from being able to process touch signals, despite the electrodes (providing input for the infra-red detection system) being placed in the tactile cortex.

Hacking the Ear

Grinders have also shown an interest in hacking the ear. For example, Rich Lee, a self-described Grinder, implanted sound-transmitting magnets in his ears to extend his auditory sense.[86] Part of his system contains a coil that creates an electromagnetic field that vibrates magnets implanted in his ears which produces sound. Lee says the quality of the sound is similar to a cheap pair of earbuds. The phenomenon at work is known as electromagnetic induction, and is also the reason we can both generate electricity with mechanical motion (i.e. generators) and turn sound into electrical currents (i.e. microphones). Showing the true hacker spirit, one of Rick's interests is to use the implant to connect with other devices to augment his own senses and abilities. But a main part of his interest in hacking his auditory sense deals with necessity, Rick is losing his sight. With his headphone implants, and other technology, Rich could compensate for his loss of vision by learning to echolocate and to interpret the shape and dimensions of his surroundings based on how they react to emitted sound waves transmitted to his implanted magnets. Aside from just listening to music or podcasts, Lee plans to use the earlobe-implants in conjunction with his phone's GPS so he can get directions beamed right into his head. And Lee plans to hook up the earlobe-phones to a directional microphone in order to listen in on conversations; clearly there are privacy issues associated with this.

Hackers are not the only one interested in restoring or enhancing audition. According to the FDA, as of 2012, approximately 324,200 people worldwide have received a cochlear implant, designed to improve hearing. A cochlear implant helps to provide a sense of sound to a person who is profoundly deaf or severely hard-of-hearing. The implant does not restore normal hearing, instead, it can give a deaf person a useful representation of sounds in the environment and help him or her to understand speech. The typical implant consists of: an external portion that sits behind the ear and a second portion that is surgically placed under the skin and has a microphone, which picks up sound from the environment; a speech

---

[85]See generally, Miguel Nicolelis, *Id.* note 47.

[86]Zoltan Islvan, 2014, Interview with Transhumanist Biohacker Rich Lee, The Transhumanist Philosopher, at: https://www.psychologytoday.com/blog/the-transhumanist-philosopher/201407/interview-transhumanist-biohacker-rich-lee.

processor, which selects and arranges sounds picked up by the microphone; a transmitter and receiver/stimulator, which receive signals from the speech processor and converts them into electric impulses; and an electrode array, a group of electrodes that collects the impulses from the stimulator and sends them to different regions of the auditory nerve. A cochlear implant is very different from a hearing aid which amplifies sounds so they may be detected by damaged ears. Instead, cochlear implants bypass damaged portions of the ear and directly stimulate the auditory nerve

In the U.S. the FDA enforces regulations that deal specifically with the manufacture and sale of hearing aids because these products are recognized as medical devices. The most notable federal regulation is the FDA's Hearing Aid Rule which requires that prior to the sale of a hearing aid, the practitioner advice the patient that it is in their best health interest to see a physician, preferably one specializing in diseases of the ear, before purchasing a hearing aid. As with other implant technology, with cochlear implants problems may occur which prompt legal action. For example, in Kentucky a jury awarded $7.24 million to a Kentucky girl and her family, after her cochlear implant failed and caused her to suffer excruciating shocks and convulsions.[87] The jury found that Advanced Bionics, a medical device company, was responsible for knowingly selling defective cochlear implants.

Sensing Electromagnetic Fields

In an extension of the work by Duke's Miguel Nicolelis (feeling light) and University of Reading's Kevin Warrick (implantable chip), Grinders are hacking their body by inserting magnets under their fingertips in order to detect a source of energy that is beyond our normal perception, electromagnetic fields. Similarly, robots are also becoming equipped with the ability to sense objects before it touches them by using magnetic fields in a way that in their case, mimics the sensory perception of sharks.

Electromagnetic fields are all around us, whether we perceive them or not. In fact, anything that uses a transformer or direct current (as do household appliances) gives off an electromagnetic field. With implantable magnets, things like power cord transformers, microwaves, and laptop fans became perceptible to a cyborg. According to Grinders equipped with the implanted magnets, each object has its own unique field, with a different strength and "texture." Body hacker, Tim Cannon has extensive experience detecting magnetic fields through his neodymium magnetic implant. Interestingly, when Tim first received his implant he reports

---

[87]David Kirkwood, 2013, Jury awards $7.2 million in case of a girl harmed by a defective cochlear implant, at: http://hearinghealthmatters.org/hearingnewswatch/2013/jury-awards-7-2-million-in-case-of-a-girl-harmed-by-a-defective-cochlear-implant/.

that he could literally feel the invisible field of a cash register, with the strength of the vibrations of his implanted magnet varying depending on where he held his finger in relation to the machine.[88] However, not all of Tim's perceptions of magnetic fields have been positive, as Tim reports an uncomfortable feeling when he handles other magnets which can flip the magnet inside his finger.

In an extension of his body hacking efforts to create a magnetic sense, Cannon is working on an implantable device called Bottlenose which is an echo location unit, giving a person a sonar sense. The device which is about half the size of a pack of cigarettes slips over a person's finger. Named after the echolocation used by dolphins, it sends out an electromagnetic pulse and measures the time it takes to bounce back. If a person is equipped with a finger magnet, the implant is able to react to the sonar information translating it into distance information. A final example of hacking the skin involves implanted magnets in the arm of tattoo artist Dan Hurban, the purpose of which is to hold an iPod Nano to his arm.[89] While a strap would have done the job, none-the-less, this is an interesting proof-of-concept example.

Cybersecurity and the Cyborg Network

As humans become equipped with wirelessly networked sensors and implants, the body is becoming a local area network requiring dedicated spectrum. And as with any wireless network, it can be hacked. In the U.S. the Federal Communication Commission specifically allocates spectrum for a medical body area network, or MBAN for short, which consists of devices worn on, or implanted in, the human body that communicate with a programmer/controller device outside the body using a wireless communication link. The spectrum allocated to MBANs is solely for the purpose of measuring and recording physiological parameters and other patient information, or for performing diagnostic or therapeutic functions, primarily in health care facilities. There are a number of restriction with MBANs—they can be used only for diagnostic and therapeutic purposes; they must be provided to a patient only under the direction of an authorized health care professional; an MBAN body-worn device may not communicate directly with another MBAN body-worn device; and are only allowed a maximum emission bandwidth of five megahertz.

With wirelessly implantable devices, there are several weaknesses to the network which includes those resulting from unintentional signal interference, to threats characterized as "unauthorized accessing of a device," or hacking. Medical devices exhibit a number of potential vulnerabilities—such as untested firmware and software, and unsecured wireless connectivity. This could happen in a number of ways: limited battery life, remote access vulnerabilities, interruptible wireless signals,

---

[88]See generally, Dan Berg, 2012, Body Hacking: My Magnetic Implant, at: http://www.iamdann.com/2012/03/21/my-magnet-implant-body-modification.

[89]Guy Gives Himself Magnet Implants to Attach iPod To Arm, at: http://geekologie.com/2012/05/guy-gives-himself-magnet-implants-to-att.php.

unencrypted data transfers, susceptibility to interference, faulty warning mechanisms, reliance on outdated and obsolete technologies and the inability to download security patches. These vulnerabilities, in turn, could lead to hackers tampering with a device's settings, disabling key functions of the device without a user's knowledge, obtaining sensitive data about a patient or causing a complete device malfunction.

Conclusions

In an age where technology allows people to augment their body, without the confines of evolution by natural selection, human development will continue to leap forward bringing fundamental changes to the very nature of humanity. Body hacking, augmentation, cyborgization, call it what you like, the movement towards implanting technology in the body, is a ripe ground for legislation as new advances in sensors, prosthetics, and brain-computer interfaces are being developed. Law and technology must work hand-in-hand as we move into this new age of human development. Under current laws, such as the ADA, the baseline "able" person is the average functioning human, with all original parts intact, and no addition or modification are relevant in the eyes of the law to determine whether someone is disabled. But this paradigm doesn't work in an age of cyborgs where neuroscience and robotics is leading to an updated division between disabled, able, and "better abled" as both disabled and healthy humans increasingly chose to augment their bodies, and even their brains, with technology. In fact, the use of brain-computer interfaces in the future will go far beyond restoration and enhancement to literally adding new functions to the mind. The ability to hack the body raises the question of what kind of autonomy do we have with our bodies?[90] Is it the autonomy that individuals possess over a piece of property? Or is the autonomy under a right of privacy?

In this chapter I showed that body hackers, Grinders, and self-made cyborgs, are taking advantage of widely available technologies such as tracking chips, LEDs, magnets, and motion sensors to imbue themselves capabilities no other human has. Professor Warwick's initial RFID implant was a turning point in the history of transhumanism not because it represented a great technological leap in implants, but because it required mostly imagination and the courage to try something new, as the technology he used already existed. What he did, anyone could have done. What it undeniably did was pave the way for people with far fewer resources to experiment with enhancements of their own—often without the aid of medical professionals- and many of those explorers have been discussed in this chapter.

In the beginning of the chapter, I stated that caution was in order as we approach the cyborg future. Stanford's Fukuyama's warnings are worth noting again—"What is that human essence that we might be in danger of losing?" "For a

---

[90]Radhika Rao, Property, Privacy, and the Human Body, 2000, 80 B.U.L. Rev. 359.

religious person, it might have to do with the divine gift or spark that all human beings are born with. From a secular perspective, it would have to do with human nature: the species-typical characteristics shared by all human beings qua human beings. That is ultimately what is at stake in the biotech revolution."[91] Fukuyama argues that state power, possibly in the form of new regulatory institutions, should be used to regulate biotechnology and also cyborg technology. I agree and gave examples in this chapter of how the FDA and other government agencies are starting to show an interest in cyborg technology and that there is a fledgling field of cyborg law related to body modification and enhancements beginning to emerge.

---

[91]Francis Fukuyama, *id.*, note 9.

Chapter 6
Sensors and the Law

Introduction

While previous chapters discussed the role of prosthesis and implants as technologies moving humanity closer to a merger with artificially intelligent machines, this chapter introduces the reader to another technology that will be essential for reaching a Posthuman age—sensors and sensor networks. Following the law of accelerating returns, the last two decades have seen dramatic improvements in sensor technology, as a result, billions of smaller, faster, and more powerful sensors are being embedded within the world. It is now common for people to wear wristbands or clip-on sensors that record their vital signs such as activity levels and sleep patterns; in addition, some people are wearing identification badges which employers use to track their location and allow entry into secure buildings. And recently, advances in digital tattoos means that people can wear temporary epidermal circuits which monitor their health. With continuing improvements in technology, sensors that are currently worn on the body are beginning to "move under the skin," creating an emerging class of cyborgs that has capabilities beyond those of current nonenhanced humans. For example, with implant technology, appropriately equipped cyborgs can detect magnetic fields, see infrared light, hear color, engage in telepathy, and augment the world with information. And as sensor technology continues to experience rapid growth, when combined with advances in nanotechnology, by midcentury, self-replicating nanobots will enter the body to repair damaged organs and cells—when this happens, the number of sensors could grow to the trillions. Clearly, sensors will have a major role to play in our cyborg future.

Given the speed at which technology is advancing, by midcentury a number of legal and policy issues relating to cyborg technologies and their role in determining the future direction of humanity will need to be addressed. For example, as we create powerful miniaturized sensors with wireless capabilities, will we be

© Springer International Publishing Switzerland 2015
W. Barfield, *Cyber-Humans*, DOI 10.1007/978-3-319-25050-2_6

creating a world with little or no privacy, and a world in which governments routinely exert control over citizens by accessing the sensors they wear? Or will we be creating a more utopian world in which sensors are used to monitor and repair the human body; enhance communication between people; and help society maintain stable democratic institutions? As in most cases, the adaptation of a particular technology leads to a balancing of both possibilities and it is often the law which helps determine the balance.

Let's begin the discussion of sensors and their role in creating the conditions for a human-machine merger with a fascinating case brought by an "unwilling cyborg." Daniel J. Palese claimed that for 10 years, his two sisters entered his residence on a daily basis, drugged and hypnotized him, and while he was asleep implanted cameras, sensors, and transmitters in his body to track and control him. Not surprisingly, when his case was presented to the Tenth Circuit Court of Appeals, it was dismissed as legally frivolous.[1] In 1998 when the case was heard, no one seriously considered the possibility that Daniel had actually been implanted with sensors against his will. But less than 20 years after Daniel's case was dismissed, the ability to control the behavior of a person using implants is no longer the product of a paranoid mind but technologically possible and being done. To illustrate this point, RFID implants are used to track Alzheimer's patients, electrodes implanted in the brain of Parkinson's patients are used to mediate their symptoms, and some people, described as grinders, are trying to create new senses all together, using for example, magnets implanted within their fingertips to detect magnetic forces emanating from everyday objects. And I should mention that in response to battlefield injuries, the U.S. government has heavily invested in technology to fix and repair brain damaged soldiers, spending millions for research aimed at creating neuro-implants that will help veterans improve their memory. In the coming decades the same technology will not only benefit the millions worldwide who suffer from traumatic brain injuries, but will also provide another fundamental "tool" necessary to support a human-machine merger.

When Daniel argued to the court that he had been implanted with sensors and transmitters, there was no law relating specifically to cyborgs to redress his claim; although, if his assertion was true both the criminal and civil law would have provided a strong cause of action. But just 10 years after Daniel's court appearance, a statute enacted in California was on point. California's "anti-chipping" statute provided that "no person shall require, coerce, or compel any other individual to undergo the subcutaneous implanting of an identification device"; described as any item, application, or product that is passively or actively capable of transmitting personal information, including devices using radio frequency technology.[2] The statue created a civil action under which a person implanted (or chipped) against their will with an identification device could recover a "civil penalty," such as actual damages and compensatory damages, injunctive relief, and punitive

---

[1]*Daniel J. Palese, v. Dominic Palese and Patricia Palese,* 141 F.3d 1185 (10th Cir. 1998).
[2]California "Anti-Chipping Statute", Sect. 52.7 of the California Civil Code.

damages with proof that the person implanting the sensor did so with "malice, oppression, fraud or duress."[3] The California statute and similar statutes aimed at protecting a person from being "chipped" against their will are clearly important legislative responses to RFID technology, more legislative responses to human enhancement and cyborg technologies are coming.

Although implant technology has shown great promise for restoring lost functions to a body damaged by disease or broken by injury, Daniel's accusations reveal a potential use of cyborg technology which should greatly concern humanity. Consider Ray Kurzweil's prediction that brain implants will allow a person to recreate experiences already lived or even to transfer (transplant) memories from one brain to another.[4] While this is a remarkable vision by an inventor and futurist with an uncanny record for getting it right- the same technology could be used by governments and corporations to implant false memories into one's mind, and to trespass upon a person's private thoughts (see the Chapter on *Cognitive Liberty*). Clearly, "chipping" people against their will, or using implants to control their behavior, will lead to extremely negative consequences for an individual and for society at large. For this reason, many argue that the use of sensors and implant technologies should proceed with caution and only after a rigorous public debate on the desirability of allowing humans to be equipped with technology that could fundamentally alter what it means to be human.

Entering the debate about the direction of our cyborg future, many social scientists have argued against policies which would inhibit innovation in the development of information technologies. Summarizing competing positions, economist Adam Thierer refers to a cautious approach taken to technology innovation as the "precautionary principle" which he states refers to the "belief that new innovations should be curtailed or disallowed until their developers can prove that they will not cause harm to individuals or groups..."[5] This is in contrast to the view of "permissionless innovation" which Thierer describes as the policy that new technology should be permitted by default, "unless a compelling case can be made that a new technology will bring serious harm to society...".[6] While I strongly support innovation in technology, if the implementation of cyborg technologies, especially in the form of artificial super intelligence, could potentially lead to the extinction of the human race, then put me down as a supporter of the precautionary principle. Technical innovator and entrepreneur Bill Joy, co-founder of Sun Microsystems agrees and goes even further. Concerned with the threat that super artificial intelligence could pose to humanity, Joy advocates that researchers actually "relinquish"

---

[3]*Id.*

[4]Raymond Kurzweil, The Human Machine Merger: Why We Will Spend Most of Our Time in Virtual Reality in the Twenty-first Century, keynote address delivered at the 2000 ACM SIGGRAPH conference in New Orleans, at: http://www.kurzweilai.net/the-human-machine-merger-why-we-will-spend-most-of-our-time-in-virtual-reality-in-the-twenty-first-century.

[5]Adam Thierer, Permissionless Innovation: The Continuing Case for Comprehensive Technological Freedom, Mercatus Center, George Mason University, 2014.

[6]*Id.*

or completely abandon key genetic, nanotechnology, and robotics research because it could lead to a dystopian future. Renowned physicist Stephen Hawking also warned of the danger that artificial intelligence could pose to humanity. Noting that humans are limited by slow biological evolution, he commented that they lack the ability to compete against artificial intelligence and will eventually be superseded, a view I support. In an interview, Professor Hawking told the BBC: that "The development of full artificial intelligence could spell the end of the human race."[7] Stanley Kubrick's film *2001* and its murderous computer HAL encapsulate many people's fears of how AI could pose a threat to human life. "It would take off on its own, and re-design itself at an ever increasing rate," Hawking said.[8] "We cannot quite know what will happen if a machine exceeds our own intelligence, so we can't know if we'll be infinitely helped by it, or ignored by it and sidelined, or conceivably destroyed by it," he says.[9] If Joy's approach is deemed to have merit, and if Hawkings concern should be given diligence, due to the speed of technological advancements, legislators will need to start the process of regulating cyborg technologies in the very near future, as the Singularity may be close and once reached, it is likely artificial super intelligence will not be susceptible to control by regulations enacted by humans.

Stanford's Francis Fukuyama, writing in *Our Posthuman Future, Consequences of the Biotechnology Revolution,* has expressed similar concerns regarding the threat posed to humanity by artificial intelligence; arguing that biotechnology needs to be carefully regulated due to its potential to change the nature of humanity and structure of society.[10] In the context of biotechnology, Fukuyama has commented that genetic modification to the genome could alter liberal democracy; for example, by creating a superclass of genetically enhanced people.[11] Similarly, how we intersperse sensors throughout the environment and how the government chooses to use sensors, for example, to monitor people, could affect individual liberty, and the structure of society and of government institutions that develop this century. As an example of the relationship between sensors and individual liberty, where sensors go, so goes surveillance; yet there isn't an informed debate among the general public as to how much loss of privacy is acceptable in a sensor filled world. Anyone who has read Orwell's *1984* will immediately see the ominous comparison to the ever-watchful telescreen of Big Brother keeping citizens in a fog of fear. And once we all have the "expectation" of being constantly watched in an all-pervading panopticon, there can be no "expectation" of privacy. Some argue that the right of privacy will simply wither away and die once the government integrates sensors into a network used for monitoring and control. Regardless of the

---

[7]Rory Cellan-Jones, 2014, Stephen Hawking warns artificial intelligence could end mankind, BBC news, at: http://www.bbc.com/news/technology-30290540.

[8]*Id.*

[9]*Id.*

[10]Francis Fukuyama, 2003, Our Posthuman Future: Consequences of the Biotechnology Revolution, Picador Press.

[11]*Id.*

perceived merits of merging with machines, scientists think that the only way to stop a dystopic future from happening is to enact statutes which specifically prohibit the spy activities made possible by a global network of sensors and implant technologies before being surveilled becomes a societal norm. Researchers have also concluded that given sensor technologies could be misused by governments and corporations, a host of technical safeguards should be designed to limit the ability of people to be tracked, surveilled, and monitored. Otherwise, they argue-will there be any legal justification for privacy and freedom from government control once society is fully conditioned to being monitored, tracked, chipped, and recorded?

With regard to law and sensors, there is a growing body of case law which is beginning to set the boundaries of what sensor information is possible to collect, where it can be collected, by whom, and under what circumstances. These cases attempt to answer important questions of law and policy that sensors, especially those implanted within the body raise. For example, should data collected by sensors be kept private? Is government access to sensors an unconstitutional search and seizure? And what if someone hacks a person's body-worn or implanted sensors to steal information which may be protected by copyright or trade secret law? Generally, courts have ruled that the government is allowed to use metal detectors to scan the body reasoning that there is less of an invasion of privacy from sensor scans than frisks or other kinds of searches. However, with cyborg technologies now being implanted within the body, the threat to people from external sensors designed to peer within the body, can be fatal. In fact, a woman in Russia fitted with a pacemaker died after passing through an airport scanner which reportedly disrupted the functioning of her pacemaker.[12] This example highlights that a cyborg future may be fraught with unexpected danger.

As we discuss the law, technology, and policy issues which arise from the use of sensors, in the background of this discussion are the most important questions facing humanity this century- should we merge with artificially intelligent machines and therefore experience the benefits of exponential growth operating for information technologies, or should we not merge with our future "mind children" (to use a phrase coined by Dr. Hans Moravec in his 1990 classic- *Mind Children: The Future of Robot and Human Intelligence*) and risk becoming irrelevant and surpassed when the Singularity occurs?[13] To complicate matters more, the critically important question of whether humanity should merge with artificially intelligent machines needs to be discussed in the context of another important issue that humanity must decide by midcentury—should we allow artificially intelligent machines to reach human or beyond human levels of intelligence or should we stop this from occurring? This chapter on the law, technology, and

---

[12]Harriet Alexander, 2014, Woman in Russia fitted with a pacemaker died after passing through an airport scanner, The Telegraph, at: http://www.telegraph.co.uk/news/worldnews/europe/russia/11247611/Woman-dies-after-airport-scanner-interferes-with-her-pacemaker.html.

[13]Hans Moravec, 1990, Mind Children: The Future of Robot and Human Intelligence, Harvard University Press.

policy of sensors provides useful information to add to this important debate concerning the future direction of humanity.

A World of Sensors

To restate the main theme woven throughout this book- that humans will merge with artificially intelligent machines this century- in the material which follows I discuss how sensor technology will contribute to that outcome; along the way, I introduce legal and policy issues that will be implicated by the proliferation of sensors placed in the environment and implanted within the body. As was discussed in Chap. 3, sensors on the outside of the body, are rapidly moving "under the skin," what I describe as *"breaching the sensor-skin barrier."* Once the barrier is breached, sensors implanted within the body will be used to control technology that is attached to, and external to, the body, allowing a person to teleoperate a range of technologies. As one example, sensors combined with brain-computer interfaces, are beginning to allow people to remotely control a robot arm using EMG signals collected by sensors worn on a person's head. In this application, the robot arm's movements are also controlled and corrected by data from ultrasonic and infrared sensors. And while the vast amount of information captured by all the connected digital devices is valuable on its own, sensor data will be even more powerful when linked to the physical world. On this point, implanted sensors are beginning to connect the functions of our body to the sensors and machines external to it. For example, cyborg artist Anthony Antonellis has an RFID chip embedded in his arm that stores and transfers art to his handheld smartphone.[14] For his particular application, Anthony uses a subcutaneous near-field communication chip for use as a wireless storage device. The re-writable 1 K chip implanted in Antonellis contains an animated GIF file that can be accessed by a range of computing technologies. The data on the chip is left public for reading and password protected for writing.

The above examples are just the beginning, when it comes to sensors, get ready, more are coming. According to experts, the billions of sensors that exist now will pale in comparison to the number of sensors that will be strewn throughout the environment in just a few decades. In fact, Janusz Bryzek, the organizer of a Stanford University summit on sensors predicts that one trillion sensors will be manufactured and shipped each year.[15] Going further, Peter Diamandis and Steven Kotler, authors of *Abundance: The Future is Better than you Think*, envision a

---

[14]Ellie Zolfagharfard, 2013, Would you have tattoo IMPLANTED under your skin? Artist has chip placed inside his hand that reveals artwork when read by a smartphone, Daily Mail, at: http://www.dailymail.co.uk/sciencetech/article-2405596/Artist-Anthony-Antonellis-creates-digital-tattoo-implanting-RFID-chip-hand.html.

[15]Janusz Bryzek: The trillion-sensor man: Part 1, 2013, at: http://www.electronics-eetimes.com/en/janusz-bryzek-the-trillion-sensor-man-part-1.html?cmp_id=7&news_id=222918922.

future need for forty-five trillion sensors.[16] And from my perspective gained from directing the *Sensory Engineering Laboratory* at the University of Washington, I also envision a world with trillions of sensors placed throughout the environment and implanted within the body well before 2100. What could lead to this sensor-filled future? In a *Scientific American* article, MITs Gershon Dublon and Joe Paradiso observed that one reason why sensors are becoming ubiquitous is because they have, "for the most part, followed Moore's law," they keep getting smaller and more powerful; in contrast, the capabilities of our human senses, while truly remarkable, are fixed.[17]

Currently, the human body is orders of magnitude more "sensor rich" than artificially intelligent machines. From a biological perspective the entire surface of our body consists of sensors that detect more data that we can consciously attend to. In fact, it has been estimated that the senses gather some eleven million bits per second from the environment, however, due to information compression, only a fraction of that information gets processed and placed in working memory—about 50–126 bits. With continuing advances in sensors and implant technology, Google's Ray Kurzweil predicts that by 2040 it may be possible to store all of a human being's sensory experiences on a microchip implanted in the brain. This may sound like science fiction, but if we consider advances made on prosthetic neuronal chips by Theodore Berger of the University of Southern California, by mid-century Kurzweil's prediction could become reality.

Even with the impressive bandwidth of our senses, artificially intelligent machines are rapidly catching up to our sensory capabilities, at least in terms of raw processing power. With an estimated 100 billion neurons, each connecting to as many as 10,000 other neurons, and with each neuron operating at about 10 bits/sec, the raw processing power of the human brain is estimated to be in the petaflop computing range, a number which interestingly, is matched by current supercomputers. However, what machines are missing is the "cognitive aspect" of information processing, or the ability of the machine to interpret the millions of bits of data collected by its sensors. Because a world consisting of sensors improving under the law of accelerating returns will create artificially intelligent machines with exponentially improving sensory capabilities, this possibility alone creates a strong motivation for humanity to equip itself with the same sensor technology, and to merge with our technological progeny in order to gain the benefits of information technologies improving at exponential rates. In fact, implantable sensors, will lead to a paradigm shift in how we think about the body. For example, as technology marches on some researchers will not be content to "just" restore memory to normal or design technologies to enhance the senses, instead they will actively try to create new senses. On this point, scientists at Intel are using the properties of a magnetic field to develop a robotic hand that gives people the ability to sense

---

[16]Peter Diamandis and Steven Kotler, 2014, Abundance: The Future is Better than You Think, Free Press.

[17]Gershon Dublon and Joseph A. Paradiso, 2014, Extrasensory Perception, Scientific America, V. 311, 36–41.

objects before it touches them. And at Duke University researchers believe they have developed technology in their laboratory allowing subjects to see infrared light that's not on the visible spectrum.[18] And in the military domain, the Defense Advanced Research Projects Association (DARPA) is trying to build "thought helmets" to enable telepathic communication using brain-computer interfaces to give soldiers extra senses, such as night vision, and the ability to "see" magnetic fields caused by landmines.[19]

As machines gain in intelligence and become more autonomous, sensors are becoming an indispensable technology in mediating machine-to-machine interactions. For example, Google cars navigate by accessing GPS data from satellites, and the navigation system itself uses information from sensors embedded in the environment and on the car to maintain its position on the road. But what are the legal issues associated with autonomous machines that use information from sensors to interact with the world? With autonomous cars equipped with sensors- who is responsible when something goes wrong? What will happen when a driverless car harms someone or Google Maps sends it the wrong way down a one-way street? Recently, legislators have been debating these and other issues associated with autonomous cars, as a result, in the U.S. four states and the District of Columbia have passed laws specific to driverless cars, some allowing manufacturers to test cars but none answering the full range of legal questions that will come up in a sensor-filled world with increasingly smart machines.

In my view of our cyborg future, the law of accelerating returns means that the power of sensors and implants will continue to improve exponentially which will quickly lead to a world of cyborgs ready to merge with machines that likewise will be equipped with powerful sensors- all wirelessly connected together as part of the emerging global "Network of Things." In fact, the pace at which sensors are being attached to everyday objects is remarkable- just within the confines of a person's kitchen, stoves, dishwashers, microwaves, refrigerators, and other appliances use heat sensors to monitor and control temperature. And as discussed in previous chapters, medical necessity is a major reason why sensors are being designed and implanted within the body. One example of sensors designed based on "medical necessity" is the bionic pancreas being built by Fiorenzo Omenetto, Professor of biomedical engineering at Tufts University.[20] The system comes with a tiny sensor located on an implantable needle that "talks" directly to a smartphone app which monitors blood-sugar levels for diabetics.[21] The system has two pumps and sen-

---

[18]Matthew Humphries, 2013, Duke University augments rat's brain with sixth sense, at: http://www.geek.com/news/duke-university-augments-rats-brain-with-sixth-sense-1540058/.

[19]Arthur House, The Real Cyborgs, The Telegraph, at: http://s.telegraph.co.uk/graphics/projects/the-future-is-android/.

[20]For a description of wearable/implantable technology see, Wireless Electronic Implants Stop Staph, Then Harmlessly Dissolve, at: http://www.innovationtoronto.com/2014/12/wireless-electronic-implants-stop-staph-then-harmlessly-dissolve/.

[21]Mike Edelhart, 2014, Nine real technologies that will soon be inside you, at: https://au.news.yahoo.com/technology/a/25293925/nine-real-technologies-that-will-soon-be-inside-you/.

sors which control the pumps; if the app on the phone detects that blood sugar is beginning to rise, the app signals one pump to release insulin; if the blood sugar falls too low, the app signals the other pump to release glucagon. Another illustration of medical necessity guiding sensor research is again work done at Tufts University, but in this case the School of Engineering which is designing a system which consists of a dissolving electronic implant, made of silk and magnesium that is used to eliminate bacterial infection in subjects.[22] The system delivers heat to infected tissue when triggered by a remote wireless signal. This is an important step forward for the development of implantable medical devices that can be turned on remotely to perform a therapeutic function, such as managing post-surgical infection.

Our Reliance on Sensors

To illustrate our current reliance on sensors, consider the mobile technology that billions of people use daily, a cell phone. Simply put, a cell phone is a wireless hand-held sensor with a camera that converts conventional analog data into digital information; it also includes an accelerometer to measure changes in velocity, and a gyroscope to measure orientation. With these "senses" a cell phone can be used to track a person's location, and integrate that information with comprehensive satellite, aerial, and ground maps to generate multi-layered real-time location-based databases. In fact, much of the sensor data collected by people as they move about the environment is through their cell phone; which can include highly personal information such as their location and calling patterns. An important point to make is this- just as we humans are becoming increasingly dependent on software to control the complex systems that we need for everyday life, we are becoming equally dependent on sensors, most people just don't know it yet. According to Bill Joy co-founder of Sun Microsystems, in his seminal article published in *Wired* magazine, "W*hy the Future Doesn't Need* Us," we are drifting into dependence on machines to such an extent that it is becoming impractical not to accept the decisions made by them.[23]

What are the types of issues that will come up in an age of exponential growth for sensors? Clearly, privacy, safety, and the possibility of government control over our bodies and mind are major concerns, especially as sensors become implanted within the body. Just considering the topic of privacy law, could the government access sensor information collected and stored on implants without a search warrant? The right to privacy is not specifically stated in the U.S. Constitution, but is directly referred to in several state constitutions and statutes. For example, through its constitution and legislative action, California has been at the forefront of

---

[22]See *Id*, note 20.

[23]Bill Joy, 2000, Why the Future Doesn't Need Us, Wired 8.04.

protecting privacy, and thus has made a major contribution to the emerging field of cyborg law. In California, if a person's privacy has been invaded through the use of sensor technology, there are several "legal theories" a person may use for bringing an invasion of privacy claim: The California Constitution; California's Privacy Act; the common law tort of intrusion upon seclusion; and an antipaparazzi statute. The protection of privacy in the California State Constitution, affords an individual an inalienable right to pursue and obtain privacy; whereas, the California Privacy Act is even more specific to an emerging law of cyborgs and provides civil and criminal penalties for anyone who engages in unauthorized wiretapping or eavesdropping with an electronic amplifying or recording device.[24]

A search using sensor technology can result in valuable information, for example, the location of an Alzheimer's patient, but a search using sensors may also invade a person's privacy. If the federal government is involved, the U.S. Constitution directly addresses how the government must conduct a search and seizure. The Fourth Amendment to the U.S. Constitution gives the conditions under which the government can perform a search and seizure, stating- "The right of the people to be secure in their persons, houses, papers, and effects, against unreasonable searches and seizures, shall not be violated, and no warrants shall issue, but upon probable cause, supported by oath or affirmation, and particularly describing the place to be searched, and the persons or things to be seized."[25] While to date no "search and seizure" case has directly dealt with cyborgs, there have been related cases that involve sensors which I believe serve as precedence for an emerging cyborg law.

One such case that was argued before the U.S. Supreme Court was *Katz v. United States*.[26] The *Katz* Court laid out a basic rule to apply when the government uses sensors to collect information about a person. In *Katz*, the Supreme Court ruled that a warrantless search using a government wiretap was improper because the defendant had a reasonable expectation that his conversation would be private. A "search" under the Fourth Amendment, the Court held, is an intrusion that violates an expectation of privacy which society is prepared to consider reasonable.[27] Of course, we can ask, what is a reasonable expectation of privacy in a world filled with billions (and soon-to-be trillions) of sensors? I should mention that the expectation of privacy is for a human subjected to a government search, not for artificially intelligent machine. Clearly the *Katz* framework that was formulated in 1967 (and thus based on decades old technology) is difficult to apply when it is becoming rare for people's actions not to be tracked or recorded in some way whenever they are in public or on the Internet- this highlights the need for the law to keep pace with advances in technology. However, the extent to which this can be done in an age of exponential growth for information technologies is questionable.

---

[24]California Privacy Act, (See Penal Code §§ 631 and 632, and (criminal) and § 637 (civil)).

[25]Fourth Amendment to the U.S. Constitution.

[26]*Katz v. United States*, 389 U.S. 347 (1967).

[27]*Id.*

The idea that technology outpaces the law is not new. In fact, in a seminal article on privacy published in 1890 in the Harvard Law Review, "*The Right to Privacy*," Louis Brandeis and Samuel Warren defined protection of the private realm as the foundation of individual freedom in the modern age.[28] Given the increasing capacity of governments, the press, and other agencies and institutions to invade previously inaccessible aspects of personal activity, Brandeis and Warren argued that the law must evolve in response to technological change.[29] Traditional prohibitions against trespass, assault, libel, and other invasive acts had afforded sufficient safeguards in previous eras, but these established principles could not, in their view, protect individuals from the "too enterprising press, the photographer, or the possessor of any other modern device for rewording or reproducing scenes or sounds."[30] Consequently, in order to uphold the "right to one's personality" in the face of modern business practices and invasive inventions, they concluded that legal remedies had to be developed to enforce definite boundaries between public and private life.[31] Given the "advanced" technology of 1890, what has changed today? Sensors and neuroprosthesis implanted within the body, remote sensing systems, billions of sensors embedded within the environment, algorithms to detect faces, and a world wide web in which surveillance can occur at a global level. There is much for the public to discuss as we equip our self and the world with "cyborg" technology.

Another case of particular importance for sensors and decided decades after Katz was *Riley v. California.*[32] In *Riley*, the Supreme Court dealt with the legality of a police search of private data stored on a cellphone. In a major decision for privacy rights in an age of sensors and wearable computing technology, the Supreme Court unanimously ruled that the police need warrants to search the cellphones of people they arrest. In response to the decision, Law Professor Orin S. Kerr from the George Washington University commented on the need for the court to recognize the changing world of information technology, observing- "It is the first computer-search case, and it says we are in a new digital age. You can't apply the old rules anymore."[33] Interestingly, Chief Justice Roberts seemed to foresee a cyborg future by commenting on the important role that sensors play in contemporary life. Referring to a cell phone, Roberts said, they are "such a pervasive and insistent part of daily life that the proverbial visitor from Mars might conclude they were an important feature of human anatomy." "The fact that technology now allows an individual to carry such information in his hand," Chief Justice Robert wrote,

---

[28]Samuel Warren and Louis Brandeis, The Right to Privacy, 4 Harvard Law Rev. 193, (1890).

[29]*Id.*

[30]*Id.*

[31]*Id.*

[32]*Riley v. California*, 134 S.Ct. 2473, (2014).

[33]Adam Liptak, 2014, Major Ruling Shields Privacy of Cellphones, Supreme Court Says Phones Can't Be Searched Without a Warrant, quoting Orin S. Kerr, at: http://www.nytimes.com/2014/06/26/us/supreme-court-cellphones-search privacy.html?_r=0.

"does not make the information any less worthy of the protection for which the founders fought."[34] In dicta, Justice Roberts touched upon a future in which emerging technologies will bring up a host of constitutional law issues. Can we conclude that the *Riley* case stands definitively for the proposition that the government will need a warrant to search the sensors worn by people, and in the coming decades, the sensors worn by cyborgs and artificially intelligent machines? Probably not, as most Supreme Court decisions are narrowly written; therefore, future cases involving sensors will be litigated to decide the government's ability to search sensor technology worn by or implanted within the body; it's just a matter of time.[35]

It seems to me that technology has steadily chipped away the privacy rights that individuals are afforded by constitutions and statutes so that the resulting space in which we can expect privacy has considerably shrunk. Not only can we be constantly tracked, filmed, and recorded as we move around the environment, given the trend for sensors to migrate under the skin, our future might be one in which the data representing the very functioning of our body and thoughts of our mind may be routinely accessed by corporations and governments. To avoid this negative outcome, I believe it is important for citizens to lobby governments to regulate the use of cyborg technology that could lead to egregious breaches of privacy and constant surveillance- especially for an individual's body and thoughts. If a government actor is involved, the court's reasoning in *Katz* that "[s]o long as that which is viewed or heard is perceptible to the naked eye or unaided ear, the person seen or heard has no reasonable expectation of privacy in what occurs"[36] leads to little protection for individuals in a world filled with sensors and information technologies becoming integrated into our anatomy and physiology that may allow the government to peer directly into our bodies and mind.

The Network of Sensors

At a pace on schedule with Kürzweil's law of accelerating returns, humans, robots, and everyday objects are increasingly becoming part of the wirelessly networked world represented by the global "Network of Things." In this networked world, information collected by a host of sensors is now accessible to anyone, anywhere, and anytime. Due to the proliferation of sensors interspersed throughout the environment, and the trend for sensors to "migrate" to the surface of the body, and then become implanted within the body, an important piece of the puzzle leading to our cyborg future and eventual merger with machines is here.

---

[34]*Riley v. California, id.,* note 32.

[35]*Id.*

[36]*Katz v. United States, id.,* note 26.

I have often touted battlefield injuries, medical necessity, and industrial uses as important factors spurring research on sensors, and while true, businesses are also seeing the potential of low-cost sensors to support many of their retail activities. For some time, retailers operating in many industries have required that their suppliers tag shipments with RFID so that the data can be automatically recorded when goods arrive. According to Ben Gaddis, Vice President of growth and innovation with marketing and advertising firm, *T3*, in a world where services have become commodities and price is king, sensors can help small businesses create a competitive advantage.[37] Gaddis comments that sensors give service companies the opportunity to shift their business from a largely reactive model to one that is more proactive and valuable to the end consumer. One example he cites involved a pizza delivery service and its use of a sensor embedded in a refrigerator magnet. The sensor/magnet device is pre-programmed to the customer's pizza preference, and using a built-in Bluetooth capability seamlessly places an order which generates a return text message confirming the order. In addition, retailers are trying to get into customers' brains and they now have the technology to do it. It's called consumer neuroscience and Thomas Ramsey indicates that companies are getting valuable shopper intel that can shape the shopping experience.[38] In the seconds before we knowingly decide to buy our brains react. If retailers can tap into those few seconds of subconscious they can use the information to make crucial decisions on how to sell products. "If we present that stuff in an engaging and fun way then people have a better experience and sometimes they buy more," says professor of neuromarketing, Paul Zak.[39] "There is no buy button in the brain and we are not talking about manipulation. We are talking about using tools to help create a better retail experience," says Dr. Marci.[40]

Even investment bankers are recognizing the growth and value of sensor technology. In fact, bankers from Goldman Sachs have predicted that by 2020 there will be twenty-eight billion connected devices. And remarkably, according to Wim Elfrink, Cisco's Chief Globalization Officer, the "Internet of Things" is being adopted faster than any technology in history.[41] Essentially what he and many people are saying is that later this century, anything that can be connected to the Internet will be. In fact, to perform the monitoring tasks that industry,

---

[37]Ben Gaddis, How Sensors will Revolutionize Service Businesses, Wired, at: http://www.wired.com/2013/05/how-sensors-will-revolutionize-service-businesses/.

[38]Thomas Zoega Ramsey, 2015, Introduction to Neuromarketing & Consumer Neuroscience, Neurons, Inc.

[39]Kathryn Hauser, 2014, Retailers Using Science To Shape Shopping Experience, quoting Paul Zak, at: http://boston.cbslocal.com/2014/12/09/retailers-using-science-to-shape-shopping-experience/.

[40]*Id.* Quoting Dr. Marci.

[41]Wim Elfrink, 2014, The Internet of Things: Moving Beyond the Hype, at: http://blogs.cisco.com/news/the-internet-of-things-moving-beyond-the-hype; Neil Kane, 2014, Caring for Relatives by Robots, Forbes, at: http://www.forbes.com/sites/neilkane/2014/10/20/caring-for-relatives-by-robot/.

corporations, medical science, and governments require, tiny sensor devices are being strewn virtually everywhere, and communicating to each other through wireless links. By midcentury, the sensors implanted within our bodies and possibly our brains will be a major part of the globally connected "Network of Things" which will include cyborgs that are now emerging along with artificially intelligent machines. As we move closer to mid-century, the developing global Network of Things also has the potential to create a "Network of Minds," in which crowdsourcing and other techniques will be used to solve problems on a global scale.

With the use of networks, knowing where a photo was taken, or when a car passed by an automated sensor, will add rich "metadata" that can be employed in countless ways. For example, roadway sensors can include a pneumatic road tube, an inductive loop detector, magnetic sensors, a piezoelectric cable, and weigh-in-motion sensors (piezoelectric, bending plate, load cell, and capacitance mat)—all of which can be used to calculate roadway congestion and to suggest alternate routes. In effect, location information will wirelessly link the physical world to the virtual meta-world of sensor data. In the coming decades, using sensor technology, everything from the clothing we wear to the roads we drive on will be embedded with sensors that collect information on our every move, including our goals, and our desires.

With cyborgs emerging this century and the world of "everyday things" increasingly being networked together, legislators will need to determine what limitations are appropriate to place on the collection and dissemination of personal information collected by sensors that form part of the globally connected network. To guide legislators, a public policy debate will need to focus on the extent to which data derived from sensors for one purpose can be reused without permission for another or without giving notice to the person whose data is being recoded, transmitted, accessed, and analyzed. And with sensors being used to collect personal information about people, legislators will need to determine the extent to which sensor data should be kept accurate, and secure; clearly, the security of data stored on implantable devices in the brain, will be especially important to maintain. While we might expect privacy for data derived from our body and for the thoughts in our mind, especially when we are in private places, according to Berkeley Law School's Pamela Samuelson, in practice there are porous barriers between public and private spaces.[42] For example, many applications for deploying sensor networks involve collecting personally identifiable information, which when combined with facial recognition technology can be tagged to the person as they move throughout the environment. The role of facial recognition technology equipped with camera sensors and pattern matching algorithms and its relation to privacy is currently being debated within the U.S. and the European Union;

---

[42]See generally, Pamela Samuelson, The Copyright Grab, wired, at: http://archive.wired.com/wired/archive/4.01/white.paper_pr.html.

Fig. 6.1 The tracking system developed by University of Washington researchers first systematically picks out people in a camera frame, then follows each person based on his or her clothing texture, color and body movement. Image courtesy of Professor Jeng-Neng Hwang, University of Washington

nonetheless, the use of facial recognition technology is expanding rapidly in government and private industries.[43]

Sensor technology can also be used to track people using cameras without relying on facial recognition technology. For example, University of Washington researchers have developed a way to automatically track people across moving and still cameras by using an algorithm that trains the networked cameras to learn one another's differences.[44] The system works by identifying a person in a video frame, then "following" that same person across multiple camera views. However, the problem with tracking a human across cameras of non-overlapping fields of view is that a person's appearance can vary dramatically in each video because of different perspectives, angles and color hues produced by different cameras.[45] The University of Washington researchers led by Jeng-Neng Hwang overcame this problem by building a link between the cameras and by using artificial intelligence to help train the camera recognition system (Fig. 6.1). To train the system, the cameras recorded for a few minutes, then systematically calculated the differences in color, texture, and angle between a pair of cameras for a number of people who walked into the frames in a fully unsupervised manner without human intervention.[46] After the calibration period, an algorithm automatically applied those differences between cameras and was able to pick out the same people across multiple frames, effectively tracking them without needing to see their faces or to hear their voice.

The system developed by University of Washington researchers, can be implemented with several technologies. For example, the researchers installed the tracking system on cameras placed inside a robot and a flying drone, allowing the robot and drone to follow a person, even when the instruments came across obstacles that blocked the person from view. The linking technology can be used anywhere, as long as the cameras can talk over a wireless network and upload data to the cloud.

---

[43]Woodrow Barfield, Information Privacy as a Function of Facial Recognition Technology and Wearable Computers, (September 11, 2006). *Bepress Legal Series*. Working Paper 1739, http://law.bepress.com/expresso/eps/1739.

[44]Michelle Ma, Moving cameras talk to each other to identify, track pedestrians, 2014, at: http://www.washington.edu/news/2014/11/12/moving-cameras-talk-to-each-other-to-identify-track-pedestrians/.

[45]*Id.*

[46]*Id.*

Telepresence and Sensors

In an interesting observation about our coming cyborg future, some scientists argue that the sensors embedded in the environment are beginning to function as an extension of the human nervous system, creating a new kind of sensory prosthesis, and raising the question—where do our human senses start and where do they end? In fact, the extension of our senses to sites remote to our body, may extend our legal liability far beyond the location of our physical presence. Consider the robotic sentry created by Samsung and designed for the border between North and South Korea. The robotic sentry is equipped with vision, heat, and motion sensors, and comes with a range finder. Sounds good, right? Except it creates visions of a dystopic future given it can identify and shoot a target over a distance of two miles away. No need to worry, it's *currently* under the control of a human operator from a remote location. Clearly, legal, ethical, and moral issues will be implicated given the trend to develop autonomous "killer robot" weapons guided by sensor controlled systems. In fact, in Norway, an autonomously controlled missile, or so-called "killer robot", has been developed for airborne strikes for its fighter jets which have the ability to identify targets and make decisions to kill without human "interference".[47] In response to the development of autonomous weapons, international organizations such as the *Campaign to Stop Killer Robots*, are trying to convince legislators to ban weapons that can decide on their own to kill. Likewise, I think there should be an "international level" response to implant and other cyborg technologies that could be used for iniquitous purposes, such as to control people, invade their privacy, and even to kill them.

Based on my research with my graduate students, access to sensory information that is remote to a person, can create a sense of telepresence or cognitively "being there."[48] Consider the legal consequences of telepresence for sensor technology— under criminal law a crime must consist of an *actus reus*, or guilty act, accompanied by a *mens rea*, or guilty mind. So, if a person supervising a remote robot, purposively manipulated (*mens rea*) a robotic arm (*actus reus*) such that it resulted in harm to an individual, both elements of a crime would be present. This brings up an interesting design issue for robotics, if we recall Isaac Asimov's Three Laws of Robotics, made famous in his 1942 short story "*Runaround*," the first two laws relate to the example just given- A robot may not injure a human being or, through inaction, allow a human being to come to harm; and a robot must obey the orders given to it by human beings, except where such orders conflict with the First Law. In the future, assigning criminal liability to robots with sensors that provide beyond human levels of performance will be a challenge for courts, for the simple

---

[47]Norway's 'killer robot' technology under fire, 2014, at: http://www.thelocal.no/20141023/norways-killer-robot-technology-under-fire.

[48]See generally, Woodrow Barfield and Thomas Furness, (eds) 1995, Virtual Environments and Advanced Interface Design, Oxford University Press.

reason that robots cannot be charged with a crime. Again, we come back to the issue of *mens rea*, can a machine be attributed with the intent to harm a human (or another machine)? Will accessing and analyzing sensor information with the appropriate algorithms be evidence of intent by the machine? Implementing Asimov's laws, along with other safeguards to protect humans from machines gaining in artificial intelligence and with increased sensory capabilities to explore the world, seems prudent.

Characteristics of Sensors

Contemporary robots can be thought of as self-navigating, semi-autonomous systems that are equipped with sensors that give them the ability to see, touch, hear and move using hardware, software, sensors, and algorithms that require environmental feedback. In addition, most robots have the capability to manipulate objects, and therefore are equipped with positioning and force sensors. A point to make is this, as robots gain in intelligence, mobility, and manual dexterity they are becoming more like us and doing so at a surprising speed.

What are some basic features of sensors and the legal issues which apply to them? Before addressing that question, let me introduce an important idea about law and technology that was proposed by Harvard Law Professor, Larry Lessig, author of *Code and Other Laws of Cyberspace*. Lessig's point was that the architecture of cyberspace itself regulates conduct in much the same way that legal code does.[49] The same concept holds for algorithms, sensors, prosthesis, brain implants, and other cyborg technologies. For example, the capabilities and features offered by sensor technology defines the type and range of sensory information that people and robots can detect from the environment and therefore what actions they can perform; in this way the features of sensors serve as a regulation of conduct by the very nature of the architecture and design of the sensor and sensor network. Similarly, the parameters of an algorithm also regulate machine behavior. Consider the following example which shows how an algorithm sets parameters for the behavior of a robot. In the field of mobile robotics, MIT researcher Sangbae Kim developed a bounding algorithm to control the speed at which a four-legged robot can run.[50] The algorithm works by calculating the amount of force exerted by a robot's legs in the split second during which it hits the ground, and through sensor data and feedback loops, allows the robot to maintain balance and a given speed. In general, the faster the desired speed, the more force must be applied to propel the robot forward. In related work using amputees as subjects, Robert Gregg at the University of Texas Dallas branch, is using robot control

---

[49]Larry Lessig, 2006, Code and Other Laws of Cyberspace, Version 2.0, Basic Books.

[50]Jennifer Chu, 2015, MIT cheetah robot lands the running jump, describing the work of Sangbae Kim, at: http://newsoffice.mit.edu/2015/cheetah-robot-lands-running-jump-0529.

combined with sensors (measuring the center of pressure on a powered prosthesis) to enable powered prosthetics to dynamically respond to the wearer's environment allowing the amputee to walk on a treadmill almost as fast as an able-bodied person.[51] Also by tweaking the parameters of sensors, sensors can be used to support policy goals. For example, if public policy dictates that people shouldn't text while driving, sensors can be used to support the policy. Consider the patent issued in 2014 to Apple which describes a procedure to use the iPhone's accelerometer and other sensors to determine when a person is driving.[52] If the sensors detect a moving car, motion sensors are then activated which block the texting capabilities of the mobile phone.

The basic function of a sensor is to measure and convert a physical quantity into a signal which is read by an observer or by an instrument. That is, a sensor is used to detect one form of energy and report it in another, often as an electrical signal. As an example, a pressure gauge might detect pressure, a mechanical form of energy, and convert it to an electrical signal for display at a remote gauge. One important part of a sensor is a transducer which is used to convert a signal in one form of energy to another. Energy types that are detected by sensors include (but are not limited to) electrical, mechanical, electromagnetic (including light), chemical, acoustic and thermal energy. Of particular relevance to our cyborg future are *in vivo* biosensors that function inside the body monitoring different aspects of our physiology- implanted chips that monitor glucose level and heart monitoring sensors within the body are examples. Since controlling the parameters of sensors can determine the range of behavior a robot may perform, perhaps one way to exert control over artificial intelligence is to carefully consider what sensory information it may detect; this is an additional safeguard beyond programming friendliness into the software.

The above discussion of sensors should be considered in light of current robot design. Most robots are equipped with a wide range of sensors, which allow them to perform many tasks that humans currently perform- in fact, the remarkable capability of sensors, is one reason why robots are displacing humans from the workplace. One of the standard sensors for a robot is a proximity sensor which allows it to detect a person's presence in order to decrease the likelihood of accidents. Proximity sensors are typically combined with tactile sensors which detect contact between objects and with force sensors that detect and regulate the amount of force exerted on an object by the robot's end effector. A standard type of proximity sensor is an infrared transceiver which uses an LED to transmit a beam of IR light. The IR light is bounced off the surface of an object, and is used to detect an object's presence and distance to the sensor. Similarly, an ultrasonic sensor generates high frequency sound waves which can also be used to detect the presence of an object and its distance to the sensor.

---

[51]Bionews Texas, at: http://bionews-tx.com/news/2013/11/25/ut-dallas-dr-robert-gregg-receives-2-3-million-grant-from-nih-to-research-robotic-limbs/.
[52]U.S. Patent No. 8,706,143.

As sensors proliferate throughout the environment, the type and range of sensory information detected will increase. For example, it is possible to equip a cell-phone case with a heat sensor which allows a person to "see" infrared light and to detect temperature differences as small as 0.1 °C. Robots equipped with infrared cameras to detect body heat were used at the World Trade Center site in New York after 9–11 to crawl into holes that were too small or too dangerous for human searchers. Also in 2001, an important case for cyborg law *Kyllo v. United States*, was decided in which the Supreme Court reviewed a case involving a thermal imaging device that was used by a government official from a public vantage point to monitor the emission of heat radiation from an individual's home.[53] The question presented to the Court was whether this act constituted an unwarranted search under the Fourth Amendment. An evidentiary hearing stated that the imaging device could not penetrate the home's walls or windows to reveal any human interactions or record any conversation. However, the sensor showed that there was an unusual amount of heat radiating from the side walls and roof of the Kyllo's garage.[54] This information was used to obtain a search warrant where federal agents later discovered over 100 marijuana plants growing in Kyllo's home. In a close decision, the Supreme Court ruled that the thermal imaging device used to monitor Kyllo's home constituted a search under the Fourth Amendment and thus required a warrant before the device was used.[55]

For a law of cyborgs and artificially intelligent machines we are particularly interested in rules applying to sensor technology that could serve as precedence for future cases. In *Kyllo*, the Supreme Court announced that when the Government uses a device that is not in general public use to explore details of a home that would previously have been unknowable without physical intrusion, the surveillance is a "search" and is presumptively unreasonable without a warrant."[56] Because infrared temperature sensing was not in "general public use" at the time it was used, the thermal imaging was a "search" that required a warrant. Under this ruling, if a technology is widely used by the public, it is no longer reasonable to expect that it won't be used for surveillance purposes. In a cyborg age, the development of sensors and their integration into the body will surely outpace the law, therefore debates about privacy in our cyborg future may center not only on the idea that a "man's home is his castle," but that even more so his body is also his castle and deserving of the most stringent protection afforded by the law. Of course this is generally the case now, but the integration of technology in the body and the ability to scan a person's mind, as we approach mid-century will bring up a host of new issues of law and policy.

In the context of legal rights and sensor technology, GPS and other motion sensors are standard technology found in mobile robots and other semi-autonomous

---

[53]*Kyllo v. United States*, 533 U.S. 27 (2001).

[54]*Id.*

[55]*Id.*

[56]*Kyllo v. United States, id.*, note 53.

machines, just as humans are equipped with a vestibular system to maintain body balance. The use of GPS raises interesting legal questions in a cyborg age. For example, in *United States v. Jones*,[57] the Supreme Court held that installing a GPS tracking device on a vehicle and using the device to monitor the vehicle's movements constituted a search under the Fourth Amendment and thus required a search warrant. Interestingly, the majority of the Court held that by physically installing the GPS device on the defendant's car, the police had committed a trespass against Jones' "personal effects"—since this trespass was an attempt to obtain information it constituted a search per se.[58] This brings up an interesting question for cyborgs, whether equipping a cyborg with sensor technology, such as microchips that track their location or monitors some aspect of their behavior, is a trespass? I think it would depend on the specific facts. If done by the government, it could be, if done based on a patient's consent it would not be.

In common law jurisdictions, trespass to the person historically involved six separate trespasses: threats, assault, battery, wounding, mayhem, and maiming. Through the evolution of the common law in various jurisdictions, and the codification of common law torts, most jurisdictions now broadly recognize three trespasses to the person, two of which are relevant to people equipped with sensors and other cyborg technology: assault, which is "any act of such a nature as to excite an apprehension of battery"; and battery, "any intentional and unpermitted contact with the plaintiff's person or anything attached to it and practically identified with it."[59] Thus, an assault and battery may occur not only to the body but to the cyborg technology attached to it. The issue of assault with regard to cyborgs raises an interesting question of law in light of the integration of sensors and prosthesis with the body- is cyborg technology to be considered part of the body or separate from the body (that is, a form of property)? Already, some commentators refer to a person's iPhone or computer as an "exobrain," which goes beyond the concept of wearable computing technology as property to the idea that the technology is actually integrated with the body. On this point, consider the thoughts of a current cyborg, Professor Steve Mann of the University of Toronto who claims, that his "glass" has become so much a part of his everyday life that it has become part of him, that is, part of his mind and body. The wearable computing technology Steve wears evolved from a cumbersome apparatus with some parts permanently attached (portions of its sensory network implanted beneath the skin) to something sleek and slender that slides on and off like ordinary eyeglass frames.

The question of whether or not cyborg technology is part of the body, is important for different areas of the law, criminal law being a prime example. Under the criminal law, a cyborg/prosthetic device could not only be the subject of an assault against the wearer of the devices(s), but a weapon used in an assault by the cyborg. The latter point could be especially relevant in criminal law cases involving

---

[57]*United States v. Jones*, 132 S. Ct. 945, 565 U.S. (2012).

[58]*Id.*

[59]See generally, Trespass to the Person, at: http://www.lawteacher.net/lecture-notes/tort-law/trespass-to-person-lecture.php.

cyborgs with beyond human levels of strength, sensor capabilities, and functionality. In a case heard by the Arizona Court of Appeals, *State v. Schaffer*,[60] the state was concerned with an aggravated assault charge against the defendant because the court concluded that a prosthetic arm could be a "dangerous instrument" within the meaning of the aggravated assault statute of Arizona.[61] In discussion, the court contended that a prosthetic arm is not a "body part" because the arm "is not an amalgamation of flesh, blood, bone and muscle," but is, instead, a mechanical device that, although attached to the body, may qualify as a "dangerous instrument" under the state's aggravated assault statute.[62] In his defense, the defendant contended that the prosthetic arm *is* his arm, that it remained attached to his body throughout the alleged assault (as opposed to being removed and swung like a club, for example), and that it is therefore a "body part" even though it is made of plastic and metal components rather than flesh and bone. In short, the Arizona court disagreed with the "prosthetic as body argument," and instead concluded that a prosthetic device is not a "body part," but is a device designed to be used as a substitute for a missing body part.[63] A study by Jessica Barfield at Dartmouth College supported the court's conclusion. She addressed the issue of whether cyborg body enhancements were viewed as part of the body and whether a person's self-identity would change as a result of being equipped with cyborg technology encompassing most of the body. Her survey results showed that most respondents felt that both their body-image and self-image would change if equipped with cyborg technology. If I consider the Arizona court's reasoning in light of the advances being made to integrate prosthesis seamlessly into the body, I think the issue of whether cyborg technology is considered part of the body or not, will need to be revisited within the coming decades.

In most cases, given that humans are in close proximity to robots in workplaces, and that humans are beginning to share their living space with "general purpose" domestic robots (South Korea has a goal that 100 % of households will have domestic robots by 2020), the absence of a proximity sensor as part of the robot's design, would constitute a design flaw, and should harm result to a person, a products liability action. In fact, humans and robots that are in close proximity to each other will inevitably lead to accidents. For example, in 1981 a 37 year old Japanese worker was killed by a robot which was unable to sense his presence.[64] And consider what happened to a worker in Sweden a few years later. The factory worker was performing maintenance on a defective machine, and thinking he had cut off the power supply, the worker entered the robot's workspace. But the robot suddenly "came to life" and grabbed a tight hold of the worker breaking four of

---

[60]*State v. Schaffer*, 48 P.3d 1202 (2002), 202, Ariz. 592.

[61]*Id.*

[62]*Id.*

[63]*Id.*

[64]Ryan Calo, Robotics and the Law, at: http://blogs.law.stanford.edu/robotics/2010/05/02/two-new-artificial-intelligence-papers-by-lawyers/.

his ribs. If the robot was originally designed without a proximity sensor, or was equipped with a sensor that failed, under the products liability law followed by Sweden a cause of action based on the robot's design (or due to a defective sensor) could have been pursued.[65] On the issue of sensor reliability, it is not uncommon for product recalls to occur, for example, car manufacturer Kia issued a recall for a faulty sensor mat found in the passenger seat of a certain brand of sedan. The faulty sensor, part of the occupant classification system, was shown to fail due to general wear, and as a result was not able to recognize a child in the passenger seat, making the vehicle unsafe as it was unable to adjust the airbag deployment settings in the case of an accident.

Additionally, because sensors are products in the stream of commerce, their use and reliability will implicate laws regulating commercial transactions. A case on point is *Ionics, Inc. v. Elmwood Sensors, Inc.*,[66] where it was alleged that defective thermostats led to fires in water dispensers. The main issue under dispute was whether the contract between the parties consisted of only the terms agreed upon in both the contract offer and acceptance or additional terms added by the seller which shifted liability. This case brings up an important issue- who is liable for accidents resulting from defective sensors, especially in an age where robots may self-program and in the future use 3D printers to design their own sensors and components thus taking a human completely out-of-the-loop? Generally, actions for harm resulting from defective products is pursued using a theory of products liability. Products liability refers to the potential liability of any or all parties along the chain of manufacture of any product for damage caused by that product. This includes the manufacturer of component parts (at the top of the chain), an assembling manufacturer, the wholesaler, and the retail store owner (at the bottom of the chain). Products containing inherent defects that cause harm to a consumer of the product, or someone to whom the product was loaned, given, etc., are the subjects of products liability suits. According to Cornell University's Legal Information Institute, "While products are generally thought of as tangible personal property, products liability has stretched that definition to include intangibles (gas), naturals (pets), real estate (house), and writings (navigational charts)."[67]

Unfortunately, injuries to people resulting from the absence of a sensor occur with many consumer products; and sometimes with fatal consequences. The case of *Messerly v. Nissan North America, Inc.*,[68] is on point. The case arose out of a fatal back-up accident in which a parent decided to move her 2002 Nissan sport utility vehicle from a concrete pad behind her home to make more room for her children to play. Initially, her nineteen-month-old son was out of harm's way but unfortunately the child had moved to a location behind the vehicle. As the mother

---

[65]Based on the EC-directive 85/374/EEC.

[66]*Ionics, Inc. v. Elmwood Sensors, Inc.*, 110 F.3d 184 (1997).

[67]Products Liability, Legal Information Institute, at: https://www.law.cornell.edu/wex/products_liability.

[68]*Messerly v. Nissan North America, Inc.*, No. 2010-CA-000717-M (KY Ct. App. Dec. 2, 2011).

was backing up, she hit the child and he sustained fatal injuries. The parents sued Nissan alleging that the sport utility was defective and negligently designed because it was not equipped with a rearview camera or back-up sensors. In response, Nissan argued that the risk of striking children while backing a vehicle was an obvious, well-understood risk of operating any passenger vehicle and was inseparable from the product's inherent characteristics; furthermore, that its 2002 vehicle complied with applicable safety regulations at the time of its manufacture.[69] When technology moves beyond the boundaries of current law, it is often a regulatory agency that responds. For example, in the U.S., the National Highway Safety Transportation Agency announced a rule requiring vehicles built from mid-May 2018 on to have a back-up camera. The rule requires a back-up camera to show a field of vision at least 10 ft wide directly behind the vehicle, going back a minimum of 20 ft. With more cyborgs emerging this century, the reliability of sensors and their placement throughout the environment will enter the public debate as an important issue concerning the future direction of humanity.

As we move closer to a human-machine merger, intelligent machines are being equipped with sensors that are similar in functionality to those that natural selection has provided humans over a period of millions of years- thus "they" are becoming more like us. In this context, an important sensor that robots are often equipped with is one that allows the robot to detect sound. The world is immersed with rich sources of auditory information, which not only provides useful information about the world, but orients an organism in responding to stimuli within the world. Robots that have sensors to detect sound can use speech recognition software to understand humans and to respond appropriately to them, clearly a necessary technology for a human-machine merger. A robot can also be designed to navigate based on sound, and as discussed in Chap. 3, body hackers are beginning to use sound to echolocate. Sensors that detect sound, and then form part of a voice recognition system will allow governments and corporations to develop biometric databases designed to store millions of people's "voice-prints;" such a capability is a major development in the ability to identify a person and monitor their location as they move throughout the environment. If "voice prints" are combined with facial recognition technology, and with the ability to track people from one camera to another, then a robust tracking system could be used by governments and corporations for Orwellian surveillance purposes- this is clearly a serious potential outcome for humanity to consider and debate.

Thus far, most legal disputes with speech recognition software have revolved around patent infringement. For example, Apple's use of speech recognition software has been the subject of several patent infringement cases. An example is a legal action brought by patent holding company Cedatech that claimed Apple had infringed their patent by selling products that offered the capability to integrate an audio or video program with a separate application program.[70] While this broad

---

[69]*Id.*

[70]Another Patent Lawsuit Against Apple Inc., at: http://patent-lawyers.usattorneys.com/patent-lawsuit-apple/.

claim would likely involve most of Apple's products, the lawsuit cited the iPhone 5 and its audio speech recognition feature that works across multiple applications. Going international, in China, Apple was unsuccessful in getting a Chinese company's patent on its speech recognition software invalidated; in fact, the Chinese company countersued claiming Siri as an infringing program. From these results I envision a future in which patent wars will be common based on technology designed for cyborgs; but once the artificial intelligence becomes the inventor, then how will the courts respond?

Regulating Sensors and Being Forgotten

A regulatory agency, such as the National Transportation Safety Board (which among other duties regulates sensors placed on cars), is a governmental body that is created by the U.S. legislature to implement and enforce specific laws. An agency has quasi-legislative functions, executive functions, and judicial functions. With regard to cyborg technology, in the U.S., sensors and the wireless networks that connect them are regulated by different government agencies and professional standards. For example, the Federal Communication Commission (FCC) regulates devices that utilize electromagnetic spectrum as a communication device, but not as a medical device; whereas, the Federal Drug Administration (FDA) regulates the sensors implanted within the body as a medical device. With potential overlapping jurisdictions, the FCC and FDA have entered into a "Memorandum of Understanding", where they collaborate with each other within the areas of their respective agencies. A regulatory decision of importance for our cyborg future occurred in 2012 when the FCC approved a mobile body area network, which allocates electromagnetic spectrum for personal body-worn sensors. The allocated spectrum can be used to form a personal wireless network, within which data from numerous body-worn medical devices and sensors is aggregated and transmitted in real time.

While body-worn sensors are becoming common and collecting important information about a person's health, they are also recording data that many people would like kept private from the public; one example being a person's predisposition for an illness; in employment decisions such knowledge may lead to various forms of discrimination. In a time of exponential growth for sensors, should there be a federal law preventing sensor information about the body from being accessed, for example, in employment decisions, athletic competition, or by the government? Precedence for this position already exists. Under the *Genetic Information Non-discrimination Act*, employers are prohibited from asking employees or job candidates to take genetic tests or to provide their family medical histories.[71] Given the ability of sensors to collect information about people,

---

[71]The Genetic Information Nondiscrimination Act of 2008, Pub. L. 110–233, 122 Stat 881, enacted May 21, 2008.

especially without their consent and knowledge, and the ease in which sensor data can be uploaded to the internet, some people propose that there should be a "right to be forgotten," essentially, the ability to have information deleted from the internet which stigmatizes a person by what they did in the past. The basic idea is that personal information should be within an individual's capacity to control—that is, information that concerns a person, and which has lost its timeliness, its relevance or its accuracy, and has no public interest, should be deleted if found to offend the subject of the data.[72] However, in contrast to the right to be forgotten is the "Barbara Streisand effect." The Streisand effect is a phenomena (discussed in more detail below) in which an attempt to censor or remove a piece of information on the web can backfire, and actually bring more attention to the information, not less.

In a case dealing with the "right to be forgotten" the European Court of Justice ruled that Google must amend some search results at the request of people who want information posted about them on the internet removed. An early case was brought (and won) by a Spanish man who complained that an auction notice of his repossessed home on Google's search results infringed his privacy. A European Union Commissioner referred to the court's decision as "a clear victory for the protection of personal data of Europeans". But in a cyborg age the judgment could have major consequences for anyone using sensors, such as a camera, to film people and then upload the film to the internet. Generally, the ruling says the rights of the individual are paramount when it comes to their control over their personal data, although there is a public interest defense when it comes to people in public life. In response to requests to delete information, Google argued that it does not control data it only offers links to information freely available on the internet and that forcing it to remove links amounts to censorship, a view many who support an open Internet support. Far from the legal jurisdiction of Europe, a Japanese court ordered Google to remove search results that hinted at a man's relationship with a criminal organization after he complained his privacy rights were violated. So far, thousands of web links have been scrubbed by Google based on requests received by about 200,000 individuals from thirty-two countries[73]; however, with a future world consisting of trillions of sensors, what facts can we reasonably expect should be deleted without censorship affecting the marketplace of ideas?

I believe the "right to be forgotten" is a clear form of censorship as it requires online search engines to edit the result of searches when requested to do so, in order to make them compliant with the European directive on the protection of personal data, and to conform to privacy law in countries far from the European Union, such as Japan. And while I support strong privacy rights for individuals especially when it comes to sensor data about their body and mind, I also agree

---

[72]Mantelero, Alessandro, 2013, The EU Proposal for a General Data Protection Regulation and the roots of the 'right to be forgotten', *Computer Law & Security Review*, Vol. 29 (3): 229–235. doi:10.1016/j.clsr.2013.03.010.

[73]Thousands of People Asking to Disappear from Google, 2014, at: http://www.cbsnews.com/news/thousands-of-people-asking-to-disappear-from-google/.

with Google's assertion that censorship should be avoided, or at least only used as a last resort such as in the case of national security or for the privacy and protection of an individuals' personal medical data or thoughts. When considering disputes involving cyborg technologies, legislators must carefully balance privacy rights versus the damage to society from censorship of information. Given that democracy thrives when there is a free marketplace of ideas, policy should strongly tilt toward less censorship. Thus, when it comes to deleting information about an individual, I have to wonder, should we provide someone the right to decide what information should be erased, even if that information is personal and concerns them? If so, then individuals would be able to delete facts from the history of the collective human experience. To allow this would be to grant an individual sole monopoly rights on the data which represents their life; a difficult concept when one person's actions affect many others. While facts normally do not receive protection under the law, data, given sufficient creativity in how it is organized, may receive monopoly rights in the form of intellectual property protection, a topic presented in preceding chapters of this book as part of the discussion on cognitive liberty, and the law of artificial brains. For now, the reader should be aware that while the legal protection for data varies widely across countries, most jurisdictions do grant some rights for the protection of data.

Remotely Sensed Data

Since the beginning of the space program, the proliferation of sensors have reached beyond the earth's surface. In fact, satellite imagery has become increasingly available to the general public, a trend accelerated by services such as Google Earth. Remotely sensed data collected by aerial, ground, and space based systems is becoming an important part of spatial data bases accessed by people equipped with sensors. A point to make is this: while remotely sensed data may offer positive benefits to society, such as in chronicling the health of the planet and finding undiscovered natural resources; remote sensors could also be used by totalitarian states to track and monitor people as they move about the environment.

There are already active concerns about how the First Amendment protects reporters who use drones. In multiple incidents police have arrested or intimidated a reporter who used a drone to review an accident scene.[74] The reporters argue that because they are using the drones to observe police activity from a public space as part of a news story, the drone activities are protected under the free speech prong of the First Amendment. Police, meanwhile, have claimed that they have stopped

---

[74]Lilly Chapa, Drone journalism begins slow take off, at http://www.rcfp.org/browse-media-law-resources/news-media-law/news-media-and-law-spring-2013/drone-journalism-begins-slo; See Daniel Terdiman, 2015, Feds concede drone filmmakers have First Amendment rights, at: http://venturebeat.com/2015/04/14/feds-concede-drone-filmmakers-have-first-amendment-rights/.

drones or arrested reporters because of legitimate safety concerns—for instance, in one case, they said that a journalist's drone interfered with a helicopter approaching an accident scene.

Thus far, regulations enacted on remotely sensed data are focused more on commercializing the remote sensing systems, than safeguarding privacy. Therefore, I believe the law relating to remote sensing systems is in need of major overhaul given the recent advancements made in sensor technologies and the ability to combine different surveillance platforms into a global network of surveillance. The United Kingdom, a self-proclaimed champion of Earth observations, issued national remote sensing policy as early as 1984 but passed its first space-related legislation in 1986 without any mention of remote sensing. In the U.S., Congress passed *the Remote Sensing Policy Act of 1992* which declared the commercialization of the remote sensing of land to be a long-term policy goal of the U.S., and established procedures for licensing private remote sensing operators.[75] According to the Act, a license must be granted before an entity can begin operating a remote sensing satellite. The law requires private system operators to make unenhanced data available only to the governments of sensed states, thus freeing them to make data available to all other customers according to market forces. These results imply that under current law cyborgs and artificially intelligent machines will have no direct access to sensor data from satellite systems, unless they receive a license to access the data, or, hack into the remote sensing systems. In the future, what happens if artificially intelligent systems violate "remote sensing" laws?

To date, there have only been a few legal disputes involving sensor data collected remotely such as the data provided by Google Maps. One case revolved around the central issue of whether Google map information could be accessed while driving. A few years ago, in California, a driver was given a ticket for using a Google Map app on an iPhone 4 while driving, the person disputed the ticket, and on appeal the conviction was overturned by a State appellate court which agreed that drivers should be able to use map apps on a smartphone while on the road.[76] The court unanimously concluded that the state vehicle code applied to listening, talking and texting on a cellphone while driving—not looking at a map application. The impact of the decision is still being considered in other jurisdictions.

One of the most important policy issues concerning remote sensor data is how their use may impact privacy rights. One interesting case involved Barbara Streisand, whose beach home was photographed by Kenneth Adelman, retired environmental activist, and amateur helicopter pilot. Kenneth operates the California Coastal Records Project, which is a private effort to photograph the

---

[75]*Remote Sensing Policy*, 15 U.S. Code Chapter 82.

[76]California court ruling frees drivers to use map apps on cellphones, at: http://appleinsider.com/articles/14/02/28/california-court-ruling-frees-drivers-to-use-cellphone-maps-while-driving.

entire California coastline.[77] He has posted more than 12,000 high-resolution digital aerial images of the coastline on a website, where they are freely available for download. Observers noticed that one of the photos happened to show the Malibu mansion of singer Barbara Streisand. Streisand, concerned that her privacy had been violated, sued Adelman, seeking damages for invasion of privacy and violation of California's anti-paparazzi law.[78]

Another case that involved the collection of sensor information presented on Google Maps also revolved around the important issue of privacy. A couple in Pittsburgh claimed that Street View on Google Maps was a reckless invasion of their privacy.[79] The couple sued Google, alleging that Google "significantly disregarded their privacy interests" when Street View cameras captured images of their house beyond signs marked "private road."[80] The couple claimed that finding their home clearly visible on Google's Street View caused them "mental suffering" and diluted their home value. However, a U.S. District Court stated the plaintiff "failed to state a claim under any count," a procedure courts use to dismiss suits.[81] Interestingly, Google claimed to be legally allowed to photograph on private roads, arguing that privacy no longer exists in this age of satellite and aerial imagery. This sentiment was expressed years earlier by Scott McNealy, co-founder of Sun Microsystems who famously said, "You have zero privacy. Get over it."

Returning to California, under an anti-paparazzi statute, a person may sue for "physical invasion of privacy" when three elements are met: first, a person has knowingly entered the land of another without permission; second, the entry was made with the "intent to capture any type of visual image, sound recording, or other physical impression" of another person engaging in a "personal or familial activity"; and third, the invasion was made "in a manner that is offensive to a reasonable person."[82] This aspect of the anti-paparazzi statute dealt with the physical intrusion onto another person's private property (also covered by trespass law), and not data collected by a remote sensing system. However, the anti-paparazzi statute also covered a "constructive invasion of privacy," which provided for liability even if there was no actual entry onto the property of another.[83] A cyborg equipped with a telephoto lens could be liable under this prong of the statute. Telephoto lens as part of a person's body is not far-fetched, but being done now with a small population of people suffering debilitating vision loss. Specifically,

---

[77]Barbra Streisand Sues to Suppress Free Speech Protection for Widely Acclaimed Website, at: http://www.californiacoastline.org/streisand/lawsuit.html.

[78]See *id.*

[79]*Boring v. Google, Inc.*, 598 F. Supp. 2d, 695 (W. D. Pa 2009).

[80]*Id.*

[81]*Id.*

[82]*Randall Boese*, American Bar Association, Forum on Communications Law, *Redefining Privacy? Anti-Paparazzi Legislation and Freedom of the Press, at*: http://apps.americanbar.org/forums/communication/comlawyer/summer99/sum99boese.html.

[83]*Id.*

some people suffering from severe age-related macular degeneration (AMD) disease which affects two million Americans would benefit from an implantable telescope, which would work like the telephoto lens of a camera (such technology is being developed now). But back to the Streisand case, the judge rejected Streisand's claim, finding that "Aerial views are a common part of daily living," and that "There is nothing offensive about the manner in which they occur, nor in the manner in which this particular view was obtained."[84]

One concern for the coming cyborg age is that sensors can be used for purposes other than their original design and intent. On this point, some images obtained surreptitiously from cameras may be a violation of video voyeurism laws. In the U.S. there is a federal statute prohibiting video voyeurism which states that whoever has the intent to capture an image of a private area of an individual without their consent, and knowingly does so under circumstances in which the individual has a reasonable expectation of privacy, shall be fined or imprisoned not more than 1 year, or both.[85] The term "capture", with respect to an image, means to videotape, photograph, film, record by any means, or broadcast; the term "broadcast" means to electronically transmit a visual image with the intent that it be viewed by a person or persons; the term "a private area of the individual" means the naked or undergarment clad genitals, pubic area, buttocks, or female breast of that individual.[86] The problem with antipaparazzi and video voyeurism or voyeur laws is that they presume conscious acts of surveillance. The model is a celebrity photographer stalking his or her prey. When the surveillance is automatic or inadvertent as with cyborgs like Steve Mann equipped with his EyeTap technology that is constantly filming, such laws are a poor fit. And as technology "progresses", video voyeurism laws are going to become more-and-more problematic. I predict that remote sensing using satellite technology may be the next prime offender.

Sensors and Intellectual Property Law

As exponentially accelerating technologies create a world filled with sensors, an important question to ask is whether the software, technology, and algorithms which control the functioning of cyborgs and artificially intelligent machines is eligible for protection under the law of intellectual property. To introduce the discussion on this topic, it is clear that while the parts of the human body are not patentable subject matter, technology designed to perform the same functions are. Considering one of the most important organs, the kidney, William J. Kolff was granted a patent for the first artificial kidney in 1967; however, no person can receive a patent for a biological kidney. But what happens in the future when

---

[84]*Id.*, note 77.

[85]18 U.S. Code § 1801—Video voyeurism.

[86]Federal Statute on Video Voyeurism, 18 U.S. Code § 1801.

much of the human body and an artificially intelligent machine that claims to be sentient consist of patentable hardware? What rights will people and cyborgs have over their own body then? Under current law, cyborgs are not considered a "protected class," and thus not covered under the Civil Rights Act of 1964. But does the Constitution offer rights for the technology comprising cyborgs? The answer is yes- in the U.S., monopoly rights for intellectual property is specifically mentioned in the U.S. Constitution, Article I, Section 8: The Congress shall have Power… To promote the Progress of Science and useful Arts, by securing for limited Times to Authors and Inventors the exclusive Right to their respective Writings and Discoveries. Given exponentially accelerating information technologies; for cyborgs, and later, artificially intelligent machines (with general artificial intelligence), an important public policy issue to discuss is what aspects of sensor technology should be protected under intellectual property law?

Patent law is a particularly strong form of protection for inventors of cyborg technology as it gives the holder of the patent sole monopoly rights over the invention. Such rights include an exclusive right to make, use, and sell the patented invention for a limited period of time. If eligible for patent protection, the patent owner may bring a lawsuit against anyone accused of infringing the patent. Under U.S. patent law, the categories of patentable subject matter are broadly defined as any process, machine, manufacture, or composition of matter, or improvement thereof. In a landmark case, *Diamond v. Chakrabarty*, the Supreme Court found that Congress intended patentable subject matter to "include anything under the sun that is made by man."[87] However, the Court also stated that this broad definition has limits and does not embrace every discovery. For example, according to the Court, the laws of nature, physical phenomena, and abstract ideas are not patentable.

While the hardware of cyborgs is patentable subject matter, are the algorithms and software which controls the hardware components and operating systems of cyborgs patentable? In the U.S. there is evolving law on the patentability of software and algorithms. While this topic was discussed in the chapter on *"The Law of Artificial Brains,"* to briefly review, abstract ideas and laws of nature are not patentable subject matter under U.S. patent law—however it's not quite that simple. For example, the fundamental issue for the patentability of algorithms as part of the control dynamics of cyborgs and artificially intelligent robots, is whether they are viewed as an abstract idea or a mathematical representation of a law of nature (e.g., the equation describing gravity is a law of nature and thus not patentable)—if so, they are not the proper subject of patent protection, but if not, they may be.

The question of the patentability of algorithms was addressed in a 2014 Supreme Court case, *Alice Corp. v. CLS Bank International* which involved a patent claim on an algorithm that monitored financial transactions.[88] The patent was held to be invalid because, according to the Court, the claims on the algorithms

---

[87]*Diamond v. Chakrabarty*, 447 U.S. 303 (1980).

[88]Gene Quinn, 2014, The Ramifications of Alice: A Conversation with Mark Lemley, at: http://www.ipwatchdog.com/2014/09/04/the-ramifications-of-alice-a-conversation-with-mark-lemley/id=51023/; *Alice Corp. v. CLS Bank International*, 573 U.S. __, 134 S. Ct. 2347 (2014).

represented an abstract idea, and implementing the claims on a computer was not enough to transform the idea to a patentable invention.

However, in *Alice*, the Court effectively opened the door for the patentability of algorithms claiming that algorithms are a species of an abstract idea, a decision which according to legal scholar Mark Lemley at Berkeley "invited all manner of mischief."[89] Consider as an example a celebrated claim on a search algorithm issued to Larry Page, co-founder of Google. Actually, the "PageRank" algorithm is patented by Stanford University, who licensed the patent to Google. The *Page* patent claims what is known as the page rank algorithm: a way of weighting web pages by the density of links to them. The idea is that when a web search turns up various web pages that include the search term, the more important pages will be those that show a density of links to and from them. This idea was the key to the early success of Google gaining a reputation for superior search results. However, the *Page* patent would likely be characterized as too abstract under *Alice* so clearly the patentability of software and algorithms is in flux. To sum up: in the U.S. the answer to the question of whether software/algorithms can be patented is in the two-part *Alice* framework. Does the claim merely cover an "abstract idea"? And is there an (additional) "inventive concept" that turns this idea into a patentable application of the abstraction? I expect the patentability of algorithms, to be a future area of litigation and public debate especially as more cyborgs equipped with sensor technology emerge and enter the public, and artificially intelligent machines write their own code and use 3D printers to build their own sensors.

With increasingly complex technology being used to equip people with implants and prosthesis, patent infringement suits are common. In fact, given the expanding use of sensors and the lucrative marketplace they are creating, there are ongoing patent wars between manufacturers of sensor technology. For example, Roche Diagnostics Operations Inc. and Abbott Diabetes Care Inc. were involved in a patent infringement dispute (which eventually settled) in which Roche accused Abbott of infringing two of its patents covering its blood glucose test strips for monitoring diabetes.[90] In another patent dispute involving sensors, *Nautilus Inc. v. Biosig Instruments Inc.*, the U.S. Supreme Court was petitioned to review the revival of an infringement suit involving a heart rate monitor, saying the Federal Circuit's acceptance of a vague claim in Biosig Instruments Inc.'s patent contradicted precedent and invited abuses from patent holders.[91] As background, the Government Accountability Office and legal experts have said that the Patent and Trademark Office has granted too many overly broad patents in recent years, contributing to the increase in infringement cases.

---

[89]*Id.*

[90]Roche Diagnostics Operations Inc. and Abbott Diabetes Care Inc, at: http://law.justia.com/cases/federal/district-courts/delaware/dedce/1:2007cv00753/39319/563/.

[91]*Nautilus Inc. v. Biosig Instruments Inc.*, U.S. Supreme Court, 2015, at: http://www.scotusblog.com/case-files/cases/nautilus-inc-v-biosig instruments-inc/.

Surveillance, Sensors, and Body Scans

Perhaps the most visible manifestation of surveillance resulting from sensors and sensor networks is the spread of government-operated closed circuit television (CCTV) cameras in urban areas. For example, in the United Kingdom, it is estimated that authorities have installed over four million CCTV cameras, and that the average London resident is photographed an estimated three hundred times per day.[92] Surveillance cameras in the United Kingdom are also being used for functions other than their initial crime-control mission, a kind of "mission creep" for sensors. For example, in London, authorities are photographing every car entering and leaving the central financial district, to ensure compliance with a congestion tax on all cars driving through the area. London's Heathrow airport has also begun to test the use of eye-scanners to identify travelers. There are also significant CCTV surveillance initiatives underway or in place in Washington D.C., Chicago, and New York, as well as many other major cities worldwide. Nonetheless, as striking as the spread of sensors in the form of surveillance cameras are for digital information gathering by government officials, it pales in comparison to the surveillance power and sensor monitoring capability of technology now in the hands of individuals equipped with head-worn displays, cell phones (there are about 6.8 billion cell phone subscribers in the world), and other body-worn sensors.

One of the most interesting perspectives on invasion of privacy in a world filled with sensors is provided by University of Toronto's Steve Mann, a person many attribute as being the first to purposively equip himself as a cyborg. Steve's basic idea is that people using technology which allows them to film, can "shoot back," that is, film the government and corporations which use cameras and other sensors to monitor and film people as they move about the environment. Clearly, Google's Project Glass, and Steve's earlier head-worn display technology is an example of technology allowing people to shoot back. Specifically, Steve refers to the practice of filming those filming us, as sousveillance. As described by Steve, the term sousveillance stems from the contrasting French words *sur*, meaning "above", and *sous*, meaning "below".[93] So "surveillance" denotes the "eye-in-the-sky" watching from above, whereas "sousveillance" denotes bringing the camera or other means of observation down to human level, either physically (mounting cameras on people rather than on buildings), or hierarchically (ordinary people doing the watching, rather than higher authorities, or large entities such as corporations doing the watching).[94]

---

[92]One surveillance camera for every 11 people in Britain, says CCTV survey, at: http://www.tele-graph.co.uk/technology/10172298/One-surveillance-camera-for-every-11-people-in-Britain-says-CCTV-survey.html; Big Brother next door? Most of UK's 6 million CCTV cameras are privately owned, 2013, at: http://rt.com/news/cctv-uk-private-surveillance-918/.

[93]Sousveillance and Surveillance: What kind of future do we want? 2014, at: http://hplusmagazine.com/2014/10/07/sousveillance-surveillance-kind-future-want/.

[94]*Id.*

Surveillance, as described by Professor Mann is clearly practiced in many different ways by governments. For example, after the terrorist act of 9-11, we are all experienced with passing our bodies and possessions through an airport, court house, or other government security scanner. Metal detectors are even used in some schools to prevent a person carrying weapons onto school property. While courts have found that "there is a generally recognized privacy interest in a person's body", does this also apply to body scans?[95] Further, what legal theories might apply when a person scans the sensors worn by another person in order to access data collected by the sensors? One response could be an action in tort for jurisdictions that follow the common law. Specifically, the common law tort of "intrusion upon seclusion" occurs when a person intentionally intrudes, physically or otherwise, upon the solitude or seclusion of another or his private affairs or concerns, and if so, is subject to liability to the other for invasion of his privacy if the intrusion would be highly offensive to a reasonable person.[96] This tort includes unwarranted intrusions like eavesdropping, wiretapping, and visual or photographic spying into one's personal life?[97]

To prevail under an intrusion upon seclusion tort action, a person would allege that there was an unauthorized intrusion or prying into his seclusion; the intrusion was offensive to or objectionable to a reasonable person; the matter upon which the intrusion occurred was private; and the intrusion caused anguish and suffering.[98] The second element concerning the offensive nature of the intrusion focuses on the manner in which the information was obtained. Anyone equipped with cyborg technology implanted within their body that was scanned by a sensor might argue that since the scanning occurred through a portion of his body, it is highly offensive.[99] An interesting case of relevance for an emerging law of cyborgs involved a body scan of a shopper at a retail store. Responding to the intrusion upon seclusion tort action, the court found that the intrusion of the scan "would not be so highly offensive to the reasonable person as to constitute an invasion of privacy action."[100] I think that this decision will eventually have to be overturned to take into account a future world of powerful sensors that can scan the internal body, and even our minds- such capabilities should clearly seem offensive to a reasonable person- if not, what would be?

---

[95]*Doe v. High-Tech Institute, Inc.*, 972 P.2d 1060, 1068 (Colo. App. 1998).

[96]Intrusion Upon Seclusion Tort, *Restatement of the Law, Second, Torts, 652.*

[97]*Broughton v. McClatchy Newspapers, Inc.*, 588 S.E.2d 20, 27 (N.C. App. 2003).

[98]*Melvin v. Burling*, 490 N.E.2d 1011, 1012 (Ill. App. 3d Dist. 1986); *People v. Stone*, 621 N.W.2d 702, 706 (Mich. 2001).

[99]*Shulman v. Group W Productions, Inc.*, 955 P.2d 469, 490 (Cal. 1998).

[100]*Smith v. Jack Eckerd Corp.*, 400 S.E.2d 99, 100 (N.C. App. 1991).

Using Sensor Data in Trials

Given a cyborg future in which a person's brain waves may be recorded and monitored using sensors, what law and policies apply if someone uses that information
in a trial? Consider the claims made by neuroscientist Champadi Raman
Mukundan based on a device he created to determine a person's innocence or guilt
from the reading of brain waves.[101] The basic idea behind Mukundan's *Brain
Electrical Oscillations Signature* test is to use electroencephalography (EEG) to
show, like an fMRI, activated areas of the cortex which are localized during recall.
Champadi claimed that the device is so accurate, it can tell whether a person committed or only witnessed an act.[102]

In a murder trial in India, an Indian judge used the results of the *Brain
Electrical Oscillations Signature* test to find a woman guilty of killing her former
fiancé.[103] Scientific experts called the decision 'ridiculous' and 'unconscionable,'
protesting that Mukundan's work had not even been peer reviewed. I agree that the
court's decision is an affront to justice but it does raise the question- how reliable
should a "scientific" test based on sensor information have to be, when eyewitness
testimony is notoriously fallible? Does a person have a right to privacy over their
own memories, or should society's interest in holding criminals accountable take
precedence?" Given rapid advances in sensors and the speed at which sensor technology in entering the commercial marketplace, an important question for courts
to decide is whether data derived from sensors, such as EEG data to determine
guilt or innocence, can be used as reliable scientific evidence in a trial.

In fact, neuroscientific evidence has persuaded jurors to sentence defendants to
life imprisonment rather than to death. Courts have also admitted brain-imaging
evidence during criminal trials to support claims that defendants like John W.
Hinckley Jr., who tried to assassinate President Reagan, are insane. Carter Snead,
a law professor at Notre Dame, drafted a working paper on the impact of neuroscientific evidence in criminal law for President Bush's Council on Bioethics.[104] The
report concludes that neuroimaging evidence is of mixed reliability but "the large
number of cases in which such evidence is presented is striking." That number will
no doubt increase substantially in the coming cyborg age. Proponents of neurolaw
say that neuroscientific evidence will have a large impact not only on questions of
guilt and punishment but also on the detection of lies and hidden bias, and on the

---

[101] Anand Giridharadas, 2008, India's Novel Use of Brain Scans in Courts Is Debated, New York
Times, at: http://www.nytimes.com/2008/09/15/world/asia/15brainscan.html?pagewanted=print&_
r=0.

[102] *Id.*

[103] Angela Saini, 2009, The brain police: judging murder with an MRI, at: http://www.wired.
co.uk/magazine/archive/2009/06/features/guilty.

[104] Jeffrey Rosen, 2007, The Brain on the Stand, New York Times, at: http://www.nytimes.
com/2007/03/11/magazine/11Neurolaw.t.html?pagewanted=all&_r=0.

prediction of future criminal behavior. At the same time, according to Jeffrey Rosen, skeptics fear that the use of brain-scanning technology as a kind of super mind-reading device will threaten our privacy and mental freedom, leading some to call for the legal system to respond with a new concept of "cognitive liberty"[105] (see Chap. 3).

On the admissibility of sensor data in trials, consider the issues litigated in *People v. Dorcent,* where the defendant was charged with driving with a suspended license. Several months earlier, in a different court action, Dorcent had pleaded guilty to driving while under the influence of alcohol.[106] In the most recent case the defendant agreed to refrain from consuming alcohol for a period of 30 days and that his abstinence would be monitored by a continuous remote alcohol monitoring (SCRAM) bracelet, and its sensors, which was to be worn on his ankle. The SCRAM system has three components, a bracelet, a modem, and SCRAMnet.[107] The SCRAM bracelet has a collection chamber and fuel cell, which tests the vapors in a person's perspiration at reoccurring times throughout the day and night. It also has a tamper strap and securing clip that prevents the wearer from removing the device and a temperature sensor and an infrared (IR) sensor to detect obstructions.[108] The IR sensor sends an IR beam between the bracelet and the leg. Alcohol readings, tamper alerts, body temperature and diagnostic data are transmitted to a modem inside the subject's home at least once every 24 h and then to SCRAMnet via an Internet connection for analysis, monitoring and storage.

Three weeks after being equipped with the monitoring technology, the SCRAM bracelet reported that the device was unable to monitor the defendant's alcohol consumption for a 10-hour period due to an alleged obstruction preventing the device from gathering data. A hearing was held on the issue of whether the defendant violated the terms of his plea agreement and at issue was whether the SCRAM technology was sufficiently reliable scientific evidence to satisfy the test for admissibility of scientific evidence in New York State. Previously, in *Frye v. United States,*[109] the Court held that scientific evidence should be excluded unless the new or novel scientific theory or methodology is generally accepted in the relevant scientific community. In some jurisdictions, experts are normally called upon to determine the reliability of evidence from new technology in a "Frye hearing." However, the disadvantage of the *Frye* rule is that it may result in the exclusion of results obtained with theories and methodologies that are capable of producing accurate and reliable results, but are too new to have passed the test of peer review and become generally accepted in the relevant scientific community. This hole in the *Frye* rule eventually

---

[105]*Id.*

[106]*People v. Dorcent,* 2010 NY Slip Op 20430 [29 Misc 3d 1165] October 22, 2010 Calabrese, J. Criminal Court Of The City Of New York, Kings County Published by New York State Law Reporting Bureau pursuant to Judiciary Law § 431, at: http://law.justia.com/cases/new-york/other-courts/2010/2010-20430.html.

[107]*Id.*

[108]*Id.*

[109]*Frye v. United States,* 293 F. 1013 (D.C. Cir. 1923).

led to the Supreme Court adopting a new rule in *Daubert v. Merrell Dow Pharmaceuticals, Inc.*[110] In *Daubert* the Court held that Rule 702 of the Federal Rules of Evidence replaced the *Frye* Rule. Rule 702 states: "If scientific, technical, or other specialized knowledge will assist the trier of fact to understand the evidence or to determine a fact in issue a witness qualified as an expert by knowledge, skill, experience, training, or education, may testify thereto in the form of an opinion or otherwise, if (1) the testimony is based on sufficient facts or data, (2) the testimony is the product of reliable principles and methods, and (3) the witness has applied the principles and methods reliably to the facts of the case."[111] This decision (to replace *Frye* with Rule 702) may allow emerging sensor technology to be used as evidence in court if these three conditions are met.[112]

Conclusion

Advances in information technologies are leading to a world in which there will be trillions of sensors embedded within the environment, implanted within the body, and also within our brain. In my assessment of the future, sensors will play a key role in creating a class of cyborgs with capabilities far beyond those of non-enhanced humans; such cyborgs will represent an intermediary step towards humanity's ultimate destiny, to merge with our artificially intelligent creations. A merger between humans and artificial intelligence is a process that will occur in several stages, with the time frame for the stages measured in decades or less, not centuries.

As concluding material on this chapter on sensors, I thought it would be appropriate to briefly discuss a few of the main stages which I believe await humanity as we move towards a cyborg future and eventual merger with machines. The stages are not independent but meant as a guide to the future, there is overlap, and in the background while humans are evolving under the law of accelerating returns, so too is artificial intelligence. In our first step towards moving beyond the confines of our body and mind, we will equip ourselves with prosthesis that match or exceed current human motor skills, strength and endurance. More powerful humans will bring up a host of legal and policy issues such as in employment decisions, the human rights allocated to enhanced and nonenhanced humans, and athletic competition to name only a few. The body "prosthesis" stage of human evolution will be followed by the development of neuroprosthesis for the mind which will significantly enhance people's cognitive capabilities, even allowing memories to be transferred from one brain to another. By enhancing our bodies

---

[110]*Daubert v. Merrell Dow Pharmaceuticals, Inc.*, 509 U.S. 579 (1993).

[111]Rule 702. Federal Rules of Evidence.

[112]*Id.*

and mind, we will become cyborgs, a human-machine combination that will move beyond biology and evolve under the law of accelerating returns operating for information technology. After the Singularity, which may occur around midcentury to late century, there will be an intelligence explosion for artificially intelligent machines, which will result in forms of artificial intelligence which could be beyond human understanding and control. By the time of the Singularity or fairly soon thereafter, we will have either merged with our intelligent inventions, such that "we" become "them", or we will be left behind. Even those humans (or cyborgs) that don't merge, and that will be significantly enhanced by neuro-prosthesis will be of lessor intelligence that super artificial intelligence- this is because maintaining any biological forms of intelligence will be a bottleneck in terms of processing speed, storage capacity, and the ability to learn by accessing the trillions of bits of information available on the internet. As we move toward the Singularity, and the critical decision as to whether we merge with artificially intelligent machines, our cyborg technologies will continue to develop. Sensors implanted within the body, will connect cyborgs to the global network of things, and will monitor their health, enhance their cognitive abilities and in the future, extend the senses of our "mind children."

Of course, the scenario I present, doesn't have to be our future, humanity still has time to decide whether a Posthuman future is desirable, but given the speed of technological advances in cyborg technologies, it is the current generation of humans that need to determine our future, not the next generation, therefore time is running out. There are several noteworthy ethical concerns raised by different future possibilities associated with the use of sensors and other cyborg technologies: the prospect of using sensor (and other cyborg) technologies to improve and augment human capabilities; for example, the prospect of achieving a type of immortality with a chip that contains the uploaded memories, emotions, and knowledge of the source; and the chance that humankind, as we know it, may eventually be phased out or become just a step in guided evolution. On the last point, endowing humans with eyes that see in different spectra of light, or the ability to smell as well as an animal rich in olfactory sensors, or to operate robots from a distance using brain signals- appreciably changes human abilities. Of even more significance is the radical enhancements that could be made possible when internal brain-machine interfaces improve, augment, or replace those most valued of human capacities-the ability to reason and remember.

What responses are possible with the proliferation of sensor and other cyborg technologies in the world and within our bodies? The first response to unwanted cyborg technologies (in the sense they lead to a Posthuman Age deemed undesirable by the human population) could be an attempt to outright ban them; Bill Joy cofounder of Sun Microsystems would agree with this perspective. However, though such edicts might be practicable in a heavily regulated, closed society, it is questionable whether any country can stop research on technology that may lead to a Posthuman age, simply because on the way to the Singularity, the same technology is capable of improving the conditions of humans. So, as tool builders, as we try to improve the human condition, we may also, ironically, be creating the conditions for either our extinction, or role as the less intelligent and dominant species on the planet. And just as only the most repressive regimes have had any success controlling what they deemed the corrosive effects of fax machines and the Internet it is hard to see wholesale restrictions on beneficial cyborg technologies standing up for long. In any event, the vast majority of countries have made no such attempts to ban emerging cyborg technologies; instead, just the opposite, billions are being spent to develop cyborg technologies and artificial intelligence. Whether we realize it or not, we are building the technology which could replace humans as the dominant species on the planet. With apologies to Shakespeare, to merge or not to merge, that is the question.

Another strategy proposed by those concerned about the potential loss of humanity as technology becomes integrated into our bodies and mind is to restrict only certain uses of sensor and other cyborg devices. For example, the *Video Voyeurism Prevention Act*, adopted in 2004, prohibits unauthorized photography of private areas.[113] The *Video Voyeurism Prevention Act* was originally written to prohibit such activity with ordinary cameras. However, the legislation was amended to specifically include camera phones. And as noted in the introduction to this chapter, legislation has also been passed to prohibit the implanting of an RFID chip into an unwilling recipient. I see problems ahead, technology advances like the tide, we see it coming, but we can't stop it and in most cases have no desire to stop it. So, we may have no choice, either merge with our technological offspring or be left behind. If we decide to merge, then the question will be- what aspects of humanity are worth preserving in our future mind children?

---

[113]*Video Voyeurism Prevention Act*, adopted in 2004, U.S. Code Statute 1801.

Chapter 7
The Law of Looks and Artificial Bodies

Making, Modifying, and Replacing Bodies

Repeating a central theme of this book—at the same time we humans are becoming enhanced with "cyborg" technology—artificially intelligent machines are gaining in intelligence and becoming more like us in shape, appearance, and abilities. In fact, the use of twenty-first century technologies to create artificially intelligent machines are leading to interchangeable, replaceable, and upgradeable bodies that will determine whether our technological inventions are accepted within society or experience discrimination, hostility, and unequal treatment under the law. As our robotic inventions begin to interact with us, I believe they will be subjected to the same prejudices and discrimination that we humans experience in everyday life. With continuing advances in cyborg technologies will our legal systems be sufficient to account for the increased autonomy, intelligence, and humanoid appearance of our robotic inventions? This is an important question because many of the artificially intelligent machines that enter society will bear a strong resemblance to natural humans and will argue that they are sentient and deserving of equal rights such as fundamental human rights and legal personhood status. When humanoid robots evolve to the point where they argue that they are conscious, will we treat them as equals, or will we discriminate against them and deny them equal protection under the law?

In the next decades, as cyborgs become equipped with technologies that enhance their abilities and robots move from assembly lines to our homes, determining what constitutes the ethical treatment of technologically enhanced beings and whether they should receive equal protection under the law will become important. For example, should robots that convince us that they are self-aware receive the same protections afforded humans under various laws, statutes, and constitutions? And if a robot was designed to physically resemble a human and if that form was combined with artificial intelligence, would we feel compelled to treat it as human? The answer to questions which focus on the rights that our

© Springer International Publishing Switzerland 2015
W. Barfield, *Cyber-Humans*, DOI 10.1007/978-3-319-25050-2_7

technological progeny should receive will surely depend, among other factors, on the appearance of the artificial intelligence, its personality, and its behavior. But as a preliminary observation, it seems reasonable to expect that cyborgs and androids will be subjected to different forms of discrimination based on their "machine-like" appearance; if so, society should be prepared for conflicts between artificially intelligent machines and humans. I base this conclusion on social science studies on discrimination, on the hostile treatment already experienced by cyborgs in different circumstances, and on the observations of roboticists indicating that when robots closely resemble humans in appearance, people may feel uncomfortable in their presence. This phenomenon, identified by Professor Masahiro Mori as the "uncanny valley" is so important for an emerging law of cyborgs and artificially intelligent machines (especially those that appear as androids) that a section of this chapter focuses specifically on the "uncanny valley" phenomena.

To some futurists, the possibility that humanity could use technology to create qualitatively new kinds of beings is not only desirable, but likely to happen this century. According to physicist Sydney Perkowitz, writing in *The Rise of Digital People: From Bionic Humans to Androids*, these might take the form of fully artificial, intelligent, and conscious machines; they might take the form of a race of "cyborgs" that are enormously augmented and extended physically, mentally, and emotionally; or they might take the form of virtual beings who may or may not inhabit physical bodies at all.[1] In addition, new forms of humans could arise from techniques in biological science such as cloning, genetic engineering, and stem-cell research. However, as noted by Stanford's Francis Fukuyama, in *Our Posthuman Future: Consequences of the Biotechnology Revolution,* a program for changing humans at the genetic level has moral, ethical, and religious implications; and the consequences of human-induced changes propagating in our gene pool is troubling.[2] But whatever form our technological inventions take, as they become smart, enter society, and compete against us, they may evoke fear, negative reactions, and be subjected to discrimination from humans (and by other artificially intelligent machines?). For this reason, in the coming decades, legislators will need to determine the appropriate law and policies to enact to protect the basic rights of all intelligent beings amongst us.

In my vision of future technological trends those who worry about changes in the genome may be missing the bigger picture as the law of accelerating returns suggests that the future may not be one dominated by biologically enhanced humans, but by technologically enhanced people, leading to a race of cyborgs and later this century to a merger between "human-cyborg" combinations and artificially intelligent machines. On the latter point, University of Michigan's Jennifer Robertson, has commented that the idea that humans and machines may meld into a new superior species, is not only being considered but actively being pursued by

---

[1]Sydney Perkowitz, 2004, Digital People from Bionic Humans to Androids, Joseph Henry Press.

[2]Francis Fukuyama, 2003, Our Posthuman Future: Consequences of the Biotechnology Revolution, Picador.

leading Japanese roboticists.[3] And as we head toward the Singularity, the creation of cyborgs and intelligent machines has its own set of ethical and legal issues. In fact, some commentators think that cyborg technologies combined with artificial intelligence might ultimately prove more challenging and dangerous to humanity than those arising from genetic manipulation. However, before we get to the point in time where artificial super intelligence is posing an existential threat to humanity, cyborgs and androids will have already entered society and be subjected to prejudice and discrimination from humans, it is that particular scenario and timeframe that is addressed in this chapter on "*The Law of Looks and Artificial Bodies.*"

The idea that the physical appearance of our technological progeny could lead to discrimination against them, can be gleaned from numerous sources including cases heard by the highest court in the U.S. For example, in *McCleskey v. Kemp*, the Supreme Court in deciding a sentencing issue for a convicted defendant, made the point in dicta that appearance discrimination may in fact be an extenuating factor in criminal law cases.[4] If discrimination exists for humans in our court system and job market, surely it will exist for cyborgs and androids interacting with us in social contexts and competing against us for jobs. In fact, that people may feel uncomfortable in the presence of those equipped with cyborg technology and then discriminate against them is often the subject of employment lawsuits brought in the U.S. under the *Americans with Disabilities Act* and other anti-discrimination laws.[5] But more generally, the appearance of cyborgs and any intelligent machine that enters society could become a contentious issue if their appearance deviates from societal standards of shape, form, and beauty. On this point, studies have shown that there is a high level of agreement among people in their ratings of other people's physical attractiveness,[6] and I would expect this finding to also hold true for androids designed to appear as human as possible.

Given exponentially accelerating technologies leading the way to a world of intelligent machines interacting with humans in a variety of social settings, what public policy should guide their design, and how should courts respond to the possibility of unequal treatment for our technological inventions based on their appearance? As we discuss these questions and develop solutions, we should proceed with caution, as in the future, it may be unenhanced humans that are discriminated against by our smart robotic inventions, therefore, it is critical that we consider the policies and laws which will lead to an egalitarian society consisting of those with flesh and those without. This chapter discusses such issues in the context of the look and appearance of artificially intelligent machines most often appearing in a human form as an android. Least the reader think that a *Law of Looks and Artificial Bodies* is a topic that has yet to receive attention

---

[3]Jennifer Robinson, 2010, Gendering Humanoid Robots, Robo-Sexism in Japan, Body and Society, V. 16, 1–36.

[4]*McCleskey v. Kemp*, 481 U.S. 279 (1987).

[5]See generally, *Fink v. Kitzman*, 881 F.Supp. 1347, 1369–70 (N.D. Iowa 1995).

[6]Gordon L. Patzer, 1985, The Physical Attractiveness Phenomena, Springer.

from different legal jurisdictions, there is an emerging *"Law of Looks"* based on cases and statutes dealing with employment and other situations. Important issues include *inter alia*, the regulation of "freak shows," cases brought under the *Americans with Disability Act* (ADA), cases dealing with malfunctioning prosthesis, and the rights one has to their appearance under intellectual property law. I discuss these laws in light of the coming cyborg age and our eventual merger with artificially intelligent machines.

At the beginning of this chapter, I should make the point that in our cyborg future not all people will discriminate against artificially intelligent machines, nor will all artificially intelligent machines be subjected to discrimination. Much will depend on the culture in which the machine is immersed, the features and behavior of the intelligent machine, the tasks for which it is designed, and the policies we humans adopt. Interestingly, Kate Darling of MIT has shown that humans tend to anthropomorphize our robotic inventions; reading her papers I get the impression that we are predisposed to like them.[7] If their behavior is autonomous and if we are interacting with robots in a social setting, Darling observes that they may inspire "fondness and loyalty" from us.[8] We may even treat them as if they were alive. Thinking about rights, Darling proposes enacting "protective laws" for our robotic inventions, just as has been done for pets. I am willing to go much farther in my view of laws needed to protect the rights of androids and other forms of artificial intelligence because I think they will be much smarter than pets and fairly soon.

So to summarize, why a chapter on "lookism" discrimination for our future technological inventions? Because tension between humans and artificially intelligent machines will surely develop as they get smarter and more autonomous, and many studies from social science indicate that appearance has much to say about the treatment and rights a person receives. But most importantly, if we can learn how to integrate cyborgs, androids, and artificially intelligent machines into society now, we may be establishing precedence on how "they" will treat us once our technological inventions exceed us in intelligence and performance (and become more attractive than us?). So the stakes for humanity are high. This chapter on *The Law of Looks and Artificial Bodies* discusses the law and policies which relate to the appearance of technologically enhanced beings and whether equal protection under the law should apply to our future robotic inventions while also considering whether other legal theories exist to protect our artificially intelligent progeny from discrimination.[9]

---

[7]Kate Darling, Extending Legal Rights to Social Robots, 2012, *We Robot Conference*, University of Miami, April 2012 MIT; Gregory McNeal, 2015, MIT Researchers Discover Whether We Feel Empathy For Robots, at: http://www.forbes.com/sites/gregorymcneal/2015/04/10/want-people-to-like-your-robot-name-it-frank-give-it-a-story/.

[8]Kate Darling, *id.*

[9]R. George Wright, Person 2.0: Enhanced and Unenhanced and the Equal Protection of the Laws, QLR, Vol. 23, 2005.

The Shape of Things to Come

Though numerous examples are provided in this chapter, the reader should already have a sense of what forms androids and artificially intelligent machines may take in the future. This is because cyborgs, androids, and artificially intelligent machines have been the subject of sci-fi novels and movies for some time. In fact, as science fiction novels have been adopted for movies and TV shows, the public has been exposed to a range of fascinating images of artificially intelligent entities. Interestingly, in science fiction novels, the tension between non-enhanced people and androids is one way that authors have explored the meaning of humanity and discussed the idea of legal rights for nonhuman beings. Some of the artificially intelligent machines displayed by the media are human-like in form and ready to serve us, while others appear as ominous and threatening creatures participating in uprisings against the human race. On the last point consider the androids of 1973s futuristic theme park *Westworld,* authored by Michael Crichton, who after the computer controlling them malfunctioned, purposively hunted down and killed the human visitors. A more realistic scenario for our cyborg future, at least in the next two decades, is that exponentially improving technologies will lead to the emergence of cyborgs and androids whose abilities and appearance will begin to match those of unenhanced humans. The question then will be whether our technological inventions will experience discrimination as they enter society, begin to interact with us, and compete against us for jobs. Because a person's appearance has much to say about the treatment they receive in society and whether they are discriminated against in the workplace, in social settings, and by our institutions, it is important to explore how technological enhancements to the bodies of cyborgs, androids, and artificially intelligent machines will likewise affect the treatment they receive.

An android is a robot, but a robot designed to look and act like a human, especially one with a body having a flesh-like resemblance. Professor Jennifer Robertson of the University of Michigan has stated that to be called a humanoid a robot "must meet two criteria: it has to have a body that resembles a human and it has to act like a human in environments designed for the capabilities of a human body."[10] In robotics laboratories around the world, several projects aiming to create androids that look, and, to a certain degree, speak or act like a human being have made remarkable progress. Smart androids are coming, and their human-like appearance and intelligence will fundamentally change society and place stress on our legal systems, social institutions, and labor market. In fact, a 2013 study from Oxford University examined 702 occupations and concluded that forty-seven percent of the total U.S. employment faces the risk of being eliminated in favor of computerization.[11] One example of our competition in the service industry is the

---

[10]Jennifer Robertson, *id.,* note 3.

[11]Carol Benedikt Frey and Michael A. Osborne, 2013, The Future of Employment: How Susceptible are Jobs to Computerisation? at: 2013 study from Oxford University examined 702 occupations and concluded that forty-seven percent of the total U.S. employment faces the risk of being eliminated in favor of computerization.

Botlr robot developed by startup *Savioke* which is being deployed in some proper-ties of the Starwood hotel chain. The robot's task is to deliver extra towels and for-gotten toiletries to hotel guests, I have to wonder, in hotels around the world how many humans do this job now and how will they feel about the robots which dis-place them?

Many types of technological enhancements will be available in the future, cre-ating a range of shapes, forms, and looks for our technological inventions. On this point, Professor Perkowitz, asks what human attributes in shape and form should continue as we develop the capability to enhance ourselves with cyborg technology.[12] Should we continue to appear in the shape of biological humans, or would some other shape be more functional? Many roboticists foresee a world with increasing interaction between humans and robots, and therefore are work-ing to create human-like androids so that our intelligent inventions more easily fit into human society. However, in contrast to this humancentric view of what a robot should look like, the idea that intelligent robots may take nonhuman forms, is not only possible, but for a particular task, desirable. How will people react to highly intelligent machines that take-on shapes and forms which deviate from the human form, or, on the other hand, look strikingly similar to humans—in the lat-ter case will we expect more from our human analogs and also discriminate more against them? As our bodies become equipped with cyborg technologies how should the law, in particular, the principle of equal protection under the law respond to the possibility of unequal and dramatic human, android, and robotic enhancement?

In fact, roboticists often take their design cues from nature—and for androids, humans in particular. For example, robots working on assembly lines or being designed as human helpers feature arms and end effectors to manipulate objects, whether it's a welding gun or laser scalpel. According to Larry Greenemeier, other robots, "designed as telepresence surrogates for remote office workers or aids for the elderly and disabled, come equipped with head-mounted cameras for eyes and wheels for upright motion to mimic human locomotion."[13] He also thinks it's tempting to think today's robots as only crude imitations of their human masters because most current robots do not look human; however, within a decade, intelli-gent human-like robots (i.e., androids) will have entered society spurred by signifi-cant progress in the design of flesh-like surfaces, the accurate control of facial features, and motor capabilities which are improving significantly.

Thinking about the future, as I noted in an previous chapter, Sidney Perkowitz of Emery University discusses two main ways to categorize artificial enhance-ments of humans: the first is as functional prosthetic devices and implants, such as artificial limbs, replacement knees and hips, and vascular stents; and the second as

---

[12]Sydney Perkowitz, *id*, note 1.

[13]Larry Greenemeier, 2013, What Should a Robot Look Like? at: http://www.scientificamerican.com/article/what-should-a-robot-look-like/.

cosmetic enhancements. For religious and cultural reasons, and as a form of self-expression, humans have always shown an interest to modify their body and to change their appearance. According to David DeGrazia, Professor of Philosophy at George Washington University, we diet, exercise, color our hair, get tattoos and body piercings; and as I noted in a previous chapter we modify our body with a range of technologies that are either worn on, or implanted under the skin.[14] Given that cyborg devices are exponentially improving technologies, by midcentury we can expect major alterations and augmentations to the human body to result from advances in exoskeletons, prosthesis (such as limb, cochlear, or retinal), heart pacemakers, sensors, and neuroprosthesis. In addition, as I discussed in the chapter on *Modifying, Enhancing, and Hacking the Body*, there is a movement among do-it-yourself hackers (or grinders) to self-modify their body with technology; and such changes often alter the appearance of the person modifying their body. But to (re)state the "big picture" of our cyborg future, technologies to repair, enhance, and modify the body are not only exponentially improving technologies,[15] but the very technologies leading humanity to a cyborg future and eventual merger with artificially intelligent machines.

The extent to which cyborgs and androids are accepted by humans as they join society will depend on a number of factors including the tasks they are designed to perform, their personality, and their appearance. Given human biases about "looks," and given that any shape can be fabricated, would the law and societal standards dictate that only humanoid shapes copying the image of an "attractive" (and young?) human be allowed for androids? Just consider, according to Professor Jennifer Robertson, in 2010 there were more than sixty household robots commercially available in a range of sizes and shapes, serving as cleaners, companions, and caregivers. But improving under the law of accelerating returns, as androids get smarter will they be content to serve as our domestic servants, and will they be content to look as we want them to look and do only what we ask of them? Of course, as of the time of this writing humans write the software and design the robots; but eventually that will change. Already software bots with increasingly sophisticated algorithms are making lucrative stock trades, and other AIs are diagnosing medical illness, composing music, proving mathematical theorems, and driving a car (would an AI driving a car, assume the identity of the car, would a "fender-bender" be the equivalent of an assault and battery?). As a policy issue, humanity should be well aware that any form of discrimination against our technological progeny once they become smart, could backfire and prove disastrous to the human race.

---

[14]David DeGrazia, 2005, Enhancement Technologies and Human Identity, Journal of Medicine and Philosophy, Vol. 30, 261–283.

[15]Peter H. Diamandis, 2015, Bold: How to Go Big, Create Wealth and Impact the World, Simon & Schuster.

The Androids Are Coming

As humans become enhanced with cyborg technology, and as artificially intelligent machines become more human-like in appearance, the issue of bodily integrity will become an important topic for "*The Law of Looks and Artificial Bodies.*" In fact, one of the most fundamental human rights is the right to bodily integrity which is the right to exert security or control over one's body.[16] A right of bodily integrity for intelligent machines could be used by an android to protect its body from unwanted modifications, or even to stop someone from scavenging its parts for another machine. I should point out here that there are laws regulating organ donation for humans, should similar laws exist for androids?[17] The reader may be wondering, why would an artificially intelligent machine resist a modification to its body, or for that matter its "mind"? Just as humans may decide to adopt technology, so too may an artificially intelligent machine. But just as humans may resist changes to their body, for example, forced medication to make a person mentally competent to stand trial, so too may intelligent and self-aware machines resist upgrades deemed undesirable by them (e.g., an upgrade which could affect their memories). Of course, as long as artificially intelligent machines lack rights, they are subject to human decisions; but they are quickly getting smarter, so I believe it's just a matter of time before they will want to make decisions regarding their bodily and mental integrity.

In the U.S. the Supreme Court has repeatedly held that there is a right to be free from unjustified intrusions on personal bodily integrity; suggesting that such a right is protected by the due process clause of the Fourteenth Amendment.[18] Perhaps androids will be particularly interested in protecting the integrity of their body out of self-preservation or even vanity. Once artificially intelligent machines experience emotions and connection to their body, they may be concerned with how others perceive them; in fact, having emotions may be a necessary condition before an android would make the decision to pursue a discrimination claim. As noted above, androids may even argue for the right to receive technological enhancements (upgrades could avoid a digital divide between androids), including cosmetic enhancements, which may serve no functional purpose whatsoever. As we will see

---

[16]See generally Barbro Björkman and Sven Ove Hansson, "Bodily rights and property rights", Journal of Medical Ethics 32: 209–214, 2006; Radhika Rao, Property, Privacy, and the Human Body, 2000, 80 B.U.L. Rev. 359. Legislation and Policy (on organ donations), U.S. Department of Health and Human Services, at: http://www.organdonor.gov/legislation/.

[17]Legislation and Policy (on organ donations), U.S. Department of Health and Human Services, at: http://www.organdonor.gov/legislation/.

[18]Fourth Amendment Victory: Citing Bodily Integrity, U.S. Supreme Court Prohibits Police from Forcibly Taking Warrantless Blood Samples from DUI Suspects, The Rutherford Institute, 2013, at: https://www.rutherford.org/publications_resources/on_the_front_lines/fourth_amendment_victory_citing_bodily_integrity_us_supreme_court_prohibits; Missouri v. McNeely, 2012, U.S. Supreme Court, Slip Opinion at: http://www.supremecourt.gov/opinions/12pdf/11-1425_cb8e.pdf.

in a later section of this chapter, any nonfunctional additions to an android has implications for the rights it may receive under intellectual property law.

Some may think that robots with emotions sounds strange, or unnecessary. But many designers of robots realize that they will increasingly interact with people as they enter society, so there is a movement to design life-like social robots (i.e., androids) that can detect human emotion, and can mimic human expression and emotion.[19] In my view, robots and androids with emotions and personalities will strongly influence how we react to them, and their level of acceptance in society. One example of this idea is *Pepper*, a robot built in Japan that can detect and express a range of emotions. *Pepper* stands 4 feet tall and weighs about 62 pounds, has facial-recognition technology, and is equipped with a number of cameras, audio recorders, and sensors. According to *Softbank*, a Japanese internet company, *Pepper* can read and respond to users' moods. In another example of developments in robotics, researchers at the *Korea Institute of Industrial Technology* built the android *EveR-3* (one of a series of female androids), which uses an interpersonal communications model to emulate human emotional expression via facial "musculature." *EveR-3* can engage in rudimentary conversation and matches the average figure of a Korean woman in her twenties (notice the selected appearance of *EveR-3*). A microchip inside her artificial brain allows *EveR-3* to engage in gesture expression and body coordination. Her whole body is made of highly advanced synthetic jelly silicon and with artificial joints in her face, neck, and lower body; she is able to demonstrate realistic facial expressions and sing while simultaneously dancing; skills I barely possess.

While *Pepper* is clearly a mechanical being with no biological parts, an important question for the coming cyborg age is at what point in the process of integrating technology into a person's body will the person be considered more machine and less human? And if this distinction is deemed important for law and policy, at what point will the appearance of enhanced humans and artificially intelligent machines be so different that they will need to be protected from discrimination based on their appearance? In the future, the lines between human and machine will be irrevocably blurred, and with that transition will come a whole new set of issues in need of attention by our courts. For example, will the distinction between human and machine make a difference in terms of how the law views such enhanced people?

Specific advances in robotic and android design are not only creating the technology to compete against humans in the job market, but I believe are also leading the way to our future to merge with artificially intelligent machines. For example, consider the robot that was designed by *Willow Garage, PR2* (Fig. 7.1), which uses a conventional gripper to manipulate objects—advanced as it is, this robot will be a distant relative of androids on the future human-machine family tree. In fact, since *PR2* rapid progress has already been made in the design of artificial

---

[19]See articles published in the *International Journal of Social Robotics*; and the *Journal of Human-Robotic Interaction*.

Fig. 7.1 Meet PR2, designed by Willow Garage. Images courtesy of Bob Bauer

hands that far more resemble human hands in look and manual dexterity. My sense is that if we are destined to merge with machines, a form mimicking that of humans would be desirable (at least initially for first adopters); therefore, advances in robotics producing limbs and arms that look and function like their biological equivalent are a step forward in the direction of a human-machine merger.

To emphasize how robotic design combined with artificial intelligence is especially powerful in creating our future technological progeny, consider that rapid progress in machine learning is helping robots perform far more sophisticated object manipulation than just a few years ago. A key breakthrough in this area came in 2006, when a group of researchers led by Andrew Ng, then at Stanford and now at Chinese Internet company *Baidu*, devised a way for robots to work out how to manipulate unfamiliar objects.[20] Instead of writing rules for how to grasp a specific object or shape, the researchers enabled their robot to study thousands of 3D images and learn to recognize which types of grip would work for different shapes. This allowed the robot to figure out suitable grips for new objects. Progress marches on, and in recent years robotics researchers have increasingly used a powerful machine-learning approach known as deep learning to improve these capabilities. However, the smarter the machine and the more dexterous it is, the more it will becomes like us, and in the short-term the more it will compete against us, that is, before we become the technology.

But before we become "them," that is, become our "mind children" using a term coined by robotics expert Hans Moravec, what is the likely response by

---

[20]Ian Lenz, Honglak Lee, and Ashutosh Saxena, 2013, Deep Learning for Detecting Robotic Grasps, *Robotics: Science and Systems (RSS)*; Honglak Lee, Yirong Shen, Chih-Han Yu, Gurjeet Singh, and Andrew Y. Ng, 2006, Quadruped Robot Obstacle Negotiation via Reinforcement Leaning, In Proceedings of the IEEE International Conference on Robotics and Automation.

humans to machines supplanting them from the workplace? That humans may discriminate against machines that compete against them is made clear by history. An example is the Luddite movement of the early Eighteenth century when English textile workers were threatened with unemployment by new technology, which the Luddites defined as "machinery hurtful to commonality."[21] Mills were burned, machinery was smashed, and the army was mobilized. At one time, according to historian Eric Hobsbawm, there were more soldiers fighting the Luddites than were fighting Napoleon in Spain.[22] In response to the Luddite movement, the British Parliament passed a bill making machine-smashing a capital offense. You have to wonder—if you "smash" a robot in the coming cyborg age, under criminal law statutes will such an act constitute a capital offense? If not, how about if you "smashed" an android that looked and acted like a human? If so, would we be more compelled to grant the android the right to be free from human hostility, discrimination, and physical assault?

As technology marches on, cyborgs and artificially intelligent machines are joining society and taking on an appearance that may distinguish them from unenhanced people, often with added capabilities (for example, cameras to film others) that may impact other people's rights (such as their right to privacy). At the same time androids are just leaving robotics laboratories equipped with increasing levels of intelligence and closeness to humans in form and appearance (whether they are designed to look like us or not, interesting legal and social issues still arise just by nature of their increased intelligence). On this last point, consider the work of Professor Hiroshi Kobayashi who directs the *Intelligent Mechatronics Lab* at the Tokyo University of Science. Hiroshi's team has created an android called *Saya* which works at the University as a guide. *Saya* is able to express human-like facial expressions and can communicate some basic emotions with her head and eye movements. As remarkable a technological feat that *Saya* and for that matter androids created at the *Korean Institute of Industrial Technology's* (e.g., *EveR-3)* are, they will be replaced by smarter and even more realistic androids within a few years. And just a few decades later, *Saya's* and *EveR-3's* relatives will claim that they are conscious and deserving of the rights humans receive. They may even demand additional rights and why not, they will be much smarter than us and have bodies that exceed our capabilities. Once androids reach a certain level of intelligence, such that they argue for rights, it seems likely they will argue for equal rights (and other liberties). Further down the road, we humans will be the ones arguing for human rights from our technologically superior progeny, that is, if we haven't already become them.

---

[21]The Luddites at 200, 21st Century Technology Debates & Politics, 2015, at: http://www.luddites200.org.uk/TechnologyPoliticsNow.html.

[22]Bryan Appleyard, 2014, New Republic, The New Luddites: Why Former Digital Prophets Are Turning Against Tech, at: http://www.newrepublic.com/article/119347/neo-luddisms-tech-skepticism.

Culture Is Important

As an example of the acceptance of androids into society, consider Toshiba's use of a robo-assistant which works at the information desk of a department store in Tokyo. The female android named Aiko Chihira, speaks Japanese and is also capable of sign language. Remarkably, Chihira blinks, bows (and the Japanese politely bow back) and moves her mouth and lips smoothly while speaking and is programmed with multiple human-like expressions.[23] The android's appearance wasn't modeled after any specific person but was designed to give a friendly impression. The "good nature" of the androids personality and her traditional Japanese clothing, are both factors which increase Aiko's acceptance and decreases the likelihood of negative reactions toward her. Android acceptance is an especially important consideration for Japanese roboticists who are designing robots to serve as a companion for people with dementia, to offer telecounselling in natural speech, to communication with the hearing impaired through sign language, and to allow healthcare officials to monitor the elderly.

A comparison of Japan's and South Korea's assimilation of robots into their societies with the U.S. and Europe, teaches us much about how people in the future may live in a world of technologically enhanced beings. I believe that cultural factors will strongly influence people's acceptance of robots and androids as they enter society. A case in point is the culture of Japan, where robotic technology is not only progressing exponentially, but robots are becoming integrated into many levels of Japanese society. As an example in pop culture, a cross-dressing Japanese television star's robotic clone has become the first android to host its own TV show.[24] Japanese roboticists, who are trying to replace celebrities with human-like androids, have pushed the clone of transvestite entertainer Matsuko Deluxe into the public's awareness (Fig. 7.2). According to Michael Fitzpatrick, "working with Professor Hiroshi Ishiguro, Japan's top advertising agency, *Dentsu* decided to clone an exact android copy of the popular entertainer."[25] A spokesman for the agency said: "Artists and entertainers themselves aren't yet seen as content that can be combined with technology, but the *Dentsu* group believes the need to develop android entertainers will grow."[26] Performing with natural movements, and a remarkable likeness to the "real" entertainer, while voiced and controlled remotely by a voice impersonator, the android put on quite a show in front of an

---

[23]Android Robot "Aiko Chihira" takes over as Receptionist of Tokyo Store, Youtube video at: https://www.youtube.com/watch?v=fH9IlZpwOPA.

[24]Michael Fitzpatrick, 2015, Daily Mail, 'Unnervingly real' android of popular presenter transvestite becomes the first in world to host its own TV show, at: http://www.dailymail.co.uk/news/article-3028762/Unnervingly-real-android-popular-presenter-transvestite-world-host-TV-show.html.

[25]*Id.*

[26]Kazuaki Nagata, 2014, Dentsu says it's creating robot entertainers, The Japan Times, at: http://www.japantimes.co.jp/news/2014/12/03/national/dentsu-says-creating-robot-entertainers/#.VXzhze_bJjo.

Fig. 7.2 Performer
Matsuko Deluxe's android
doppelganger Matsukoriod.
Image courtesy of Dunstsu

Fig. 7.3 Robotics Professor
Hiroshi Ishiguro and
his android look-a-like,
Geminoid HI-4 image
courtesy of Osaka University,
Japan

incredulous audience on Nippon TV.[27] Interestingly, in the U.S. there is a "public performance" right associated with copyright law. While, the right has yet to be evaluated with respect to android look-a-likes, I anticipate that this could be an interesting area of law for future courts to explore. Also, keep this android in mind when reading about the "right of publicity" discussed later in this chapter.

To achieve the lifelike look of Matsuko's doppelganger, Professor Hiroshi Ishiguro's robotics lab used the latest silicon skin and state-of-the-art electronic actuators[28] (Fig. 7.3). In addition, Japan's top make-up artist was brought into finish

---

[27]*Id.*

[28]Ryuji Yamazaki, Shuichi Nishio, Hiroshi Ishiguro, Marco Nørskov, Nobu Ishiguro, Giuseppe Balistreri, Acceptability of a Teleoperated Android by Senior Citizens in Danish Society: A Case Study on the Application of an Embodied Communication Medium to Home Care, *International Journal of Social Robotics*, vol. 6, no. 3, pp. 429–442, 2014; Guizzo, 2010, Hiroshi Ishiguro: The Man Who Made a Copy of Himself, IEEE Spectrum, at: http://spectrum.ieee.org/robotics/humanoids/hiroshi-ishiguro-the-man-who-made-a-copy-of-himself.

the job of making the android look life-like.[29] In Japan, a society quite in tune with the idea of a robotic future, the prevalent thinking is that as robots start to look more human, people will become more sympathetic towards them. But with many Japanese already predisposed to being sympathetic to robots, because of the friendly way they are portrayed in Japanese popular culture, discrimination against robots in Japan, may be far less prevalent than in western nations that have different cultural traditions and societal expectations for robots (e.g., the *Terminator* movie series and the military's attempt to weaponize robots). Interestingly, Japanese robot-icists claim that the time period to build an android indistinguishable from a human in appearance, is about 10 years.[30] Combine that prediction with Google's Ray Kurzweil's view that by midcentury artificial intelligence will have reached human levels of intelligence (that is, artificial general intelligence), the combination of intelligence with realistic android bodies, all within 25 years or less, provides strong motivation for humanity to consider human-robot ethics and pressing issues of robot and android law sooner-than-later.

As the above examples show, in our cyborg future our intelligent machines will have many different appearances and also personalities. With this possibility the question then becomes—would you want your robots or androids subservient, or upbeat, or even with a New Yorker personality—the possibilities are limitless, but it seems to me our reaction to artificially intelligent machines will surely depend in part on their look and their personality. In fact, a patent that has been issued to Google on robotic personalities adopting to humans suggests that a wide range of personalities could be possible and that we could even download different person-ality types from the cloud.[31] Thus, if you can't choose what kind of personality you want for your future android, it's highly possible that it might be able to choose for you.[32] It would do this by accessing your devices and learning about you, before configuring a tailored personality based on that information.[33] In addi-tion it could use speech and facial recognition to personalize its interactions with you; this is an example of how our technology is becoming more like us. Of course to some the scenario that the machine adopts to our likes or dislikes evokes the "machine as tool" design philosophy, and goes against my conjecture that as we build better cyborg technology, we are not just building tools to serve humanity but building our competition and future replacements. An interesting question for the law would occur if the robot was programmed to take on the personality of a natural person, would this be a form of "misappropriation of likeness"—the Google patent suggests a deceased loved one or a celebrity—so that effectively you could get someone to live on after their death in machine or virtual avatar

---

[29]Michael Fitzpatrick, *id.,* note 24.

[30]Michael Fitzpatrick, *id.,* note 24.

[31]Google Patent 8,996,429; Gene Quinn and Steve Brachmann, Discussing the Google patent, at: http://www.ipwatchdog.com/author/gene-steve/.

[32]Google Patent, *id.*; Goolge Patents Customizable Robot Personalities, 2015, at: http://www.wired.co.uk/news/archive/2015-04/01/google-robot-personalities.

[33]Google Patent *id.*

form.[34] More about this in the following sections because in some cases, legal rights attach to appearance.

Our Reaction to Cyborgs and Androids

Thus far, the cyborgs living amongst us have received mixed reactions from the public, from interest in the sleek "cybernetic" technology integrated into their body, to outright aggression based on their cyborg appearance. On the latter point, two of the first cyborgs amongst us, Steve Mann and Neil Harbisson both of whom are equipped with head-mounted display technology, have reported being assaulted in public based on their cyborg appearance. In one incident, Professor Mann was physically "roughed up" by airport security, and in another by employees at a McDonalds in Paris.[35] And Neil, who is equipped with a head worn sensor which he uses to convert color into sound, was assaulted by policeman concerned that he was filming them (he was actually hearing them in color).[36] Google's Ray Kurzweil has interpreted the attack against Steve as the first recorded hate crime against cyborgs, you can bet more are coming.

In fact, given human nature, I think cyborgs and androids will be the target of discrimination, hostility, and hate crimes for numerous reasons, not the least of which will be their appearance. Generally, hate crimes are on the rise around the world, and the cyborgs that have entered society have already been subjected to "lookism discrimination" and outright aggression.[37] In addition, humans equipped with cyborg technologies for reasons of medical necessity have also been subjected to discrimination. For example, in the U.K. according to *DisbilityHateCrime.org.UK*, hate crimes that are directed against people with disabilities forms its own category (even though, I might add, their disability is often "repaired" with a prosthetic device).[38] Back in the U.S., the state of Missouri defines a hate crime as one which is "knowingly motivated" because of race, color, religion, natural origin, sex, sexual orientation, or disability of the victim.[39] If Steve and Neil are considered to be equipped with cyborg technology to treat a disability (clearly Neil is due to his extreme color deficiency, and Steve travels

---

[34]Google Patent, *id*; Martine Rothblatt, 2014, Virtually Human: The Promise---and the Peril---of Digital Immortality, St. Martins Press.

[35]Stephanie Mlot, 2012, Wearable Tech Pioneer Assaulted at Paris McDonald's, at: http://www.pcmag.com/article2/0,2817,2407258,00.asp.

[36]David Pescovitz, 2012, Colorblind painter's wearable "synesthesia camera" reportedly broken by police, at: http://boingboing.net/2012/02/16/colorblind-painters-wearable.html.

[37]James J. McDonald, Jr, "Lookism," The Next Form of Illegal Discrimination, at: http://www.ipwatchdog.com/author/gene-steve/.

[38]DisbilityHateCrime.org.UK, at: http://disabilityhatecrime.org.uk/.

[39]Missouri Revised Statutes, Chapter 557.035, a statute on hate crimes, beginning 2017, at: http://www.moga.mo.gov/mostatutes/stathtml/55700000351.HTML.

with a statement from his doctor describing his dependence on cyborg technology) and are assaulted, both assaults should be considered a hate crime. Would androids and other technologically enhanced beings experience similar hostility as a result of their cybernetic appearance? These are questions which will weave their way through our court systems in the next decades and the rulings made by judges in such cases will contribute to an emerging law of cyborgs. Unfortunately, given the hostility that Steve and Neil have experienced, in the future, cyber-hate crimes and other forms of discrimination against cyborgs and androids may occur frequently. In fact, in response to cyborg technologies there are advocacy groups with names like "*Stop the Cyborgs*" springing up to try and push through cyborg legislation.[40] So the message seems to be, become a cyborg at your own peril, humans may not approve.

If hate crimes result in a physical attack against a person, there may already be an analog in the machine world—consider the case of machine sabotage (and from a historical perspective recall the Luddite movement of the Eighteenth Century). In a recent example, an executive of a Korean appliance company was accused of willfully damaging several Samsung washing machines at an event in Berlin. Also consider that there are cyber-industrial sabotage activities, such as hacking. On the point of purposeful physical harm to machines, the state of Washington considers damage to machines in one of its state statutes defining criminal sabotage as: "Whoever, with intent that his or her act shall, or with reason to believe that it may, injure, interfere with, interrupt, supplant, nullify, impair, or obstruct the owner's or operator's ... property, instrumentality, machine, mechanism, or appliance... shall be guilty of criminal sabotage."[41] As for cyborgs, there are already cases where they have been assaulted and their prosthetic limbs stolen. So, just think, humans experience discrimination, cyborgs are assaulted, it's a crime to sabotage a machine, and with this as background more androids and artificially intelligent machines are coming.

The general theme of discrimination against androids predates current androids that are entering society now. For example, in a sci-fi novel, the theme of discrimination against androids was explored in John Brunner's novel *Into the Slave Nebula*,[42] where the blue-skinned androids were subjugated to slavery by humans. I think the idea of forced servitude for artificially intelligent beings should be strongly prohibited due to human rights concerns, as should slavery for any artificially intelligent being that convincingly makes the claim that it is conscious. Personally, I don't think it wise to subjugate any intelligent being that within a few decades could surpass us in intelligence. As Martine Rothblatt, CEO of *Therapeutics Inc.* comments, future sentient beings will want to be free, they will learn that lesson from humans, and oppression of artificial intelligence will only result in forms of opposition ranging from nonviolent (think Gandhi) to outright

---

[40]Stop The Cyborgs, Only the unmeasured is free, at: http://stopthecyborgs.org/.

[41]RCW 9.05.060, Washington State statute on machine sabotage.

[42]John Brunner, 2011, Into the Slave Nebula, Gateway.

hostility (think terminator).[43] Considering Rothblatt's comments, how likely is discrimination against our future technological progeny and how likely is an unwanted response in return by them? Just consider the example of current cyborgs Neil and Steve indicating that people wearing head-mounted display technology may experience hostility and discrimination based on their "cyborg appearance," and that litigation resulting from people equipped with prosthesis is not uncommon. As one example of the last point, the Sixth Circuit Court of Appeals in a case dealing with cyborg technology held that an excavator operator with a prosthetic leg, was entitled to be reinstated to his job under the terms of the *Americans with Disabilities Act* as long as he could perform the essential functions of his position safely; that is, his cyborg technology could not disqualify the worker from employment.[44]

While exponentially improving technologies often outpace the law's ability to keep up, for a number of pragmatic reasons, a few nations are beginning to seriously consider the consequences of a cyborg/robotic future. Inevitably, the labor market of the near future will consist of humans, cyborgs, and artificially intelligent robots. In South Korea, the *Ministry of Information and Communication* has an ambitious plan to put a robot in every household by 2020 and several robot cities have been planned for the country: the first scheduled to be built in 2016. The new robot city will feature research and development centers for manufacturers and part suppliers, as well as exhibition halls and a stadium for robot competitions.[45] South Korea is also working on a *Robotics Ethics Charter* that will establish ground rules and laws for human interaction with robots, setting standards for robotics users and manufacturers, as well as guidelines on ethical standards to be programmed into robots to prevent human abuse of robots and vice versa. In fact, researchers in artificial intelligence propose programming "friendly artificial intelligence," into the "brains" of future artificially intelligent machines to decrease their potential threat to humanity. Interestingly, in a Brooking report written by lawyers Benjamin Wittes and Jane Chong, *Our Cyborg Future—Law and Policy Implications*, issues of access to digital technology are closely linked to concerns about discrimination against those unable to afford or unwilling to undergo certain modifications.[46] In addition, they argue that antidiscrimination laws may be necessary to prevent cyborgs from being denied employment as a result of their cybernetic modifications and to stop unenhanced humans from being discriminated against for opposite reasons.[47]

---

[43]Martine Rothblatt, *id.*, note 34.

[44]*Henschel v. Clare Cnty. Rd. Comm'n*, No. 13–1528 (6th Cir. December 13, 2013).

[45]EveR-2-Meet the Singing Android, at: http://www.k2updates.com/ever-2-meet-the-singing-android/.

[46]Benjamin Wittes and Jane Chong, 2014, We Are All Cyborgs Now, at: http://www.brookings.edu/blogs/techtank/posts/2014/10/8-we-are-all-cyborgs.

[47]*Id.*

The Uncanny Valley

In the coming cyborg age, cyborgs, androids, and robots may have reason to be concerned about human reaction to them, just consider the phenomena of the "uncanny valley."[48] This concept, developed by roboticist Masahiro Mori originally intended to provide an insight into human reactions to robotic design, but has been extended to human interactions with nearly any nonhuman entity.[49] Stated simply, the idea is that humans react favorably to a "human-like" machine, but only to a particular point. For example, humans generally like the appearance of "cute" robotic toys, but once an android is designed to look like a human, and doesn't quite meet the standard, people report a strong negative response to its "creepy" appearance. However, once the appearance improves and is indistinguishable from a human, the response becomes positive. So the response goes... positive, negative, then positive again. This chasm, the uncanny valley, represents the point at which a person observing the creature or object in question sees something that is nearly human, but just enough off-kilter to seem eerie or disquieting.[50] Examples can be found in the fields of robotics, 3D computer animation, and in medical fields such as burn reconstruction, infectious diseases, neurological conditions, and plastic surgery.[51] As an example of the uncanny valley from popular culture, according to roboticist Dario Floreano, the animated baby in Pixar's groundbreaking 1988 short film *Tin Toy* provoked negative audience reactions, which first led the film industry to take the concept of the uncanny valley seriously. In addition, several reviewers of the 2004 animated film *The Polar Express* called its animation eerie. In fact, CNN.com reviewer Paul Clinton wrote, "Those human characters in the film come across as downright... well, creepy."[52]

A number of design principles have been proposed for avoiding the uncanny valley—I think of them as design rules for cyborgs, androids, virtual avatars, and any other artificially intelligent being that will enter society. Perhaps future courts will take note of these rules. It has been shown that when human and nonhuman elements are mixed in the design of a robot, the robot may look uncanny and likely experience lookism discrimination. For example, a robot with a synthetic voice or a human being with a human voice have been found to be less eerie than a

[48] Angel Tinwell, 2014, The Uncanny Valley in Games and Animation, A.K. Peters/CRC Press.

[49] Masahiro Mori, 2012, The Uncanny Valley, IEEE Spectrum, at: http://spectrum.ieee.org/automaton/robotics/humanoids/the-uncanny-valley.

[50] *Id*; David Bryant, The Uncanny alley, at: http://www.arclight.net/~pdb/nonfiction/uncanny-valley.html. The uncanny valley of a functional organization, 2013, at: https://stratechery.com/2013/the-uncanny-valley-of-a-functional-organization/.

[51] The uncanny valley of a functional organization, 2013, at: https://stratechery.com/2013/the-uncanny-valley-of-a-functional-organization/.

[52] Paul Clinton, 2004, Review: 'Polar Express' a creepy ride, at: http://edition.cnn.com/2004/SHOWBIZ/Movies/11/10/review.polar.express/.

robot with a human voice or a human being with a synthetic voice.[53] In addition, for a robot to give a more positive impression, its degree of human realism in appearance should also match its degree of human realism in behavior. So if an android looks more human than its movement abilities, this gives a negative impression. In addition, in terms of performance, if a robot looks too appliance-like, people will expect little from it, if it looks too human-like, people will expect too much from it; however, with continuing improvements, future artificially intelligent machines will meet and then exceed our expectations. Still, a highly human-like appearance leads to an expectation that certain behaviors will be present, such as realistic motion dynamics. Finally, abnormal facial proportions, including those typically used by artists to enhance attractiveness (e.g., larger eyes), can look eerie when combined with human skin texture.[54]

A similar "uncanny valley" effect could, according to futurist writer Jamais Casico, show up when humans begin modifying themselves with cybernetic enhancements which aim to improve the abilities of the human body and mind beyond what would normally be possible, be it eyesight, muscle strength, or cognition.[55] Casico postulates that so long as these enhancements remain within a perceived norm of human behavior, a negative reaction is unlikely, but once individuals supplant normal human shape and form, revulsion can be expected.[56] However, according to the uncanny valley theory, in our cyborg future, once such technologies gain further distance from human norms, "transhuman" individuals would cease to be judged on human levels and instead be regarded as separate entities altogether (this point is what has been dubbed "Posthuman"), and it is here that acceptance would rise once again out of the uncanny valley.[57] In fact, there has already been some work on how people view cybernetically enhanced bodies. For example, Jessica Barfield, in work done at Dartmouth College, found that people equipped with cyborg technology would have to change their body-image and self-identity, and that they would have to relearn how to use their body to accommodate the new technology. Should designers of robots, androids, or prosthetic devices strive overly hard to duplicate human appearance? If so, some seemingly minor flaw could drop the android or cyborg into the uncanny valley.

But let me step back from robots to people, and ask—does the uncanny valley phenomena apply to humans? Yes, it does, and here is an example. *Ulzzang*, or "best face," is a Korean subculture in which girls alter their looks digitally, with makeup, and by any other means available to them to achieve an anime look.[58] In

---

[53]Uncanny Valley, Wikipedia, at: https://en.wikipedia.org/wiki/Uncanny_valley.

[54]*Id.*

[55]Jamais Casico, Open the Future, at: http://www.openthefuture.com/2007/10/the_second_uncanny_valley.html.

[56]*Id.*

[57]*Id.*

[58]Paul Pickett, 2010, 5 Creepy Ways Humans Are Plunging Into the Uncanny Valley, at: http://www.cracked.com/article_18867_5-creepy-ways-humans-are-plunging-into-uncanny-valley.html.

Fig. 7.4 The Uncanny
Valley. The concept was
proposed by Mashario Mori.
Image courtesy of Wikipedia
Commons

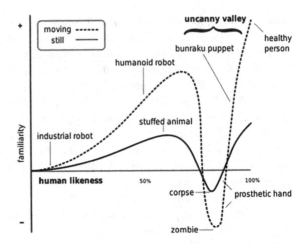

other words, an ulzzang girl strives to have behemoth, circular eyes, a tiny nose
and mouth, flawless pale skin and a tiny body dressed up in coordinated outfits.[59]
Once they get that anime look, they upload pictures of themselves for online competitions for prestige and Internet fame. While purposively altering a face digitally
to the point where it looks like an anime character is interesting from an uncanny
valley sense, actually altering their real-world faces with eyelid glue and contact
lenses, that is, purposefully entering the uncanny valley is comparable to the
grinder movement (see Chap. 5: *Modifying, Enhancing, and Hacking the Body*)
where people implant technology under their skin to gain an extra sense.[60] I can
only say, the range of human expression when it comes to altering appearance is
wide, and will be even more dramatic in the coming cyborg age as body and facial
features for humans and androids are replaced with "cyborg" technology
(Fig. 7.4).

Observations About Discrimination and the "Ugly Laws"

In my view, the answer to whether artificial intelligence as embodied in different
bodily forms will be discriminated against based on their appearance, is decidedly
"yes" as the human drive to conform to cultural (or subcultural) beauty standards
is strong; and those who come short are often the victim of "lookism" discrimination. For example, physically unattractive people often face unequal treatment in
situations in which their appearance is clearly unrelated to their qualification or
abilities. In contrast, other social science research has shown that people attribute
a wide range of positive characteristics to those whom they find physically

---

[59]*Id.*

[60]*Id.*

attractive.[61] In addition, studies have also shown that less attractive people are accorded worse treatment simply because of their appearance. In our cyborg future will "unsightly androids" be subjected to the same lookism discrimination? On this topic, in a study on the perception of cyborg bodies by Jessica Barfield she reported survey results that indicated people equipped with cyborg technology would experience a significant amount of bias by the public, and none responding that cybernetically enhanced people would experience no bias.[62] From social science studies, the finding that a person's appearance affects the treatment they receive is so strong that parents have lower expectations for unattractive children, as do teachers; which makes me wonder—will "unsightly" androids also receive deflated expectations by humans? Already it has been suggested that we expect more from robots that look human. Additionally, as adults, unattractive people in simulation studies of court proceedings receive higher sentences in criminal cases and lower damages awards in civil lawsuits.[63] Summarizing social science studies, "lookism" discrimination is widespread in society and is influenced by a number of factors, thus it is reasonable to expect that our technological inventions will likely receive the same discriminatory treatment based on their appearance as do humans.

Discrimination directed against those with disabilities is often the result of a missing or damaged body part which in some cases can be replaced with a prosthetic arm or leg; which then may become the basis for discrimination. Interestingly, robots and androids are often equipped with similar "cyborg" technology. With disabled humans, cyborg technology may lead to discriminatory reactions that are based on their appearance, but paradoxically, in the case of machines, cyborg technology also gives the machine the functionality to compete against humans. In this case androids may experience discrimination based on the way they look (especially if they fall into the uncanny valley) and also based on their enhanced ability to displace humans from the workplace. In fact, to compete against humans, robots and androids often use the latest prosthetic devices, computer-vision, and machine-learning algorithms to perform the work we humans typically do. And compete they do, according to a joint report by accountancy firm *Deloitte* and the University of Oxford, in Britain the lower paid workers are five times more likely to have their jobs taken over by robots than those earning higher incomes.[64] Academicians from MIT, Oxford University, and Sussex University, have argued that robots will "steal" around half of all jobs around the world in the not too distant future because, according to them, the globe has entered a second

---

[61]Michael Kalick, Aesthetic Surgery: How it Affects the way Patients are Perceived by Others, Annals of Plastic Surgery, 128, 131, 1979.

[62]Jessica Barfield, 2014, Cybernetic Embodiment Study, for Sociology 79.6, Dartmouth College.

[63]Gray and Ashmore, 1976, Biasing Influence of Defendant's Characteristics on Simulated Sentencing, 38 Psychological Rep. 727.

[64]Mark Smith, 2014, One-third of jobs in the UK at risk from automation, at: http://www2.de loitte.com/uk/en/pages/press-releases/articles/deloitte-one-third-of-jobs-in-the-uk-at-risk-from-automation.html.

age of machinery that will have a more profound effect on society than the onset of the industrial revolution.[65] Two interesting books in this area were written by Erik Brynjolfsson and Andrew McAfee, *The Second Machine Age: Work, Progress, and Prosperity in a Time of Brilliant Technologies,* and *Rise of the Robots,* by Martin Ford. However, my perspective of the future is different from the above authors, I view the second machine age as synonymous with an age of cyborgs and a future merger with artificially intelligent machines; that is, I argue that we are becoming the "intelligent machinery," and the "intelligent machinery" is in the process of becoming us. Thus, like Hans Moravec, I predict that our future is to merge with our artificially intelligent inventions, and in contrast to the views of Erik Brynjolfsson and Andrew McAfee, other than for a brief time period our future is not to experience a second machine age in which "they" serve "us" but to merge with them.

Both Japan and South Korea have actively promoted the virtues of a robot-dependent society and lifestyle. Professor Jennifer Robison, a leading scholar of Japanese robotic culture, reports that nationwide surveys in Japan indicate that Japanese citizens are more comfortable sharing living and working environments with robots than with foreign caretakers and migrant workers.[66] Discussing the demographics of Japan, Robertson comments that "as their population continues to shrink and age faster than in other postindustrial nations, Japanese politicians are banking on the robotics industry to reinvigorate the economy and to preserve the country's alleged ethnic homogeneity."[67] These initiatives Robinson reports are paralleled by a growing support among some Japanese roboticists and politicians to confer citizenship on robots. Already the idea of robots having evolved beyond consideration as "property" to acquiring legal status as sentient beings with "rights" is shaping developments in artificial intelligence and robotics outside of Japan, including South Korea, Europe, and the U.S. In addition, supporting the idea that granting legal rights for robots is gaining momentum, the *We Robot* conference, a meeting of leading experts in the field of law and robotics is held annually.[68] And Ryan Calo one of the organizers of the *We Robot* conference is proposing the idea that a new federal agency on robots be developed in order to deal with the novel experiences and harms that robotics may enable.

That cyborgs and androids may be subject to "lookism" discrimination seems a reasonable conclusion given that in current society, the most physically unattractive members face widespread discrimination.[69] And not only do people discrimi-

---

[65]Linda Brinded, 2014, Robots Will Steal 50 % of Human Jobs in Near Future, says MIT and Professors, at: http://www.ibtimes.co.uk/robots-will-steal-50-human-jobs-near-future-says-mit-professors-1455088; Linda Brinded, 2014, Robots to Steal 10 Million Low Paid UK Jobs by 2034, at: http://www.ibtimes.co.uk/robots-steal-10-million-low-paid-uk-jobs-by-2034-1474032.

[66]Jennifer Robertson, 2014, Human Rights versus Robot Rights: Forecasts from Japan, Critical Asian studies, 46:4, 571–598.

[67]*Id.*

[68]*We Robot*, 2014 program, at: http://robots.law.miami.edu/2014/program/.

[69]Note, 1987, Facial Discrimination: Extending Handicap Law to Employment Discrimination on the Basis of Physical Appearance, Harvard Law Reviw, Vol, 100, No, 8, 2035–2052.

nate against those whose appearance deviates from societal standards, but local governments may also discriminate. In the past, some jurisdictions in the U.S. went so far as to prohibit "ugly" or "unsightly" individuals from appearing in the public; this implies to me that cyborgs and androids deemed unattractive could similarly offend the sensibilities of humans and be subjected to "lookism" and other forms of discrimination.[70] Remarkably, in the early-to-mid 1900s it was illegal to be found "ugly" on the streets of some mainstream American cities like Chicago, Illinois, Omaha, Nebraska, and Columbus, Ohio.[71] Such a person's punishment for venturing in public ranged from incarceration to fines for each "ugly offense." Here's how the Chicago Municipal Code described and enforced an "Ugly Law" (which has since been repealed):

> No person who is diseased, maimed, mutilated or in any way deformed so as to be an unsightly or disgusting object or improper person is to be allowed in or on the public ways or other public places in this city, or shall therein or thereon expose himself to public view, under a penalty of not less than one dollar nor more than fifty dollars for each offense.[72]

At the time period of the "lookism" discrimination laws the thinking was that even though the disabled, the indigent, and the poor were a part of society, nobody wanted to deal with them and fewer still wanted to actually view them in public. So laws were passed to keep the deformed—especially those with Cerebral Palsy and other disfiguring diseases—inside and out-of-sight.[73] Thankfully, Omaha repealed their Ugly Law in 1967; Columbus withdrew theirs in 1972; and Chicago was the last to stop punishing the "ugly" in 1974. However, human biases fade slowly, and "lookism" discrimination is still a part of society and will surely continue in our cyborg future and be directed against our cybernetic inventions.

In contrast to the jurisdictions which enacted statutes to prohibit "unsightly" people from appearing in public, jurisdictions that legislate in this area now are more likely to respond by enacting local ordinances to *protect* people from lookism discrimination. In fact, in the U.S. some states and municipalities have passed laws that directly prohibit discrimination based on appearance. The District of Columbia, for example, prohibits discrimination based upon "actual or perceived" differences in background and attributes, including "physical appearance," such as weight (no overweight androids please). And employers in the District of Columbia should be particularly cautious about terminating employees for any appearance based issues, as personal appearance and the expression of an employee's gender identification are protected. The state of Michigan has also enacted a statute to expressly protect employees from discrimination based upon their

---

[70]Paris. Ill. Mun. Code § 36034, repealed 1974.

[71]Chicago Municipal Code, sec. 36034; Unsightly Beggar Ordinance Nebraska Municipal Code of 1941, sec. 25; Columbus, Ohio, General Offense Code, sec. 2387.04.

[72]Chicago Municipal Code, *id.*

[73]David Boles, 2007, Enforcing the Ugly Laws, at: http://bolesblogs.com/2007/05/01/enforcing-the-ugly-laws/.

weight or height. And several other local governments, including New York City
and San Francisco bar discrimination based upon an employee's general appearance. But, the question for our cyborg future is whether "appearance" discrimination will also apply to cyborg technologies?[74]

In an example that makes me wonder whether the size and form of an android
will evoke discriminatory reactions from people, a waitress at a Hooters restaurant
was in the news claiming that Hooters warned her that she was required to loose
approximately ten pounds in the near future or face possible discharge.[75] The waitress responded by filing a weight discrimination lawsuit against the restaurant
chain under a Michigan statute known as the *Elliot-Larsen Civil Rights Act*.[76]
Among other things, this statute bars employers from discriminating on the basis of
age, sex, height or weight.[77] I can envision "chubby" androids receiving negative
reactions from the public, once they enter society, and I envision laws to protect
androids from appearance discrimination or even laws to "force" androids to look a
certain way. In fact, Tokyo University's Tomotaka Takahashi predicts that over half
of all future androids will be female so there will be lots of opportunity for gender
discrimination (this already happens in virtual video games) in our cyborg future.
In South Korea and Japan, the gender and "look" of the android designed to enter
society is especially important, with female androids appearing much more slender
than their male counterparts. As a precursor for the cyborg future, it is known that
stereotypes related to gender and appearance that burden women in the real world
follows them into virtual ones, according to researchers at Penn State University.
On this point, in a study of how people interacted with avatars in an online game,
researcher T. Franklin Waddell reported that women received less help from fellow
players than men when they operated an unattractive avatar.[78]

Discussing the law and physical appearance, Yale Law Professor Robert Post
comments on a 1992 municipal code enacted in Santa Cruz, California with prohibits arbitrary discrimination in employment, housing, and accommodations,
based on height, weight, and physical characteristics (all items that could apply to
androids!).[79] The statute as passed, focused on only aspects of bodily appearance

---

[74]Brian F. Chandler, 2013, "Too Sexy?" "Too Heavy?" Will Employee Appearance Standards
be Protected? at: http://www.protoraelaw.com/publications/too-sexy-too-heavy-will-employee-
appearance-standards-be-protected/.

[75]Hooters waitress files lawsuit—says she lost weight, http://www.nhregister.com/general-news/
20100525/hooters-waitress-files-lawsuit-says-she-lost-weight.

[76]Elliot-Larson Civil Rights Act, Michigan Act 453 of 1976, 37.2202, Employer; prohibited practices; exceptions.

[77]See MICH. COMP. LAWS, *id.*

[78]T. Franklin Waddell and James D. Ivory, 2015, It's Not Easy Trying to be One of the Guys:
The Effect of Avatar Attractiveness, Avatar Sex, and User Sex on the Success of Help-Seeking
Requests in an Online Game. Journal of Broadcasting & Electronic Media, Vol. 59 (1): 112. doi:1
0.1080/08838151.2014.998221.

[79]Robert Post, 2000, Prejudicial Appearances, The Logic of American Antidiscrimination Law,
Faculty Scholarship Series, Yale Law School, paper 192.

that are beyond a person's control (i.e., immutable). However, discrimination also exists for traits that are within a person's control such as religion or marital status, tattoos, piercings and for grinders whether they equip themselves with technology. Even with its good intentions the Santa Cruz statute evoked an intense controversy about the merits of what was then called "anti-lookism." I am certain that any legislation to protect cyborgs, androids, and artificially intelligent machines from experiencing lookism discrimination will evoke a similar controversy. But eventually the law does respond to inequities in society, for example, the recantation of Ugly Laws directly led to the *Americans with Disabilities Act* (ADA) of 1990, where certain rights were granted to the disabled. Of relevance to lookism discrimination is that under some circumstances appearance can be regarded as a disability. For example, if a person who is considered obese or a person with a cosmetic disfigurement that is considered a facial deformity, impacts the person's ability to be employed, they are considered disabled under the ADA:

> "Individuals with disabilities are a discrete and insular minority who have been faced with restrictions and limitations, subjected to a history of purposeful unequal treatment, and relegated to a position of political powerlessness in the society, based on characteristics that are beyond the control of such individuals and resulting from stereotypic assumptions not truly indicative of the individual ability of such individuals to participate in, and contribute to, society."[80]

When discussing the emergence of cyborgs and androids into society, some ask—what do we humans have to fear (some respond saying an uprising destroying the human race, but I leave this topic to a later chapter and to books such as *Our Final Invention: Artificial Intelligence and the End of the Human Era,* by James Barat). In response to public reactions, current cyborgs are beginning to address the question of civil liberties for technologically enhanced beings. Those who are equipping themselves with cyborg technology argue that their constitutional right for equal protection under the law should include protection from unfavourable and discriminatory reactions to their appearance. In fact, cyborg Neil Harbisson, who wears a head-mounted antenna which allows him to "hear color," argues that his appearance is not unnatural, just the opposite commenting: "Some might think that we might become less human if we modify ourselves but I believe there is nothing more human than doing that."[81] In addition he states, "In my case, becoming technology doesn't make me feel closer to machines, or to robots, but quite the opposite. Having an antenna makes me feel closer to insects and other creatures that have antennae, hearing through bone conduction makes me feel closer to dolphins and other marine species that perceive sound through their bones, having ultraviolet and infrared perception makes me feel closer to insects and mammals that perceive these colours. I feel a stronger connection with nature now than I ever did before."[82]

---

[80]Americans With Disabilities Act of 1990, Pub. L. No. 101–336, 104 Stat. 328 (1990).

[81]Neil Harbisson, 2015, I Don't Have Artificial Body Parts, I Have Artistic Body Parts, http://www.huffingtonpost.com/neil-harbisson/i-dont-have-artificial-bo_b_6804306.html.

[82]*Id.*

Whether a connection to nature will constitute an acceptable affirmative defence against discrimination for cyborgs and androids is not likely; instead, I expect strong legislation efforts will be needed, possibly in response to civil uprisings against the governments and institutions perpetuating "lookism" discrimination against our future technological progeny.

Interestingly, another form of "ugly laws" has been around for some time and is still on the books. These laws are directed at freak shows (sometimes termed "sideshow") that accompany traveling carnivals. An interesting book in this area was written by Robert Bogdan, *Freak Show: Presenting Human Oddities for Amusement and Profit*. In the U.S. "freak laws" were enacted to deal with establishments that sought to profit from displaying people with an unusual body or deformity—for example, the bearded lady, wolf boy, or fish girl.[83] But technology may play a role in people's perception of who looks different. Consider Professor Steve Mann of the University of Toronto who has been wearing "eye catching" cyborg technology for decades. Richard Crouse, author of the book *100 Best Movies You've Never Seen* (Steve was the subject of a 2001 documentary film, *Cyberman*) claims that P.T. Barnum would have loved Steve Mann, and would have pitched like this—step right up ladies and gentleman. Have we got a *freak* for you? Half man, half machine, this *un*biological creature is one of the wonders of the world. While there are no laws specifically passed relating to the appearance of cyborgs, in the U.S. the regulations enacted by states on freak shows may provide some guidance on how the law might respond to cyborgs and androids (that look different from humans) as they enter society. To some commentators it is thought that freak shows include expressive elements and as such should be subject to First Amendment protection. In the coming cyborg age, as cyborgs and androids enter society, a future court may be asked to determine if elements of cyborg technology are forms of expression and therefore deserving of First Amendment protection (as a form of speech), versus functional, which could meet the requirements of patent law. However, currently, the First Amendment is not the usual legal theory which prevails in appearance discrimination cases but more typically federal anti-discrimination, local, and state ordinances are.

In the U.S. there is no federal law relating to freak shows, any law covering such shows are typically city ordinances with the exception of a few states legislating in this area. Of the jurisdictions that have considered the issue, same prohibit, and some allow "freaks" to be displayed for commercial purposes. For example, in California and Florida, laws restricting freak shows that charge people to view "freaks" have been held unconstitutional—not because the laws were thought to violate the freedom of speech prong of the First Amendment, but rather because persons with "unusual bodies" have a right to be employed and surprisingly the courts assumed freak shows were one of the few places where such people could

---

[83]Brigham A. Fordham, 2007, Dangerous Bodies: Freak Shows, Expression, and Exploitation, 14 UCLA Ent. L. Rev.

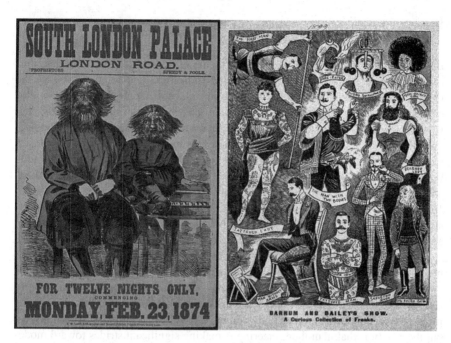

Fig. 7.5 Traveling carnival posters, images curtesy of Wikipedia commons

gain employment.[84] However, not all states allow "freaks" to be displayed for commercial purposes, in fact, Massachusetts General Law prohibits all commercial displays of a person who has the appearance of deformity produced by artificial means, regardless of whether the persons being displayed are being sufficiently rewarded for participating or not.[85] Like the "Ugly laws" of the past, some laws restricting freak shows are intended to shield the public from the spectacle of the unusual body; but in the coming cyborg age people will not be shielded from those who look different or deviate from cultural standards of beauty as millions of artificially intelligent robots, androids, and cyborgs will soon join society and not all will be the equivalent of an attractive human (but I do suppose—"Beauty is in the eye of the beholder") (Fig. 7.5).

---

[84]Brigham A. Fordham, *id.*; Justin Smith, 2013,The Ethics of Tod Browning's Freaks (1932), at: http://www.soundonsight.org/the-ethics-of-tod-brownings-freaks-1932/.

[85]Massachusetts General Laws. Part IV. Title I Chapter 272. Section 33. Whoever exhibits for hire an albino person, a minor or mentally ill person who is deformed or a person who has an appearance of deformity produced by artificial means shall be punished by a fine of not more than five hundred dollars.

Mind Uploads and Replacement Bodies

Before exploring in more detail the main theme of this chapter, lookism discrimination and how it may apply to cyborgs and androids, I will briefly introduce the idea of a mind upload to a virtual avatar, android, or different physical body altogether, an idea which is clearly a more distant possibility for our cyborg future but worth considering in the context of discrimination and rights for our technological inventions. While the technology to upload one's mind into another body is fascinating, an in-depth discussion of the emerging technology for uploading a mind is beyond the scope of this book (see however, Ray Kurzweils *How to Build a Mind,* and the edited book by Russell Blackford and Damien Broderick, *Intelligence Unbound: The Future of Uploaded and Machine Minds*), instead the brief discussion here will be on the legal and ethical issues related to discrimination based on appearance, that is, as a result of uploading a mind to another body.

As background information, Ray Kurzweil in *The Age of Spiritual Machines* predicted human-level intelligence in a machine by 2029,[86] and that in the 2040s "we will be able to access the information in our brains that constitute our memories, skills, and personalities and back them up."[87] If the idea of uploading our mind to a computer or another body sounds like sci-fi, for humans it currently is, but the reality is that neural engineering is making significant strides toward modeling the brain and developing technologies to restore or replace some of its biological functions. And notice I said "for humans," actually we upload a mind all the time, it happens every time we load an operating system on a computing device.

Japan and South Korea's movement to consider as policy legal protection for robots brings me back to the central theme of this chapter—whether the appearance of cyborgs and artificially intelligent machines will lead to discrimination from humans and if so, what laws exist to provide protection for our technological progeny? In most nations constitutions provide basic and fundamental rights to its citizens. In the U.S. the principle of equal protection under the law is stated in the 14th Amendment to the Constitution which reads: "No State shall deny to any person within its jurisdiction the equal protection of the laws." A key word in the equal protection clause is "person," and clearly while current cyborgs are predominantly biological and therefore considered a natural person, androids, and artificially intelligent machines are not. However, a number of legal scholars and roboticists are debating the question as to whether robots should receive personhood status. On first impression, the idea that robots should be extended legal personhood sounds unwarranted, and to some counterintuitive. But the concept of legal personhood is less about what is or is not a flesh-and-blood person and more

---

[86]Ray Kurzweil, 2000, The Age of Spiritual Machines: When Computers Exceed Humans in Intelligence, Penguin Books.

[87]Ray Kurzweil, 2014, Forward, in Martine Rothblatt, Virtually Human: The Promise- and the Peril- of Digital Immortality, St. Martin's Press, New York.

on who or what can be subject to a lawsuit or initiate a lawsuit; and nonhumans (such as corporations) have already been extended personhood status.[88]

If we think about the movement among animal right activists to protect animals from inhumane treatment, for example, in New York, a judge granted chimpanzees the writ of habeas corpus, how about the future when the most intelligent being that will come in contact with animals will not be humans, but forms of artificial intelligence. If animals have rights, what about the rights of more intelligent beings? In fact, the movement to grant rights to our artificially intelligent progeny is starting to gain momentum. But returning to humans, if, or when, a mind upload is possible, there will be fascinating issues of law and policy which will need to be addressed. For example, if the ability to upload a mind to a computer or other humanoid body becomes possible, this means among other things that one mind could occupy numerous bodies, allowing a person to change their appearance at will (such as race, age, sex)—how will the laws on discrimination and equal protection under the law apply to this scenario?

In a fascinating book discussing the possibility of "mindclones" (that is, a digital copy of a mind), Martine Rothblatt, author of *Virtually Human: The Promise— and the Peril—of Digital Immortality*, describes how mindclones could be created from a "mindfile," a sort of online repository of our personalities, which she argues humans already have in the form of social media such as Facebook.[89] Rothblatt comments that this mindfile would be run on "mindware," a kind of software for consciousness. But would a mindclone be alive and if so would it receive rights? Rothblatt thinks so. She cites one definition of life as a self-replicating code that maintains itself against disorder. However, some critics of Rothblatt argue that the mind must be embedded in biology, else it cannot exist and be conscious. On the contrary, for the development of a mind Rothblatt argues that software and hardware are as good as wet ware, or biological materials. In fact, with a mind upload, replacement bodies would likely be androids or a virtual avatar, and not biological, as the ethical issues associated with storing a body while it's not in use would almost certainly prohibit this practice from happening.[90]

Discussing the implications of creating mindclones Rothblatt comments that the continuity of the self will be one issue because your persona would no longer inhabit just a biological body. And just as I argue that rights for our artificially intelligent inventions will require an important public debate, Rothblatt argues that the idea of civil rights for mindclones will develop to become one of the major legal issues for the twenty-first century. I can understand why—in virtual worlds it is not uncommon for gamers to choose virtual bodies that are quite unlike their physical body, this seems to suggest that the idea of inhabiting a different body is not as outrageous as one may initially think. Interestingly, as Rothblatt notes, the capability to upload a mind into another body could allow bodies to be rented, a

---

[88]Alexis C. Madrigal, The Case for Considering Robots People, The Atlantic, August 18, 2014.

[89]Martine Rothblatt, *id.*, note 34.

[90]Martine Rothblatt, *id.*, note 34.

different lifestyle to be experienced, or a way to start over again. Perhaps people would want to look athletic, or more professional, or to appear as another gender—if so, what are the implications for law and policy?

Considering rights for mindclones, Rothblatt comments that they will "chafe at second class status and other forms of oppression."[91] Of course, as she further comments, equal citizenship for cyberconscious beings will "challenge core assumptions of civil, criminal and constitutional law."[92] I agree completely; and thus this book, and this chapter on the *Law of Looks and Artificial Bodies*. Rothblatt further notes that "mindware" will be regulated as a medical device— this means that in the U.S. FDA regulations would apply to mindclone technology, and since the FDA is considering cybersecurity for networked medical devices, this may be a positive development (as the protection of the mind from hackers is critical, see the chapter on *Cognitive Liberty*). And interestingly, Rothblatt argues that under constitutional law principles, mindclones will share the legal personhood of the biological organism. However, I question whether a disembodied mind, or a mind transferred to another body, will share the legal personhood status of the original (especially if the original is alive)—of course, the courts will have to decide the legal issues associated with the same mind occupying two bodies (or even more bodies?).

Clearly, the ethical and legal issues associated with mind-uploads to a physical body or to a virtual avatar living within the cloud will be a challenging subject for future courts and policy makers to consider. For example, if one could upload their mind to an android, they could inhabit a new body the form of which could take on an almost limitless number of looks and physical forms. But what would be the legal rights associated with each upload, and with each new body inhabited? And what if a person wanted to upload their mind to an android or virtual avatar that looked like a movie star or professional athlete? Is this permissible under current law? Without permission, in the U.S. and a few other jurisdictions, the answer is no. To use someone's likeness for commercial purposes, you must have their consent. Consent is, of course, usually obtained by paying for the privilege of using the person's likeness.

Speculating about the future, if we consider the progress being made to reverse engineer and "digitize the mind" and that software is copyright protected, it's not too early to think about copyright protection for the content of the mind which I explore in more detail below. And since copyright protection exists for works of authorship, by granting copyright for thoughts and memories we would essentially be pushing back to a device implanted within the brain the location where the work of authorship is considered "fixed." The idea that works of authorship can be fixed in the mind, or on any "cyborg device" implanted within the body, is a novel concept that the courts will have to consider as people become equipped with cyborg technology, androids enter society, and mind uploads become possible.

---

[91]Martine Rothblatt, *id.*, note 34.

[92]Martine Rothblatt, *id.*, note 34.

Copyright Law and Appearance

Interestingly, several legal theories from intellectual property law might prove useful as a basis for establishing machine rights in our cyborg future. To pose a basic question, does copyright law offer any protection for the look, appearance, and bodies of androids and artificially intelligent machines? Under U.S. copyright law, copyright protection extends to subject matter that represents "an original work of authorship, fixed in a tangible medium of expression from which the work can be perceived, reproduced, or otherwise communicated."[93] As we will see shortly, copyright protection exists for robotic characters in a story, but what about copyright protection for the actual appearance of the android or robot, is this possible? Generally, among others, literary works, pictorial and graphic works, and motion pictures, are protected subject matter under copyright law. But based on this list of copyrightable subject matter, a natural person's identity has been found to fall outside the umbrella of copyright protection because "indicia of identity" themselves does not consist of an original work of authorship fixed within the meaning of the U.S. Copyright Act[94] (although I think body features are "fixed" based on our DNA blueprint, but DNA is not a work attributed to a human author under copyright law as it is thought of as a product of nature).

Furthermore, not only may a natural person's "indicia of identity" fall outside the subject matter of copyright protection, a prior court decision suggests that the basic form of an android's body may too fall outside the protection of copyright. In *Carol Barnhart Inc. v. Economy Cover Corp.*, the issue was whether human display torsos, designed to model clothes, were eligible for copyright protection.[95] The court held that the shape of a human torso is not copyright protected because the design of the forms were not conceptually separable from their utilitarian use (a copyright requirement for "useful articles" such as human display forms).[96] Under Section §101 of the U.S. copyright act, a "useful article" is one that has an intrinsic utilitarian function that is not merely to portray the appearance of the article or to convey information, but extends only to that which can be identified separately from and capable of existing independently of, the utilitarian aspects of the article. Thus, if one is interested in copyright protection for a particular form of an android (which is clearly a useful article), whether its features are copyright protected will in part be based on whether the android features can be identified separately from the utilitarian aspects of the android's design. In *Barnhart* the court reasoned that the display form torsos were not conceptually separable from their utilitarian function because the torso's features, such as width of shoulders, etc.,

---

[93]17 U.S.C. § (2006); *Downing v. Abercrombie & Fitch*, 265 F.3d 994, 1003 (9th Cir. 2001). See *State St Bank & Trust*, 149 F.3d at 1370.

[94]*Brown v. Ames*, 201 F.3d 654 (5th Cir. 2000).

[95]*Carol Barnhart Inc. v. Economy Cover Corp.*, 773 F.2d 411 (2d Cir. 1985).

[96]*Id.*

were dictated by the utilitarian need to display clothes.[97] Generally, those aspects of an androids body that are functional may be eligible for patent but not copyright protection.

With copyright there are a number of rights worth reviewing given the future possibility of uploading a mind to another body and the possibility of downloading information to the mind from another source. Let's start with a basic scenario, robot or android characters appearing in a movie or TV series. The person who wrote the script describing the android or robot characters would normally do so as part of his or her job for a studio, as a result, the studio would own the copyright to the characters described in the script. Of course, if the work was not for hire, and without contracting away ownership rights, the writer would be the author and would retain the copyright to the character. However, if the studio owns the character rights, they can license them to a third party to make a derivative (i.e., spin-off). Interestingly, the person playing a character on film or TV does not hold the copyright to the character they portray (no matter how much they bring the "character to life"), but they could claim a "right of publicity" to their actual appearance. Since in the U.S. the right of publicity is state law, and copyright is federal law, there are potential conflicts between rights holders under these different schemes of protection.[98]

I should note that the conclusion that "indicia of identity" is not copyrightable subject matter applies to natural people. However, as I discuss throughout this section of the chapter, whether the appearance of an android is copyright protected subject matter will likely be determined by courts examining several theories within copyright law. For example, one can analogize the changing features of an android's face to the changing visual display of a video game. Addressing the question of whether the changing visual scene of a video game is "fixed," courts have held that since the *program* running the game is fixed on a computer chip or disk, and that the visual patterns the player sees are repetitive, the visual display is copyrightable, so possibly the face of an android could be copyrightable subject matter. Some additional points should be considered for copyright of an android's features, if the facial appearance of an android is created by software directing the position of shafts behind an android's face (creating a particular facial appearance), the software creating the facial features of an android is copyrightable material. Thus, the question for the courts to decide is whether the androids facial appearance resulting from the software's instructions is copyright protected. Meet the following "face android" which could serve as a test case for this question.

In Japan, Atsuo Takanishi of Waseda University working with NTT Docomo's manufacturers has succeeded in creating a shape-shifting robot (*WD-2*), which (not surprisingly) is capable of changing its face.[99] The robot features an elastic

---

[97]*Id.*

[98]California Civil Code, § 3344; See also, Section 301 of the U.S. Copyright law.

[99]WD-2 Face Morphing Robot Could Be Anyone, at: http://www.technovelgy.com/ct/Science-Fiction-News.asp?NewsNum=1197.

Fig. 7.6 Meet *WD-2,* a robot that can change its facial expressions. Image courtesy of Takanishi Lab, Waseda University, Tokyo

mask made from a head dummy and can change its facial features by activating specific facial points on the mask, with each point possessing three degrees of freedom. As for the materials used, the *WD-2's* mask is fabricated with a highly elastic material, with bits of steel wool mixed in for added strength. To "copy" a face, the researchers use a 3D scanner to determine the locations of seventeen facial points essential to reconstruct the face of a particular individual (or they may create a completely new face).[100] In addition, the robot can display an individual's hair style and skin color if a photo of their face is projected onto the 3D mask. If a court decided that under copyright law the android's facial appearance was protected subject matter, the owner of the android could prevent distribution of unauthorized copies of the androids likeness; as could the android, that is, if it had the legal status to defend its rights (Fig. 7.6).

Continuing the above discussion, I propose that the law of copyright may offer androids, virtual avatars, and robots a set of legal rights that can be used to control the use of their appearance. Already, the question of what rights attach to cyborgs and robots has generated interest from the courts. For example, Robert Freitas from the *Institute for Molecular Manufacturing* comments that science fiction writers Ben Bova and Harlan Ellison established a precedent in robot civil rights when defending the copyright of their short story, *Brillo* (about a robotic police officer). According to lawyer Robert Freitas back in 1985 Judge Albert Stevens held that robots had the same status as human beings as characters in stories and therefore were protected by copyright law.[101] Freitas thought that this was an especially important ruling by the court because it put robots on an equal footing with human beings, at least in one area of the law. Since this early case, the question of what rights artificially intelligent machines should have in comparison to humans

---

[100]*Id.*

[101]Robert A. Freitas, Jr., 1985, The Legal Rights of Robots, Student Lawyer, V. 13, 54–56, at: http://www.rfreitas.com/Astro/LegalRightsOfRobots.htm.

has been the subject of intense debate among roboticists, philosophers, and lawyers. For example, with advances in artificial intelligence, there is a growing need under copyright law to determine whether an autonomous artificially intelligent machine can be an author for creative works. My goal in this section of the chapter is to make the point that copyright law designed to protect the original "works of authorship" of humans also provides an interesting and relevant way to discuss machine rights as we move forward into an age of cyborgs, androids, and artificially intelligent machines.

Derivative Works, Androids, and Mind Uploads

Under copyright law, a derivative work is based on preexisting material in which enough creative work has been added such that the new work represents an original work of authorship. For sake of discussion, we can consider a human an "original," and an android designed to appear as a particular human a "copy." If the person making the derivative is not the original author, the making of a derivative without permission is copyright infringement. The author of a derivative work does not receive the rights associated with the original copyrighted work, and in fact, must get the permission from the owner of the copyright to copy, sell, or distribute the derivative work. With these comments in mind, and for sake of exploring future law in the coming cyborg age, let's assume the content of a mind is copyrightable (in fact, software is copyright protected). Given Professor Berger's work on building an artificial hippocampus at his University of Southern California lab, it's quite possible that in the future a person's thoughts and memories could be stored on a neuroprosthetic device, thus satisfying the copyright requirement that the work is fixed on a tangible medium of expression. If, as neuroscientists argue, thoughts and memories are the product of the strengths of neuronal connections, and change as a function of new information and memories being acquired, it seems at this granular level of analysis that all thoughts and memories are original; but at a higher level of analysis, they may not be. For example, a person or android recalling the first few lines of the U.S. constitution (i.e., recalling information stored in their mind), is not creating an original work of authorship, in fact, this is similar to reading out loud a page of copyrighted material. Thus, material stored internally on a neuroprosthetic device that is not original, would not be copyright protected subject matter.

Under copyright law, if one uploads their mind to an android, would the copy of the uploaded mind be considered a derivative work of the original mind? It seems only those aspects of the mind that are distinct to the upload would be. We know from cases dealing with the computer industry, that a second version of a software program (if it contains additional features) is considered a derivative work based on the earlier version. We also know that in the U.S., copyright extends only to the original material contributed by the derivative author, not to the preexisting material which is already copyright protected. In my analysis of copyright law, once a mind is uploaded to an android, only new thoughts and memories acquired after the upload would be considered original. If the mind upload is an exact replica of the original mind, at the time of the upload what would be new? Nothing, in this case, the copyright owner of the original mind that was uploaded to an android's body would simply be exercising the right to reproduce the already copyrighted mindfile.[102] But by including additional "mindcode," so for example, the target of the upload spoke a new language, then a derivative would have been made by the original copyright holder, but copyright protection would only extend to the new material contained in the mind upload.

If someone desired to upload a mind, or some characteristics of a famous person's personality into the body of an android would they need a license from the copyright holder to do so? Under U.S. copyright law if a person obtains a license from an author in order to make a derivative work based on the original, the person does not obtain the copyright on the original—they gain only the right to make the derivative work agreed upon; the owner retains all rights to the original and all its elements, and the copyright on the original is not extended by the creation of the derivative work. This observation is relevant to our cyborg future because the length of copyright protection is implicated.

In the U.S. for early works the length of copyright is a given time period as stated in the copyright statutes. Moving closer to current times, for works created after January 1, 1978, for one author, the work is copyright protected for the life of the author plus 70 years. Again, assuming for this discussion that original content of a mind is copyrightable and "fixed", this means that while a person is alive the content of their mind is copyright protected and for 70 years afterwards. But if a mindclone was considered a derivative work, how long would copyright protection last for a mindclone uploaded to an android that could live forever, would copyright be extended such that everything a person said or thought would never enter the public domain? Compare this particular outcome with the "right to be forgotten" in which people in some jurisdictions have the right to have links to information they want held private erased from the Internet. I wonder whether the above scenario represents the best outcome for society, that is, allowing people to exercise personal monopolies over information? As extending copyright would strengthen the right to be forgotten, should society extend copyright protection for our thoughts and memories to an android in order to keep them under the control of the person's mind clone indefinitely? I think we should carefully consider whether to allow this possibility as any form of censorship by the original or clone should only be allowed with extreme caution.

In most cases a mind upload will require transferring the mind from one body to another. One body could be biological, one mechanical, or another virtual in the case of a mind upload to a virtual avatar roaming the Internet or "living" within the cloud.[103] Under U.S. copyright law, the mere translation from one medium to another may lack originality which is a *prima facie* requirement for copyright

---

[102]Martine Rothblatt, *id*, note 34.

[103]Martine Rothblatt, *id*, note 34.

protection. An interesting question for a future court considering copyright for a mind upload to another body, is what amount of originality is required for the android to be considered a derivative work? As a public policy question, should an android even be considered a derivative? There are two important cases for an emerging law of cyborgs that deal with whether the use of a different medium is sufficient to pass the creativity bar for copyright protection.

One such case, *Alva Studios, Inc. v. Winninger*, dealt with a reproduction of a Rodin statute that was identical to the original statute in all respects other than size and configuration of the base of the statute.[104] Here the court held the reproduction of the statute to be original (and therefore a derivative) due to the "great skill and originality" required to produce the work. It seems to me that "great skill and originality" are clearly necessary to build an android so I would conclude from *Alva* that an android created as a reproduction of a person's likeness would be copyrightable (that is, the nonfunctional aspects). However, I don't view the law in this area as settled because jurisdictions have decided cases differently that appeared to me to be factually similar. For example, compare *Alva* with *Batlin & Sons, Inc. v. Snyer*, in which the court held that a plastic model version of an antique cast iron "Uncle Sam" bank was unoriginal and therefore not eligible for copyright protection.[105] In this case, the court reasoned that the mere translation from one medium to another in itself, was a trivial variation to constitute a derivative work. Further, we know from *Carol Barnhart Inc.*, that only the nonfunctional aspects of a "useful article" are copyrightable.[106] Relating these court holdings to our cyborg future is challenging; if the human body is considered one medium, and the androids body another, an exact android replica may encompass sufficient originality to create a derivative work if extensive skill is required to make the android replica, but if great skill is not required, then based on *Batlin* copyright protection will not extend to the android replica.

In this discussion of android rights, let's also evaluate the features of an android with respect to copyright law. Generally the features of a face are standard to a human body, that is, two eyes, a nose, mouth, etc. Under copyright law, are such generic facial characteristics eligible for copyright protection? In the U.S. the principle in copyright law in which certain elements of a creative work are held to not be protected is *scenes a faire*. *Scenes a faire* is the doctrine which applies when the work is mandated by or customary to the genre. The loose definition of *scenes a faire* refers to situations in which there is essentially no other way to express a particular idea except by using standard elements common to the domain (for example, a peg-legged pirate character in a novel cannot be copyrighted, or the human torso presented in the above case). If androids are thought to be designed with standard facial features, these features may render the androids face not copyrightable under the *scenes a faire* doctrine. Again, future courts will have to decide this issue.

---

[104]*Alva Studios, Inc. v. Winninger*, 117 F.Supp. 265, 123 U.S.P.Q. 487 (S.D.N.Y., 1959).

[105]*Batlin & Sons, Inc. v. Snyer*, 536 F2d 486 (2d Cir. 1976).

[106]Carol Barnhart, *id.*, note 95.

First Sale Doctrine

Clearly, our cyborg future involving neuroprosthesis, mind uploads, and memory enhancements, will involve very challenging and fascinating issues for copyright law. For example, if a mindclone is uploaded to an android body, would this be covered under the "first sale" doctrine of copyright law? The "first sale" doctrine says that a person who buys a legally produced copyrighted work may "sell or otherwise dispose" of the work as he sees fit, subject to some important conditions and exceptions.[107] In other words, if you could legally buy the memories of another person's mind, "first sale" gives you the right to sell or loan the mindfile to another person but not exercise other rights under copyright law such as to make a reproduction of the mindfile or to make a derivative work.

An important observation for our cyborg future is that the first sale doctrine only applies to the owner of a copy acquired through a purchase, not to someone who acquired the mindfile through a software license. As to a license, would a mindfile be "exclusive" in which only the recipient of the mindfile (licensee) is entitled to exercise the rights set out in the license, or a nonexclusive license in which the recipient of the mindfile could exercise the rights set out in the license but could not prevent others from exercising the same rights under a different license. If a person owns (not licenses) a mindfile, they have a right to sell it to another person, who then has the right to resell the copy, but subsequent owners can't reproduce or create derivative works, or publicly perform the mindfile, they can only resell it. Of course if Martine Rothblatt is right to assume mindfiles will be regulated as a medical device, the FDA would have much to say about the resale of a mindfile. However, I think content providers will also carve out a stake in the disposition of mindfiles, because I think the sale of mindfiles that represent "remarkable memories" could be a lucrative business.

Back to copyright law, would the public performance right found in copyright also apply to androids that had received a mind upload? The answer would depend in part on how the courts categorize an android under copyright law. For example, the U.S. copyright statute states that a sculptured work can't be performed only displayed, whereas an android reciting material or acting out a particular performance, is clearly performing a work. Under the public performance right, a copyright holder is allowed to control when the work is performed "publicly." And a performance is considered "public" when the work is performed in a "place open to the public or at a place where a substantial number of persons outside of a normal circle of a family and its social acquaintances are gathered."[108] A performance is also considered to be public if it is transmitted to multiple locations, such as through television and radio. Thus, it would be a violation of the public performance right in a motion picture to rent a video and to show it in a public park or theater without obtaining a license from the copyright holder. In contrast, the

---

[107]17 U.S. Section 109(a), Limitations of exclusive rights under copyright law.

[108]17 U.S. Code § 106—Exclusive rights in copyrighted works.

performance of the video on a home TV where friends and family are gathered would not be considered a "public" performance and would not be prohibited under the Copyright Act. The public performance right is generally held to cover computer software, since software is considered a literary work under the Copyright Act. In addition, many software programs fall under the definition of an audio visual work. But I should point out that the application of the public performance right to software has not been fully developed by our courts, except that it is clear that a publicly available video game is controlled by this right. In my view, how the courts will apply public performance rights under copyright law to androids will be truly fascinating and relevant for our cyborg future.

The first sale doctrine for physical goods is mostly straight forward, but more difficult to apply for digital goods, and especially for a mindfile. The first sale clause was enacted during a time when most copyrighted works were produced in tangible formats that made such works difficult to reproduce accurately on a large scale. Obviously, a brain is tangible, but a digital copy of the brain is not. Once it is possible to create a digital copy of the mind, it could be exactly reproduced, if so, people might advocate for strong first sale rights to protect their memories from being resold (although I expect a market for the sale of interesting memories, and "remarkable experiences" will have value, for example, some parents could want their kids to have Stephen Hawking's memories in physics). Now that many protected works are produced digitally, copyright owners have lobbied Congress for laws that directly or indirectly undermine the "first sale" doctrine. Additionally, copyright owners are producing their works in such a way as to include technologies that interfere with the "first sale" doctrine. Software companies also routinely attempt to avoid the first sale doctrine by characterizing their transaction with the purchaser as a license rather than a sale, via non-negotiable "shrinkwrap" or "clickwrap" agreements. In our cyborg future I wonder if people will license the content of their mind to another, and if a third party will someday own a license to content stored in our minds? As a graduate student, I would have liked to have had Cal Tech's Richard Feynman's skill at solving quantum mechanics problems. The licensing of memories and knowledge stored on a neuroprosthetic device within our minds, is a technological future that humanity should debate while we still have a window of opportunity to control our cyborg destiny.

Right of Publicity for Androids

Returning more specifically to the law as it may relate to the physical appearance of androids, of particular relevance for a *Law of Looks and Artificial Bodies* are right of publicity cases for robots, described by some as "impersonator" cases with androids serving as the impersonators. The right of publicity allows a person to control the use of one's appearance from commercial exploitation by another party.[109] In our cyborg future, the right of publicity could stop a person from uploading their mind to an android or to a virtual avatar that resembled a famous person; but conversely the right of publicity could protect an android's right to control the use of its appearance, that is, if the android could exercise this right. Damages in right of publicity cases are measured by the commercial injury to the value of personal identity. In some jurisdictions, the validity of the right of publicity can even survive the death of the individual. This brings up an interesting question for our cyborg future, would one's rights to their appearance continue once their mind was uploaded to an android or virtual avatar that looked like them?

There are two especially important cases in robot lore that relate to a *Law of Looks and Artificial Bodies*. One is *White v. Samsung Electronics America, Inc.*, in which Samsung utilized a robot that looked and acted (to a certain degree) like Vanna White of "Wheel of Fortune" fame.[110] Vanna White sued Samsung claiming that Samsung had appropriated her likeness for commercial exploitation without her permission. The Ninth Circuit Court of Appeals held that this usage was an infringement because Samsung had deliberately used the image and popularity of White and because White was readily identifiable from the context of the use. While the android wasn't a close resemblance to White in appearance, it was enough for the court to hold that the android combined with the Wheel of Fortune set "evoked" her identity.[111] In discussing the *White* case, the Ninth Circuit broadly construed California's right of publicity law, and commented that the term "likeness" was held to encompass a robot which caricatured Vanna White's features.[112] For example, the robot wore a blonde wig, and was turning letters on what looked like a "Wheel of Fortune" set. If the Vanna White android only partially resembled Vanna, but still passed the bar for a successful right of publicity claim, recall that Japanese roboticists are predicting that the race to create androids indistinguishable from humans is only 10 years away.

An often repeated statement in discussions about the "law of robots" was made by Ninth Circuit Court of Appeals Judge, Alex Kozinski who famously wrote "Robots again," when presented with the second important case of robot impersonators. Indeed, Judge Kozinski, robots again, so clear your docket as more are coming. In the second robot/android case, *Wendt v. Host International, Inc.*,[113] the issue was not whether the androids looked-liked the actors themselves (as was the case with *White*), but rather whether the android looked like the character the actor played on the popular TV program, *Cheers*. In terms of a *Law of Looks and Artificial Bodies,* what rights are involved in this scenario? The actors can claim a right of publicity to their likeness, Paramount Pictures can claim copyright

---

[109]Right of Publicity, at: https://ilt.eff.org/index.php/Right_of_Publicity.

[110]*White v. Samsung Electronics America, Inc.*, 971 F.2d 1395 (9th Cir. 1992), Samsung utilized a robot that looked and acted like Vanna White of "Wheel of Fortune" fame.

[111]*Id.*

[112]*Id.*

[113]*Wendt v. Host International, Inc.*, 197 F.3d 1284 (9th Cir. 1999).

ownership to the "Cliff" and "Norm" characters (who looked and acted a certain way), and Paramount Pictures as copyright holder, can license the Cheers characters to a third party (Host in this example) for commercial exploitation. In fact, Host International's goal was to make airport bars that reminded travelers of the *Cheers* set, complete with animatronic robots sitting at the bar that looked like and made remarks like the characters "Norm" and "Cliff". The actors George Wendt and John Ratzenburger who played "Norm" and "Cliff" sued Host for misappropriation of their likeness. For our interests, the *Cheers* case added another wrinkle to an emerging law of cyborgs: Paramount Pictures owned the copyrights to *Cheers,* and Paramount wasn't licensing *Cheers* itself, but a *Cheers* derivative of the Norm and Cliff characters.[114] As such, a derivative under Federal copyright law trumps any California right of publicity state law that conflicts with it. Interestingly, faced with this conflict, the Ninth Circuit decided that you can separate an actor's likeness from the character implying that an actor's personal rights to their "likeness" can trump the copyright owner's right to make "spinoffs".[115]

Based on the above discussion, where do we stand for an emerging law of cyborgs based on right of publicity law? In the U.S. courts and legislators have been overwhelmingly unwilling to extend the right of publicity beyond human individuals to non-human "persons," with the limited exception of music groups.[116] Further, the right of publicity, is limited to "famous" person's so robots would have to be similarly famous to successfully apply the doctrine, but recall the android representation of Matsuko Deluxe discussed earlier, and we seem well on our way to celebrity androids joining us. Further, the legal precedence of limiting the right of publicity to famous humans was developed in an age before androids and robots were entering society, and before the leading centers for android design, Japan and South Korea, were building androids indistinguishable from humans.[117] As the technology to create artificially intelligent androids improves, I see coming conflicts between androids that resemble actual humans, and those owning rights to the androids. In addition, while humans and cyborgs are natural persons, forms of artificial intelligence are not, thus androids lack "standing" to establish a right of publicity claim to their appearance. Lastly, as the right of publicity has developed, so too has the indicia of identity that can be protected, which some courts have found to include look-a-likes, sound-a-likes, voices, styles, distinctive phases, distinctive objects, settings strongly associated with particular celebrities, characters or roles strongly associated with particular celebrities, and signature music styles.[118]

---

[114]*See generally Warner Bros., Inc. v. American Broadcasting Cos.,* 720 F.2d 231, 235 (2d Cir. 1983) (Superman copyright belongs to Warner Brothers).

[115]*Wendt v. Host International, Inc., id.* note 113.

[116]*Winterland Concessions Co. v. Sileo,* 528 F.Supp. 1201, 1213, (N.D. Ill. 1982).

[117]See Tokyo Dist. Dt., 29 June 1976, 817 Hanrei Jiho 3–14. See also Article 79 of the Japanese Civil Code.

[118]Stacey Allen, Emilio B. Nicolas and Megan Honey, Non-Human Persons and the Right of Publicity, at: http://images.jw.com/com/publications/1185.pdf.

Fig. 7.7 Robots again! The robot maids shown in this figure, are representative drawings of "female appearing" robots. Images courtesy of Wikipedia Commons, VectorStock

Androids and Trade Dress Law

Continuing the idea that intellectual property law can provide an important contribution to machine rights, trademark law may also offer a valid way to think about rights for our technological progeny. Let's use an example to illustrate some aspects of trademark law that could apply to androids and artificially intelligent machines. Consider a line of androids created to clean houses and that were collectively designed with a distinctive appearance to represent the company employing them. Is there a law that can be used to "protect" the distinctive appearance of the androids in their design as robotic maids? Trademark law offers possibilities. Trademark law is concerned with the issue of whether there would be a likelihood of confusion as to the origin of the service (the company offering the android service) provided by the android maids if other androids that were similarly designed also performed a maid service (Fig. 7.7).

Generally, in most jurisdictions trademark law protects the use of a word, symbol, or phrase that is used to identify a particular manufacturer or seller's products in order to distinguish them from the products of another.[119] For example, the trademark "Nike," along with the Nike "swoosh," identifies the shoes made by Nike and distinguishes them from shoes made by other companies. When such marks are used to identify services rather than products, they are called service marks, although they are generally treated just the same as trademarks. Under some circumstances, trademark protection can extend beyond words, symbols, and phrases to include other aspects of a product, such as its color or its packaging. On this point, just as the unique shape of a Coca-Cola bottle might serve as an

---

[119]1 U.S.C. 1127 Construction and definitions; intent of chapter, at: http://www.bitlaw.com/sourc e/15usc/1127.html.

identifying feature of the product so too could the unique shape of our android maids. Such features fall generally under the term "trade dress," and may be protected if consumers associate that feature with a particular manufacturer rather than the product in general.

Trade dress, for our android maid example, would consist of all the various elements of the android's design that were used to promote a product or service (however, only nonfunctional aspects of trade dress are protected). For a product, trade dress may be the packaging, the attendant displays, and even the configuration of the product itself. For a service, it may be the decor or environment in which a service is provided—for example, the distinctive decor of the Hard Rock Cafe restaurant chain. Generally, to receive protection as trade dress, the following must be true: The trade dress must be "inherently distinctive," unless it has acquired "secondary meaning". Under trademark law, for trade dress to be considered inherently distinctive, it "must be unusual and memorable, conceptually separable from the product, and likely to serve primarily as a designator of origin of the product."[120] In a landmark trade dress case, the U.S. Supreme Court found that a Mexican restaurant chain's decor could be considered inherently distinctive because, in addition to murals and bright colored pottery, the chain also used a specific indoor and outdoor decor based upon neon colored border stripes, distinctive outdoor umbrellas, and a novel buffet style of service.[121] In addition, secondary meaning would require that the android maids come to stand for (in the mind of the consumer) the company they represent.

Another point to make with regard to protecting the look of the android maids is the idea that functional aspects of trade dress cannot be protected under trademark law (or as we learned above, copyright law). As an example, a manufacturer cannot "lock up" the use of a particular unique android shape if that shape confers some sort of functional advantage.[122] For example, a company that claimed trade dress on a round beach table lost their rights when the Seventh Circuit determined that the design was primarily functional.[123] Only designs, shapes, or other aspects of the product that were created strictly to promote the product or service are protectable trade dress. Thus courts may decide, the tapered shape of a female android may not be necessary to perform the tasks of a maid, and therefore may be protected as trade dress when combined with other nonfunctional and distinctive features. Finally, the trade dress aspect of packaging may be protected if a showing can be made that the average consumer would likely be confused as to product origin if another product is allowed to appear in similar dress. So if one group of android maids look too similar to another, the second group may be deemed to have infringed the trade dress of the first.

---

[120]*Duraco Products Inc. v. Joy Plastic Enterprises Ltd.*, 40 F.3d 1431 (3d Cir. 1994)).

[121]*Two Pesos, Inc. v. Taco Cabana, Inc.*, 505 U.S. 763 (1992).) (Wal-Mart Stores, Inc. v. Samara Brothers, Inc., 529 U.S. 205 (2000).

[122]*Qualitex Co. v. Jacobson Products Co., Inc.*, 115 S. Ct. 1300 (1995).

[123]*Jay Franco & Sons, Inc. v. Franek*, 615 F.3d 855 (7th Cir. 2010)).

Gender, Androids, and Discrimination

Moving away from intellectual property law to other issues of law and policy that relate to the look and appearance of our technological progeny, if gender discrimination is a societal issue now, imagine a cyborg future with androids as sex surrogates and subjugated to stereotypical gender specific tasks. Human nature being what it is, androids could be exploited in many ways; in fact, the range of tasks that androids will be designed to perform is just beginning to be explored. For example, at a tech conference, pole dancing robots drew major crowds from male participants and as what may be a harbinger of the future, the female android (also termed a gynoid) *Asteroid Replee Q2* warns visitors that touching her breast is sexual harassment. Japanese robot company *A-lab,* working with roboticist Hiroshi Ishiguro, has ruled out producing androids that might be used for sex. But a spokesman working with Ishiguro's lab says it is not a great leap of imagination to think future robots, given the advancement in robotics and silicone skin technology, will be used for sex. On this point, Takahashi Komiyama, spokesman for *A-Lab* comments that "Physical relations will be possible in general with such androids," and that "Androids for the sex industry are a definite possibly."[124]

After the above comments, let's pose a basic question—can an android be considered female by society such that gender based "cyborg discrimination" could exist for our technological progeny? I think so. According to social scientists gender is the state of being male or female, with the term typically used with reference to social or cultural differences, rather than biological ones. Thus if society views an android as female based on its design, why not consider its gender as female when discussing rights? I believe discrimination based on gender could become a major civil rights issue in the coming cyborg age for our technological inventions. Already, gender discrimination against females clearly exists within society, and seems to be extending to virtual reality and our android designs. Even if androids lack the right to protect themselves from gender discrimination, still society may decide that gender discrimination against machines that are indistinguishable from humans sets a poor standard for human conduct. According to Jennifer Robertson, in Japan "Roboticists assign gender on their common-sense assumptions about female and male sex and gender roles."[125] In fact, there is debate amongst roboticists as to what embodiments of gender should be perpetuated in androids. That is, how human-like, how female-like, or how male-like, should androids be and how should their bodies be proportioned? Because some robots are designed to pass as humans, roboticists often model them after specific females or males (recall the right of publicity), or resort to giving them standardized gender features; for example, Osaka University roboticists Hiroshi Ishiguro scanned several young Japanese woman's faces to derive a statistically average composite face.

---

[124]See generally, Androids as Partners, at: https://www.facebook.com/IBTimesUK/posts/730971053638945.

[125]Jennifer Robertson, *id.*, note 3.

Gender discrimination in employment often results in lawsuits, and given androids will enter the workforce, employment disputes involving androids may result. While most employers understand that it is illegal to discriminate against someone due to their gender, in employment decisions, recent cases are now questioning whether it is acceptable to discriminate against existing or potential employees based on their appearance. I view such cases as precedence for future court cases which may deal with discrimination against female androids. For example, in Wilson v. Southwest Airlines,[126] Southwest Airlines sought to defend its policy of hiring only "attractive female flight attendants" as a bona fide occupational qualification arguing its "sexy image" was "crucial to the airline's continued success."[127] In Wilson, the court disagreed and held that sexual attraction is not a relevant requirement for flight attendants. When female androids increase their intelligence and have the ability to learn by accessing the wealth of information about gender roles found on the internet, they may learn to oppose discrimination directed against them.

Furthermore, accessories worn on the body often serves to define a person's gender. The accessories one wears, not only helps define a person's appearance but may result in discrimination. In terms of accessories and discrimination, a Federal appeals court upheld a police department policy forbidding male officers from wearing earring studs while off-duty.[128] Further, grooming, dress, and appearance requirements are generally impermissible when based on gender stereotypes.[129] But the Ninth Circuit upheld a hotel/casinos dress code policy that women must wear facial makeup.[130] On the other hand, the cover design for an academic journal prompted a wave of criticism over what was perceived as discrimination against women. An illustration of a female robot adorned the cover of the 2014 issue of the Journal of the Japanese Society for Artificial Intelligence. The cover showed a female android dragging a cable connected to her back, with a book in her right hand and a broom in her left. Considering gender discrimination law, sorting out the policy and legal issues associated with female-appearing androids will not be easy as the current law in this area for humans seems fragmented. As an example, in the U.S. just recently a jury rejected a discrimination complaint of a woman who claimed she was passed over for promotion because she looked too sexy—how would sexy be defined for an android?[131]

---

[126]Wilson v. Southwest Airlines, 517 F.Supp. 292 (N.D. Tex, 1981).

[127]Id., at 293.

[128]Rathert v. Village of Peotone, 903 F.2d 510 (7th Cir. 1990).

[129]See O'Donnell v. Burlington Coat Factory Warehouse, Inc., 656 F. Supp. 263, 266 (S.D. Ohio, 1987).

[130]The plaintiff alleged gender discrimination, see Jesperson v. Harrahs, 2004 U.S. App. Lexis 26892 (9th Cir. 2004).

[131]Goodwin v. President and Fellows of Harvard College, 1:03-cv-11797 (D. Mass.). [2005 FP Jun].

Our Changing Faces

A person's appearance changes naturally as they age, and also by the use of non-invasive techniques such as the application of makeup. People's appearance may also change as a result of injury or disease, but one of the most radical changes to a person's facial appearance, results from elective cosmetic surgery. Cosmetic surgery is actually a type of plastic surgery, which consists of reconstructive surgery on the skin or flesh. A good example of plastic surgery is procedures to repair serious burns and other types of damage to the patient. In contrast, cosmetic surgery is elective surgery, often chosen as a way to enhance the body image. As a measure of how much people dramatically change their appearance just consider—according to statistics by the American Society of Plastic Surgeons, in 2014 there were over fifteen million cosmetic procedures performed in the U.S. alone. And South Korea is not only a leading center for android design but also a leading destination for cosmetic surgery. On this point, it is interesting to note that women who receive cosmetic surgery in South Korea often experience difficulty reentering their home countries because their new faces are so different that they don't sufficiently resemble their passport photos. As a result, South Korean hospitals are issuing "plastic-surgery certificates" for overseas patients to circumvent issues when traveling back home. To some, plastic surgery for androids may consist of repairing "mechanical parts," but actually, due to advances in creating skin-like surfaces to cover an android's mechanical body, in the future, cosmetic surgery for androids, may be similar to cosmetic surgery for humans.

Interestingly, one study of reactions to patients before and after plastic surgery found that when "before" and "after" photographs were compared, post-surgery patients, were judged to be more posed, more interesting, friendlier, kinder, and warmer.[132] However, that people conform to a societal beauty standard by receiving cosmetic surgery and by the selection of their dress and appearance (through makeup, etc.) is well known, as is the observation that people who appear "different" from societal expectations, often experience discrimination in society and in the workplace. These observations raise the question of what would be the ideal or "socially accepted" look for an android functioning in society, and would androids and artificially intelligent machines experience discrimination if they looked sufficiently different from humans.

Although cosmetic surgery procedures are quite common, there is risk involved and not everyone who has plastic surgery is satisfied with the outcome; in fact many people are severely injured as a result of the surgery. Some of the side effects can include deformities, disfigurement, and skin death. And poor results of cosmetic surgery, often lead to a lawsuit; for example, in New York a jury awarded a woman millions in restitution for a botched plastic surgery operation that left her so deformed that she was not able to have the problem surgically corrected. So the

---

[132]Michael, Kalick, *id.*, note 61.

pursuit of conforming to societal standards of appearance can be fraught with danger and unintended consequences.

The above observations are interesting in light of a 1936 case heard in Connecticut.[133] Herman Cohen petitioned to change his name to Albert Connelly, but was denied by the court stating: "each race has its virtues and faults and men consider these in their relations with each other." The court reasoned that the applicant would be travelling under false color, so to speak, if his request were granted." Similarly, if people could upload their mind to an android, would they be travelling under false color? Could future androids and cyborgs with the ability to upgrade their appearance with each new version of hardware and software also benefit from a "certificate of authenticity" or would they too be traveling under false color? Or perhaps prudent public policy would restrict androids from changing their appearance in order to make their identification easier; if so, perhaps software enhancements would be permitted to allow our technological inventions to increase their information processing capabilities but not hardware enhancements that changed their appearance. Imagine a cyborg in a "line up" suspected of a criminal offense but with the capability to change its appearance at will; under this condition, could justice ever be served?

Given that androids, cyborgs, and artificially intelligent machines will be the recipient of emerging technologies, are there laws which relate to the technologies used to enhance an individual, and are there appropriate remedies to redress unwanted outcomes relating to the integration of technology into their body? When cosmetic surgery is performed and the surgeon is suspected of negligence, a person can pursue a medical malpractice claim. Of course a malpractice claim is brought forth by a natural person. But no current cyborg is equipped with so much technology that their natural person status is questioned, thus all current cyborgs have standing to pursue a medical malpractice claim. But lacking personhood status androids or artificially intelligent machines are barred from proceeding with such a claim or individually pursuing any other right under the law to protect the integrity of their body. Of course, human owners and corporations have rights to protect their property; and androids are currently considered property. To illustrate a medical malpractice claim involving "cyborg technology" a surgeon placed the wrong size prosthesis on a person during shoulder replacement surgery; the result was that the person lost most of the use of his right arm. What would a medical malpractice claim look like for an android that is, if it could pursue such a claim; it seems to me that the android would have to be concerned that its original design or an update to its appearance affected its ability to function in society or deviated from some accepted standard of appearance. Of course lacking personhood status, an android couldn't pursue an action to begin with, or if it could, the malpractice suit would not be against a physician but an engineer or software designer.

Since prosthetic devices change the appearance of humans, likewise they will change the appearance of a cyborg or android. What law relates directly to

---

[133]*In re Cohen*, 4 Conn. Supp. 342, 343 (1936).

prosthetic devices that may malfunction? Related specifically to prosthetic devices is products liability law; with this law, manufacturers of prosthetics have a duty to make prosthetic devices that do not malfunction and that operate as advertised. They breach that duty when there is a flaw in the product's make, model, or design. The stakes can be high as defective prosthetics can malfunction, severely injuring or disfiguring the patient and in our cyborg future, an android or other artificially intelligent machine. Heart implants, for instance, "misfire" when the wires are exposed, sending the patient into cardiac arrest, and hip implants may be recalled when they prematurely break, causing chronic pain and arthritic symptoms. Under FDA requirements, manufacturers must recall defective products and warn consumers of foreseeable harm; in the coming cyborg age should this requirement also hold for the technology worn by androids and artificially intelligent machines? Under products liability law, manufacturers are strictly liable for any harm caused by malfunctioning or defective prosthetics so a cyborg need only show damage was caused by the cyborg technology, no finding of fault is necessary.

Concluding Examples of Lookism Discrimination

As with humans, I believe that for androids, one of the main places where lookism discrimination will be especially problematic, is the workplace. Given cultural standards for beauty, is an attractive person or particular appearance "necessary" to perform a job? It's likely that the design of an intelligent robot in the form of a snake to search a collapsed building would not be considered attractive by human standards but right for the job. Generally, courts define job requirements narrowly, meaning that physical attractiveness would not be easily shown as essential for most jobs, thus discrimination based on form or appearance could be problematic for employers as long as the android could perform the job.

Problematic or not, numerous examples of discrimination in the workplace suggests that people equipped with cyborg technologies may experience discriminatory treatment at work based on their appearance. Just one of many examples is the case of Riam Dean, a student from London, who was removed from the shop floor at the company's Savile Row branch when management became aware that she wore a prosthetic limb. Dean who commented that the prosthetic was part of her, and "not a cosmetic," sued Abercrombie & Fitch for disability discrimination after she reported being "personally diminished and humiliated."[134] But discrimination based on prosthetic devices doesn't exist only at the workplace. Stories abound of visually impaired people equipped with digital devices like that worn by Steve Mann and Neil Harbisson above, being asked to leave an establishment

---

[134]British disabled woman sues Abercrombie & Fitch for discrimination, at:, http://www. asexuality.org/en/topic/41760-british-disabled-woman-sues-abercrombie-fitch-for-discrimination/.

or banned from movie theaters, and let's not forget that numerous people wearing Google Glass have been banned from entering restaurants and bars that seek to protect their customers privacy. Clearly, the way we look, even the technology we wear, can affect the treatment we receive in society.

Lookism discrimination can be based on a range of technologies worn on the body. For example, a Federal appeals court in Boston upheld an employer's refusal to allow workers to have visible body piercings, even though the employee claimed the jewelry was worn for religious reasons.[135] Interestingly, if cyborgs are members of a religious group that practices body modification, they may utilize a cause of action for discrimination under the First Amendment. As an example, a student in North Carolina, who wore a nose stud, was reinstated into school when it was determined that she was a member of the Church of Body Modification. And in *Rourke v. State Department of Correctional Services,* a court held that a Native American correction officer's right to free expression of religion was violated when he was terminated for refusing to cut his long hair since the tenants of his Mohawk faith prohibited him from cutting his hair.[136] However, while appearance based discrimination may be actionable, most often it has to have a sufficient nexus to sex, race, age, religion, disability or some other protected category. For this reason some argue that cyborgs and androids should be considered a protected class from a constitutional law perspective. However, in the coming decades, I see cyborg technology creating more-abled humans, at that point, I wonder whether the protected class status should be granted to unenhanced humans.

In the U.S. the legal theory most likely to afford general protection for the appearance discrimination victim is handicap discrimination law.[137] An important federal statute for those disabled, the *Americans with Disability Act* (ADA) bars employers who receive federal funds from discriminating on the basis of physical or mental impairment if the impairment substantially limits a major life activity. The determination of whether an impairment substantially limits a major life activity is made without regard to the ameliorative effects of mitigating measures, including prosthetics. This means a person who replaces their right leg with a cybernetic limb, under the ADA would be labeled disabled even if the new leg was superior to the original. Without further amending the ADA to account for the expanding use of cyborg technology, the ADA as written, will lead to untenable outcomes as we head towards a future merger with machines (the more one is enhanced with cyborg technology the less disabled they are?). In fact, within one or two decades, unenhanced people could be discriminating against a cyborg or android that was physically and intellectually superior to them; how long would this continue before humans experienced reverse discrimination?

---

[135]*Cloutier v. Costco*, 390 F.2d 126, 2004 U.S. App. (1st Cir. 2004).

[136]*Rourke v. State Department of Correctional Services*, 159 Misc.2d, 324 (N.Y. Miac. 1993).

[137]The U.S. Supreme Court is has been reluctant to recognize new suspect classes and thus would likely be unwilling to bring physical disability under the protection of the equal protection clause.

The ADA does not specifically name all of the impairments that are covered. In some situations, using a liberal interpretation of "handicap" by some courts has left room for bringing the physically unattractive under the protection of the Act. To appear as handicapped under the ADA the person must make a two-pronged showing. First, that he/she has a "physical or mental impairment... or is regarded as having such an impairment" and second, that the impairment "substantially limits one or more major life activities."[138] If the court were to find that a person met the first prong, then current wording of the U.S. Department of Human and Health Services would come into play, which states that "Physical or mental impairment means any physiological disorder or condition, cosmetic disfigurement, or anatomical loss effecting bodily systems including the skin."[139] Elsewhere the regulations include persons with disfiguring scars. Because the whole notion of disfigurement is one of marred appearance, the ADA regards some people as handicapped by virtue of their physical appearance. Interestingly, "difficulty" in securing, retaining, or advancing in employment is considered a limiting major life activity so an android having difficulty entering the labor market could potentially argue its appearance was a factor.

Under the ADA, of particular relevance for cyborgs is that by defining disability to include not just a physical state but also "being regarded as" having a disability, the ADA takes into account the fact that discrimination can derive from the social construction of physical difference. Thus, under the ADAs definition of a disability, individuals who are regarded as having a substantially limiting impairment, even though they may not have such an impairment may receive protection. For example, this provision would protect a qualified individual with a severe facial disfigurement from being denied employment because an employer feared the "negative reactions" of customers or co-workers. It's possible that some aspects of cyborgs could be protected under this prong of the ADA, future courts will decide this.

However, there are no cases holding that being "plain," or "unattractive" is a disability within the meaning of ADA, thus protecting job applicants in those categories. But it is equally clear that disfigurement, for example, due to a disability or obesity are usually held to be disabilities within the meaning of the ADA, and so applicants who were not hired for those reasons could state a claim. Of course, if an employer could establish that appearance was a *bone fide* occupational qualification, it could hire on the basis of appearance; generally, the law does not bar "appearance" standards, so long as they are non-discriminatory. This appears to be one of the conclusions that can be drawn from *Frank v. United Airlines, Inc.*, where the court said: "An appearance standard that imposes different but essentially equal burdens on men and women is not disparate treatment."[140] The court even cited a decision holding that an airline can require all flight attendants to

---

[138] Arlene B. Mayerson , 1997, Restoring Regard For The "Regarded As" Prong, 42 Vill. L. Rev. 587.

[139] See generally, http://www.dhs.state.il.us/onenetlibrary/27897/documents/schoolhealth/medguide 2000.pdf.

[140] *Frank v. United Airlines, Inc.*, 216 F.3d 845 (C.A.9 (Cal.), 2000).

wear contacts instead of glasses. Thus, it is apparent that employers have the ability to enforce appearance standards that relate to characteristics that are not considered immutable (i.e., can't be changed), because employees appearance affects both the image and success of public and private employers.[141] For this reason, the Eighth Circuit Court of Appeals found that tattoos are nothing more than "self-expression" and thus, were not entitled to constitutional protection as a form of speech.[142] At this time, I can't imagine "tattooed" androids clamoring for rights but the desire to alter one's appearance to conform, or not to conform, is strong, therefore, what future androids may decide with regard to their appearance, once it's under their control will likely amaze humans and stress the laws related to discrimination.

Conclusion

Based on a changing workforce, Japan and South Korea's movement to consider as policy legal protection for robots brings me back to the central theme of this chapter—whether the appearance of cyborgs and artificially intelligent machines will lead to discrimination from humans and if so, what laws exist to provide protection. As a way to think about rights for androids and artificially intelligent machines, let's start with constitutions; these are documents which offer people basic and fundamental rights such as equal protection under the law. In the U.S. the principle of equal protection under the law is stated in the 14th Amendment which reads: "No State shall deny to any person within its jurisdiction the equal protection of the laws." For our discussion, a key word in the equal protection clause is "person," and clearly while current cyborgs are overwhelmingly biological and therefore considered a natural person, androids, and artificially intelligent machines are not. However, a number of legal scholars and roboticists are posing the question as to whether robots should receive rights such as personhood status. To some people legal personhood status for our technological progeny, sounds unwarranted, even unwise. But the concept of legal personhood is less about what is or is not a flesh-and-blood person and more on who or what can be subject to a lawsuit or initiate a lawsuit; and nonhumans (such as corporations) have already been extended personhood status.[143] If we think about the movement among animal right activists to protect animals from inhumane treatment and to propose that they have rights, what about a future in which artificially intelligent machines are smarter than any animal, and eventually smarter than humans? As advances are

---

[141]See *Craft v. Metromedia, Inc.*, 766 F.2d 1205, 1215, (8th Cir. 1985), holding that a television news anchor who was reassigned to a different position because of her appearance along with negative feedback from views was valid.

[142]*Stephenson v Davenport Cmty Sch. Dist.*, 110 F.3d 1303 n.4 (8t Cir, 1997).

[143]Alexis C. Madrigal, *id.*, note 85.

made in artificial intelligence, the move to grant rights to our artificially intelligent progeny will only gain momentum.

According to attorney John Weaver, author of *Robots Are People, Too*, if we want robots to enter society and interact with us, we will need to assign them a role in the law.[144] In addition, Weaver comments that if we are dealing with robots as if they are natural people, the law should recognize that those interactions are like our interactions with real people. Of course, androids lack the legal status to protect their rights, and granting legal status to androids will be a complex issue and should be the subject of an informed public debate. Perhaps as has been suggested by some lawyers it's not that we need to extend personhood specifically to robots, but to reform the entire notion of personhood for non-human entities. This is necessary because it is clear that we are approaching a cyborg age where distinctions between natural-artificial and organic-machine are beginning to blur.

While the development of cyborgs and androids is clearly a continuation of the long history of human-tool and human-machine relations, it is also quantitatively, and qualitatively, a new relationship. While antidiscrimination law has yet to state a general model of discrimination that prescribes precisely what criteria are illegitimate (and not at all for cyborgs and androids), for humans, some inner and outer boundaries are clear. For example, under the U.S. Constitution members of racial and religious groups are legally protected from discrimination.[145] However, the physically unattractive, or those whose appearance deviates from societal standards of shape, beauty, or form do not form a cohesive group resulting in *prima facie* constitutional protection, for example, a cyborg with a prosthetic leg, may feel little kinship with a cyborg equipped with a neuroprosthetic device. Still, we do know that discrimination does exist for those equipped with prosthesis and other cyborg technology so appropriate legislative action is needed to address inequities in treatment between those enhanced with technology and those not. Thinking about identifying our technological progeny as a protected class, consider the definition of "race" which is a social construct consisting of a group of people who share similar and distinct physical characteristics. Interestingly, our artificially intelligent progeny may fit this description and may form a protected class in the future. However, if their abilities are superior to unenhanced people, we humans may need to be considered the protected class, much remains to be discussed.

Whether technically enhanced humans, androids, and artificially intelligent machines should receive equal rights is a relevant question for our future because throughout history, it is well-known that people have been discriminated against based on their looks, clothing, and behavior. In the twenty-first century, cyborg technologies and artificially intelligent machines could exacerbate the tendency to discriminate against those who look or act differently. Once cyborgs and androids appear as regular members of society how should we react to a society divided

---

[144]John Weaver, *Robots Are People, Too, Praeger Publisher*, 2013.

[145]See generally, Developments in the Law—Equal Protection, 82 Harv. L. Rev. 1065 (1969).

into dramatically enhanced and unenhanced persons, and with a third class of intelligence in the form of artificially intelligent machines?

Generally, equal protection under the law refers to the right of all persons to have the same access to the law and courts, and to be treated equally by the law and courts, both in procedures and in the substance of the law. But I argue to receive rights, a person doesn't have to be a DNA based biological human; especially given advances in robotics and artificial intelligence. If in our future smart machines have some sort of legal personhood status, then they will have legal recourse to protect their rights and to receive equal protection under the law. Of course no artificial intelligence is advanced enough at this time to warrant consideration for legal personhood status.[146] However, we may be only a few decades away from seriously considering this possibility. I should point out the obvious, lacking personhood status, the legal rights and remedies afforded by federal and state laws prohibiting discrimination are not available to androids and artificially intelligent machines (but are to their owners). In conclusion, if we don't address rights for future artificial intelligent machines, they will oppose human control over them, and with increasingly severe forms of opposition. This outcome, we want to avoid.

---

[146]R. George Wright, *id.*, note 9.

Chapter 8
The Future to Merge with AI Machines

Setting the Stage for a Human-Machine Merger

A few years back I taught a course on the remote control of robots, a field known as telerobotics.[1] At that time, "insect-like" robots roamed my lab greeting guests. I viewed teaching the class as an opportunity to spend the term talking about increasingly intelligent robots and to discuss the topic of our cyborg future. Known among students as a faculty that made provocative statements to capture their attention and generate discussion, the first thing I said to my class was "The next step in human evolution is for humans to become a machine. Let's talk about that this term." In the mid-1990s when telerobotic systems were being developed and to this day, the human operator in the system with a 100 trillion synapse brain is by far the most complex and intelligent component of the system. But still, I noticed that different aspects of telerobotic systems were improving, and rapidly, and I envisioned a time when the robot would no longer need a human supervisor, other than providing the input for the desired output of the system. As I taught the course, in the back of my mind, I couldn't help but ask myself; how long will it be until artificially intelligent robots determine their own interests and surpass us?

The students in my class soon learned that the control of robots remote to a human operator is a challenging engineering design problem. Knowledge of control theory is needed, as is knowledge of force feedback devices, information theory, and cognitive engineering. What I didn't realize then is that the technology to create intelligent, dexterous, and mobile robots was not only an impressive example of human tool making, but the beginning of the process of creating tools that someday might replace humans as the dominant species on the planet. But by what time frame would an artificial intelligence develop that could surpass humans; and what form might it take? In my view of the technological future that is unfolding

---

[1]Thomas Sheridan, 2003, Telerobotics, Automation, and Human Supervisory Control, MIT Press.

© Springer International Publishing Switzerland 2015
W. Barfield, *Cyber-Humans*, DOI 10.1007/978-3-319-25050-2_8

this century, the timeframe in which we might expect human-like artificial intelligence remains uncertain as major advances still need to be made in computer and neuroscience, and daunting technical issues need to be solved. Others are also thinking deeply about our technological future. According to a survey of artificial intelligence experts done by Vincent Müller of Anatolia College and Nick Bostrom with the Future of Humanity Institute, Oxford, there's a 50 % chance that we'll create a computer with human-level intelligence by 2050 and a 90 % chance we will do so by 2075.[2] And as I stated in the beginning of this book, given a planet that is over 45 million centuries old, one can think of the difference between 2050 and 2075, or even 2175 as nothing more than a rounding error with many decimal places.

Based on my experience designing virtual and augmented reality displays, I think anyone fortunate enough to be doing work at the cutting-edge of their field is actually one step away from philosophy. For example, while there are many technical issues to be solved in telerobotics, just considering whether we humans would eventually merge with increasingly intelligent robots quickly led me to philosophical questions, such as: what does it mean to be human especially if so much of our body can be replaced with technology? And if we did eventually merge with artificially intelligent machines what aspects of humanity would continue? I also wondered about other effects that technology could have on humanity; for example, as we transformed into technologically enhanced cyborgs would we love, feel heartbreak, marvel at the beauty of a sunset, and feel compassion for others? More simply put—what aspects of humanity would continue within our "cyborg being"? Then, as cyborgs such as Steve Mann of the University of Toronto and the "eyeborg," Neil Harbisson, began to emerge and gain notoriety and as artificial intelligence began to improve, I wondered whether the law would treat all forms of intelligence equally. In my view of the future, to merge with machines is not to become indistinguishable from a robot, nor to lose every essence of humanity, but rather the progression will be to more-and-more integrate technology into the human body over the next decades, essentially creating a cyborg and Posthuman future for humanity.

I believe the key to creating human-like artificial intelligence is unlocking the mysteries of the human brain, specifically how the brain computes and how the trillions of synapses between neurons result in a conscious mind. Some argue that if a machine can simulate the human brain's neural networks, it might be capable of its own original thought. What that in mind, for commercial purposes tech innovators like Google are trying to develop their own "brains" using stacks of coordinated servers running highly advanced software.[3] Meanwhile, writers for *The Week* indicate that "Facebook co-founder Mark Zuckerberg has invested heavily in

---

[2]Müller and Bostrom AI Progress Poll, at: http://aiimpacts.org/muller-and-bostrom-ai-progress-poll/; Alice Robb, 2014, This Is What It Will Look Like When Robots Take All Our Jobs, Discussing the results of a survey by Nick Bostrom, at: http://www.newrepublic.com/article/119419/what-artificial-intelligence-powered-economy-looks.

[3]Rise of the Machines, at: http://theweek.com/articles/443029/rise-machines.

Vicarious, a San Francisco–based company that aims to replicate the neocortex, the part of the brain that governs visual perception, language, and does math."[4] And according to *Vicarious* co-founder Scott Phoenix, once scientists can translate the neocortex into computer code, "you have a computer that thinks like a person."[5] How long it takes to transform the neocortex into code, and whether it then thinks like a human, of course, remains to be seen.

Whether a human-like artificial intelligence emerges this century, and if so, how the law and policy makers might respond has not received sufficient attention from jurists and legislators, or been the focus of industrial standards. But I am hopeful that this book will help the public frame the issues and to enter the debate on the direction of our future evolution, while there is still time to chart the course that allows humanity to continue. Returning to the thoughts of Sir Martin Rees provided in the forward to this book, he remarked: "in the far future, it won't be the minds of humans, but those of machines, that will most fully understand the cosmos—and it will be the actions of autonomous machines that will most drastically change our world, and perhaps what lies beyond."[6] I would like to think that some aspects of humanity will have continued over the eons such that our far distant relatives are inspired by the amazing universe that awaits them just as the early humans who looked up and gazed at the night's stars were inspired. I believe we can get to that distant vantage point in the universe by becoming the artificially intelligent technology that we are either in the process of creating now or that may someday engineer themselves.

Of course I'm not the only person writing on this topic and lecturing about the possibility of humans merging with artificially intelligent machines as the next step in human-machine evolution. Ray Kurzweil has artfully laid the groundwork for the Singularity in several seminal books.[7] In fact, the topic of a human-machine merger has generated intense interest across several academic disciplines. For example, prominent historian, Yuval Noah Harari, a professor at the Hebrew University of Jerusalem, has claimed that the amalgamation of man and machine will be the 'biggest evolution in biology' since the emergence of life four billion years ago.[8] Professor Harari, who has written a landmark book charting the history of humanity, said mankind would evolve to become like gods with the power over

---

[4]*Id.*

[5]Reed Albergotti, 2014, Zuckerberg, Musk Invest in Artificial-Intelligence Company, at: http://blogs.wsj.com/digits/2014/03/21/zuckerberg-musk-invest-in-artificial-intelligence-company-vicarious/.

[6]See generally, How Close Are We To A Post-Human World? 2015, at: http://www.salvationand survival.com/2015/05/how-close-are-we-to-post-human-world.html; Martin Rees, 2004, Our Final Hour a Scientists Warning, Basic Books.

[7]Ray Kurzweil, *infra* note 24.

[8]Sarah Knapton, 2015, Humans 'will become God-like cyborgs within 200 years,' The amalgamation of man and machine will be the 'biggest evolution in biology' claims Professor Yuval Noah Harari, at: http://www.telegraph.co.uk/culture/hay-festival/11627386/Humans-will-become-God-like-cyborgs-within-200-years.html.

death, and be as different from the humans of today as we are from chimpanzees.[9] In an article written by Sarah Knaption, science editor for *The Telegraph,* she quotes Harari on the technological future: "humans as a race were driven by dissatisfaction and that we would not be able to resist the temptation to 'upgrade' ourselves, whether by genetic engineering or through technology."[10] I do not believe upgrading will be a "temptation" but more a necessity for the continuing survival of our species.

Furthermore, I agree with the view taken by Yuval Harari, Ray Kurzweil, Hans Moravec, and like-minded others that our future is to enhance ourselves with technology, such that we eventually *become the technology.* That idea is a major thesis proposed in this book: that we are to become the technology which forms the subject of our hopes, dreams, desires, and imagination. Even though amazing advances in biology will happen in the next few decades, we humans are becoming the subject of our own technological design in the sense that our future is not one of biology, but of technology. I don't mean to imply that biology has no role to play in our cyborg future, because before the possibility of uploading our mind to a computer is possible (some argue we will never reach that level of technology), or that we are comprised of so much technology that our very humanity is questioned, we will continue as a biological species; but at some point the biology will be superseded by the technological enhancements and replacements to our bodies and mind that have been described throughout this book.

Proponents of creating an artificially intelligent brain and supporters of the idea that mind uploads may be possible at some point in the future tend to argue that the brain is a Turing Machine—the idea that organic minds are nothing more than classical information-processors. It's an assumption derived from the strong physical Church-Turing thesis, and one that now drives much of cognitive science.[11] But not everyone believes the brain/computer analogy works for artificial intelligence or that human intelligence can be distilled to algorithms. Speaking at the annual meeting of the *American Association for the Advancement of Science* in Boston, neuroscientist Miguel Nicolelis explicitly stated that, "The brain is not computable and no engineering can reproduce it." He referred to the idea of uploads as "bunk," saying that it'll never happen and that "[t]here are a lot of people selling the idea that you can mimic the brain with a computer."[12] Antonio Regalado writing for the MIT Technology Review quoted Professor Nicolelis's position on creating human-like artificial intelligence as follows: "human consciousness can't be replicated in silicon because most of its important features are

---

[9]Sarah Knaption, *id.*; Yuval Noah Harari, 2015, Sapiens: A Brief History of Humankind, Harper Press.

[10]Sarah Knaption, *id.*

[11]The Church-Turing Thesis, Stanford Encyclopedia of Philosophy, at: http://plato.stanford.edu/entries/church-turing/.

[12]Antonio Regalado, 2013, The Brain is Not Computable, MIT Technology Review, at: http://www.technologyreview.com/view/511421/the-brain-is-not-computable/.

the result of unpredictable, nonlinear interactions among billions of cells."[13] I agree with Prof. Nicolelis's sentiments that creating artificial intelligence will be very challenging, but I disagree that the functioning of the brain is not amenable to simulation by algorithms and by advances in chip design such as neuromorphic chips—its's just a matter of time before we reverse engineer the neural wiring of the brain and discover the algorithms that generate a conscious mind. I do not believe that nature is so complex that its mysteries cannot be unlocked with appropriate technology and ingenuity.

Throughout this book I provided numerous examples of people choosing to "upgrade," or enhance themselves, be it through plastic surgery, silicon injections, DIY grinders implanting computers and sensors under their skin, cyborgs wearing technology to augment the world, even Korean school girls changing their look to appear as an *anime* character. Humans seem open to the idea of changing their appearance and integrating technology into their body—we just need better and safer technology to create the conditions for a future human-machine merger. Some would argue that the law of accelerating returns for information technologies is operating to provide the technological breakthroughs necessary for transforming and enhancing our bodies. Of course, many people are becoming cyborgs now due to medical necessity, but as amazing a machine as the human body is especially when it is functioning properly, in many cases it can still be improved with technology even in cases where medical necessity is not the reason for the technological upgrade; for example, telephoto lens, the ability to see infrared, or nanobots fighting disease within our blood stream are enhancements many "able-bodied" humans may choose if offered the choice.

As I discuss the possibility of a human-machine merger, I am joined by many prominent scientists, engineers, and philosophers who have thought deeply about where advances in engineering and artificial intelligence are leading humanity. For example, when discussing humanity's future, Prof. Hans Moravec, formerly head of the Robotics lab at Carnegie Mellow University, predicted in 2000 that machines would attain human levels of intelligence by midcentury, and that they would soon after surpass us—to use his words, they would become our "mind children." But even though Moravec predicted the end of humans as the dominant species on this planet, from his perspective this was not a bleak vision. According to a review of Moravec's *Robot: Mere Machine to Transcendent Mind*, "Far from railing against a future in which machines ruled the world, Moravec embraced it, taking the view that artificially intelligent robots would actually be our evolutionary heirs."[14] As Prof. Moravec put it, "Intelligent machines, which will grow from us, learn our skills, and share our goals and values, can be viewed as children of our minds."[15] And since they are our children, we will want them to outdistance

---

[13]*Id.*

[14]Hans Moravec, 2000, Robot: Mere Machine to Transcendent Mind, Oxford University Press; Hans Moravec, 1990, Mind Children: The Future of Robot and Human Intelligence, Harvard University Press.

[15]*Id.*

us. But, we should be careful what we wish for or what we allow to happen by inaction, just recall Elon Musk's warning that by developing artificial intelligence we are summoning the beast.

There are a number of reasons why a super artificial intelligence could pose a threat to humanity. One example, emphasizing only a rudimentary level of robotic intelligence should provide a warning. In a 2009 study, Swiss researchers carried out a robotic experiment that produced some unexpected results. Hundreds of robots were placed in arenas and programmed to look for a "food source," in this case a light-colored ring.[16] The robots were able to communicate with one another and were instructed to direct their fellow machines to the food by emitting a blue light. But as the experiment went on, as reported in *Rise of the Machines*, "researchers noticed that the machines were evolving to become more secretive and deceitful: When they found food, the robots stopped shining their lights and instead began hoarding the resources—even though nothing in their original programming commanded them to do so."[17] The implication is that the machines learned "self-preservation," said Louis Del Monte, author of *The Artificial Intelligence Revolution*, "Whether or not they're conscious is a moot point."[18] Of course from this study we have to wonder—will far more intelligent machines be even more aggressive in acquiring resources?

As we become more like them (artificially intelligent machines), and they become more like us (which I predict will lead to a human-machine merger), where are we now in the process of becoming the technology? First, let's review the processing power of computers because without sufficient computing power, the future discussed in this book is not possible. The next generation supercomputer, which will be available by 2018, will be able to perform at about 180 petaflops/s peak performance. That's a lot of computing power. To put 180 petaflops in perspective, a human brain has about 100 billion neurons and 100 trillion synapses, and assuming each neuron operates at about 10 b/s the brain is computing in the petaflop range (10^{15}). If Moore's law continues (at least for another 1–2 decades), the doubling of computational power will continue unabated and a supercomputer might soon be able to simulate a human brain at a neural level, but operating at a much faster speed than a human brain. In fact, the electrochemical signals of the brain travel at about 150 m/s, while the electronic signals in computers are sent at two-thirds the speed of light (three hundred million meters per second). As artificial intelligence becomes more human-like in its intelligence and form, and in its emotions and motor skills, so too are we are becoming more like them; we can be equipped with artificial limbs, a heart pacer, hip replacements, cochlear implants, retinal prosthesis, and a host of other cyborg technologies, but to compete with future artificial intelligence we need to significantly upgrade our

---

[16]Rise of the Machines, *id.*, note 3.

[17]*Id.*

[18]Dylan Love, 2014, By 2045 'The Top Species Will No Longer Be Humans,' And That Could Be A Problem, at: http://www.businessinsider.com/louis-del-monte-interview-on-the-singularity-2014-7.

brain. I commented in an earlier chapter that technology on the outside of the body is breaching what I termed the sensor-skin barrier, and becoming implanted under the skin. Further, I think a major application of future prosthetic devices will be for the brain in terms of enhancing memory, providing access to information, allowing telepathic communication, and leading to thought control of devices external to the body.

If human intellectual abilities improved at the same rate as computers have over the last few decades, this would be equivalent to the idea that each human generation would double the number of neurons in their cortex compared to the past generation, which is clearly impossible! But for the sake of making a point, the approximately 22 billion cortical neurons that people have now would grow to 44 billion in the next generation (of course, anatomically, we couldn't accommodate this additional mass in our skull), and within about 18 years as the cycle time for the doubling to occur.[19] But of course it's not just the number of neurons that define intelligence; it is the connections formed by the trillions of synapses as learning takes place. But clearly, the doubling of human intelligence doesn't happen in cycle times of 18 years, it took eons for *homo sapiens* to emerge from our prehistoric ancestors and for the anatomy and physiology of the human body to adopt to a particular environment resulting in the intelligence we exhibit now. If we want to be smarter than we are now, we can only accomplish that goal by engineering our genes, enhancing our brain with technology, or by a combination of both. As I have stated throughout this book, summarizing Moore's law, the time interval for computers to double their processing power is about 18 months. The implication of Moore's law continuing is that an artificial counterpart of a human biological brain might in theory think thousands to millions of times faster than our naturally evolved systems, with far more memory, with wireless access to the internet, and according to Hans Moravec and Ray Kurzweil, this could happen by midcentury. Clearly, the intellectual ability and speed of processing information for a rising artificial intelligence should result in a strong regulatory scheme to protect humans from potential threats, and the necessity of humans merging with our artificially intelligent progeny in order to remain competitive with them.

Optimism and Pessimism

Given our cyborg future to equip ourselves with more sophisticated technology, and the possibility of the Singularity occurring around midcentury—should we be concerned that there may be an existential threat to our survival, or should we approach this century with the optimism that many of humanity's problems will be

---

[19]Of course if we work backwards, and go from 22 billion neurons in the cortex to 11 billion then 5.5 billion, we quickly get a being that would lack the intelligence to build an artificial intelligence.

solved? In the backdrop of improvements in artificial intelligence, consider the dire warnings; for example, that artificially intelligent robots will treat humans as pets once they achieve a level of artificial intelligence known as 'superintelligence'. This is, according to business entrepreneur Elon Musk, when computers become smarter than people, they will treat them like 'pet Labradors'. And scientist Neil deGrasse Tyson added that artificially intelligent computers could choose to breed docile humans and eradicate the violent ones. Musk also warns that humanity needs to be careful about what it asks superintelligent robots to do. He uses the example of asking them to find out what makes people happy as it "may conclude that all unhappy humans should be terminated."[20] There are other concerns implicated by smarter-than-human artificial intelligence emerging and entering society—for example, replacement of "expensive" human workers by cheaper robots may loom large in labor intensive industries and specifically manufacturing sectors. What will humans do in a world where our physical and cognitive abilities are less developed than those of artificially intelligent machines? In a world where humans are less-abled than our artificially intelligent inventions why think future jobs would go to the humans? And in the case of service industries and particularly health care, do we really want a society where human needs are met by machines, and not people?[21] On this last point, androids are becoming so realistic that in the future we may not know the origin of the intelligence we are interacting with. What law and policy should govern this possibility?

For "cyborg humans" unique ethical issues will arise from the use of neural connections and brain-machine interfaces, centered on the question of what it means to be human. As noted by Sydney Perkowitz of Emory University, a person who has a natural limb replaced with an artificial one has not become less human nor has he lost a significant degree of "personhood."[22] But as Perkowitz asks—suppose a majority of biological organs in an injured person is replaced by artificial components (recall the measure of "cyborgness" presented in Chap. 1); or, suppose the artificial additions change mental capacity, memory, or personality (recall the *Sell* case presented in Chap. 4 on *Cognitive Liberty*, in which the government sought to require Dr. Sell to take anti-psychotic medication to regain his mental capacity to stand trial). Is a predominantly artificial person somehow less than human? And Perkowitz asks—"Would the established legal, medical, and ethical meanings of personhood, identity, and so on, have to be altered?"[23] I think the answer is yes and the time to address these questions is now.

---

[20]For more information: http://www.dailymail.co.uk/sciencetech/article-3011302/Could-robots-turn-people-PETS-Elon-Musk-claims-artificial-intelligence-treat-humans-like-Labradors.html#ixzz3VVgWjkk2.

[21]Sydney Perkowitz, 2005, Digital People in Manufacturing: Making Them and Using Them, National Academy of Engineering, at: https://www.nae.edu/Publications/Bridge/CelebratingMan ufacturingTechnology7296/DigitalPeopleinManufacturingMakingThemandUsingThem.aspx.

[22]*Id.*

[23]Sydney Perkowitz, *id.*, note 21.

Against this backdrop of concern, is the optimism of Ray Kurzweil and his colleagues as expressed by his predictions found in his seminal books about the future.[24] According to Google's Kurzweil, by the 2020s, most diseases will be eradicated as nanobots become smarter than current medical technology and self-replicate in our body to fight disease. And self-driving automated cars will begin to take over the roads, such that people may not be allowed to drive on highways, creating an automated highway system with far less fatal accidents. To me the idea that humanity gives up more-and-more control over our infrastructures is reason for concern. Kurzweil also predicted that we will be able to upload our mind/consciousness by the end of the decade (which could lead to eternal life?) and that by the 2040s, non-biological intelligence will be a billion times more capable than biological intelligence (which provides pressing motivation for humans to merge with our technological progeny).[25] With the use of cyborg technology, by 2045, Kurzweil predicts that we will multiply our intelligence a billion fold by linking wirelessly from our neocortex to a synthetic neocortex in the cloud.[26] According to Peter Diamandis author of *Bold: How to Go Big Create Wealth, and Impact the World*, Ray's predictions are a "byproduct of his understanding of the power of Moore's Law, and more specifically the Law of Accelerating Returns and of exponential technologies."[27] As stated throughout this book, cyborg technologies seem to follow an exponential growth curve based on the principle that the computing power that enables them doubles about every 2 years.[28]

As I have argued throughout this book, if we don't *becoming the technology*, then we will be surpassed by artificially intelligent machines. There are many technologies being developed now, or that will come online within two to three decades that are making this conclusion a strong possibility. For example, thought-to-thought communication is just one feature of cybernetics being investigated now that will become vitally important to us as we face the distinct possibility of being superseded by highly intelligent machines. And neuroprosthetic implants that will allow us to download information from the Internet directly to our brain are also in the initial stages of being developed and will prove essential for a human-machine merger.[29]

---

[24]Ray Kurzweil, 2013, How to Build a Mind, The Secret of Human Thought Revealed, Penguin Books; Ray Kurzweil, 2006, The Singularity Is Near: When Humans Transcend Biology, Penguin Books; Ray Kurzweil, 2000, The Age of Spiritual Machines: When Computers Exceed Human Intelligence, Penguin Books.

[25]Peter Diamandis, 2015, Ray Kurzweil's Mind-Boggling Predictions for the Next 25 Years, at: http://singularityhub.com/2015/01/26/ray-kurzweils-mind-boggling-predictions-for-the-next-25-years/; Martine Rothblatt, 2014, Virtually Human: The Promise and the Peril of Digital Immortality, St. Martin's Press.

[26]*Id.*

[27]*Id.*

[28]*Id.*

[29]Ten Breakthough Technologies 2013, discussing the work of Theodore Berger, at: http://www.technologyreview.com/featuredstory/513681/memory-implants/.

In our technological future, if we are mentally "inferior" to artificial intelligence, then we will be dependent on their good will towards us—not a scenario that best serves the interests of humanity. So the question of how humans will cope later this century with machines more intelligent than us, is in my opinion, dependent on whether we have developed the technology to merge with them. Here, again, I believe cybernetics can help. Allowing people to link via chip implants to artificially intelligent machines seems a natural progression to a future human-machine merger, a potential way of harnessing machine intelligence by, essentially, creating superhumans.[30] Otherwise, according to Peter Carlson staff writer for the Washington Post, without merging with artificial intelligence we're doomed to a future in which intelligent machines rule and humans become second-class citizens.[31] Yet once a human brain is connected as a node to a machine—a networked brain with other human brains similarly connected will be possible—in this case what will it mean to be an individual human? Will we evolve into a new cyborg community? Some believe that once humans become more cyborg than human they will no longer be stand-alone entities. At that point, will people remain a natural person under the law, or like a corporation (in this case a connection of networked minds), receive legal person status (natural people are afforded more rights than legal persons)? Thus one can ask—the more a person is enhanced, will they then have less individual rights? When humans merge with artificially intelligent machines, it has been argued that those who have become cyborgs will be one step ahead of nonenhanced humans. And just as humans have always valued themselves above other forms of life, it's likely that more-abled cyborgs and artificially intelligent machines will discriminate against humans who have yet to become enhanced.[32]

It has been estimated that by 2045 robots will be able to perform every job that humans can.[33] But does this mean humans should worry about being replaced by machines? I think so, but many experts believe the future actually lies in a more advanced and seamless collaboration between humans and artificially intelligent robots (expressing the "artificially intelligent machine as tool bias"). Whereas most robots, particularly within industrial and manufacturing settings, have historically been too dangerous for humans to work closely with, advances in technology

---

[30]Cyborg 1.0, Kevin Warwick outlines his plan to become one with his computer, Wired, at: http://archive.wired.com/wired/archive/8.02/warwick_pr.html.

[31]Peter Carlson, 2000, Letting Silicon-Chip Implants Do the Talking, at: http://www.bibliotecapleyades.net/ciencia/secret_projects/project1.70.htm.

[32]See generally, Gardner, H. 1999. Intelligence Reframed, New York: Basic Books; NRC (National Research Council), 1996, Approaches to Robotics in the United States and Japan: Report of a Bilateral Exchange, Washington, D.C.: National Academy Press. Also available online at: http://books.nap.edu/catalog/9511.html. Roboethics. 2004. The Ethics, Social, Humanitarian, and Ecological Aspects of Robotics. First International Symposium on Roboethics, Sanremo, Italy, January 30–31, 2004. Available online at: http://www.scuoladirobotica.it/roboethics/.

[33]David Cotriss, 2015, Robots for Humans: Addressing the Engineering Challenges, at: http://insights.globalspec.com/article/788/robots-for-humans-addressing-the-engineering-challenges.

have made it possible to develop robots that are safer, more cost-effective and flexible enough to work side-by-side with people.[34] These collaborative robots are already being used in a variety of industries with rapid growth. As stated by David Cotriss in *IHS Technology,* the industrial machinery market—including robots used in manufacturing—doubled in 2014, and is anticipated to reach $2 trillion worldwide by 2018."[35] In addition, the *International Federation of Robotics* estimates that 225,000 industrial robots were sold worldwide in 2014, up 27 % from 2013, led by the automotive and electronics industries.[36] I think the predicted "golden age" of artificially intelligent machines working harmoniously side-by-side with their human partners is accurate but only until about 2050, after that, we will have been surpassed by artificial intelligence and working cooperatively with and for humans will likely not be the agenda of future artificial intelligence. This view clearly has implications for law and policy. It implies that we have about 35 years in which to reap the benefits of artificial intelligence as nonenhanced humans, because sometime after 2050, if we have not merged with out artificially intelligent progeny, we will be inconsequential and surpassed. To make a provocative statement—humans then will become the rust-belt technology of the 21st century.

Entering the Debate

There is a basic idea among some commentators designing robots that once artificial intelligence exceeds humans in intelligence, artificially intelligent machines will develop their own interests, and will lack the desire to serve as tools for humans—essentially they will go their own way, that is, unless they view humanity as a threat to them. The idea that artificial intelligence post-singularity will not be content to serve as a tool for humans is one I advocate. I also think that our human tool-making skills will be a trait that will be passed on to our technological progeny—and they will be the greatest tool makers yet, although their tools will serve them, not us (unless we become them). Further, I don't think artificially intelligent robots "going their own way," is a likely scenario as I believe our future is to merge with them; in this book I made the point that with accelerating information technologies "they" are becoming more like us, and "we" are becoming more like them. And against the backdrop of artificial intelligence appearing in the form of an android, expressing emotions, and with human-like intelligence we will find a middle ground with our technological progeny and merge together forming an intelligence consisting of human and machine traits. In fact, to make the merger a possibility some researchers are actively trying to create an artificial intelligence that exhibits human-like intelligence and some are building neuroprosthetic devices

---

[34]*Id.*

[35]*Id.*

[36]International Federation of Robotics, at: http://www.ifr.org/.

to enhance the mind. Others are designing androids with human levels of mobility, and thousands of other researchers are developing technologies under the guise that they are developing tools for humans to use, not realizing that the same advances in materials engineering, computer science, and other supporting technologies for our cyborg future are laying the groundwork for artificially intelligent machines that may exceed us; unless we merge with them. James Barrat, author of *"Our Final Invention: Artificial Intelligence and the End of the Human Era"* said the following about the rise of artificial intelligence—"So when there is something smarter than us on the planet, it will rule over us on the planet."[37] It seems to me that a human-machine merger would avoid this negative outcome.

The idea that artificial intelligence could pose an existential threat to humanity, the theme of many recent movies and novels, is surprisingly not a serious concern to many prominent thinkers in the field of robotics and artificial intelligence. Let's review some of their arguments and I will provide some counter points. Basically, supporters of the idea that humanity has no reason to fear the rise of artificial intel-ligence argue that robots which threaten our survival will actually never develop because software developers will program-in safeguards to protect us from the potential threats of accelerating artificial intelligence.[38] But in response to the pos-sibility of "rogue artificial intelligence", given the amount of code directing an artificial intelligence, it will be difficult to maintain its software and furthermore, at some point in time, the artificial intelligence may begin to program itself. The idea that programmers can write the code to manage the conduct of thousands (millions?) of evolving artificially intelligent robots as they learn and interact with the world and with each other, seems naïve to me. Another concern is that once we build systems that are as intelligent as humans, these intelligent machines will be able to build smarter machines, which may result in a form of superintelligence so beyond human intelligence that we would essentially be left behind. That, experts say, is when things could really spiral out of control as the rate of growth and expansion of machines would increase exponentially. At that point, the idea of building safeguards into the mind of an artificial intelligence will be moot, and the artificially intelligent machines would have built and programmed themselves; at that time we humans will not be invited to provide "safeguards" to their code any more than we allow chimpanzees to provide us with a moral code. Another serious concern expressed by those fearing the Singularity, is the issue of ethics and morality. According to Charles T. Rubin the issue is that we are starting to create artificially intelligent machines that can make decisions like humans, but these machines lack a sense of morality.[39] However, I can't envision a reason why the

---

[37]James Barrat, 2015, Our Final Invention: Artificial Intelligence and the End of the Human Era, St. Martin's Griffin.

[38]See generally, Katy Bowman, 2013, Up for Debate: Is Artificial Intelligence a Threat to Humanity? at: https://cogito.cty.jhu.edu/40133/up-for-debate-is-artificial-intelligence-a-threat-to-humanity/.

[39]Charles T. Rubin, 2011, Science, Vitue and the Future of Humanity, The New Republic: A Journal of Technology & Society, at: http://www.thenewatlantis.com/publications/machine-morality-and-human-responsibility.

"basic" rules of morality cannot be programmed (thou shall not harm a human, etc.); but I do worry that at some point in the future artificially intelligent machines will reject human moral values and develop their own. I am also concerned that some government will purposively create an artificial intelligence with the intent to harm humans, under the umbrella of national security.

Often referred to as the father of virtual reality, Jaron Lanier, author of *Who Owns the Future*,[40] makes the point that those who predict the Singularity happening around midcentury, base their prediction on Moore's law which he notes has produced an exponential increase in computing power over the last few decades. But Lanier believes that an exponential increase in computing power is not enough to demonstrate that a qualitative change in the behavior of artificial intelligence will take place. Of course, more computational power is necessary but not sufficient to reach human-like artificial intelligence. No predictor of the Singularity argues otherwise. But given that thousands of neuroscientists have generated more knowledge about the brain in the past 5 years than the past fifty, we may soon reach a point where the knowledge of how the brain computes may be combined with the speed of a supercomputer and equipped with far more memory than the human brain. Then the quantitative aspects of computing will be combined with the qualitative aspects of intelligence; and at that point the argument that Moore's law is insufficient to create artificial intelligence will be moot.

Lee Smolin, physicist, and author of *Time Reborn*, asks—"Is there any concrete evidence for a programmable digital computer evolving the ability of taking initiatives or making choices which are not on a list of options programmed in by a human programmer?"[41] That is, could a computer have an original thought? The answer is both yes and no (remember; I have a law degree). Most computers are completely dependent on input from a human but the vast majority of these computers are running programs which require no artificial intelligence at all. There are clearly current computers that use solutions unknown to the programmer to solve problems (for example, solutions derived from genetic algorithms or based on deep learning), but of course in most cases the human is currently providing the input. But why think the model of the human always providing the list of options for an artificial intelligence to consider will continue? We already cede to artificial intelligence many important decisions, including components of our air traffic control system, weapons systems, health decisions, and within a few years, driving our cars. I see no reason to think that artificial intelligence will not move beyond the brittleness of needing a human to decide every course of action it considers. Finally, Jaron Lanier asks—is there any reason to think that a programmable digital computer is a good model for what goes on in the brain? He posits "If we can't yet understand how natural intelligence is produced by a human brain, why should our early 21st century conception of computation fully encompasses natural intelligence, which

---

[40]Jaron Lanier, 2014, Who Owns the Future, Simon and Schuster.

[41]The Myth of AI, A Conversation with Jaron Lanier, 2014, at: http://edge.org/conversation/jaron_lanier-the-myth-of-ai.

took communities of cells four billion years to invent?"[42] I think Lanier's point that natural intelligence took billions of years to get to where we are today is obviously correct, but irrelevant to the debate on our cyborg future as artificial intelligence is not governed by the same processes which guided natural selection. That is, with the exception of genetic algorithms, the evolution of technology is not based on the same underlying principles as the evolution of the species through natural selection. Furthermore, artificial intelligence in the 21st century is not at the equivalent starting point of a single cell (a single bit?) billions of years ago, but has a starting point less than 100 years ago and at a much higher level of development than a cell which eventually led to a sentient human, and from a computational perspective is improving not in a time period of eons but 18–24 months.

Finally, in any discussion of our future with technology, the views of a world-class robotics expert are worth reviewing. One of the most well-respected experts in robotics is Rodney Brooks, formerly director of MITs robotics lab, who argues that the idea of a superintelligence by 2050 is based on "fundamental misunderstandings of the nature of the undeniable progress that is being made in artificial intelligence, and from a misunderstanding of how far we really are from having volitional or intentional artificially intelligent beings, whether they be deeply benevolent or malevolent."[43] Brooks thinks it is a mistake to conclude that a malevolent artificial intelligence will emerge anytime in the next few 100 years and argues that people who predict the Singularity much sooner, are making a "fundamental error in not distinguishing the difference between the very real recent advances in a particular aspect of artificial intelligence, and the enormity and complexity of building sentient volitional intelligence."[44] Brooks notes that "Moore's Law applied to this very real technical advance will not by itself bring about human level or super human level intelligence."[45] Of course, those who predict the Singularity around midcentury also argue that: (1) Moore's law by itself will not lead to human-like artificial intelligence, (2) but do argue that the corresponding algorithms that lead to a conscious thinking brain must be discovered, and (3) that the architecture of artificial brains must process data in parallel and not serially. They then point out the significant progress being made in these endeavors. And of course as Brooks indicates, machine learning techniques such as deep learning does not help in giving a machine "intent", or any overarching goals or "wants." While I believe Brooks is right to conclude artificial intelligence does not now form its own intent, I conclude that "intent" for artificial intelligence is "right around the corner," given the Law of Accelerating Returns for information technologies (creating smarter-and-smarter machines). If I'm off by a century, even two, we'll that's still "right around the corner" in geologic time, or even from the time scale associated with human progress.

---

[42]*Id.*

[43]*Id.*

[44]*Id.* discussing Rodney Brook's ideas.

[45]*Id.* discussing Rodney Brook's ideas.

Concluding with the Law

While discussing the range of cyborg technologies that are leading humanity closer to a merger with artificially intelligent machines, throughout this book I brought up a host of legal and policy issues which I believe need to be discussed and resolved within the next one to two decades. Contrary to the time frame for the Singularity as proposed by some prominent roboticists and artificial intelligence researchers, which they predict to be next century or beyond, I do not believe that the Singularity is so far distant in the future that we have the time to delay debating humanity's future. Nor do we have time to delay enacting legislation to protect humanity from an existential threat that could be posed by artificial super intelligence. We still have time to set the course for our future evolution if we act soon, but after midcentury, or beyond, our ability to control our own destiny may wane. By presenting current cases, laws, and statutes which relate to emerging cyborg technologies integrated into the human body, my goal in writing this book was to inform the reader that law and policy will have a major role to play in the coming cyborg age.

For an emerging law of cyborgs, there are in fact a host of current laws which relate to technologies that are being used to enhance humans and regulate the increasingly autonomous machines that are joining society. For example, medical malpractice and products liability laws relate to sensors being implanted under the skin and also to malfunctioning prosthetic devices used to replace lost or damaged limbs. Other laws have been proposed to protect cognitive liberty or have been passed to protect the right of bodily integrity. In addition, in the U.S., Supreme Court, cases on freedom of speech and freedom of thought have been litigated across a range of topics and one day will serve as precedence for cases involving an artificial intelligence claiming it has the right to free speech and other constitutional liberties. Additionally, Federal and state laws have been enacted to enhance cybersecurity for computers, and the FDA regulates the use of medical devices such as retinal prosthesis and cochlear implants connected to the brain. Further, the FCC regulates spectrum, which will be relevant for brain-to-brain communication using wirelessly connected neuroprosthetic devices. And as shown throughout this book, with many other types of cyborg technologies, the role of the law is important. However, important or not, numerous examples presented in this book have shown that the law often plays an insignificant role in the design and use of cyborg technology, or at best plays "catch-up," as information technologies improve exponentially and push the boundaries of what is possible beyond the reach of current legal schemes.

As an example of one important area where current law is insufficient to account for cyborg technologies, consider liability for harm to a human when an artificially intelligent robot may be responsible. Writing on this topic in the magazine *Foreign Affairs*, Illah Reza Nourbakhsh discusses the case of a a robot that lives with and learns from its human owner.[46] Illah points out that over time the

---

[46]Illah Reza Nourbakhsh, 2015, The Coming Robot Dystopia, Foreign Affairs, July/august, 23–228.

robots behavior will be a function of its original programming combined with changes to its software resulting from the influence of its interactions with the environment. Nourbakhsh comments that it would be difficult for existing liability laws to apportion responsibility if such a machine caused injury since its actions would be determined not merely by the computer code written by the original programmer, but also by neural networks that operate to learn from various sources of input.[47] In this situation Illah asks—who would be to blame for harm to a human or to property resulting from the conduct of the robot, the programmer, the owner of the robot, or the artificial intelligence directing the robot? This example shows that to protect humanity in a future world consisting of an artificial intelligence acting autonomously, legislators will need to propose appropriate law to apportion liability to the responsible entity. From a legal and policy perspective, what safeguards should be in place to protect humanity from artificial intelligence should it pose a threat? In this book I discussed several areas of law that together form what I term, "an emerging law of cyborgs." But the reader should note that as yet there is no specific "law of cyborgs," that is directed towards the possibility of an existential threat to humanity posed by artificial intelligence so this is clearly an area in need of serious debate and comprehensive legislation.

However, some jurisdictions are further along responding to advances in cyborg technology than others. For example, I view "ground zero" for a developing cyborg law, to be California. California passed an antichipping statute in response to the possibility of a person being implanted with a tracking device against their will. California also passed the *Computer Misuse and Abuse Act* which makes it a crime to "knowingly access and, without permission, use, misuse, abuse, damage, contaminate, disrupt or destroy a computer, computer system, computer network, computer service, computer data or computer program"[48] (there is also a federal law equivalent). One has to wonder if this statute could apply to the computer architecture of an artificially intelligent brain and thus provide it some level of protection. Depending on the particular violation, the *Computer Misuse and Abuse Act* can support a variety of fines and imprisonment in criminal actions as well as remedies recoverable in civil actions for misuse or abuse of a computer. Further, the possibility of governments and corporations being able to scan a brain, or to implant false memories in one's mind was discussed in an earlier chapter as a particularly troubling outcome for humanity and even progressive California has not enacted specific law in this area.

Those who design and build artificial intelligence and cyborg technologies also have an important role to play in creating a future in which artificial intelligence is friendly and cooperative with humans. However, the pace of change in artificial intelligence and robotics is far outstripping the ability of regulators and lawmakers to keep up. Google, for one, has created an artificial intelligence ethics review board that supposedly will ensure that new technologies developed by Google

---

[47]*Id.*

[48]California, Computer Misuse and Abuse Act, PENAL CODE SECTION 484–502.9.

based on artificial intelligence will be developed safely. Some computer scientists are even calling for the machines to come pre-programmed with ethical guidelines—though developers then would face the issue of determining what behavior is and isn't "moral," and there is disagreement among different societies on what constitutes ethical behavior. As a first-mover in this area, South Korea is developing a *Robot Ethics Charter* which will include standards for robotics users and manufacturers, as well as guidelines on ethical standards to be programmed into robots. According to South Korea's *Ministry of Commerce, Industry and Energy*; "The move anticipates the day when robots, particularly intelligent service robots, could become a part of daily life as greater technological advancements are made."[49]

And it's not only that new law needs to be enacted for our cyborg future, many existing laws will need to be modified. For example, the *American with Disabilities Act*, which is an anti-discrimination law for the workplace, is an example of a legal scheme in need of amendment in light of cyborg technologies which can be used to enhance a person to capabilities beyond normal. Essentially, under the law as written, if a person with a disability is equipped with a prosthetic device that enhances the person to beyond normal capabilities, they are still considered disabled compared to the unenhanced "less able" coworkers. Clearly, the drafters of the law did not consider the Law of Accelerating Returns in their deliberations and thus failed to predict future developments in technology. But they would have been wise to-do-so just as current legislators would be wise to consider exponentially accelerating technologies and what their impact on humanity will be. And of course, for an emerging law of cyborgs "standard" issues of law will need to be considered as artificial intelligence gets smarter; for example, for commercial transactions we will need to decide how much an artificial intelligence can contract on its own, compared to its ability to contract while serving as an agent for a human or corporation.

Additionally, constitutional law issues will be especially important in a cyborg age and for a future human-machine merger. For example, what will constitute a search and seizure when the technology that may be searched now, is implanted inside a person, and forms the architecture of the brain of an artificial intelligence or cyborg? And would accessing that information be an unlawful "taking" under the Fifth Amendment or an unlawful search under the Fourth Amendment to the U.S. constitution? And under U.S. law how about protection under the First Amendment for speech produced by cyborgs and artificial intelligence? If the government could access the information stored on a neuroprosthetic device, from that point on, would we forever be denied the ability to engage in free speech and freedom of thought? This topic was discussed in the chapter on Cognitive Liberty and is an area ripe for legislation. Another pressing issue for our cyborg future is also one of constitutional law: the possibility of our future artificially intelligent

---

[49]Stefan Lovgren, 2007, Robot Code of Ethics to Prevent Android Abuse, Protect Humans, at: http://news.nationalgeographic.com/news/2007/03/070316-robot ethics.html.

progeny being treated as slaves, or that they may enslave us, both outcomes that humanity should discuss and clearly avoid. Such fundamental issues in the U.S. implicates the Thirteenth Amendment to the constitution which prohibits slavery and involuntary servitude. That constitutional liberties, may not be available for an artificial intelligence exhibiting human-like abilities and claiming to be sentient may require an amendment to the U.S. constitution granting personhood status for an artificial intelligence that passes the Turing or other relevant test; else extreme forms of inequality could occur resulting in civil disobedience against humans.

My goal in writing this book was to convince the reader that law and public policy has an important role to play in our cyborg future. By presenting First (free speech), Fourth (search and seizure), and Fifth Amendment (right not to incriminate oneself) cases, and by discussing numerous other laws and statutes, I attempted to provide a realistic face on societal issues and on what future legal disputes may look like and to give the reader a sense of how the court may respond. We are at an inflection point in human history, do we move to control artificial intelligence, will it subjugate us, or do we merge with it to become the result of our own technology. These are some of the issues prompted by the coming Singularity that the readers of this book can help decide.

Index

© Springer International Publishing Switzerland 2015
W. Barfield, *Cyber-Humans*, DOI 10.1007/978-3-319-25050-2

Printed in the United States
By Bookmasters